COMMEMORATIVE MODERNISMS

For my family, especially my Grandma, who passed onto me her love of Katherine Mansfield, and for my dear friend, Garon Coriz

COMMEMORATIVE MODERNISMS

Women Writers, Death and the First World War

Alice Kelly

EDINBURGH
University Press

Edinburgh University Press is one of the leading university presses in
the UK. We publish academic books and journals in our selected subject
areas across the humanities and social sciences, combining cutting-edge
scholarship with high editorial and production values to produce academic
works of lasting importance. For more information visit our website:
edinburghuniversitypress.com

© Alice Kelly, 2020, 2022

Edinburgh University Press Ltd
The Tun – Holyrood Road, 12(2f) Jackson's Entry, Edinburgh EH8 8PJ

First published in hardback by Edinburgh University Press 2020

Typeset in 10/12.5 Adobe Sabon by
IDSUK (DataConnection) Ltd

A CIP record for this book is available from the British Library

ISBN 978 1 4744 5990 7 (hardback)
ISBN 978 1 4744 5991 4 (paperback)
ISBN 978 1 4744 5992 1 (webready PDF)
ISBN 978 1 4744 5993 8 (epub)

The right of Alice Kelly to be identified as the author of this work
has been asserted in accordance with the Copyright, Designs and Patents
Act 1988, and the Copyright and Related Rights Regulations 2003
(SI No. 2498).

CONTENTS

List of Figures	vi
Acknowledgements	viii
Introduction: A Culture Surcharged with Death	1

Part One Death in Proximity: Wartime Commemorations

1 The Shock of the Dead: Deathbeds, Burial Rites and Cemetery Scenes in Nurses' Narratives	39
2 Uncomfortable Propaganda: Edith Wharton's Wartime Writings	81

Part Two Grief at a Distance: Civilian Modernisms

3 Mansfield Mobilised: Katherine Mansfield, the Great War and Military Discourse	121
4 The Civilian War Novel: H.D.'s Avant-Garde War Dead	154

Part Three Modernist Death: Postwar Remembrance

5 Modernist Memorials: Virginia Woolf and Katherine Mansfield in the Postwar World	193
Conclusion: Modernism's Ghosts	230
Bibliography	244
Index	285

FIGURES

I.1 David McLellan, Members of the Women's Army Auxiliary Corps carrying wreaths to place on the graves of British soldiers buried at Abbeville, 9 February 1918. © IWM (Q 8471)   4

I.2 Olive Edis, Women's Army Auxiliary Corps gardeners tending the graves of the war dead at Étaples, 1919. © IWM (Q 8027)   11

I.3 Official letter (Army Form B.104) from the Infantry Record Office informing Mrs Ethel A. Ottley of the death of her husband, 8 December 1917. NAM. 2004-11-115-6. Reproduced courtesy of the Council of the National Army Museum, London   12

I.4 Next of Kin Memorial Plaque for Sergeant Herbert Walter Stacey, 13 Squadron, Royal Air Force. © IWM (EPH 2223)   17

I.5 Next of Kin Memorial Scroll for Sergeant Herbert Walter Stacey, 13 Squadron, Royal Air Force. © IWM (EPH 2223)   18

I.6 Imperial War Museum appeal for mementos of the war dead. © IWM (Q 24093)   20

I.7 Sir John Lavery, *The Cemetery, Étaples, 1919*. Imperial War Museum Women's Work Section commission. © IWM (Art.IWM ART 2884)   28

1.1 Arthur G. McCoy, *If I Fail He Dies, Work for the Red Cross* (Duluth, MN: J. J. LeTourneau Printing Company, 1918)

	(copyright Rev. S. A. Iciek, 1918). Courtesy of the Pritzker Military Museum & Library	42
1.2 and 1.3	Two pages from Patricia Young, Album of photographs, autographs, and notes compiled by a nurse of the Volunteer Aid Detachment, Dumfries, Scotland, 1914–17. Yale Center for British Art, Friends of British Art Fund	70–1
2.1	Edith Wharton and Walter Berry among the ruins. Edith Wharton Collection. Yale Collection of American Literature, Beinecke Rare Book and Manuscript Library, Yale University	90
2.2 and 2.3	Edouard Brissy, Museum of the Battle of Ménil-sur-Belvitte, created by the priest present during the combat, 31 August 1915. © Ministère de la Culture – Médiathèque de l'architecture et du patrimoine, Dist. RMN-Grand Palais/Opérateur D	95–6
3.1	Alfred Hughes (1870–1933), Portrait of Katherine Mansfield wearing a military style jacket in 1915, probably taken in Hughes's London studio. Ref: PAColl-10046-07. Alexander Turnbull Library, Wellington, New Zealand	130
3.2	Photograph from Katherine Mansfield's passport and her signature (as Kathleen Mansfield Murry), issued in 1919. Ref: MS-Papers-11326-070-02. Alexander Turnbull Library, Wellington, New Zealand	139
4.1	Septimus E. Scott, *These Women are Doing Their Bit* (London: Johnson, Riddle & Co., 1916). Sponsored by the Ministry of Munitions. © IWM (Art.IWM PST 3283)	166
4.2	Samuel Begg, 'A Hospital-Ceiling as a Screen for Moving Pictures: A Cinema for Bedridden Wounded Soldiers at a Base in France', Cover of *Illustrated London News*, 10 August 1918. © Illustrated London News Ltd/Mary Evans	174
5.1	Crane Arthur, Unveiling of the Cenotaph and the funeral of the Unknown Warrior, Armistice Day, 1920. © IWM (Q 14966)	194
5.2	'The Last Journey', *The Times*, 10 November 1920, p. 12. © The Times/News Licensing	195
C.1	Sir William Orpen, *To the Unknown British Soldier in France* (1921, exhibited 1923). © IWM (Art.IWM ART 4438)	231
C.2	Sir William Orpen, *To the Unknown British Soldier in France* (1927–8). © IWM (Art.IWM ART 4438)	232

ACKNOWLEDGEMENTS

The research for this book has been made possible by institutional and financial support. Both my Masters and my PhD research was funded by the Arts and Humanities Research Council. In the final year of my PhD, I was awarded a Fox International Fellowship at Yale University, endowed by Joseph C. Fox and Alison Barbour Fox. Since then my research has been supported at the University of Oxford, first by the Women in the Humanities Postdoctoral Writing Fellowship at The Oxford Research Centre in the Humanities (TORCH), and the Rt Hon. Vere Sidney Tudor Harmsworth Postdoctoral Research Fellowship on the History of the United States and World War One, supported by the Harmsworth family, at the Rothermere American Institute and Corpus Christi College. The necessary research in archives and presentations at conferences has been funded by a Wood-Whistler Scholarship at Newnham College, Cambridge, and travel grants from Linacre College, Oxford; the Faculty of English, Oxford; the AHRC; Newnham College, Cambridge; the Faculty of English, Cambridge; Darwin College, Cambridge; and Corpus Christi College, Oxford. My research has been further supported and extended by a Corpus Christi Fellowship at the Huntington Library and Gardens in Pasadena, California, and a Remarque Visiting Fellowship at New York University. A British Academy Rising Stars Engagement Award enabled me to run my Cultures and Commemorations of War Seminar Series. I am indebted to all of these sources.

More importantly, this book has come into being through conversation with, and the encouragement of, other scholars. First of all, I would like to thank my brilliant PhD supervisor, David Trotter, whose intellectual rigour, unfailing good humour, and kind words sustained me throughout the writing of my dissertation. Elleke Boehmer's encouragement of this project from my Masters onwards has been much appreciated. Michael Whitworth has been continually supportive and encouraging, always willing to offer feedback on ideas. I am similarly indebted to the generous support of Jay Winter, who supported my application for a Fox Fellowship and enabled me to stay at Yale beyond it. I feel very fortunate to have returned to Oxford at a time when there was a very active Globalising and Localising the Great War group of scholars, established by Adrian Gregory and John Horne. A number of other scholars have offered support and advice, and have read my work or shared their own with me, including Carol Acton, Tim Barringer, Claire Buck, Ardis Butterfield, Bruno Cabanes, Santanu Das, Jay Dickson, Anne Fernihough, Andrew Frayn, Alan and Irene Goldman-Price, Christine Hallett, Alison Hennegan, Margaret Higonnet, Sydney Janet Kaplan, Tim Kendall, Gerri Kimber, Marina MacKay, Lucy McDiarmid, Jan Mieszkowski, Gill Plain, Jane Potter, Pierre Purseigle, Laura Rattray, Vincent Sherry, Helen Small, Angela Smith, Randall Stevenson, Trudi Tate, Jonathan Vance, Rishona Zimring and Bart Ziino. Our conversations and exchanges have been invaluable in writing this book. I would like to thank Jackie Jones and the editorial team at Edinburgh University Press, as well as my copy-editor Sarah M. Hall, for all of their help in turning my manuscript into a book.

My work has benefited from participation in scholarly societies and conferences. The Board and members of the Katherine Mansfield Society, the British Association of Modernist Studies, the Edith Wharton Society, the War and Representation Network, and the First World War Studies Society, have all provided productive and welcoming environments to develop my ideas. The new body of academic and public scholarship in First World War Studies, as well as new archival material prompted by the centenary, has stimulated my thinking within my own field. The participants in my Cultures and Commemorations of War series have enabled me to think beyond the First World War to broader questions about war and memory. I am grateful to the innumerable scholars I have met at conferences and events who have given me useful references and much encouragement. The excellent questions, comments and enthusiasm shown by my students in classrooms at Cambridge, Yale, Wesleyan, and Oxford, have provided another valuable space to test out my ideas. Much of the writing of this book happened in my TORCH Academic Writing Group, where our friendly and supportive group provided a huge sense of camaraderie, teamwork, and good cheer.

A number of librarians and libraries have provided wonderful resources and spaces in which to work. Over the past decade, I have been lucky enough to spend many hours in the Reading Rooms of the Bodleian Library, Oxford; in libraries by the river in Cambridge; in my family home in the Malvern Hills; in the cool calmness of the subterranean Bass Library, and the translucent marble of the Beinecke Rare Book and Manuscript Library, at Yale; and, for shorter stints, among the cacti of the Huntington Library and Gardens in Pasadena, California, and in an office on Fifth Avenue high above the honking horns of New York City. I am grateful to the very helpful librarians and staff at all of these libraries, as well as those at the University Library and English Faculty Library in Cambridge; the English Faculty Library in Oxford; the Sterling Memorial Library at Yale; the Department of Rare Books and Special Collections at Princeton University Library; and The Alan Mason Chesney Medical Archives of The Johns Hopkins Medical Institutions, for creating friendly and welcoming spaces for research and writing. Linacre College in Oxford; Newnham, Darwin and Sidney Sussex Colleges in Cambridge; and Davenport College at Yale have all provided welcoming social and intellectual communities. In particular, Darwin College provided the warm and supportive atmosphere needed for extended scholarly work. The colleagues and friends I have made around the lunch table at Corpus Christi College in recent years have provided intellectual support and encouragement. I am grateful to all the Fellows and especially the staff who make these communities thriving and friendly places to work.

My friends and family have been invaluable in both helping me to rethink my project and giving me a space away from it. There are too many people to thank individually, but in particular Charlotte Gould, Catherine Licata, Rory O'Connor, Naomi Portman, Susie Rumsby, Hanna Smyth, Philip Sidney and Laura McLindon have been brilliant cheerers and supporters. In the last stage of this project, the sudden loss of a very close friend, Garon Coriz, means that a personal grief is present in its pages. My final and greatest thanks go to my family, who have been there for me throughout the process of writing this book, from beginning to end. My partner Joel Dodson has supported me in too many ways to mention. My sister Clare Kelly and her family, Tim, Ruben and Lucy, and my brother Tom Kelly and his family, Angela, Massimo and Emeric, have all been encouraging in different ways, as well as making me laugh. Thank you to Pippa for all the walks, and for snoozing under the desk while I work. My parents Jim and Sarah Kelly have been endlessly supportive and encouraging in ways too numerous and far-ranging to list. Thank you in particular to my Dad for patiently reading draft after draft, often late into the night. This book is dedicated to my parents and to my grandparents.

And to all the friends and strangers who have taken an interest in my project and offered a personal anecdote or some encouragement, thank you very much.

ACKNOWLEDGEMENTS

Notes on the Text

An early version of part of Chapter 1 was published as '"Can one grow used to death?": Deathbed Scenes in Great War Nurses' Narratives', in *The Great War: From Memory to History*, ed. Jonathan Vance, Alicia Robinet and Steven Marti (Waterloo, ON: Wilfrid Laurier University Press, 2015), pp. 329–49. Versions of parts of Chapter 2 were published in my Introduction 'Wharton in Wartime' in my critical edition of Edith Wharton, *Fighting France: From Dunkerque to Belfort* (Edinburgh: Edinburgh University Press, 2015), pp. 1–73. An early version of part of Chapter 3 was published as 'Mansfield Mobilised: Katherine Mansfield, the Great War and Military Discourse', *Modernist Cultures*, Vol. 12: *Modernism and the First World War*), ed. Andrew Frayn (Edinburgh: Edinburgh University Press, 2017), pp. 78–97.

I am grateful to the Trustees of the Imperial War Museum for permission to quote from the Papers of Miss M. A. Brown (ARRC). I would like to thank the Watkins/Loomis Agency, who represent Edith Wharton's Estate, for permissions to quote from Wharton materials; the Department of Rare Books and Special Collections at Princeton University Library for permissions to quote from the Edith Wharton Manuscripts and the Archives of Charles Scribner's Sons; and the Beinecke Rare Book and Manuscript Library at Yale University for permissions to quote from the Edith Wharton Collection and the H.D. Papers.

Every effort has been made to trace the copyright holders, but if any have been inadvertently overlooked, the publisher will be pleased to make the necessary arrangements at the first opportunity.

My private opinion is that it is a lie in the soul. The war never has been, that is what its message is. I dont want G. forbid mobilisation and the violation of Belgium – but the novel cant just leave the war out. There *must* have been a change of heart. [. . .] I feel in the *profoundest* sense that nothing can ever be the same that as artists we are traitors if we feel otherwise: we have to take it into account and find new expressions new moulds for our new thoughts & feelings.
     Katherine Mansfield on Virginia Woolf's *Night and Day*,
     in a letter to John Middleton Murry, 10 November 1919

Commemoration: Commemoration. What *does* it mean? What does it mean? Not, what did it mean to them, there, then, but what does it mean to us, here, now? It's a *facer*, isn't it boys? But we've all got to answer it. What were the dead like? What sort of people are we living with now? Why are we here? What are we going to do?
     W. H. Auden, 'Address for a Prize Day',
     The Orators: An English Study (1932)

INTRODUCTION: A CULTURE SURCHARGED WITH DEATH

One of the key questions of modern literature was the problem of what to do with the war dead. In March 1915, just eight months into the First World War, in a paper delivered in Vienna, Sigmund Freud presciently noted that 'we cannot maintain our former attitude towards death, and have not yet discovered a new one'.[1] Freud expressed a common sentiment: that the ongoing war had already fundamentally changed the ways that people thought about death. The accompanying questions of how to bury, memorialise and grieve the dead began as soon as the war itself did – in August 1914 – and would continue long into the postwar period.

This book is about the ways that women writers wrote about death during and after the First World War. It examines the impact of the vast, unanticipated mortality on literary representations of death in British and American writing during and immediately after the war. It considers the particular role that women writers played in enacting, rehearsing and mediating the crisis in attitudes towards death caused by the war, while it was still ongoing and into the postwar period. The major premise of this book is that the extent and nature of the enormous death toll of the war changed the way that death was represented in literature: what Katherine Mansfield referred to as 'a change of heart', in regards to Virginia Woolf's 1919 novel *Night and Day*.[2] A second premise is that the unprecedented war losses and the subsequent cultures of both private memorialisation and public commemoration are a crucial yet overlooked context for literary development in this period, including but not limited to modernism. This book argues for the intertwining of modernist, war and memorial culture, suggesting that much of what we call modernist experimentation in terms of death can be traced to its specific sociohistorical wartime and postwar context.

The writers I examine here wrote death within a range of genres: some predominantly realist, some decidedly more modernist, and others working on a scale somewhere in between. Rather than radically redefining these terms, my argument extends and refines the concepts as understood in recent scholarship.[3] The texts I examine include works by writers of different ages, classes and nationalities: accounts and memoirs by British and American nurses, including Enid Bagnold, Ellen N. La Motte and Mary Borden; works by Edith Wharton, an American who lived in France from 1911; the New Zealander Katherine Mansfield, and the American H.D. (Hilda Doolittle), who both spent most of their adult lives in Europe; and the British author Virginia Woolf. On the way I also touch on texts by Rudyard Kipling, Rose Macaulay, E. M. Forster, Jean Rhys, Christopher Isherwood and Elizabeth Bowen, among others. I have focused my discussion on predominantly Anglo-American women writers. The American writers I discuss here lived in Europe; writers from elsewhere, such as Mansfield and Rhys, made Europe their home. My geographical focus is therefore predominantly European and specifically British, but in bringing these writers together, I have kept in mind their particular national literary traditions, histories and commemorative cultures.

Modernist culture in the heart of the modern period (roughly 1910–30) was inherently a war culture, and the study of First World War literature is necessarily historicist and interdisciplinary. My primary sources are literary texts (novels, memoirs, short stories, letters, diaries, manuscript drafts, and newspaper and magazine articles). I read these fictional and non-fictional texts as war writings, produced in the context of total war, which constitutes their shared subject matter or subtext, whether explicitly or implicitly. I simultaneously draw on visual (photographs, postcards, paintings, drawings, film, propaganda posters) and material cultures of memorialisation (break-the-news-letters, scrapbooks, memorial volumes, mourning artefacts and memorabilia, and new cemeteries and war memorials). My methodology combines close readings of texts, including manuscript versions, and archival research with analysis of the new death and commemorative culture that developed as a result of the war.

Although there is not an inherently sexed mode of dying or response to death, I focus primarily on women writers because of the dramatically different experience of death and bereavement for women and men during and after the war. This includes women in the war zones such as nurses, who dealt with death on a daily basis, and civilian women, the 'community of mourners' distinguished by Freud as 'those who [. . .] have only to wait for the loss of their dear ones by wounds, disease, or infection'.[4] Combat, and co-extensively death in combat, was an experience from which women were excluded; the ideology of making the 'ultimate sacrifice' in the name of King and Country was a clearly sexed position asked only of men. A relatively small number of women died while working in the war zones or on the home front during air raids, but importantly these accidental deaths were not part of the ideology of warfare, except as victims. The linking of women with the death (or life) of another person was part of war ideology, however, and the image of women as life-givers was frequently used in recruiting efforts for war work, particularly nursing.

The culturally constructed position of the mourning woman was consolidated during the Great War. This followed immediate historical precedent: women were the primary carers around the nineteenth-century deathbed.[5] Carol Acton notes that we must consider 'the individual experience of loss and grief [...] as gendered, both in terms of the particular wartime environment and the more general way cultures prescribe different grief responses and mourning behaviour for men and women', arguing that 'such "gendering" privileges women, particularly mothers, as mourners'.[6] Joy Damousi notes 'the universality of women as central to the cultural practices of mourning' during and after the war despite 'profound cultural differences in mourning rituals surrounding the war dead'.[7] A number of postwar official commemorative efforts were specifically aligned with female mourners. The guests of honour at the unveiling of the Tomb of the Unknown Warrior in Westminster Abbey on 11 November 1920 included a group of 100 bereaved women, chosen because they had each lost a husband and a son in the war.[8] Similarly, the memorandum suggesting the Two Minutes' Silence included as its intended beneficiaries 'the women who have lost and suffered and borne so much'.[9] Women's groups, such as the Gold Star Mothers in the United States (founded in 1928), established particular commemorative rituals and tributes and organised for memorials to be constructed.[10] The burden of mourning was symbolically focused on women, making them predominantly responsible for the emotional labour of the war (see Fig. I.1). Their different, largely civilian experience of death – as survivors – resulted in different modes of written representation.

In some ways, a focus on women might seem outmoded. Early literary and cultural histories of the war were primarily concerned with the male combatant experience.[11] In line with feminist scholarship and the development of women's studies, the surge of critical attention paid to women's First World War writing from the 1980s onwards argued for the importance of a gendered reaction to the war and its impact on women's writing, consciousness, and social position.[12] Historical studies of the broad variety of women's wartime experience have investigated women's war work and identity.[13] The accessibility of women's war writing has increased through a number of anthologies and editions.[14] The question of gender continues to be an important category of analysis in recent scholarship.[15] Historical scholarship has examined women's

Figure I.1 David McLellan, Members of the Women's Army Auxiliary Corps carrying wreaths to place on the graves of British soldiers buried at Abbeville, 9 February 1918. © IWM (Q 8471)

roles in grief and bereavement during and after the war, typically in national contexts.[16] However, only a small number of critics have explicitly addressed this link in the context of British and American First World War writing: excellent work by Jane Marcus, Margaret R. Higonnet and Carol Acton focuses largely on the experience of nurses.[17] I am indebted to all of this scholarship. My particular aim here is to analyse the impact of the war on women's written representations of death, both by civilians and those in the war zones.

In separating this project into varying degrees of proximate and distanced encounters with death, both geographically and temporally, I suggest that the proximity in which an author encountered the war dead influenced their mode of representation.[18] I examine proximity both literally and metaphorically. Although the geographical distance between civilians on the home front and soldiers in war zones was not that great – a popular truism ran that officers could be in the trenches in the morning and eating at their favourite club in London by the evening – there was a disjunction, frequently figured as a gulf in experience, between those who had been in the war zones and those who had not. The imaginative distance between these two groups was vast. I am simultaneously interested in the idea of proximity on a metaphorical level, in terms of sympathy and engagement. For example, a nurse may be physically close to her patient, but remain distanced emotionally. In many cases, proximate or intimate depictions of death draw on more traditional motifs and (borrowing from Jay Winter) 'sites' such as the deathbed and the graveyard – even if only to demonstrate that those sites are no longer useful – whereas distanced representations of death tend to result in abstract, less corporeally focused modes of representation, pointing towards what Allyson Booth usefully terms 'civilian modernism'.[19] This relates to what Booth refers to as 'corpselessness' to describe the home front in Britain, and 'corpses' to describe the war zones, resulting in, in many cases, a correlation between the presence or absence of a corpse and the degree of literary realism or modernist abstraction.[20] Of course there are exceptions to this.

This study also considers temporal proximity. Rather than focusing belatedly on modernist texts from the 1920s or the 'War Books Boom' of 1928–30, this study is divided into texts written during the war and those written after it had ended, although these divisions were not always as straightforward as calendar dates might suggest. It begins with texts written while the war was still ongoing, in line with Hazel Hutchison's argument about American First World War writing that 'the really creative moment, the ignition spark of innovation, happened *during* the war'.[21] Literature written under the conditions of war and without knowledge of when it would end provides some of the most generically and linguistically experimental examples of First World War writing. If not the genesis of postwar modernism, then this writing demonstrates a serious acceleration in its development.

The tension between tradition and change in representing the war dead belongs to the broader debate concerning the war as a break with, or continuation of, historical and literary development. Key cultural critics have depicted the war and its mass death as inaugurating a new 'modern' era and modes of thought: prominently, Paul Fussell's argument for the war as the beginning of 'modern memory' and Modris Eksteins's depiction of the war as the birth of 'the modern age'.[22] Fussell's landmark study of British combatant narratives set the precedent for studies of the war's cultural legacy, with his thesis that irony, the 'dominating form of modern understanding', has its origins 'largely in the application of mind and memory to the events of the Great War'.[23] However, only a handful of instances here show women writers using irony as their primary mode of expression. Samuel Hynes's study *A War Imagined: The First World War and English Culture* argues that the war was not only 'the great military and political event of its time' but also 'the great *imaginative* event': 'how English culture was transformed, and English imaginations were altered, by what happened between

1914 and 1918'. Hynes's wide-ranging exploration of the war's cultural legacies includes 'Modernist works that are not a part of what we would ordinarily call war literature' by D. H. Lawrence, Woolf and others. The war 'added a new scale of violence and destruction to what was possible', and in so doing, 'it changed reality'. For Hynes, one of the most prominent cultural tropes generated is the 'Myth of the War': a 'sense of radical discontinuity of present from past' which became common in postwar literature.[24]

In contrast, Jay Winter's *Sites of Memory, Sites of Mourning: The Great War in European Cultural History* argues that the predominant social and cultural response to the enormous death toll was a reversion to traditional ('classical, romantic, or religious') modes of mourning, and their 'enduring appeal [. . .] lay in their power to mediate bereavement'. Winter usefully reminds us, however, that the distinction between 'modernist' and 'traditional' forms 'was at times more rhetorical than real': 'Modernists didn't obliterate traditions; they stretched, explored, and reconfigured them'.[25] By examining whether authors wrote in 'traditional' modes (through the representation of sites such as the deathbed and the graveyard) or in more abstract 'modernist' terms (sites not usually associated with war death, such as the female body or the cinema), or a combination of both, we can begin to trace changing attitudes towards death, grief and memorialisation.

In *Postcards from the Trenches: Negotiating the Space between Modernism and the First World War* (1996), Allyson Booth articulates one of the underlying premises of my project: that 'we read modernism without fully realizing the extent to which it handles the bones of the war dead'.[26] Despite the growth of the field in recent years, there is much to be done to fulfil the necessity of a truly historicised modernism in the context of the First World War. In what follows I present a short history of death before, during and after the war; a review of the fields of modernist death, and modernism and the First World War; and a chapter summary.

Death before the First World War

We cannot overestimate the effect of the First World War on contemporary and later perceptions of, and attitudes to, death. David Cannadine has argued that 'its significance was profound for at least a generation [. . .] that interwar Britain was probably more obsessed with death than any other period in modern history'.[27] Adrian Gregory refers to the war and postwar period as 'a transitional moment in the history of attitudes towards death'.[28] Pat Jalland argues that the war was 'a major turning-point in the history of death', which 'shattered what remained of the Victorian way of death'.[29]

The Victorian culture of death was extensive, extravagant and highly prescribed, with strict socially enforced rituals.[30] Jalland describes the idealised conventions of the mid-Victorian, Evangelical 'good death':

Death ideally should take place at home, with the dying person making explicit farewells to each family member. There should be time, and physical and mental capacity, for the completion of temporal and spiritual business, whether the latter signified final Communion or informal family devotions. The dying person should be conscious and lucid until the end, resigned to God's will, able to beg forgiveness for past sins and to prove his or her worthiness for salvation.

The moment of death was significant in religious terms because of the expectation of immediate divine judgement. Conversion often happened on the deathbed. The *ars moriendi*, literature on the art of dying, as well as deathbed scenes in religious tracts, therefore provided instruction on 'dying well'.[31] Through well-known deathbed scenes, literature became a means of consolidating the myth of the good death and its conventions. Following death, the body was kept in the home and displayed at the wake, before being buried in as elaborate a funeral as the family could afford.

Victorian funerary and mourning practices were ostentatious, expensive and prolonged, with bereavement paraphernalia a lucrative industry. Two key aspects of this culture stand out for our purposes. First, the task of mourning was undertaken and embodied predominantly by women, who wore mourning dress and remained isolated from society for a lengthy period: a culture of female mourning aptly represented by the reigning monarch, Victoria, the so-called 'Widow of Windsor'. Second, this culture of bereavement was linked physically to the body of the loved one. Fashionable mourning jewellery – a ring containing a tooth or a necklace containing the hair of the deceased – was worn by women. Postmortem memorial photography showed mourners with their arms around or touching the corpse, which was posed in a naturalistic manner as though still alive. Following a child's death, parents commissioned mourning dolls: life-size wax effigies dressed in the child's clothing and incorporating their hair, lying in coffin-like boxes. The doll, filled with sand for a life-like feel when held, was kept in the home until burial and then typically left at the child's grave. This surfeit of the material in the scene of Victorian death was matched by the surfeit of words in deathbed scenes in the Victorian novel, most prominently the lengthy, sentimentalised deathbed of Little Nell in Charles Dickens's *The Old Curiosity Shop* (1841).[32] This physical intimacy and closeness with the body of a loved one would be, in most cases, erased in wartime.

However, these death and mourning customs were changing well before 1914. The unprecedented decrease in mortality rates was largely due to medical improvements, better standards of public health and housing conditions, higher wages, shorter working hours and a more nourishing diet. Life expectancy increased, and the lower rate of child mortality made it uncommon for the young to die before the old. By the outbreak of war, Cannadine argues, 'the English were less intimately acquainted with death than any generation since the industrial revolution'. The National Funeral and Mourning Reform Association, founded 1875, campaigned for 'moderation' and 'simplicity' instead of 'unnecessary show' at funerals; a trend reflected by Queen Victoria's far less elaborate funeral in 1901 than Wellington's in 1852.[33] From the 1890s onwards, the length of mourning had been 'considerably shortened, and the mourning garb shorn of its distinctiveness'.[34] In wartime, the continuing 'simplification of mourning dress and the rejection of black crepe' was promoted by the state out of concern that 'thousands of widows in formal widows' weeds would demoralise the nation'.[35] Modes of dealing with the dead were slowly changing alongside burial rituals. New crematoria, built in England from 1884, remained largely unpopular: by 1918, only 0.3 per cent of funerals involved cremation.[36] Religious belief was changing too. Jalland notes the 'gradual decline in Christian faith between 1850 and 1918', as church attendance ceased to keep pace with population growth, meaning that mourners 'were steadily losing the biblical language of consolation'. This accounted in part for the growth of spiritualism, or communication with dead spirits through rapping, automatic writing and séances, which gained further in popularity as the war began.[37] The glorification of 'death on active service, in battle, in the front line, for one's country' would contribute to the rapid voluntary enlistment of over 750,000 men by the end of September 1914.

In this context, the shock at the sheer numbers of war dead is even more understandable. Worldwide losses totalled approximately 10 million soldiers (6 million Allied soldiers, 4 million from the Central Powers) and 7 million civilians. Winter estimates that between 722,785 and 772,000 British citizens died as a result of the war, and that total losses from the Empire were over 1 million.[38] Of the 6 million Allied men who served, one in eight died. The 20,000 losses on the first day of the Somme was 'the equivalent of all British losses in the Boer War'. The shock of the dead was seemingly the same across the class spectrum: 'However illustrious or insignificant were the bereaved [. . .] their basic reactions were similar, namely numbed incredulity'.[39] It is difficult to comprehend these enormous figures. Historians tell us that 'every family was in mourning: most for a relative [. . .] others for a friend, a colleague, a lover, a companion'; that 'the wider circle of those touched by wartime death [. . .] encompassed the entire population'.[40] One prominent individual experience of bereavement is Vera Brittain, who recorded the loss of her fiancé, two close friends and brother in her memoir *Testament of Youth*.[41] Attempts to depict the enormous numbers temporally and spatially, such as Sir Fabian Ware's striking calculation that if the Empire's dead marched four abreast down Whitehall, it would take them *three and a half days* to pass the Cenotaph. Although there was not a 'lost generation' as such – the majority of men who went to war '*did actually come back'* – the symbolic as much as the literal impact of these huge numbers of dead was, and remains, pervasive.[42] This was, as H.D. wrote to the poet Marianne Moore in 1917, a culture 'surcharged with death'.[43]

WARTIME DEATH

The official response to the war dead was as unprepared in practical terms as that of individuals in mental terms. In earlier wars, soldiers had been buried in mass, unmarked graves, with only the higher ranks being commemorated – or celebrated – on columns, arches, and civic structures such as railway stations. During the Boer War, the most recent war in British memory, it had been the Loyal Women's Guild who had attempted to account for the dead.[44] As the war continued, the British government's lack of official protocol for how to deal with the dead in practical terms was a problem that increased in urgency every day.

The ways in which men could die in battle and in the war zones expanded rapidly. In comparison with the Victorian good death, war deaths were 'sudden, violent, premature, ugly deaths of young healthy adults, with bodies often smashed and unidentifiable'.[45] It was often impossible to retrieve bodies while fighting was still ongoing or in adverse weather conditions. Cannadine writes that 'after any major offensive, the combat zone might remain littered for weeks with bodies – gradually decomposing and giving off a nauseous, unforgettable stench'.[46] Men were living among the dead in what Booth calls the 'corpsescapes' of the Western Front.[47] Death was 'inescapable': 'Any soldier would see more of it in a week at the front than he might reasonably have expected to have witnessed in a lifetime'.[48]

Although soldiers attempted to bury their comrades with a chaplain present, this activity itself could result in more deaths. Bodies were initially buried where they fell in shallow, ad hoc graves, marked by any suitable nearby item: in one instance, the back of a metal Pocket Kodak camera case was used as a grave marker for two soldiers killed in April 1916.[49] Towards the end of the war, standardised wooden crosses were used. The previous sanctity of the corpse disappeared in wartime: 'New trenches might be dug through them; parapets might be made of them; even bodies decently buried might come to the surface again'.[50] New weaponry meant that men could be blown to pieces, not leaving an entire corpse to bury. Burial parties attempted to identify men using their identification tags or through their possessions, some of which might include a name. From 1915, it was an army requirement to wear green and red identification tags round the neck, giving key details including religion in order that the man might receive an appropriate burial, but this was difficult to ensure in wartime. The green tag stayed with the body, while the red tag could be cut away and retained by the authorities. Some men wore 'unofficial identity tags fashioned from coins, such was the fear of being unidentified'.[51]

The origins and evolution of the Commonwealth War Graves Commission have been well documented, but it is useful to briefly consider the role of the man known as the 'Great Commemorator'. Arriving in France in September 1914, Fabian Ware, the commander of a mobile unit of the British Red Cross, immediately noted the need for a system to locate graves of the dead. The British Red Cross had set up a Wounded and Missing Department in the first few days of the war, but it had only a handful of volunteers and lacked an adequate database or system, in the face of what were 'unimaginable' casualties by the end of the first year.[52] Ware's amateur work was recognised by the War Office and reorganised as the Graves Registration Commission (GRC) and subsumed into the British Army by March 1915. General Douglas Haig's letter to the War Office the same month emphasises the 'moral value' of the unit:

> It is fully recognised that the work of the organisation is of purely sentimental value, and that it does not directly contribute to the successful termination of the war. It has, however, an extraordinary moral value to the troops in the field as well as to the relatives and friends of the dead at home. The mere fact that these officers visit day after day the cemeteries close behind the trenches, fully exposed to shell and rifle fire, accurately to record not only the names of the dead but also the exact place of burial, has a symbolic value to the men that it would be difficult to exaggerate.

Haig was also thinking about postwar accountability: 'on the termination of hostilities the nation will demand an account from the Government as to the steps which have been taken to mark and classify the burial places of the dead, steps which can only be effectively taken at, or soon after, burial'.[53] The Commission was, of course, of great interest to families at home. In spring 1915 it began to receive and answer letters of enquiry and requests for photographs of graves from relatives, as well as send the location of cemeteries. Following the lifting of the prohibition on war photographs of graves (granted only for the Commission), by mid-August 1915 the GRC had photographed 6,000 graves, sent 800 photographs to families, and registered 18,173 graves.[54] By May 1916 the registration figure was over 50,000. By this time, the Commission had become the Directorate of Graves Registration and Enquiries, becoming the Imperial War Graves Commission in 1917, the official body for locating bodies and informing families, as well as locating the missing.[55] E. M. Forster was one of the 'Searchers' for the missing, as we will see in Chapter 5. Women serving as gardeners in Queen Mary's Army Auxiliary Corps in France were often tasked with tending the war graves, as seen in this 1919 photograph by Olive Edis (Edis, the first official female war photographer, had been commissioned by the Imperial War Museum to document women's services; see Fig. I.2).

Figure I.2 Olive Edis, Women's Army Auxiliary Corps gardeners tending the graves of the war dead at Étaples, 1919. © IWM (Q 8027)

How was death experienced by noncombatants on the home front? In early 1915, the British Government made the highly contested decision to bury bodies where they fell, rather than return them home. The American government, by contrast, decided to let families decide whether or not to repatriate their dead.[56] Cannadine stresses 'the difference between those at the front, who saw and purveyed *death*, and those at home, who saw no death, no carnage and no corpses, but who experienced *bereavement*'.[57] Civilians were not allowed to enter the war zones without a special permit, and could only visit wounded relatives in hospitals behind the lines under very special circumstances. Death on the battlefield or scenes of combat were never depicted in newspaper photographs because of the 1916 Defence of the Realm Act (DORA).[58] This perhaps helps to account for the immense popularity of the 1916 film *The Battle of the Somme*, where its combat scenes and (faked) death scene attracted huge audiences.[59] For noncombatants, the experience of war death was therefore largely one of imaginative re-construction. The distinction between the combatant and the noncombatant experience was, at least in one aspect, the difference between corporeal, visceral death and death related only in words: between matter and information.

For civilians, the wartime years were marked by intense anxiety and prolonged waiting for news. Notification of a death came in various forms. The

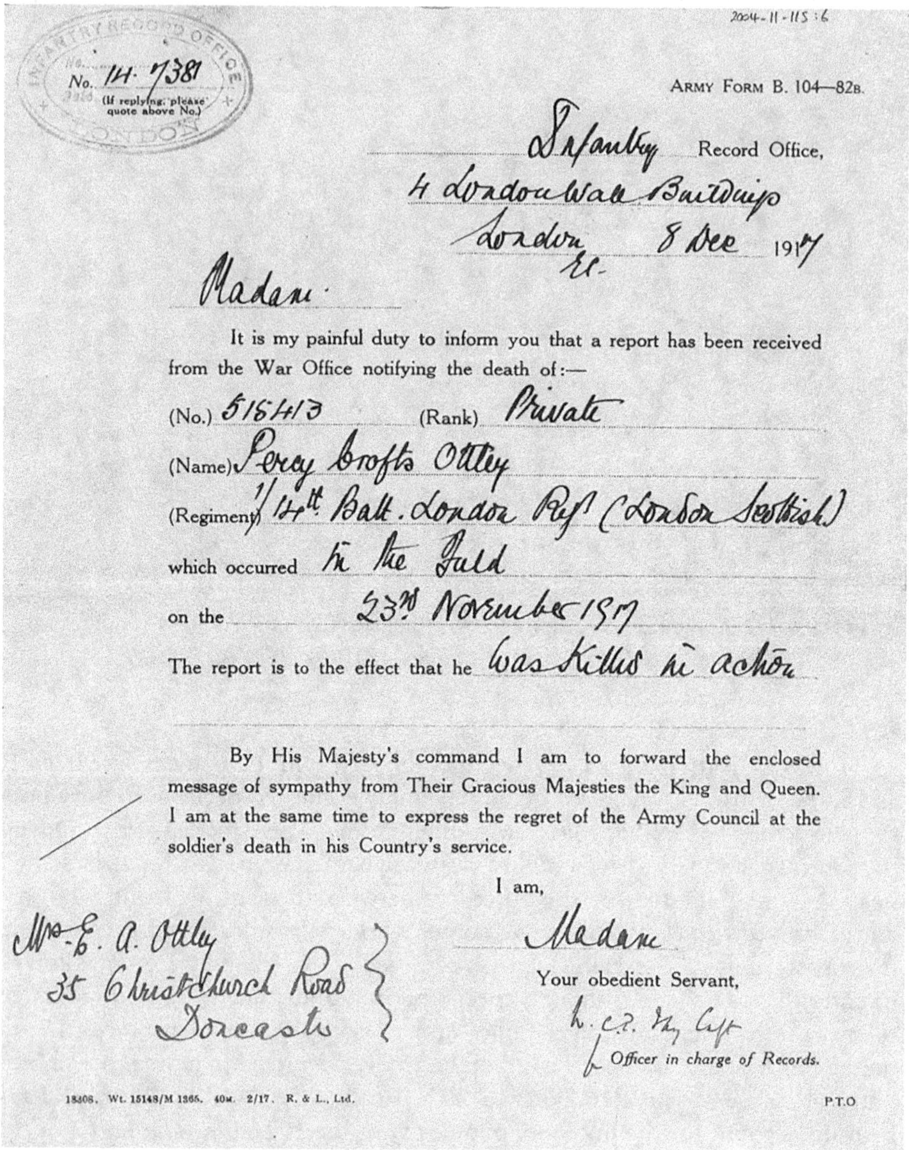

2004-11-115:6

No. 14·7381
(If replying, please quote above No.)
INFANTRY RECORD OFFICE LONDON

ARMY FORM B. 104—82B.

Infantry Record Office,
4 London Wall Buildings
London E.C. 8 Dec 1917

Madam.

It is my painful duty to inform you that a report has been received from the War Office notifying the death of:—

(No.) 515413 (Rank) Private

(Name) Percy Crofts Ottley

(Regiment) 1/14th Batt. London Regt (London Scottish)

which occurred In the Field

on the 23rd November 1917

The report is to the effect that he was killed in action

By His Majesty's command I am to forward the enclosed message of sympathy from Their Gracious Majesties the King and Queen. I am at the same time to express the regret of the Army Council at the soldier's death in his Country's service.

I am,

Madam

Your obedient Servant,

Mrs E. A. Ottley
35 Christchurch Road
Doncaster

for Officer in charge of Records.

18308. Wt. 15148/M 1365. 40M. 2/17. R. & L., Ltd. P.T.O.

Figure I.3 Official letter (Army Form B.104) from the Infantry Record Office informing Mrs Ethel A. Ottley of the death of her husband, 8 December 1917. NAM. 2004-11-115-6. Reproduced courtesy of the Council of the National Army Museum, London parents of officers were informed by telegrams, whereas letters were sent to the parents of soldiers, which could take weeks to arrive (see Fig. I.3). In some cases this notification was not even certain; 'the "missing, feared killed" telegram' only made 'the subsequent news of death even harder to bear'.[60] 'Missing *always* means dead' says the mother in Kipling's 1925 story 'The Gardener': a sentiment that was more often right than not.[61] In some towns, local vicars were sent the names of the dead to deliver the news in person. Casualty lists were published daily in *The Times*, which meant that families might read about their death of their loved one in a general list before they had received individual notification. Fellow soldiers, superiors or nurses would often write informal, consolatory letters, giving further details about a man's death, the nature of his injuries and any last words. These letters were routinely embellished, typically depicting the death as painless and quick, that he was popular and much loved among his comrades, and had died a hero.[62] These letters were the first narrative mediation of a death, and in some aspects represent an attempted return to the Victorian deathbed scene. Later fictional renditions would not always be so consolatory.

In these circumstances, conventional burial and mourning rituals became unworkable. The decision not to return bodies home meant that families had no physical manifestation or place on which to focus their grief, and often found 'the reality of death almost impossible to accept'.[63] Except for those who died in hospitals on the home front, families could not hold funerals for their dead men. Unlike the Victorian tradition of an expensive, ostentatious and individualised funeral to denote social status even in death, complete with socially demarcated burial plots and headstones, wartime death and burial was startlingly democratic.

The design and creation of war cemeteries began while the war was still ongoing. The November 1918 report written by Sir Frederic Kenyon, Director of the British Museum, entitled *War Graves: How the Cemeteries Abroad Will be Designed*, made recommendations for the new cemeteries based on architectural proposals, as well as landscaping expertise from the Royal Botanic Gardens at Kew and the garden designer Gertrude Jekyll, and advice from Kipling, the literary advisor to the IWGC, on suitable inscriptions. The three architects Kenyon recommended – Sir Edwin Lutyens, Sir Herbert Baker and Sir Reginald Blomfield – created the now familiar cemeteries, following the construction of three trial versions. Each cemetery included a secular Stone of Remembrance designed by Lutyens with an inscription suggested by Kipling ('Their Name Liveth For Evermore' from the Book of Ecclesiasticus), and the more Christian Cross of Sacrifice, designed by Blomfield. Demonstrating the role played by writers in this process of public commemoration, Kipling was tasked with effectively selling the controversial designs to the grieving public in a *Times* article in February 1919, after the outcry provoked by Kenyon's report. The article was rapidly republished as a booklet, *The Graves of the Fallen*, with illustrations intended to make the proposed cemeteries more acceptable.[64] Despite much opposition, the designs were agreed. The 'flurry of construction' after the war 'resulted in the creation of more than 500 permanent cemeteries and 400,000 headstones by 1927'.[65]

The real innovation, however, was the equal treatment of the dead. The First World War was characterised by what Thomas Laqueur calls a 'commemorative hyper-nominalism', where 'both during the war and after, the state poured enormous human, financial, administrative, artistic, and diplomatic resources into preserving and remembering the names of individual common soldiers'. This break in tradition represents 'a radical departure not only from earlier military practice [. . .] but also from nineteenth-century British domestic custom'. Although 'genuinely new' with their named, individual graves, war cemeteries were simultaneously shocking in their democratic uniformity.[66] Relatives could not choose grave memorials: instead all bodies were buried with an identical plain Portland limestone headstone, which was 2 feet, 6 inches, by 1 foot, 3 inches. A religious emblem and any military decorations were noted on the headstone. The one element of personalisation was the possibility of a sixty-six character inscription (with a fee per character), which had to be approved by the IWGC.[67] The standardised lettering designed by Leslie MacDonald Gill (younger brother of the artist Eric Gill) was inscribed at an angle designed to ensure the permanency of the inscription.

Further demonstrating the cultural construction of women as primary mourners, many of the inscriptions chosen specifically invoked the loss to mothers: 'OH TO HAVE CLASPT / YOUR HAND DEAR HERBERT / TO HAVE BROUGHT YOU HOME / TO REST. (MOTHER)' reads one. Others read: 'EVER IN MY THOUGHTS / MY ONLY CHILD / MOTHER' and simply 'MY BELOVED FIRST BORN'. Others sought reassurance for mothers through their inscriptions, either to assuage guilt ('FORGIVE O LORD / A MOTHER'S WISH / THAT DEATH / HAD SPARED HER SON') or that the dead son is in fact OK ('"I'M ALL RIGHT MOTHER / CHEERIO"', quoting a letter home).[68]

Inscriptions on headstones were only possible for those whose bodies had been found. There were 300,000 British and Empire servicemen still missing in 1921, some of whose bodies have never been recovered.[69] Their names were instead inscribed on the newly designed monuments to the missing, with epitaphs written in Books of Remembrance. The largest of these monuments is the Thiepval Memorial to the Missing of the Somme, designed by Lutyens and built in 1928–32, which includes the names of 72,337 British and South African servicemen. For some families these new cemeteries and memorials must have given a form to what had been formless in the wartime and immediate postwar years: a structure, a location, a uniform shape. For others this state ownership of their dead only exacerbated their sense of loss. The numerous examples of parents writing to ask to pay for their son's repatriation were routinely denied. It is not difficult to see why some Victorian parents found this so difficult.

Another episode in the modern history of death bears consideration here: the three global waves of the influenza epidemic from January 1918 to March 1920. The origins of the pandemic remain disputed, but the first wave reached the western front trenches by mid-April 1918.[70] In August 1918 the second-most deadly wave circulated throughout the world, accelerated by troop movements, overcrowded hospitals and military camps, before slowing down in December 1918. It was longer-lived in Europe, where food and fuel shortages meant that people were already malnourished and with weaker immune systems. The flu affected military operations, as both sides suffered high mortality rates. Germany's higher numbers of losses put paid to the Allied fear that the flu was a German weapon of war. The third and final wave took place during the first six months of 1919, impacting the peace negotiations.

The flu, as Laura Spinney notes, killed 50–100 million people, or between 2.5 and 5 per cent of the global population – a range that reflects the uncertainty that still surrounds it' and was dramatic enough to impact life expectancy rates. It 'infected one in three people on earth', and was most fatal in people aged 20–40 and pregnant women.[71] The month before the sudden death of his pregnant daughter Sophie from flu in January 1920, Freud wrote to his friend Ernest Jones, 'Can you remember a time so full of death as this present one?'[72] In contrast to absent war corpses, this surplus of flu corpses meant a return to the deathbed and dying at home. In England and Wales undertakers could not keep up with the deaths, meaning that 'bodies were often left in people's houses for days or weeks', sometimes in rooms with the living.[73]

In these circumstances, why does the flu epidemic not play a larger role in the cultural history of death? The most important factor is timing. The epidemic came in the final year of the war, when an exhausted public had become accustomed to hearing about deaths of young men. Second, it was difficult to assess the size and scale of the epidemic, especially because wartime censorship prevented it being reported. (The lack of censorship in neutral Spain is the reason it became known as the 'Spanish Flu'.) Third, although flu killed more people than the war worldwide, this wasn't the case in Europe: 'France lost six times more souls to the war than to the flu, while in Germany the multiple was four, in Britain three and in Italy two'.[74] For France, Germany, Britain and Italy, flu deaths, reported alongside war deaths, must have seemed like just another type of wartime loss. Jalland argues that people 'tended to blame the war' for flu deaths and in this way 'the memory of the killer epidemic was subsumed in that of the war'.[75] Others linked the dead of the war with the flu in a different way, suggesting that the flu was the result of 'noxious vapours rising from the cadavers left behind on the killing fields'.[76] The scant cultural legacy of the flu has also contributed to its lack of a strong place in cultural memory: the best-known story about the epidemic, the American writer Katherine Anne Porter's 'Pale Horse, Pale Rider' only appeared in 1939.

Death after the War: Public and Private Modes of Memorialisation

In the period immediately following the First World War, there was an increasingly apparent need for public, official modes of commemoration of the war dead, as well as more personal modes of individual memorialisation. Examining public and official frames of remembrance allows an analysis of whether a similar rhetoric is used in personal, unofficial modes, specifically literary memorialisation. Cannadine suggests that both these attempts, public and private, 'to come to terms with death in interwar Britain [. . .] were in large part spontaneously generated by the bereaved for their own comfort'.[77] Booth similarly notes the 'urgency with which the civilian public insisted upon the erection of war memorials to the dead and missing'.[78] The wartime and postwar need for some means of marking, dignifying and memorialising the war dead similarly underlies the writing that I examine here.

The narratives of the development and establishment of public structures of remembrance – the temporary Cenotaph (constructed for 'Victory Day' on 19 July 1919), the Two Minutes' Silence (begun on 11 November 1919), the unveiling of the permanent Cenotaph and the Burial of the Unknown Warrior (both on 11 November 1920), and the Poppy Appeal (begun in 1921), and many local memorials – have been explored at length. Hynes describes the postwar trope of 'monument-making', suggesting that a monument 'records the dead, and so gives dignity to their undignified deaths', and simultaneously 'reassures non-combatants that the dead died willingly and do not resent or repent their sacrifice'. Monuments work as 'official acts of closure' which 'embody, in permanent form, ideas about war – heroic, romantic, histrionic, occasionally tragic'. He argues that monuments 'belong to the discourse of Big Words, and by existing they affirm the meaning and value of those words'.[79] Discussing the 'language of memorialisation' used for the many new physical memorials created in the postwar period, Gregory writes:

> This language during the 1920s drew heavily on pre-war rhetoric of God, Empire, King and Country, on notions of sacrifice and on presenting the war in terms of a crusade for human dignity and liberty. The 'Big Words' were used in abundance because they were the best form of giving comfort to those who grieved.

Gregory notes that the success of the British war correspondent Philip Gibbs's collected dispatches was because 'he knew what his readers needed in 1919: brave, consolatory language that would shore up their faith in the war they had won, a monument of words'.[80] The consolatory power of these words is, of course, contested. However, the official acts of monument-making, whether physical monuments or the development of rituals, were couched in a conservative language that attempted to reinstate the wartime values of patriotism and heroism. As Winter has suggested, '[t]raditional modes of seeing the war [...] provided a way of remembering which enabled the bereaved to live with their losses, and perhaps leave them behind'.[81]

A more personalised version of the official monuments and memorials were the medals and plaques that women who had lost a loved one received, signifying state recognition of their loss (see Figs I.4 and I.5). In Britain and across the Empire, women and next-of-kin received the Memorial Plaque, along with a personalised Memorial Scroll bearing the deceased's name and a consolatory letter from King George V: 'I join with my grateful people in sending you this memorial of a brave life given for others in the Great War'. The bronze Memorial Plaque, or Dead Man's Penny as it became known due to its similarity with the penny coin, featured various images of British might: Britannia holding a trident and laurel wreath, a lion, two dolphins, oak leaves with acorns, and a lion biting into a German eagle.[82] Britannia holds the wreath over the deceased's name, in raised letters and without rank. The text around the edge of the plaque asserts those Big Words: 'He died for freedom and honour'. About 1.3 million of these plaques were issued for male veterans (and 600 for female participants), from 1919 until well into the 1930s as veterans died from wounds sustained in the war. There was similar public recognition of the contribution of mothers in Canada, the United States and Italy.[83] In Australia, mothers received the Mothers' and Widows' Badge, made of black ribbon with

Figure I.4 Next of Kin Memorial Plaque for Sergeant Herbert Walter Stacey, 13 Squadron, Royal Air Force. © IWM (EPH 2223)

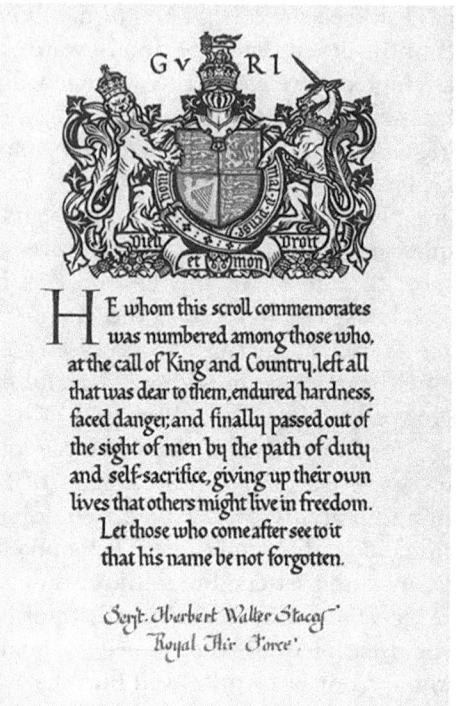

Figure 1.5 Next of Kin Memorial Scroll for Sergeant Herbert Walter Stacey, 13 Squadron, Royal Air Force. © IWM (EPH 2223)

the Rising Sun Australian Military Forces motif and words 'For Australia', suspended between one metal bar inscribed with laurel leaves and the other with a gold star for each son or husband who had died.[84]

As well as an official recognition of loss, these 'symbols of sacrifice manufactured en masse' functioned as a kind of miniature memorial, to be displayed in the home or worn at official commemorative events.[85] They provided something material in the absence of a body, which – aside from the man's returned personal effects and any letters and photographs – was the only official memory object the family had. Some incorporated these tokens into personal memorials, which, alongside photographs, 'made shrines of side boards'.[86] Of course, these objects were not universally well-received: some families sent their memorial plaques back in protest, and for some, these tokens 'soon came to be seen as hollow recognition'.[87] This state recognition of civilian grief only happened in the 'winning' nations – this practice did not happen in Germany, or at least not until the 1930s.[88]

Sponsored pilgrimage to the battlefields and cemeteries – which became known as the 'Silent Cities' – was an unofficial means of honouring bereaved women in the postwar period.[89] In contrast to the postwar trend for battlefield tourism, complete with guidebooks and luxury Thomas Cook tours, bereaved women were considered to be pilgrims.[90] In contrast to other countries, the British government didn't sponsor pilgrimages, meaning that it was predominantly middle- and upper-class families who could afford the trip.[91] Poorer women in Britain were therefore reliant on charitable organisations, such as the British War Graves Association, established by a bereaved mother in Leeds, which organised a pilgrimage to the cemeteries every Whitsuntide.[92]

Monument-making extended beyond stone and ritual. All of the arts saw the reworking of older and the development of new commemorative forms in the postwar period, a process which had begun during the war. New musical elegies included Ralph Vaughan Williams's *Pastoral Symphony*, first performed in London in January 1922 (Williams had served in the Royal Army Medical Corps); the soldier Ivor Gurney's *War Elegy*, written 1920 and first performed in 1921; and the civilian John Foulds's *A World Requiem*, written 1919–21 and performed on 11 November 1923 in the Royal Albert Hall as part of the Royal British Legion's first Festival of Remembrance. Foulds's work, which required 1,250 performers including singers performing in the 'London Cenotaph Choir', was billed as 'a Cenotaph in Sound'.[93] In art, the British War Memorials Committee, established within the Ministry (previously Department) of Information in February 1918, commissioned paintings and sculpture by artists such as John Singer Sargent, Charles Sergeant Jagger, Paul and John Nash, C. R. W. Nevinson, Percy Wyndham Lewis and Stanley Spencer, deliberately including modernist artists. These artworks were intended both to 'represent and commemorate all aspects of the war effort' and 'serve as a memorial to all Britons who lost their lives'. Three women artists – Anna Airy, Dorothy Coke and Flora Lion – were approached to contribute; the sole commission, to Airy, of women working in a munitions factory, was not finally accepted.[94]

Alongside commemorative art forms, new institutions of cultural memory – themselves memorials – were devised. The paintings and sculpture commissioned by the British War Memorials Committee were intended to be housed in a 'Hall of Remembrance' designed by the architect Charles Holden as 'a memorial gallery to the war dead'. This project was never finally realised because government funding was instead needed for postwar rebuilding.[95] The paintings were moved to the new Imperial War Museum, with some of them shown at *The Nation's War Paintings* exhibition at the Royal Academy, from December 1919 to February 1920 (extended due to its popularity).[96] Some of the paintings were particularly graphic in their depiction of the war. The deformed corpses lying in waterlogged shell holes in the foreground of C. R. W. Nevinson's *The Harvest of Battle* (1919) can hardly have been comforting to those gallery visitors seeking solace.

The creation of the Imperial War Museum in March 1917 (opened in July 1920) is an interesting example of war memory being institutionalised while the war was still ongoing. The idea for a museum was initially suggested by Charles ffoulkes, who became the Museum's first Secretary and Keeper. Sir Martin Conway (later the first Director) and Sir Alfred Mond (later first Chairman) proposed that it should be a memorial. Mond suggested calling it 'the great Imperial War Memorial', but this was rejected by the War Cabinet.[97] Again seeking to represent all aspects of war experience, the museum asked for donations of 'photographs and biographical material [. . .] of all officers and men who have lost their lives or won distinctions' and as well as 'letters, sketches, poems and other interesting documents sent from any of the war areas, and all kinds of mementoes, even of trifling character, which may be of interest in connection with the war'.[98] Clouting notes that this 'endeavour was utterly novel [. . .] to collect objects before the subject of the museum itself was fully concluded and understood'.[99] Sending a photograph of your dead son or brother or husband must have seemed to many a means of giving him a place in history. That more than 150,000 items were collected by the time the museum opened demonstrates that many people wanted their loved one enshrined in official memory (see Fig. I.6).[100]

Rather than official commemorative acts and rituals, my focus here is unofficial modes of representation and remembrance of war death in writing. Considering combatant narratives, Hynes asks: 'Are such narratives memorial gestures that fix and communicate public meaning, like war-monuments – the

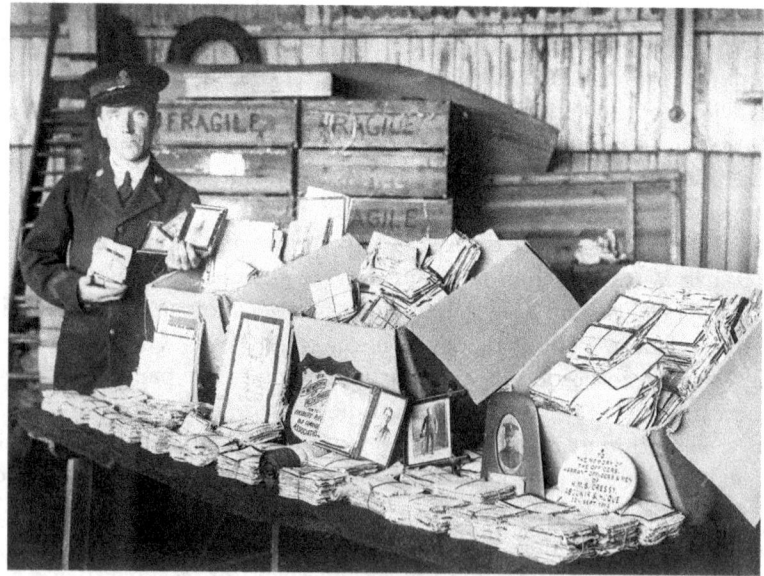

Figure I.6 Imperial War Museum appeal for mementos of the war dead.
© IWM (Q 24093)

Cenotaph or the Marine Corps Memorial or the Menin Gate? Or are they a different kind of gesture, a different act of making?'

The important difference between 'personal narratives and other acts of remembrance' is that 'only personal narratives are *stories* [. . .] only narratives happen along a line of time, in which meaning is not fixed but emergent'. Although Hynes doesn't use these terms, other types of memorials such as monuments or paintings, are synchronic, whereas written narratives are diachronic: '[m]eaning in narrative', he argues 'is that process in time, and not a frozen gesture'. This allows, as this project examines, the narration of the events leading up to a death, the death itself, and the events following a death. This diachronicity, as well as the presence of a voice in narrative which 'imposes private feelings and responses upon events', arguably creates a greater sense of immediacy and intimacy than other official acts of commemoration. As Hynes notes, '[y]ou participate vicariously in Robert Graves's war when you read *Goodbye to all that*; you don't experience a cemetery that way'. In this sense, written memorials do not only memorialise: they frequently attempt to represent and re-create the event of the death itself. Hynes argues that '[a]ll these kinds of war-narratives – the letters, the diaries, the memoirs – are acts of commemoration'.[101] Much of the literature I read here is commemorative in purpose.

In a war that, as Dan Todman notes, is largely remembered in terms of the mass death it entailed, these individual narratives of death contribute to a larger collective myth of the war.[102] Hynes writes:

> In the construction of a myth of war, memorials play a very small role, and personal narratives a very large one. Not any single narrative alone, but narratives collectively, for what war-stories construct is a combining story that is not told in any individual narrative, but takes its substance from the sum of many stories.

Considering the notion of 'collective memory', he suggests that the personal narratives of the combatants Siegfried Sassoon and Graves 'shape and colour the recollections of Private Smith, who never wrote a word about them', and therefore 'do create a kind of collective memory in the minds of men who shared a common war'. In usefully asking what exactly personal narratives commemorate, Hynes suggests that

> each narrative among the thousands that exist of modern wars, commemorates *one* life lived in the mass action of a modern war, that each is a monument of a kind to that one soldier, or sailor, or pilot, and to no one else, and by existing they refute and subvert the collective story of war that is military history.[103]

Hynes's analysis here relates to the role that literature plays in shaping cultural perceptions of, and responses to, war death. I am extending this examination of 'collective memory' in exploring the written responses of women who shared the same war, albeit in different roles. Especially in the cases of the nurses' narratives I discuss, these writings attempt to find literary forms to commemorate the lives of dozens, sometimes hundreds, of men, often focused through individual examples. Although singular narratives, they contribute to a larger myth and collective narrative of the experience of death during wartime, and they may serve as a monument to one person or to many.

Modernist Death

Although there are numerous studies considering the relation between modernism and mourning – typically about metaphorical, rather than actual mourning – much less has been written in relation to modernist death.[104] The few critical accounts of literary death focus largely on the nineteenth century.[105] The two studies of modernist death in British literature both argue for a specifically modernist mode of death, but posit the war as a contributing, rather than key, factor in changing literary representation. In *Fictional Death and the Modernist Enterprise* (1995), Alan Warren Friedman examines a range of male and female modernist writers and suggests that 'modernism begins with a shift to denial from the familial, climactic death central to Victorian life and letters'. He offers these characteristics of modernist death:

> No longer natural and culturally acceptable, fictional death became attenuated, denied, or horrific: initiatory or evaded rather than climactic. Subverting suspense, modern novels become circular and self-reflexive, returning repeatedly and ultimately to terminal events they rarely confront or transcend. Modernists elide the dying process [. . .] refract it through untrustworthy memory [. . .] base it in materiality [. . .] or foreground the complementarity of eros and thanatos [. . .]

Despite its repression, death is in fact ubiquitous in modernist literature, 'no longer tragic and consummatory', but instead 'unpredictable, incoherent, often initiatory and pervasive'. Death, Friedman suggests, 'leaks into language everywhere'.[106]

Ariela Freedman's *Death, Men, and Modernism: Trauma and Narrative in British Fiction from Hardy to Woolf* (2003) reads 'a canon of early twentieth-century works centrally concerned with a revaluation of the meaning of death'. The writers she examines all saw 'the modern relationship to death' as a 'crisis' in which '[t]raditional means of understanding or containing death no longer hold'. However, although she notes that the First World War 'made responding to death an issue of particular urgency for fiction writers', her focus is much larger than the war. What she identifies as the trope of the young dead man functions as 'a symptom and a symbol for the failure of modernity'; death plots are therefore 'symptoms of a crisis in meaning'. Her psychoanalytic thesis, arguing that frequently '[m]ale characters die in the place of female characters', means that she reads Woolf's *Mrs. Dalloway* and Mansfield's 'The Garden Party' as 'stories of innocence carefully and deliberately regained over a male dead body'.[107]

More like my understanding of British modernism, Pearl James in *The New Death: American Modernism and World War One* (2013) 'identifies modern, mechanized, mass death as one of the signal preoccupations and structuring contexts of canonical American modernist writing'. James traces the impact of the 'New Death' in work by Cather, Fitzgerald, Hemingway and Faulkner, seeking 'to reembed American novels of the postwar period within a context of pervasive death and unfinished mourning'. James considers 'how modernist novels reveal, refigure, omit, and aestheticize the violent death of young men in the aftermath of World War I'. She particularly considers 'how cultural norms of masculinity complicate the work of death in narrative', where in some cases, 'female bodies suffer more elaborately than male ones'.[108] Although our analysis stems from the same premise, James's reading differs from my own in its time-frame, geographical location and national context. James locates her reading of these postwar American modernist texts alongside different wartime repatriation and burial procedures, a development from the American Civil War. In contrast, my argument suggests that in the British case the process of representing the war dead necessarily began earlier, from as soon as the war began, and widens it to include both British and American texts.

Putting the war at the heart of this book aligns my work with this earlier scholarship and demonstrates a development of it. Here I argue for the war dead and the new culture of commemoration as a key preoccupation of, and context for, literary modernism. Although attitudes towards death were slowly changing in the late nineteenth and early twentieth centuries, I argue that it was the mass death of the war that was the primary factor in changing literary representation.

Modernism and the First World War: Handling the Bones of the War Dead

Although the key genealogies and surveys of modernism routinely refer to the significance and influence of the First World War, they fail to provide any sustained consideration of the particular means by which the war contributed to and developed modernist aesthetics, or how the experience of war, both psychological and material, provoked and stimulated new modes of literary expression.[109] Vincent Sherry has suggested these passing references are 'a sort of ritual invocation' serving 'to silence, not to stimulate [. . .] further inquiry'.[110] Beyond the assumption of pre- and postwar temporalities and the reproduction of standard clichés which posit the war as collective trauma, the war has been, and continues to be, strangely written out of modernist surveys. Andrew Frayn has argued that 'too often the relationship between modernism and the First World War continues to be avoided in the interests of not fetishizing it', as though the obviousness of the war and its clichés makes redundant any further investigations.[111] Only a few critics have considered the modernist war in any detail.

My work here is indebted to Booth's excellent *Postcards from the Trenches*, which examines the ways in which modernism is 'strangely haunted by the Great War'. Booth's study examines Anglophone literature alongside architecture, and her interdisciplinary analysis results in 'an expansive conception of modernism [. . .] that displays itself as deeply engaged in a broader Great War culture'. Her overarching metaphor of space allows her to question, with reference to Woolf's novels:

> How centrally or peripherally did the war figure in this and other of Woolf's novels? In other canonical modernist works? Did explicit accounts from the spaces of war – trenches, hospitals, and the infamous no man's land – have any relation to the literary spaces of Woolf's modernism?

Booth argues that the influence of the Great War permeates modernist form:

> even at moments when the spaces of war seem most remote, the perceptual habits appropriate to war emerge plainly; that the buildings of modernism may delineate spaces within which one is forced to confront both war's casualties and one's distance from those casualties; that the dislocations of war often figure centrally in modernist form, even when war itself seems peripheral to modernist content.

Booth suggests that the war provided a number of tropes and narrative structures in modernist writing, even in writing which doesn't ostensibly concern the war; that 'the idioms of modernism' have 'their important origins in the trenches of the Great War'. However, the modes used to represent war are not always modernist:

> War does not happen in a vacuum; men and women venture into it provided with the same perceptual equipment that they relied on to understand and articulate any other experience. In attempting to express war, they draw on the idioms and representational techniques that seem to fit best. Some conceptual categories and verbal methods

will lend themselves to the problem of articulating the new experience and be pressed into service frequently; others will seem less useful and be discarded.

Booth explicitly doesn't set out 'to construct rigid categories of modernist versus antimodernist texts', but 'rather to explore the multiple positions that modernism made available to inhabitants of a culture over which the Great War loomed'. Like mine, Booth's study concerns the multiple positions of proximity that affect representation. Unlike mine, however, it focuses on the constitution or re-constitution of categories (soldier and civilian, male and female), investigating 'the patterns that emerge as appropriate to both the experience of war and the experience of a world shaken up by war – patterns that both soldiers and civilians seem gradually to have internalized as fitting the disconcerting worlds of both combatant and civilian modernism'. Booth's modernism is a modernism

> constituted not so much in the space between men and women as in the space between civilians and combatants – or, more precisely, in the surprising array of imaginative methods that begin to bridge that space and to delineate a cultural and imaginative landscape that could take both combatant and civilian experience into account.

The emphasis throughout is on 'the ways in which war distorted previously existing shapes – ways of thinking – about death, national borders, time, military spaces such as battlefields, and civilian spaces such as buildings – and the ways in which modernism accommodated and articulated those distortions'.[112] Booth's project is the closest model for the study I undertake here, and my aim is to deepen and extend one aspect of her work: the literary 'distortions' prompted by changing ways of thinking about death.

In recent years, we have seen more examinations of the relationship between modernism and the Great War, although none of these have focused specifically on the representation of the war dead. One aim of Trudi Tate's *Modernism, History and the First World War* (1998) is 'to rethink the ways we read modernism'. She reads 'across a range of writings', including soldiers, nurses and civilians, stressing the connections between them:

> modernists and war writers reviewed one another's books, and war writings were discussed in avant-garde journals such as the *Little Review* and the *Egoist*. Reading them together, the distinction between 'modernism' and 'war writing' starts to dissolve – and was by no means clear at the time – and modernism after 1914 begins to look like a peculiar but significant form of war writing.[113]

I continue to stress the significance of these connections across different forms of writing here. In *The Great War and the Language of Modernism* (2003), Vincent Sherry locates the development of modernist technique within the changing contemporary political climate, specifically what he identifies as the 'breakdown in the established language of liberal modernity'. Examining the work of Pound, Stein, Eliot, Ford and Woolf, he argues that '[t]he writers of a specifically English modernism will distinguish themselves by identifying this crisis and realizing – incorporating – its meaning in an imaginative literature'.[114] More recently Marina MacKay has suggested that the 'decisive historicist turn in modernist studies over the past twenty years' has enabled us to see that 'even the most civilian of modernists was working in a social and cultural environment saturated and transformed by total war'.[115]

More generally, studies of First World War writing have broadened in their scope and interests to examine previously neglected aspects of the conflict. In 2005 Santanu Das identified 'the "second wave" of war criticism [. . .] marked by two important trends: interdisciplinarity and diversification of concern', trends which continue today.[116] The swathe of recent critical companions demonstrate the move of the genre into the critical commonplace and onto university syllabi.[117] Studies of publishing and reading histories have broadened the field of war writing to include popular literature and magazines.[118] The inherent difficulties of representing war experience in words have been considered.[119] Increasingly interdisciplinary studies have investigated the bodily, corporeal experience in wartime and its expression.[120] Critics, particularly Das, have begun to focus on racial and colonial aspects of the war.[121] Case studies have focused on specific genres or themes, and critics have significantly expanded the study of American First World War literature.[122] Recently, scholarly consideration of modernism and war has extended into the study of violence.[123]

Chapter Summary

Part One: Death in Proximity: Wartime Commemorations examines representations of death in writing by those who witnessed war deaths at first hand. This section includes the writings of nurses, who were participants in the war, and Edith Wharton, who visited the war zones a number of times. This section comes first in my study in order to examine the physical reality of war death for those who witnessed it, the changed modes of dying, grief and commemoration, and early attempts at memorialisation.

My first chapter focuses on a group of nurse narratives, and explores the ways in which women involved in hospitals in the war zones or at home witnessed and wrote about military death. Unlike my other author-specific chapters, this chapter is synoptic and incorporates published wartime and postwar memoirs and unpublished materials drawn from archival research in the Imperial War Museum, London. I focus on the representation of sites of death and commemoration – deathbeds, burial rites and cemetery scenes – and nurses' attempts to honour the dead in traditional modes. I argue that nurses turned back to these conservative aesthetic modes only to find they were no longer adequate for representing the war dead.

My second chapter examines Edith Wharton's wartime writing, in particular her reportage *Fighting France* (1915), short story 'Coming Home' (1915), and an unpublished, undated wartime fragment entitled 'The Field of Honour' held in the Beinecke Rare Book and Manuscript Library, Yale University. This chapter seeks to complicate our notions of Wharton as jingoistic propagandist. I demonstrate the literariness, complexity and subtlety of Wharton's propaganda, and suggest that her writing contains a number of moments of anxiety, apprehensiveness or unease concerning the war dead, that undermine the straightforwardly propagandistic statements expressed elsewhere.

Part Two: Grief at a Distance: Civilian Modernisms explores the responses of those largely removed from the war zones who didn't witness war death at first hand. These authors turned to abstract modes to represent war death, and their writing is more experimental and more closely related to what we term modernist. It is notable that the authors I discuss here, Katherine Mansfield and H.D., frequently represented the public event of the war through personal and bodily tropes.

My third chapter considers Mansfield's wartime experience as a civilian modernist, addressing the incursion of military discourse into the writings of civilians. I discuss her expression of the public event of the war through the personal situation of her own worsening illness. I examine her wartime and postwar letters, particularly focusing on three textual clusters from 1915 and 1918, when she experienced and wrote about air raids, and the second half of 1919, when she increasingly related the war and the war dead to her own illness and potential death. The importance of the seriality of the letter form, as a means of marking time and measuring progress, becomes increasingly important as the letters continue.

My fourth chapter focuses on H.D.'s avant-garde representation of the war dead in her highly experimental roman à clef, *Bid Me to Live (A Madrigal)* (first drafted from 1918, published 1960). I discuss H.D.'s depiction of wartime civilian experience, and consider her writing in terms of civilian modernism. I examine H.D.'s abstract modes of representation, including the war and the female body (particularly her depiction of her 1915 stillbirth as her war trauma), and her use of the cinema as a modern means of memorialisation of the dead, in a reworking of the trope of nineteenth-century memorial photography. Drawing on archival research, this chapter also includes discussion of H.D.'s revisions of the typescript drafts of the novel.

Part Three: Modernist Death: Postwar Remembrance analyses the literary representation of the new public memorial culture in the postwar world. I discuss the representation of memorials on the home front and in the war zones as new narrative sites, the depiction of new war cemeteries, and depictions of deaths primarily in novels and short stories by Virginia Woolf and Katherine Mansfield. I also draw on work by E. M. Forster, Rudyard Kipling and Christopher Isherwood. My discussion of the new commemorative culture develops into a larger discussion of modernist death and the intersection of memorialisation and modernity.

It is difficult to comprehend the enormity of the numbers of dead of the war, the commonness of death, or the individual experiences behind the concept of mass mourning. By analysing the literary strategies that a range of women writers used to make sense of war death, I demonstrate in the following chapters that the extent and nature of the death toll of the war changed the way that death was represented in literature, and that proximity to the war dead, both in chronological and geographical terms, affected these modes of representation. I show that the unprecedented war losses and the commemorative cultures that developed are a crucial context for literary development in this period, including modernism, and establish the intertwining of modernist, war and memorial culture. More broadly, I consider the enormous impact of the Great War on the history of attitudes towards death, and the longstanding effects of the war on those who lived through it (see Fig. I.7).

Figure I.7 Sir John Lavery, *The Cemetery, Étaples*, 1919. Imperial War Museum Women's Work Section commission. © IWM (Art.IWM ART 2884)

Notes

1. Freud, 'Thoughts for the Times on War and Death' [1915], in *Sigmund Freud: Collected Papers, Volume 4*, trans. under supervision of Joan Riviere (1959), p. 307.
2. Mansfield, letter to J. M. Murry, [10 November 1919], in *The Collected Letters of Katherine Mansfield, Volume III, 1919–1920*, ed. Vincent O'Sullivan and Margaret Scott (1993), p. 82.
3. For example, Douglas Mao and Rebecca L. Walkowitz, 'The New Modernist Studies', *PMLA* 123.3 (2008), pp. 737–48, and Peter Brooks, *Realist Vision* (2005).
4. Freud, 'Thoughts', p. 308.
5. Jalland, *Death in the Victorian Family* (1996), p. 12.
6. Acton, *Grief in Wartime: Private Pain, Public Discourse* (2007), pp. 6, 7.
7. Damousi, 'Gender and Mourning', in Susan R. Grayzel and Tammy M. Proctor (eds), *Gender and the Great War* (2017), p. 212.
8. See Adrian Gregory, *The Silence of Memory: Armistice Day, 1919–1946* (1994), pp. 34, 39–41. Gregory notes that initially the fighting services were the planned audience at the Ceremony, but this was overruled by the Cabinet in favour of the bereaved, p. 46 (note 75). 'Priority was given at the service in the Abbey: (a) to women who had lost a husband and a son (b) women who had lost only sons (c) other widows. The ordering of priorities is suggestive. It is noteworthy that fathers do not get any priority at all. Bereaved members of parliament were the only fathers invited. The identification of the bereaved with women was already becoming conventional'. From the Committee conclusions, 5 November 1920, PRO: CAB 27 / 99, p. 22, pp. 46–7 (quoted in Footnote 75).
9. Sir Percy Fitzpatrick, memorandum submitted to Lord Milner for the attention of the War Cabinet (4 November 1919), quoted by Gregory, p. 10.
10. Damousi has written in the Australian context about the Centre for Soldiers' Wives and Mothers, which in 1918 established the ritual of laying down wreaths on Anzac Day in Sydney; this became known as the 'Wives' and Mothers' Tribute', in 'Gender and Mourning', p. 215.
11. Bernard Bergonzi, *Heroes' Twilight: A Study of the Literature of the Great War* (1965; 2nd edn, 1980); Paul Fussell, *The Great War and Modern Memory* (1975; repr. 2000); John Onions, *English Fiction and Drama of the Great War, 1918–39* (1990).
12. See Nicola Beauman, *A Very Great Profession: The Woman's Novel 1914–39* (1983); Nosheen Khan, *Women's Poetry of the First World War* (1988); Sandra M. Gilbert and Susan Gubar, *No Man's Land: The Place of the Woman Writer in the Twentieth Century* (3 vols) (1989–94); Claire Tylee, *The Great War and Women's Consciousness: Images of Militarism and Womanhood in Women's Writing, 1914–64* (1990); Sharon Ouditt, *Fighting Forces, Writing Women: Identity and Ideology in the First World War* (1994); Dorothy Goldman, with Jane Gledhill and Judith Hattaway, *Women Writers and the Great War* (1995); Angela K. Smith, *The Second Battlefield: Women, Modernism and the First World War* (2000); Debra Rae Cohen, *Remapping the Home Front: Locating Citizenship in British Women's Great War Fiction* (2002); Jane Potter, *Boys in Khaki, Girls in Print: Women's Literary Responses to the Great War, 1914–1918* (2005). Essay collections include: Margaret Higonnet, Jane Jenson and Margaret Collins Weitz (eds), *Behind the Lines:*

Gender and the Two World Wars (1986); Helen M. Cooper, Adrienne Auslander Munich and Susan Merrill Squier (eds), *Arms and the Woman: War, Gender, and Literary Representation* (1989); Dorothy Goldman (ed.), *Women and World War I: The Written Response* (1993); Miriam Cooke and Angela Woollacott (eds), *Gendering War Talk* (1993); Suzanne Raitt and Trudi Tate (eds), *Women's Fiction and the Great War* (1997).

13. Angela Woollacott, *On Her Their Lives Depend: Munitions Workers and the Great War* (1994); Deborah Thom, *Nice Girls and Rude Girls: Women Workers in World War I* (1998); Susan R. Grayzel, *Women's Identities at War: Gender, Motherhood, and Politics in Britain and France during the First World War* (1999); Janet S. K. Watson, *Fighting Different Wars: Experience, Memory, and the First World War in Britain* (2004).

14. Poetry anthologies: Catherine W. Reilly (ed.), *Scars Upon My Heart: Women's Poetry and Verse of the First World War*, pref. by Judith Kazantzis (1981); Nosheen Khan (ed.), *Not with Loud Grieving: Women's Verse of the Great War: An Anthology* (1994). Prose anthologies: Trudi Tate (ed.), *Women, Men and the Great War: An Anthology of Stories* (1995); Joyce Marlow (ed.), *The Virago Book of Women and the Great War* (1998); Agnès Cardinal, Dorothy Goldman and Judith Hattaway (eds), *Women's Writing on the First World War* (1999); Margaret R. Higonnet (ed.), *Lines of Fire: Women Writers of World War I* (1999); Angela K. Smith (ed.), *Women's Writing of the First World War: An Anthology* (2000). There is one anthology of drama: Claire Tylee with Elaine Turner and Agnès Cardinal (eds), *War Plays by Women: An International Anthology* (1999). Sharon Ouditt has produced a useful bibliography: *Women Writers of the First World War: An Annotated Bibliography* (2000). New editions include: Mary Borden, *The Forbidden Zone* [1929], ed. Hazel Hutchison (2008); Edith Wharton, *Fighting France: From Dunkerque to Belfort* [1915], ed. Alice Kelly (2015); Ellen N. La Motte, *The Backwash of War* [1916], ed. Cynthia Wachtell (2019).

15. Christa Hämmerle, Oswald Überegger and Birgitta Bader Zaar, *Gender and the First World War* (2014); Susan R. Grayzel and Tammy M. Proctor (eds), *Gender and the Great War* (2017).

16. Studies include Joy Damousi, *The Labour of Loss: Mourning, Memory and Wartime Bereavement in Australia* (1999) (Australia); Suzanne Evans, *Mothers of Heroes, Mothers of Martyrs: World War I and the Politics of Grief* (2007) (Canada); Erika A. Kuhlman, *Of Little Comfort: War Widows, Fallen Soldiers and the Remaking of the Nation after the Great War* (2012) (Germany and United States).

17. Marcus, 'Corpus/Corps/Corpse: Writing the Body in/at War', in *Arms and the Woman: War, Gender, and Literary Representation*, pp. 124–67; Higonnet, 'Women in the Forbidden Zone: War, Women, and Death', in Elisabeth Bronfen and Sarah Webster Goodwin (eds), *Death and Representation* (1993), pp. 192–211; Acton, *Grief in Wartime* (2007).

18. This mode of scholarship has been employed by critics for wars in other contexts or period. See Bart Ziino, *A Distant Grief: Australians, War Graves and the Great War* (2007); Mary A. Favret, *War at a Distance: Romanticism and the Making of Modern Wartime* (2010); Jan Mieszkowski, *Watching War* (2012).

19. I appropriate Winter's term 'sites' to refer to traditional spaces of the dead. See *Sites of Memory, Sites of Mourning: The Great War in European Cultural History* (1995; repr. 1998).
20. Booth, *Postcards from the Trenches: Negotiating the Space between Modernism and the First World War* (1996), p. 5. The experience of 'corpselessness' and 'corpses' was obviously different in other nations.
21. Hutchison, *The War that Used Up Words: American Writers and the First World War* (2015), p. 3.
22. Fussell, *The Great War*; Eksteins, *Rites of Spring: The Great War and the Birth of the Modern Age* (1989).
23. Fussell, *The Great War*, p. 35.
24. Hynes, *A War Imagined: The First World War and English Culture* [1990] (1992), pp. ix–xi.
25. Winter, *Sites of Memory*, pp. 3–5.
26. Booth, *Postcards*, p. 17.
27. Cannadine, 'War and Death, Grief and Mourning in Modern Britain', in Joachim Whaley (ed.), *Mirrors of Mortality: Studies in the Social History of Death* (1981), pp. 188–9.
28. Gregory, p. 22.
29. Jalland, 'Victorian Death and Its Decline: 1850–1918', in Peter C. Jupp and Clare Gittings (eds), *Death in England: An Illustrated History* (1999), p. 251.
30. See John Morley, *Death, Heaven and the Victorians* (1971); Michael Wheeler, *Heaven, Hell and the Victorians* (1994); and Pat Jalland, *Death in the Victorian Family* (1996), 'Victorian Death and Its Decline' (1999), and *Death in War and Peace: Loss and Grief in England, 1914–1970* (2010).
31. Jalland, *Death in the Victorian Family*, pp. 17–26.
32. Dickens, *The Old Curiosity Shop* [1841], ed. Elizabeth M. Brennan (1998), chapters 71 and 72.
33. Cannadine, 'War and Death', pp. 192–3, 217. The death rate fell from 22 per 1,000 in the 1870s to 13 per 1,000 in 1910. Life expectancy rose from forty years for a man in 1850 to fifty-two years by 1910.
34. Cannadine, 'War and Death', quoting an unnamed contemporary, p. 193.
35. Jalland, 'Victorian Death and Its Decline', p. 251. By contrast, Silke Fehlemann notes that in the German Reich 'the deep mourning female provided a very strong image', where the 'wearing of black clothes and the display of deep mourning were largely accepted [. . .] until the end of the war', in Ute Daniel et al. (eds), 'Bereavement and Mourning (Germany)' in *1914–1918-Online* (2014). <https://encyclopedia.1914-1918-online.net/article/bereavement_and_mourning_germany> (last accessed 2 May 2019).
36. Jalland, *Death in the Victorian Family*, p. 249.
37. Jalland, 'Victorian Death and Its Decline', pp. 248–50.
38. J. M. Winter, *The Great War and the British People* (1985), p. 70.
39. Cannadine, 'War and Death', pp. 195–6, 215.
40. Quotes from Winter, *Sites of Memory*, p. 2; Dan Todman, *The Great War: Myth and Memory* (2005), p. 46, citing Gregory, p. 19.

41. Brittain, *Testament of Youth: An Autobiographical Study of the Years 1900–1925* [1933], pref. by Shirley Williams (1978).
42. Cannadine, 'War and Death', pp. 197–200.
43. H.D., letter to Marianne Moore, 29 August 1917, in Susan Stanford Friedman (ed.), 'H.D. (1886–1961)', in Bonnie Kime Scott (ed.), *The Gender of Modernism: A Critical Anthology* (1990), p. 138.
44. See David Crane, *Empires of the Dead: How One Man's Vision Led to the Creation of WWI's War Graves* (2013), p. 49.
45. Jalland, *Death in the Victorian Family*, p. 6.
46. Cannadine, 'War and Death', p. 204.
47. Booth, *Postcards*, p. 50.
48. Cannadine, 'War and Death', p. 208.
49. Object held in the Imperial War Museum (EPH 9029). <https://www.iwm.org.uk/collections/item/object/30088095> (last accessed 28 April 2019).
50. Cannadine, 'War and Death', pp. 207, 204.
51. Laura Clouting, *A Century of Remembrance* (2018), p. 60.
52. Crane, *Empires of the Dead*, pp. 38–9.
53. Quoted in Philip Longworth, *The Unending Vigil: A History of the Commonwealth War Graves Commission* (2003), p. 7.
54. Figures from Crane, *Empires of the Dead*, p. 55.
55. The IWGC changed its name again to the Commonwealth War Graves Commission in 1960.
56. See Lisa M. Budreau, *Bodies of War: World War I and the Politics of Commemoration in America* (2010).
57. Cannadine, 'War and Death', p. 213.
58. Discussed by Hynes, *A War Imagined*, p. 80.
59. *The Battle of the Somme*, dir. Geoffrey Malins and J. B. McDowell (1916).
60. Cannadine, 'War and Death', p. 214.
61. 'The Gardener' [1925], *Debits and Credits* (1926), p. 405.
62. For more on condolence letters, see my chapter 'Words from Home: Wartime Correspondences', in Ann-Marie Einhaus and Katherine Baxter (eds), *The Edinburgh Companion to the First World War and the Arts* (2017), pp. 77–94.
63. Jalland, 'Victorian Death and Its Decline', p. 252.
64. Kipling, 'War Graves. Work of Imperial Commission. Mr. Kipling's Survey', *The Times*, 17 February 1919, p. 4. The Times Digital Archive, <https://tinyurl.com/y582vpjb> (last accessed 3 April 2019). Kipling, *The Graves of the Fallen: Imperial War Graves Commission* (1919).
65. Clouting, *Century*, p. 94.
66. Laqueur, 'Memory and Naming in the Great War', in John R. Gillis (ed.), *Commemorations: The Politics of National Identity* (1994), pp. 160, 155.
67. The British government charged for this inscription, whereas the Australian and Canadian governments covered the cost. The New Zealand government didn't allow personal inscriptions, arguing that charging for them went against the principle of equality in death.

68. Just a few of many examples included as part of Sarah Wearne's *Epitaphs of the Great War* project <http://www.epitaphsofthegreatwar.com/all/> (last accessed 29 April 2019).
69. Clouting, *Century*, p. 65.
70. My brief summary of the epidemic here draws on Laura Spinney's account, *Pale Rider: The Spanish Flu of 1918 and How It Changed the World* (2017), particularly the Introduction and chapters 3 and 7. See also accounts by Alfred W. Crosby and Nancy K. Bristow in the Bibliography.
71. Spinney, *Pale Rider*, p. 76.
72. Quoted in Peter Gay, *Freud: A Life for Our Time* [1988] (1989), p. 390.
73. Jalland, *Death in War and Peace*, pp. 32, 33.
74. Spinney, *Pale Rider*, p. 6.
75. Jalland, *Death in War and Peace*, pp. 33, 34.
76. Spinney, *Pale Rider*, p. 75. Spinney notes that some religious communities saw the flu epidemic as a punishment from God, perhaps for the war itself, pp. 78–9.
77. Cannadine, 'War and Death', p. 219.
78. Booth, *Postcards*, p. 41.
79. Hynes, *A War Imagined*, pp. 269–70.
80. Gregory, *The Silence of Memory*, pp. 23–4, 278.
81. Winter, *Sites of Memory*, p. 5.
82. The winning design in a competition with 800 entries was by Edward Carter Preston.
83. Damousi, 'Gender and Mourning', p. 218.
84. This badge is discussed by Damousi, *The Labour of Loss*, p. 26, and Bruce Scates 'Bereavement and Mourning (Australia)', in Ute Daniel et al. (eds), *1914–1918-Online* (2016), <https://encyclopedia.1914-1918-online.net/article/bereavement_and_mourning_australia> (last accessed 2 May 2019). Scates refers to these as 'commemorative broaches', suggesting their similarity with jewellery, although they looked more like medals. A similar gesture in the US, although not given by the state, was the custom of families hanging a service flag in their windows, with blue stars denoting living servicemen and gold stars denoting those who had passed away (hence, the Gold Star Mothers).
85. Scates, 'Bereavement and Mourning (Australia)' (2016).
86. Tanja Luckins, *The Gates of Memory: Australian People's Experience of Loss and the Great War* (2004), p. 135, quoted by Scates in 'Bereavement and Mourning (Australia)' (2016).
87. Damousi, *The Labour of Loss*, p. 26.
88. Silke Fehlemann notes that 'in contrast to other victorious nations', postwar mourning and remembrance in Germany was 'characterised by the exclusion of bereaved families from commemoration practices'. She notes that families were only rewarded politically in the 1930s, when National Socialism propaganda included 'crosses of honour for surviving dependents' and 'evenings for the parents of fallen combatants', in 'Bereavement and Mourning (Germany)'.
89. For example, Sidney C. Hurst, *The Silent Cities: An Illustrated Guide to the War Cemeteries and Memorials to the 'Missing' in France and Flanders, 1914–1918* (1929).

90. David W. Lloyd notes that 'At least thirty guidebooks to the battlefields, in English, were produced [. . .] from 1919 to 1921', and that by 1921 the French company 'Michelin had produced fifteen guidebooks in English', in *Battlefield Tourism: Pilgrimage and the Commemoration of the Great War in Britain, Australia and Canada, 1919–1939* (1998), p. 30.
91. Lloyd notes the only exception: the 'small sum' given by the British Government in the early 1920s 'to voluntary organisations, such as the YMCA, the Salvation Army, the Church Army and the St Barnabus Society, to facilitate their travel programs' which 'was suspended in 1923,' in *Battlefield Tourism*, pp. 38–9. Lloyd estimates the trip was 'at least £4 per person' to join a tour or pilgrimage, p. 48. The French government funded an annual pilgrimage to a grave for bereaved relatives, but the German War Graves Commission did not. See Fehlemann, 'Bereavement and Mourning (Germany)'. In the US, the Gold Star Pilgrimages, for mothers and widows who had not remarried, who had chosen not to repatriate their dead, took place from 1930 to 1933: 6,654 women participated over the three years. The pilgrimages were racially segregated. See Budreau, *Bodies of War*.
92. Lloyd, *Battlefield Tourism*, p. 36.
93. Quoted in Clouting, *Century*, p. 210.
94. See Alex Walton's account of 'Official Memorial Art', in Clouting, *Century*, pp. 221, 222–3, which informs my discussion of the role of art in remembrance here.
95. See Imperial War Museum, Hall of Remembrance, <https://hall.iwm.org.uk/> (last accessed 26 April 2019).
96. Walton, 'Official Memorial Art', p. 225.
97. Quoted by Clouting, *Century*, p. 212.
98. Quoted by Clouting, *Century*, p. 213. The first widespread appeal was included in food ration books. Claire Buck has noted that in contrast to the IWM's mass appeal for mementos of men, the Women's Work Subcommittee appealed for photographs of women killed doing war work in much more personalised terms: Agnes Conway, the Chair of the Committee (and the daughter of Martin Conway), 'wrote to each family individually', in *Conceiving Strangeness in British First World War Writing* (2015), p. 187. The photos were included in the Women's War Shrine, part of an exhibition of women's war work at the Whitechapel Art Gallery which opened in October 1918, p. 180.
99. Clouting, *Century*, p. 212.
100. Clouting, *Century*, p. 214.
101. Hynes, 'Personal Narratives and Commemoration', in Jay Winter and Emmanuel Sivan (eds), *War and Remembrance in the Twentieth Century* (1999), pp. 205–9.
102. Todman, *Myth and Memory*, p. xii.
103. Hynes (1999), pp. 207–20.
104. For modernism and mourning, see: Seth Moglen, *Mourning Modernity: Literary Modernism and the Injuries of American Capitalism* (2007); Patricia Rae (ed.), *Modernism and Mourning* (2007); Tammy Clewell, *Mourning, Modernism, Postmodernism* (2009); Madelyn Detloff, *The Persistence of Modernism: Loss and Mourning in the Twentieth Century* (2009); Greg Forter, *Gender, Race, and Mourning in American Modernism* (2011); Lecia Rosenthal, *Mourning Modernism: Literature, Catastrophe, and the Politics of Consolation* (2011).

105. Studies of death in literature include Garrett Stewart's *Death Sentences: Styles of Dying in British Fiction* (1984), and Webster Goodwin and Bronfen (eds), *Death and Representation* (1993).
106. Friedman, *Fictional Death and the Modernist Enterprise* (1995), pp. 18–30.
107. Freedman, *Death, Men, and Modernism: Trauma and Narrative in British Fiction from Hardy to Woolf* (2003), pp. 3–9, 14–18, 118.
108. James, *The New Death: American Modernism and World War I* (2013). pp. 2–25.
109. There are too many modernist surveys from the past thirty years to single out any of these in particular. My comments here are representative of the field as a whole.
110. Sherry, *The Great War and the Language of Modernism* (2003), p. 7.
111. Frayn, 'Introduction: Modernism and the First World War', in Frayn (ed.), *Modernist Cultures*, 12.1 (2017), p. 2.
112. Booth, *Postcards*, pp. 4–17.
113. Tate, *Modernism, History and the First World War* (1998), pp. 12–14.
114. Sherry, *The Great War and the Language of Modernism* (2003), inside dustjacket, p. 22.
115. Marina MacKay, *Modernism, War, and Violence*, pp. 11, 12.
116. Das, *Touch and Intimacy in First World War Literature* (2005), p. 10.
117. Vincent Sherry (ed.), *The Cambridge Companion to the Literature of the First World War* (2005); Kate McLoughlin (ed.), *The Cambridge Companion to War Writing* (2009); Adam Piette and Mark Rawlinson (eds), *The Edinburgh Companion to Twentieth-Century British and American War Literature* (2012); Das (ed.), *The Cambridge Companion to the Poetry of the First World War* (2013); Einhaus and Baxter (eds), *The Edinburgh Companion to the First World War and the Arts* (2017).
118. Jane Potter, *Boys in Khaki, Girls in Print*; Mary Hammond and Shafquat Towheed (eds), *Publishing in the First World War: Essays in Book History* (2007); Shafquat Towheed and Edmund King (eds), *Reading and the First World War: Readers, Texts, Archives* (2015).
119. McLoughlin, *Authoring War: The Literary Representation of War from the Iliad to Iraq* (2011); Winter, *War Beyond Words: Languages of Remembrance from the Great War to the Present* (2017); Hynes, *On War and Writing* (2018).
120. Ana Carden-Coyne, *Reconstructing the Body: Classicism, Modernism, and the First World War* (2009); Das, *Touch and Intimacy* (2005).
121. Das (ed.), *Race, Empire and First World War Writing* (2011); Das, *India, Empire, and First World War Culture: Writings, Images, and Songs* (2018).
122. See, for example, Einhaus, *The Short Story and the First World War* (2013). For American First World War writing, see Steven Trout, *Memorial Fictions: Willa Cather and the First World War* (2003) and *On the Battlefield of Memory: The First World War and American Remembrance, 1919–1941* (2010); Mark Whalan, *The Great War and the Culture of the New Negro* (2008) and *World War One, American Literature, and the Federal State* (2018); Hazel Hutchison, *The War that Used Up Words* (2015).
123. Sarah Cole, *At the Violet Hour: Modernism and Violence in England and Ireland* (2012); MacKay, *Modernism, War, and Violence* (2017).

Part One

Death in Proximity:
Wartime Commemorations

I

THE SHOCK OF THE DEAD: DEATHBEDS, BURIAL RITES AND CEMETERY SCENES IN NURSES' NARRATIVES

The other day I overheard a soldier talking to another soldier about us – the men and women who stay at home. [. . .] 'They ought to see the towns in France,' said the soldier. 'They don't know there's a war on.' I was startled by the word. 'They.' We and They are two nations, not one.

But there is a third nation, the nation of nurses. They are midway between us.

James Douglas, 'How a Nurse Sees the War'
(*Birmingham Gazette*, 1918)[1]

'We will send you the dying, the desperate, the moribund,' the Inspector-General had said.

'You must expect a thirty per cent. mortality.'

Mary Borden, *The Forbidden Zone* (1929)[2]

A truism of the Great War is that it turned men into numbers. In *A Scottish Nurse at Work* (1920), the Voluntary Aid Detachment nurse Henrietta Tayler, who worked in a Belgian military hospital, explains that they received 'ten or twenty patients every night [. . .] and [during] any local attack *many* more [. . .] we had many, many deaths'.[3] The numbers of dead are only described indirectly, with the emphasis on mass death compounded by the lack of specificity.

The confrontation with injury and death that nurses encountered in casualty clearing stations and military hospitals during the war was unprecedented. Much has been written on the culture shock to 'these gently nurtured girls who walked straight out of Edwardian drawing rooms into the manifest horrors of the First World War', but very little on how nurses coped with such large numbers of dying men.[4]

This chapter explores the ways in which women involved in hospitals, casualty clearing stations, hospital ships and ambulance trains in the war zones and on the home front witnessed and wrote about military death in contemporary and retrospective diaries and memoirs. Focusing on intensely proximate encounters between nurses and the dying, I argue that most nurse narratives turned back to older, more conservative literary tropes for depicting the war dead – deathbed scenes, burial rituals and cemetery scenes – which attempted to convert the modern wartime hospital (in literary terms, at least) into a traditional site of mourning and commemoration. I suggest that nurses appropriated specific historically determined narrative tropes for representing the dead partly because they reflected the reality of what they were experiencing, but more importantly, because they imposed a meaningful and immediately recognisable structure on the deaths they were attempting to represent, dignify and memorialise. Nurses were implicitly positioned at the forefront of the contemporary debate about death, burial and adequate memorialisation and their unique viewpoint warrants further critical attention.

This chapter argues, then, for the importance of these nursing accounts as a type of immediate proto-commemoration, before more official modes of memorialisation were established. However, as we shall see, the conservative narrative tropes employed by nurses were frequently inadequate for the mass numbers of war dead, demonstrating that earlier literary modes of writing about the dead had outgrown their usefulness, and there were not yet new ones to take their place. This is writing which registers the shock of the war dead, but doesn't yet know what to do with it.

Unlike the civilian writing I discuss later, nurses' eyewitness accounts provide a record of the lived experience of those who witnessed the unrelenting numbers of deaths at first hand. Margaret R. Higonnet rightly suggests that these texts, like the nurses themselves, 'both observe and participate in the experiences of trauma'.[5] The peculiarly liminal status of the nurses, with their 'marginalised identity – one in, but not of, the war', as Sharon Ouditt observes, makes their accounts particularly valuable.[6] The First World War was the first time that nurses had been included as part of the army during a major conflict, serving in all the theatres of war under several different nursing branches.[7] Volunteer women, who wrote the majority of the memoirs I discuss here, primarily served in the Voluntary Aid Detachments (VADs, founded in 1909 and open to men and women), who were considered 'semi-trained'.[8] Because they had to pay for their own uniform and expenses, the VADs were initially made up of predominantly middle- and upper-class women, although they became more diverse as the war continued.[9] The eagerness of volunteer nurses was driven by popular mythologies of nursing as much as successful recruitment campaigns: in Britain, the legacy of the Crimean War nurse and 'Lady with the Lamp' Florence Nightingale, and in the United States, the American Civil War nurse and founder of the American Red Cross Clara Barton, both of whom had died in recent years (1910 and 1912 respectively).[10] During the war, the death and subsequent mythologising of Edith Cavell in October 1915 received much attention in the press and may have further prompted women to volunteer.

What distinguished the nurses from other medical personnel in the war zones, including doctors, male nurses and stretcher-bearers, were the cultural associations of their sex with life, death and grief. The nurse's heavily gendered role and ambiguous military positioning was compounded by her contradictory roles of healer and griever, as well as participant and witness. Quoting from Mary Borden's graphic 1929 text, *The Forbidden Zone*, Higonnet argues that it was the 'nurse's business [...] to create "a counter-wave of life".[11] This image of women as life-givers was used in nursing recruiting efforts. This was particularly explicit on a graphic American Red Cross poster from 1918, depicting a nurse propping up a wounded soldier, with the words 'If I Fail He Dies', demonstrating that the burden of the soldier's survival was placed entirely on the nurse (see Fig. 1.1).[12] By the end of the war, the nurse had acquired a certain cultural cachet, evidenced by an American *Vogue* cover from May 1918, by the artist Porter Woodruff, which is the cover of this book. With the folds in the flag behind her echoed in her flowing nursing robes, and her dark blue coat recalling the Virgin Mary, the patriotic Red Cross nurse embodies sacrifice, duty and devotion to the cause, as well as grace and style.[13] Here, while the imagery of soldiers in the trenches behind adheres to a realist idiom, the image of the First World War nurse has been stylised using the visual vocabulary of the fashion industry, combining the archetypal female model of the nurse with the independent modernity of the New Woman. Simultaneously, nurses were implicitly asked to fulfil the culturally constructed role of primary mourner, a recognisable Victorian type attributed to women, as I considered in the Introduction. The nurses' presence at the wartime deathbed was therefore already highly determined before the war had begun.

Higonnet has argued for the conflation of authentic and artificial war narratives, suggesting that all 'authentic' accounts are themselves fictionalised creations.[14] For my purposes here, I examine a selection of mostly contemporary texts which are presented as 'authentic', but are nonetheless fictionalised accounts – Olive Dent, Enid Bagnold, R. E. Leake (the pseudonym of Mollie Skinner), Pat Beauchamp, Henrietta Tayler, Lesley Smith and Dora M. Walker – and read them as representative of the larger body of nurses' writings.[15] These first-hand

Figure 1.1 Arthur G. McCoy, *If I Fail He Dies, Work for the Red Cross* (Duluth, MN: J. J. LeTourneau Printing Company, 1918) [copyright Rev. S. A. Iciek, 1918]. Courtesy of the Pritzker Military Museum & Library

accounts were written during and after the war by British, American and Australian women who served as VADs, except Beauchamp, who was a member of the First Aid Nursing Yeomanry. My use of the term 'nurses' and 'nurses' narratives' therefore applies predominantly to voluntary, rather than trained, nurses and their writings.[16] One section of this chapter, however, considers the American trained nurse Ellen N. La Motte, whose wartime memoir demonstrates a modernist version of the nurse narrative.[17] The nurses I discuss were based at hospitals on the Western Front, in Mesopotamia, Burma and on the Gallipoli Peninsula, as well as on the British home front, but I consider them all 'proximate' to the war dead in their subject position, even if not geographically.

In recent decades there has been a re-evaluation of what Higonnet has termed 'an alternate history of World War I traumas', through a critical appreciation of the nurse narratives in First World War literature.[18] Angela K. Smith has similarly argued for the nurses' 'establishment and recognition as active and important contributors to the dialogue of war'.[19] Social and cultural histories have increased our understanding of the organisation and work of various nursing groups, as have more general studies of the medical profession and discourse during the war.[20] These studies have focused on the emancipatory potential of women's war work and the ideologies within the interpellation of women as military nurses. Smith and others have noted the importance of the site of the 'forbidden zone', including the hospital unit, as 'a kind of no woman's land inhabited by select women [. . .] providing women with their own arena for war experience'.[21] The connections between nurses' writings and modernist writings has been debated: perhaps most definitively, Jane Marcus argues that 'the fragmentation described as typical of modernist texts has an origin in the writing practice of women nurses and ambulance drivers'.[22] The republication of some nurses' accounts has prompted further interest, and the prefaces and afterwords to these new editions have frequently provided excellent critical commentary on the genre as a whole.[23] This initial rediscovery work has contributed to what Santanu Das has identified as 'the "second wave" of war criticism', including, among other things, 'the ordeal of the conscientious objectors, military deserters, labourers, stretcher-bearers and medical staff'.[24] Das's work on sensory and physical experience at war is complemented by other recent literary and historical studies of the wartime body by Joanna Bourke and Ana Carden-Coyne.[25] The cultural and interracial encounters between white nurses and colonial troops are only just beginning to be explored.[26] The turn from a focus solely on nurses to the work of medical personnel more broadly is shown by a recent volume by Carol Acton and Jane Potter.[27] However, despite the number of war dead, of whom a high proportion died in field hospitals and convalescent units, any extended critical discussion of the nurses' depictions of death is limited to the excellent work of Margaret R. Higonnet and Carol Acton.[28] This chapter seeks to expand that scholarship.

'AND ALSO ALL THAT IS MEANT BY THE WORD NURSING': NURSING MANUALS AND HANDBOOKS

Alongside her other responsibilities, the nurse's role involved keeping vigil by the deathbed. Christine Hallett has written of this practice of 'specialing' in the base hospital:

> Caring for the dying was one of the most important elements of the nurse's work. [. . .] it was often the most highly trained nurses who stayed with patients who were dying; the practice was known as 'specialing'. The nurse worked to ensure that everything possible was done to provide the patient relief from pain and trauma at the time of his death. Nursing the dying was as much a process of containment as nursing the living; the nurse protected both the dying patient and those around him.[29]

In the field hospitals, however, it was frequently the volunteer nurses who recorded their experiences of attending deathbeds. The emotional burden of comforting the dying and the shock of the frequently distressing death scenes meant that these experiences could be particularly disturbing.

A survey of contemporary nursing handbooks and manuals demonstrates that volunteer nurses were not formally prepared for the conditions surrounding wartime death. These handbooks collectively attest to the care and attention nurses were encouraged to give to their patients and stress their increased responsibility. However, the difficult emotional situations that nurses would face are only implicitly discussed, with nurses at most knowing the physical and legal procedure for dealing with a dead body. The 1912 *British Red Cross Society Nursing Manual, No. 2*, written by the Scottish physician and pioneer of first aid James Cantlie, was aimed at VADs whose nursing was limited to 'the temporary care of patients' until they were moved to general hospitals. The last page, unusually, provides information on 'Laying Out the Dead':

> When a person dies, remove the blankets and throw the sheet over the corpse, covering the face as well as the body. After an interval pass a bandage or handkerchief beneath the lower jaw and tie off on the top of the head, so that the mouth is closed. Spread a mackintosh beneath the corpse to protect the bed, and proceed to wash the whole body with soap and water; dry thoroughly; shut the eyelids and place a pad of cotton-wool on either eye to ensure the lids being kept closed. Push a piece of cotton-wool up the bowel for a short distance. Put on stockings or socks, and pyjamas or nightdress; tie the feet together.
>
> A clean sheet is spread beneath the body, which is then completely covered by another clean sheet.[30]

The information is solely concerned with the physiological practice of dealing with a corpse and provides no indication of what the nurse may be required to do to console or comfort the patient before death, or the emotional burden of this experience. Duncan C. L. Fitzwilliams's 1914 manual, although aimed at 'nurses, orderlies, and Red Cross workers', does not deal with the question of dying at all. Under the index entry for 'Breathing', we find 'Cheyne-Stokes', nature of' and 'stertorous, cause and nature of' (known colloquially as the 'death rattle'), but there is no explicit reference to dying.[31] Violet Young's 1914 text *Outlines of Nursing* similarly does not discuss dying patients.[32] M. N. Oxford's *Nursing in War Time: Lessons for the Inexperienced* (1914), explicitly aimed at volunteer nurses, does, by contrast, include a short section on 'The Last Duties to a Patient'. Oxford outlines a physiological methodology similar to that in Cantlie's handbook, but the manual ends, unusually, with the need for a respectful treatment of the corpse, going beyond physical details to discuss the significance of death:

> It is unnecessary to say that we do these last offices for our patients with the same reverent care that we should like used for our own relations, and for ourselves when our turn comes; without unnecessary talking, and with exactly the same decency that we observe in washing a living person.[33]

Towards the end of the war, the French physiologist Charles Richet's translated Red Cross Lectures, *War Nursing: What Every Woman Should Know* (1918), 'particularly useful for members of the V.A.D.', does not include any reference to death, assuming perhaps – like other manuals and handbooks – that women would know the procedures from their assistance at peacetime deathbeds.[34]

Although these handbooks did not explicitly prepare the nurses for the mass death they encountered, some passages arguably refer implicitly to the care of the dying. Fitzwilliams notes that a nurse's training includes 'all that is meant by the word nursing as applied to the comfort and care of the sick'.[35] Oxford's more explicit 'Introductory' acknowledges the frequently gory situations that nurses would encounter:

> A woman who means to nurse, especially in war time, must possess courage. The sight of blood need not alarm you; a very little blood makes a very great mess [. . .] There is a great deal too in determining not to be frightened. The sight of pain is worse to bear; avoid worrying the patient by unnecessary talking or demonstrative sympathy, but help him as you can by fresh applications, altering his position or his pillows, or by gentle rubbing, if that is any relief. He will appreciate deeds more than words.[36]

The failure of the nursing handbooks and manuals to prepare volunteer nurses made the mass numbers of dying men all the more shocking. Even if they implicitly discussed the types of scenes a nurse might encounter in wartime, these examples were woefully inadequate. The nurse narratives show again and again that 'specialing' was virtually impossible in the wartime hospital. Writing and recording the deaths of the men became the best tribute that nurses were able to provide.

Deathbed Scenes

During the nineteenth century, the deathbed scene was consciously constructed as a trope for representing the dying and the dead. It was predominant in religious ideology, and further consolidated by its reproduction in painting, literature, and other cultural forms. As I discussed in the Introduction, the characteristics of the Victorian 'good death' were well defined.[37] The personal significance of the deathbed for those caring for the dying person is demonstrated in the Victorian tradition of deathbed memorials. Kept in diary form, these attest to the importance of the last weeks, days and hours, as Pat Jalland notes:

> While these memorials were chiefly intended as spiritual accounting to God, they also served as personal therapy for the writer and as a written record to preserve the memory of the loved one for the immediate family. They usually recorded daily, even hourly, events in the sick-room, including the symptoms, medical treatment, visitors, and conversations. [. . .] The medical and spiritual accounts were often uneasily juxtaposed, even within the same paragraph, as the diarist moved between a prosaic clinical narrative and a symbolic spiritual discourse.[38]

These memorials complemented the *ars moriendi* as literature that sanctified and privileged the final expressions and emotions of the dying. Few of these memorials have survived, but their influence on nurses' narratives is evident, particularly the recording of daily and hourly changes in patients. The deathbed as narrative convention was further reproduced and reinforced in the Victorian period through well-known literary deathbed scenes, which were usually lengthy, memorable descriptions, highly sentimentalised and laden with pathos. Literature thereby became a means of consolidating the myth of the good death and its conventions. Jalland observes these literary scenes were 'usually melodramatic occasions of moral judgement and emotional farewell', often including 'proof of spiritual salvation, with minor miracles, haloes of light, and edifying last words'. Unlike seemingly truthful religious tracts, fictionalised deathbed scenes were 'deliberate devices for emotionally engaging the reader in an age when sentimental stories were very popular'.[39] In depicting the deaths of their patients through deathbed scenes, nurses were invoking a longstanding, recognisable and consolatory narrative trope for representing death.

Each nurse narrative typically includes a number of individually described deathbed scenes among depersonalised passages about the numbers dying. Re-invoking Victorian pieties, these individual deathbed scenes act as a type of memorialisation. They are typically remembered by the nurse for a particular reason: regret at not doing more for the patient, the patient's seemingly superlative vulnerability, or that their injuries and death were especially painful. These individual deaths are an important means of personalising the multiple anonymous deaths that the nurse wished to portray, despite the fact that the patient concerned is not always named, but instead known by his injury or bed number. The particularising of a scene, whether or not the patient is named, insists that *all* deaths are *individual* deaths. However, these narratives signal a stylistic break with the lengthy, highly sentimentalised nineteenth-century literary deathbed sequences. In the nurses' narratives we see the tension between an engaging individualisation and sympathy (a version of nearness) and a disengaging generality (distance). Although nurses frequently employed the narrative model of the deathbed scene, their writings repeatedly demonstrate that this trope was no longer adequate.

Nurses' narratives depict the changed nature of dying that the war caused – anonymous, away from home, often very painful and usually leaving a broken or incomplete corpse – which was ideologically difficult to accommodate to Victorian convention. In *Four Years Out of Life* (1931), Lesley Smith, a VAD in France, records the break with traditional modes of dying that prompted women at home to take the war seriously:

> I looked hastily at the list and found, not only Douglas's name but the names of five other boys who had been friends of his and ours; sons of people we knew – our friends! It was a queer crashing start to one's own personal war. Before that it had been the government's affair, and now we were all in it just because some boys we knew had been killed outright instead of dying with the usual paraphernalia of doctor and nurses and wreaths.[40]

Comparing these descriptions with the Victorian urge towards realism – the desire that the corpse would look the same in death as it had in life, documented in the popularity of Victorian memorial photography – we see how the war was an unexpected assault on traditional aesthetics of death. Smith records that there was no longer the conclusiveness and neatness permitted by an entire corpse: 'Death has its own clean finality; but these men, whose admirable bodies lay inert and helpless at the mercy of a grotesque, obscenely rolling head, seemed a denial of everything beautiful and fair'. The approach to death lost its sanctity and pathos. Smith describes the death of a dehumanised patient known as 'Ninety-nine', because of his habit of continually counting aloud. His impending death is only apparent because of blood trickling through his bandages:

> I ran back to look at him, there had been nothing to be seen through the mass of bandages but two eyeholes and a gash for the mouth, but at last there was a change, a trickle of blood was dribbling slowly out of the gash and soaking the white bandage. Old Ninety-nine would not count much further. The new rhythm was strangely disturbing:
> 'Ninety ninety ninety – hic – seven, ninety ninety-nine, hic, ninety hic, ninety hic.' He was obviously just going. Well, there wasn't anything to be done and it was no use disturbing Sister, she was having a heavy night in 'Chests' [. . .] old 'Ninety-nine' gave a last triumphant shout of 'Ninety ninety hic nine' and was silent for the first time since he had come in three days ago. A breathless pause held us stationary for a moment, then Matron tramped out saying, 'I'll send Sister.'[41]

Despite Smith's urgent engagement with the scene ('I ran back'), the deflationary death sequence is notable for its ordinariness and lack of ceremony. Smith's resignation to, and disengagement from, Ninety-nine's death is stated before it even occurs, and the bathos of his last moments is seen through his gasping attempts to keep counting to the end, rather than dying a dignified death. Smith and her Matron are 'held [. . .] stationary' only to validate that the man has actually died; it is not a reverential or ritualistic pause. The moment of death has moved from being the sacred transition into another realm that the nineteenth-century narrative depicted in extended, sentimentalised sequences, to one so commonplace that it does not even qualify interrupting others from their work.

The nurses' writing reveals the multiple roles they were expected to play at the deathbed: final sitter present at the men's deaths, sometimes surrogate priest and final confessor, and primary mourner. All of the accounts record men seeking comfort from the nurse, physically and mentally. An extended passage in Smith's narrative concerns the death of Railton, a young corporal who has lost one leg and severely injured the other.[42] This particular death is given relatively extensive narrative space, because of the pathos of the story – that he 'came in determined to live' and that he 'had a girl to go back to'. Smith prefaces this account by noting that in this period they 'had one case after another who *might* have recovered, whose lives we fought for, and who died in spite of us after days of agony', adding further pathos. The detail in the long description of Railton's death suggests the multiple, conflicting pressures on the nurse, demonstrating the tension between general duties and the traditionally personalised attention at a deathbed:

I waited while the champagne revived him and then laid him back on the pillow. He still held my hand and I couldn't leave him, but a chest wound had slipped off his air pillow and was in a bad position, and an amputation back from the theatre that afternoon was being very sick. There were two fomentations due and Sister had run over to the mess for a cup of tea. I still waited, but I couldn't help being conscious of all these clamorous duties.

Railton could hardly move his head, but he lifted his eyes to my face and panted:

'Sorry to keep you, Nurse – I won't be long now – Am going fast, ain't I?'

I choked and fumbled stupidly for a word, and finally managed to tell him to hold on, there might be a change at any moment. He just brushed that aside and still holding me with his eyes said:

'I'm frightened, Sister. Is it all true what they say in church?' His voice had dropped to an agonised whisper and I had to bend down to catch what he said. 'Will I be forgiven?'

I tried to say what he wanted to hear and he slowly lifted his hand off mine and said 'Thank you.'

I fled down the ward to roll over the amputation's head and prevent him choking himself.

The individualisation of Railton in this intensely intimate encounter between a nurse and her patient initially seems to return the reader to the world of the Victorian deathbed. However, Smith's gentle care over one patient (a type of nearness) is contrasted with her distancing references to other patients in the ward identified by their injuries; a necessary troping of people as wounds that is both horrific and anonymous.[43] Her comment, 'I couldn't help being conscious of all these clamorous duties', is an admission that this individualised deathbed scene cannot be maintained in the wartime hospital, and that a focus on one patient – even at the moment of his death – is impossible due to multiple other demands on her attention. Moreover, this pressure for individualised attention seems not only difficult, but constrictive. In one reading, Smith's engagement with Railton is depicted through the language of physical restriction, signifying an unwanted rather than a voluntarily emotional exchange: 'He still held my hand and I couldn't leave him [. . .] still holding me with his eyes'. The conclusion, 'I fled', fits into this reading. Smith's description of her reaction to his anxious questions demonstrates that she considers her response inadequate. Once Railton has died, the narrative moves on quickly: 'in the morning there was another man in Railton's bed'.[44] Acton notes that there is 'literally no further space for Railton and no time for Smith to grieve'.[45]

Similarly, in her typically patriotic memoir, *Fanny Goes to War* (1919), Pat Beauchamp, a member of the First Aid Nursing Yeomanry, personalises one of her dying patients, but elides his actual death. Beauchamp's text, with its title promising a hybrid adventure and war tale, has a cheery propagandistic tone, but this deathbed scene is another curious mixture of distance and intimacy. Beauchamp records watching a man slowly dying from a distance and tells us that this deathbed image has remained with her: 'I shall always see the man in bed sixteen to this day'. The characterisation of the man through superlatives ('extremely fair [. . .] one of the worst cases [. . .] He must have been such a splendid man') and her likening him to Christ adds pathos to his inevitable fate. However, the patient remains nameless, identified only by his bed number. Beauchamp records her distance, even repulsion, from the man, noting the 'unearthly light in his eyes; that 'somehow he did not seem to belong to this world any longer'. However, Beauchamp is simultaneously attracted to him, writing in the language of popular romance that 'My heart ached for him', that 'I longed for him to get better'. His death is elided in the narrative, but represented, as in many other nurse narratives, by his empty bed. Her shocked reaction is characterised by the recorded reaction of her fellow nurse to her questions: '"Died in the night," she said briefly. "Don't look like that," and she went on with her work'. This death is the first of a series, suggesting their frequency: 'One gets accustomed to these things in time, but I never forgot that first shock'. The absent nurse and the distant reader are not sure what to conclude from his death.[46]

The fear that the nurse 'gets accustomed' is a sentiment expressed by Enid Bagnold in *A Diary without Dates*, her popular 1918 memoir of her nursing experiences at the Royal Herbert Hospital in London, which led to her dismissal from her nursing position within half an hour of the book's publication.[47] One particularly poignant deathbed scene concerns an infantilised 'boy of seventeen' with pneumonia, whose physical pain ('so ill that he couldn't speak') and his child-like vulnerability ('it gave me a shock to see how young his feet were') purposefully heighten the pathos and emotive effect. The Sister speaks in a soothing, maternal tone to the boy, who is clearly in grave danger after a rapid decline, referred to in euphemistic diction as being 'on the edge of the world – to-night looking over the edge'. Although he 'submits with a terrible docility' to whatever medical procedure the nurses and doctors attempt, Bagnold acknowledges that his illness exceeds their expertise. She documents her own helplessness at the lack of a physical wound to treat, and her feelings of inadequacy as a nurse: 'no shell, no mark, no tear . . . . The attack comes from within'.

Although there is nothing further she can do medically to ease the boy's suffering, Bagnold demonstrates her emotional and mental engagement with him, stressing that 'he is all the centre of my thoughts'. The desperate actions of the boy's mother (who has been summoned to his bedside), seeking some alleviation of her son's suffering by bringing each day 'a bribe, dumbly offered' of a cake for the Sisters, is a ritual that Bagnold states 'hurts me', further compounding her sense of impotence and guilt. The description of the sky 'like a pale egg-shell' hints at the fragility of the boy's situation, suggesting the propensity to crack at any moment, as does the inconclusiveness of Bagnold's unanswered questions: 'I think from time to time, "Is he alive?"'. When the boy comments that the ward is pretty, she takes comfort in this small gesture: 'It isn't, but I am glad it seems so to him'.

Bagnold eventually withholds from the reader whether the boy survives his illness, but the key element of the scene is the truism that results, which suggests the traumatic impact on the nurses of keeping vigil over so many deathbeds: 'Can one grow used to death? It is unsafe to think of this . . . For if death becomes cheap it is the watcher, not the dying, who is poisoned'.[48] This fear of normalised death, of becoming 'used' to death because of its frequency, was of serious concern to the nurses. Jane Marcus compares the nurses to 'mythological ferrymen', whose bodies were 'forbidden, dangerous, polluted carriers of a terrible knowledge'.[49] Even heavily propagandistic narratives, such as Olive Dent's 1917 text *A V.A.D. in France*, do not conceal the enormous emotional burden of deathbed scenes, or the universal concern at this prolonged exposure to death, for themselves as well as their patients.

The nurse's role was to keep vigil, where she might simultaneously deny the possibility of death to the patient and provide comfort to him, but privately acknowledge to her fellow nurses and the reader her anticipation of inevitable death, which was often a relief. The Victorian ritual of the extended deathbed was disturbed by the wartime deathbed, where the nurses in fact sometimes urged on their patients' death: 'how often [. . .] I prayed that it might be over quickly', Beauchamp writes.[50] Smith notes of her work in the head injuries ward, 'my only happiness was in remembering how few during that time had recovered enough to go home'. Nurses were highly aware of their disproportionate burden of responsibility for death, as Smith records in her mention of 'our exaggerated conscientiousness':

> We 'took in' three times in that one month, and each time there were half a dozen cases who swung between life and death for days and whose lives seemed, to our exaggerated conscientiousness, to be bound up with our own. Again and again we gave in to death, angry, dogged by a sense of our failure, resenting our powerlessness, and then began the struggle all over again as another convoy replaced the last.

Sometimes the nurse author notes her personal discomfort in telling the patient something they did not actually believe: 'I tried to whisper that it would probably be better to-morrow, but the lie stuck in my throat'.[51]

Nurses took on the burden of providing the circumstances for a spiritually good death and were clearly very distressed if their patient could die unconsoled. Hallett writes, '[i]n offering emotional comfort and containment to their patients, many recognised that there was a spiritual dimension to these patients' suffering', but formal death rites required 'the "expertise" of a chaplain or priest'.[52] The Australian nurse R. E. Leake, working in Burma, records her experience with a Catholic priest:

> He horrified me by refusing 'dying consolations' to one of his flock, and the poor soul so collapsed after he had left his side that I indignantly followed up the little man and begged him to come back to the patient and give him what he craved.
>
> At first he looked very astonished, and then his eyes blazed and in his own language he positively *stormed* – for one minute. Then 'Pardon,' he said, and was gone.

This clash of different religious traditions was common in the wartime hospital, especially when nurses were treating enemy soldiers. We do not know whether the man received his dying consolations; we only see the impact on the nurse herself, who records 'sitting down by the poor broken body [. . .] suddenly overflowing with pity for it'.[53] Henrietta Tayler records a distressing scene of delayed absolution due to a language barrier:

> Every day and every night, for a long time, some one died – and some of the death-beds were almost unbearably pathetic. One fair-haired boy from East Austria clung to me, panting and crying, 'Schwester, Schwester, ich soll nicht sterben. Lass mich nicht sterben' – and when he found it was inevitable, begged for a priest. One of the *infirmiers* in a French ward was found and came at once, but of course the two had no channel of communication except through me, for the boy, though a devout Catholic, said he knew even his Paternoster in his own tongue only. When he had had Absolution, *Letze Ölung* and everything, he said earnestly, 'Nun, lass mich sterben, morgen sall ich nicht mehr so gut sein.' He lived till next morning, but was hardly conscious again.[54]

Although Tayler does not explicitly sentimentalise it, the pity of the scene would have affected (and affects) its readers because of the difficulty in administering dying consolations and the desperation of the 'boy' who 'clung' and 'begged'. Although the rites are successfully administered, it is clear that this is only one of a regular series of deathbeds the nurse witnessed, again highlighting the numbers of men dying and drawing attention to the difficulties of each individual death.

The narrative tension, between responsibility and blame for a death (a version of nearness) versus negation of responsibility and disengagement (distance), is present in all of the nurse narratives, together with frequent expressions of the nurses' feelings of inadequacy in their inability to relieve the suffering of the men. Bagnold writes:

> the conversation has taken on a tragic tone. The sister from the recovery hut has told how one patient on the dangerously-ill list did not want her to write to his wife 'because there is a new baby coming this week,' of how word has come through from home that 'little sonny's' mother is dead, and he must not be told yet, and of how another boy – only nineteen – had opened dying eyes to see some flowers she had taken into the ward, and how pleased he had been for it reminded him of the garden at home. We sit on the floor of the bell tent and gaze out into the night, a night when the sound of the guns is insistent. Our eyes seek the horizon, and we suddenly feel a helpless band of futile women, agonisingly impotent.[55]

They attempt to make the best of situations, such as withholding bad news from home, but the conclusive feeling is the inability of the nurses to alter the fates of those they nurse, fighting against the 'insistent' relentlessness of the guns. Tayler notes the relentlessness of incoming patients: 'though many died, being only sent to us at the last gasp, there always seemed to be others to take their places'. She emphasises that little can be done for many of the patients: 'Poor miserable objects, dying like flies, because only arriving when at the point of death'. The sense of helplessness is sometimes tempered by a justification that 'nothing at all could be done' for the patient, that there was sufficient medication and that 'we were able to soothe the last days and hours'. Elsewhere Tayler discusses the deaths of many of her patients in a depersonalised, passive voice, suggesting that the deaths were entirely out of the nurses' control: 'a sad number of deaths occurred of hopeless heart disease, cancer, dropsy, nephritis, lupus, tuberculosis and other cruel illnesses'.[56]

The dominant impression of these deathbed scenes, then, is the sheer number of deaths and the emotional burden this put on the nurses to play multiple, often contradictory roles. At times, even Dent's usually propagandistic narrative becomes intensely graphic and honest:

> Without – a night of glorious July summer, with palest saffron, flamingo and purple lights, and one gem-like star, a night of ineffable beauty and peace, and within – a vision of Hell, cruel flesh-agony, hideous writhings, broken moanings, a boy-child sitting up in bed gibbering and pulling off his head bandages, a young Colonial coughing up his last life-blood, a

big, so lately strong man with ashen face and blue lips, lying quite still but for a little fluttering breathing.

This positive account full of patriotic rhetoric does not conceal the enormous emotional burden of deathbed scenes. She writes,

> I am too tired to sleep [...] too tired to do anything but think, think, think, too tired to shut out of sight and mind the passionate appeal of two dying eyes, and a low faint whisper of 'Sister, am I going to die?'[57]

Consciously or unconsciously, nurses used the trope of the deathbed scene to attempt to give meaning to otherwise meaningless deaths, and thereby constitute a type of proto-commemoration of the men who died. Giving the men – only a few of very many men – a deathbed scene meant that they weren't forgotten. Turning to a traditional structure – one that had been consolidated through the *ars moriendi* literature, Evangelical tracts, deathbed memorials, and Victorian paintings and literature – demonstrates some attempt to find comfort in the salvaging of traditional death rituals and to derive meaning from these deaths. However, the narratives repeatedly demonstrate that these deathbed scenes were no longer adequate for the mass death the nurses attempted to represent, that war death could not be contained by its conventions. Many of these scenes therefore end inconclusively. Earlier modes of writing death and commemoration had outgrown their usefulness, but there were not yet new ones to take their place.

A Stranger among Strangers: Anti-Deathbed Scenes

Not all nurses' memoirs were consolatory. Some nurses saw the opportunity for literary experimentalism that the war offered, and the deathbed scenes in their narratives are decidedly more stylised. The four nursing memoirs that came out of L'Hôpital Chirurgical Mobile No. 1 in Belgium – by Ellen N. La Motte, Mary Borden, Agnes Warner and Maud Mortimer, provide a case study of different ways of writing about death from within the same social setting.[58] These writers have received some critical attention in recent years and new archival material has come to light.[59] Here I briefly examine the first of them.

The American professional nurse Ellen N. La Motte's *The Backwash of War: The Human Wreckage of the Battlefield as Witnessed by an American Hospital Nurse* was immediately suppressed in Britain on publication in September 1916 and in America in the summer of 1918, and not republished until 1934, because of its graphic, anti-war nature. La Motte structured the text as a short style cycle, or a series of loosely interlocking vignettes.[60] This intensely modernist text, both in form and content, was written mostly in Paris during La Motte's breaks away from the hospital. Eight of the fourteen vignettes in the book present deathbed scenes, and much of the text deals with what La Motte calls 'this awful interval' between life and death, which is 'gross, absurd, fantastic'.[61]

The vignette 'Alone' presents the opposite of a consolatory deathbed scene. Beginning with a simple statement of the man's death – 'Rochard died to-day' – the scene details how his death, from gas gangrene and a fractured skull, is intensely painful and unmourned.[62] The nurse repeatedly articulates her sense that death will be the only thing that can bring relief:

> So all night Rochard screamed in agony, and turned and twisted, first on the hip that was there, and then on the hip that was gone, and on neither side, even with many ampoules of morphia, could he find relief. Which shows that morphia, good as it is, is not as good as death.

Although the nurse 'cared for him very gently, very conscientiously, very skilfully', the surgeon and orderlies can do nothing to ease his protracted pain as he 'died slowly'. The man is depicted as unremarkable, suggesting the nurse's inability to engage with each death: 'He had been there only a few hours. He meant nothing to any one there. He was a dying man, in a field hospital, that was all'. Rochard dies offstage while the nurse is at lunch and the two orderlies are seemingly indifferently drinking wine at 'the other end of the ward'. There is no redemptive quality in this scene, no human connection between the dying man and the people around him, no relief for his suffering. He is, as La Motte notes, 'a stranger among strangers'.[63]

Other vignettes present extended deathbed sequences. 'La Patrie Reconnaissante' ('The Grateful Nation') tells the story of Marius, a Paris taxi-driver in peacetime who has had a shell in his stomach and has waited ten hours for the stretcher-bearers to arrive. His death is a highly unpleasant, uncomfortable one, repeatedly described as disturbing the other patients: 'For three days, night and day, he screamed in his delirium [. . .] And all the while the wound in the abdomen gave forth a terrible stench, filling the ward'.[64] His death is protracted like Rochard's: 'And all that night he died, and all the next day he died, and all the night following he died'. There is no aestheticising of his death:

> His was a filthy death. He died after three days' cursing and raving. Before he died, that end of the ward smelled foully, and his foul words, shouted at the top of his delirious voice, echoed foully. Everyone was glad when it was over.

His death which 'came suddenly' offers a final commentary on the way that his lengthy and painful war death will be presented in official, propagandistic terms. The nurse knows that the state will sanitise the death: seeing a funeral procession out of the window, she notes that '[t]he Bier was covered with the glorious tricolour of France [. . .] It would be just like that when he died'. To her surprise, the patriotic slogans she sees on a French newspaper are matched by Marius's final words: 'Then Marius gave a last, sudden scream. [. . .] *"Vive la Patrie Reconnaissante!"* he yelled. *"Hoch le Kaiser!"* Then he died'.[65] Is he still delirious, or has he become the patriotic and compliant soldier that the state demands? La Motte leaves it ambiguous, but Marius and his deathbed scene have been stubbornly non-compliant up to this point, presenting a deathbed that is disturbing in all senses.

In 'Pour La Patrie', the Victorian death ritual becomes an act of violence and coercion. Here an older man who has been shot knows he is dying because he has been awarded the *Médaille Militaire* in a 'perfunctory' ceremony, ensuring his wife a pension. There is an unusual admission of the nurse's own sense of complicity in the face of his extreme pain:

> He clenched his hands and writhed, and cried out for mercy. But what mercy had we? We gave him morphia, but it did not help. So he continued to cry to us for mercy, he cried to us and to God. Between us, we let him suffer eight hours more like that, us and God.

The nurse summons the priest to give the man the sacrament, but religion here offers no mercy either: 'No, it did not bring him comfort, or resignation'. In fact, the process of accepting the sacrament is presented as an act of subjugation: 'He was being forced into it. Forced into acceptance. Beaten into submission, beaten into resignation'.[66] La Motte's description of the 'volley of low toned Latin phrases, rattling in the stillness like the popping of a *mitrailleuse*' – a comparison to the shots of a French volley gun – suggests the violence of this action. Although the man eventually dies peacefully, he reveals that his bravery on the battlefield was itself the result of coercion: '"Now I have won the *Médaille Militaire*. My Captain won it for me. He made me brave. He had a revolver in his hand"'.[67] Here La Motte satirises the model of the wartime hero, suggesting that examples of wartime heroism are in fact instances of compulsion.

Other sections show La Motte not only revising the Victorian deathbed scene, but turning it on its head. In 'At the Telephone', a wounded French soldier is having his leg amputated with not 'even a fighting chance' of survival. He has had a spinal anaesthetic and is conscious, but he 'babble[s] of his home, and of his wife':

> After a short while, however, his remarks grew less coherent, and he seemed to find himself back in the trenches, telephoning. He tried hard to telephone, he tried hard to get the connection. The wires seemed to be cut, however, and he grew puzzled, and knit his brows and swore, and tried again and again, over and over. He had something to say over the

telephone, the trench communication wire, and his mind wandered, and he tried very hard, in his wandering mind, to get the connection. A shell had cut the line evidently.[68]

Although we know from other accounts from the same hospital that this incident did happen, the use of repetition and the circular nature of the prose – mirroring the 'wandering mind' of the patient – demonstrate that La Motte's account is stylised and modernist in both content and style. It is not surprising to find that La Motte had spent time before the war with her friend from Johns Hopkins Medical School and high modernist Gertrude Stein and her avant-garde circle in Paris. Stein had given her two of her books to read and the pair were in correspondence during this period and intermittently until Stein's death in 1946.[69] The new medium of the telephone, here referring to the field telephone used in the war zones, provides a particularly modern means of writing about death (not unlike my later discussion of H.D.'s use of the cinema). The soldier's concern to 'get the connection' is a means of communicating with home and family, but here it is an imagined or fantasy connection. Finally, in the climactic end of the scene, the man gets through:

> He struggled hard to get the connection, in his mind, over the telephone. The wires seemed to be cut, and he cried out in anxiety and distress. Then he grew more and more feeble, and gasped more and more, and became almost inarticulate, in his efforts. He was distressed. But suddenly he got it. He screamed out very loud, relieved, satisfied, triumphant, startling them all.
> '*Ça y est, maintenant! Ça y est! C'est le bon Dieu à l'appareil!*' [That's it now! That's it! It is the good God on the telephone!]

Simultaneously a 'sudden, vivid' drop of blood spotted the sheet and the surgeon, unaware that the man has died, declares 'with satisfaction' that he is finished with the operation. The Directrice, who we can presume to be La Motte's boss Mary Borden, repeats his words '"Finished here"' in a grim parody.[70] Having found his connection, aptly, with God at the end of the telephone line, the man has simultaneously found his end on the operating table. In an inversion of the motif of connection and disconnection, connection here symbolises death. Seeking connection with God, the man is enacting a type of last sacrament using modern technology. This isn't a commemorative scene, but a reworking of the Victorian deathbed scene, where we can see La Motte experimenting with a particularly modern mode of writing about death. Of the vignettes that are dated, this was one of the final texts to be written.[71] By the next month, July 1916, La Motte had left the hospital – and the war – and returned to the States, before going to China. This satirical text was suppressed until 1934, when its modernist and graphic account of the nurse's experience and its distressing deathbed scenes were more acceptable to the public.

Burial Rites and Funeral Ceremonies

Nurses' descriptions of burial rites and funeral ceremonies demonstrate their continued attempts to do justice to, dignify and memorialise the men. This question of paying respect would later be one of national concern in terms of monuments and ceremonies, but at the local level, nurses were concerned with the immediate ceremony of the burial, attempting to create traditional rites at the front and record them in writing. Like the memorialising impulse seen in deathbed scenes, these moments demonstrate an attempted reversion to conventional rituals and sites of the dead. The cemetery or graveyard scene is a conventional literary motif and a traditional site for meditation on death and mortality. As with the deathbed scenes, it became clear that these earlier, more traditional modes could not always provide consolation or adequately represent the deaths the nurses witnessed. Nurses were simultaneously concerned with both the bodily, corporeal aspect of dying – before the problem of the disposal of the mass dead became apparent to the government – and the consolatory aspects, both of the patient before his death and his family through letters afterwards.

Numerous nurses record laying out the dead and helping to move bodies to the mortuary, reminding us how involved they were with corpses. These descriptions were included seemingly to reassure relatives at home that justice was done to their dead. However, these descriptions are not always positive. Although a routine task, laying out a body was time-consuming and impossible to schedule. A number of nurses recall the inconvenience of this process. Smith makes repeated references to laying out, usually with some note of how it fits in to, or disturbs, her timetable. 'The worst nephritis case died in the afternoon in a pool of steam,' she writes, 'and we laid him out before I went over to tea'. If we return to the death of Railton, Smith's description of his death demonstrates its inconvenience:

> Railton's mother came back and sat quietly beside him till he died at ten minutes to eight. If he had lived till five minutes past eight the night people would have had to lay him out. As it was we had to indent for a shroud before going over for a hurried supper and then come back to him afterwards. [. . .] when at last we were finished Sister asked her if she would like us to take her back to the Y.W. hut. She 'thanked us kindly but would rather stay with Jim!' We tried to explain that the body would be taken to the mortuary almost at once, and she would be told about the funeral, but she only thanked us kindly again and said she'd rather stay with Jim. Sister and I looked at each other despairingly. We

couldn't leave her alone with her dead son, and when he was taken away the night nurse could not possibly desert the ward to take her across to the Y.W.C.A. hut.

'The men'll be here for him in no time, Kay. I'm going to wait. I'll get on with the dispensaries for the morning; there's lots to do and I'm not going to leave that poor old woman to lose her way at this time of night.'

Traditional and wartime modes of death clash here. The unsentimental and disgruntled tone of Smith's description demonstrates that despite her evident care for Railton, preparing his body for burial is a chore. The inconvenience to the tight hospital schedule is worsened by the presence of Railton's mother. She represents a traditional mode of mourning, that of sitting by the dead and allowing the body to remain in state for a number of hours – a model which is unworkable in the wartime hospital, where there is no time for grieving. The nurses, however, take pity on his mother and determine not 'to leave that poor old woman' alone. Similarly, the death of the New Zealander Grainger presents problems for the hospital schedule, despite his death being anticipated. Grainger dies at 5.10pm, and Smith is told off by her Matron for taking too long over the task of laying him out, giving an indication of how long the procedure of preparation for burial takes: '"The Sergeant was notified at 5.50 that the body was ready for removal, Matron," I answered'.[72] Smith's complaints about the forty-minute interruption to the hospital schedule caused by a death are therefore not unfounded.

Inconvenience was not the only reason that nurses may have disliked the process of laying out a body. The frequent lack of an entire corpse meant that preparing the body for burial could be unpleasant or even traumatic, revealing the extent of a patient's injuries that were not apparent when he was alive. Smith records a particularly traumatic experience concerning the laying out of the patient known as 'Ninety-nine':

> I rolled him over gently towards me, and the unwieldly [sic] white roll of bandages that was his head suddenly fell on the pillow as if it had decided reluctantly to follow the body. [. . .]
>
> 'We'll have to do this head again. I'm sorry,' she added as I appeared with the tray, 'we can't let him go to the mortuary like this. [. . .] Now, Nurse, lift his head a little.'
>
> I put my hand at the back of his head and then dropped it and laughed and laughed. The funniest thing had happened. My hand had gone right through the bandages. There was no head there!

Smith has been increasingly fraught by her time spent on night duty in the 'Heads' ward, which culminates in her hysteria at finding part of Ninety-nine's head missing. The experience continues to preoccupy her: 'I felt sick when I thought how my hand had gone through the hole into Ninety-nine's head. I had scrubbed and disinfected but I'd never feel clean again'. Although Smith later jokes that she sees herself 'playing at Lady Macbeth', this seems to be a textbook case of nursing trauma, provoked by the discovery of the incomplete corpse of a patient.[73] Smith's hysterical laughter is a response to the unanticipated breakdown of traditional modes of dealing with the dead.

The wartime corpse prevented the traditional laying out of the body and undermined the symbolism of the whole and aesthetically presentable corpse, one of the key features of Victorian deathbed narratives and images. The nurses' role in preparing the body for burial involved the aestheticisation of often mangled human forms, as Tayler notes:

> There were many, alas, whom we could not save [. . .] for whom nothing at all could be done save to wash off the mud and the blood, close the tired eyes, straighten the distorted limbs and cross the weary hands.

The nurse's job was to 'make good' the body: a physical equivalent of some of the more propagandistic memoirs, which attempted to aestheticise the great number of war deaths through consolatory and patriotic rhetoric. This corporeal house-keeping was required by tradition and driven by the Victorian desire for the realism of the corpse. However, as Smith's example shows, nurses' attempts to make the corpse respectable for the mortuary frequently proved to be futile, as the body was often beyond repair.

Following preparation for burial, the corpse was moved to the mortuary before the funeral ceremony. Here, the burden of the dead was physical. Carriers of the dead, most notably Charon in Greek mythology, are traditionally male. However, nurses described transporting bodies in order to demonstrate adequate care for the dead. Tayler writes of her time in a French hospital: 'Many, many times in the cold winter nights did we have sad little processions through the snow to the small mortuary chapel', with an illustration entitled 'A sad little procession', depicting two nurses bearing a body on a stretcher across a barren landscape.[74] Of only seven illustrations in the text, one is deliberately dedicated to demonstrating to the civilian public that justice is done to their war dead. Smith's detailed description of moving the corpse of 'No. 7' to the mortuary demonstrates that nurses sometimes found this experience 'nerve-racking':

> 'Walk behind me, Nurse,' whispered Sister, and the procession passed out into the first faint beginning of the dawn. We filed down the narrow path to the mortuary and stopped while Sister unlocked the door. The porters laid down their burden and stretched their backs while Sister struck a match and lit a bare gas jet that whistled forlornly. [. . .]

> Six cold marble slabs like a fishmonger's counter surrounded the tiny room. Three of them were empty, but I had hardly time to realise what was happening when I heard an urgent whisper from Night Sister.
> 'Nurse, attend please.'
> I stopped thinking at once and went towards her. The porters held the stretcher alongside a marble slab and Sister murmured: 'Hold here, Nurse.' I slipped my hands under the dead body until I felt her warm clasp. She then said 'Ready,' and we lifted No. 7 on to his slab.
> I waited until Sister had arranged the grave clothes and put some flowers on his breast and pulled the sheet again over his face. There were now only two slabs empty. Sister carefully lowered the light, and the silence was nerve-racking after the high piercing scream of the escaping gas. She locked the door behind her. The porters had already vanished, and the cold wind cut our breaths from us as we walked back to Isolation.[75]

The porters are responsible for carrying the body over to the mortuary, but the nurses make the final arrangements before burial. It is clear that Smith doesn't know what to do in the circumstances, instead following the Night Sister's commands. The Sister's command that they walk in a procession is an attempt to bestow formality on the occasion, like Tayler's 'processions'. However, the very negative comparison with the 'fishmonger's counter' depicts the human cadavers as like meat, and the mention of there being 'only two slabs empty' suggests ominously that these will soon be filled. The scene is notable for its repression: although Smith states that the silence is 'nerve-racking', her intense discomfort is only acknowledged obliquely. The reference to 'the high piercing scream' of the gas refers to her own tension, which she cannot articulate: 'the cold wind cut our breaths from us'. In a scene demonstrating the nurse's emotional difficulty in dealing with the dead, the nurses do not discuss this experience, returning instead, fittingly, to 'Isolation'.

If fitting burial rites were not possible or nurses were not personally involved, they sometimes engaged in a form of imaginative compensation, seen in Bagnold's depiction of actual and imagined rituals of military death. When she 'ask[s] after the man who has his nose blown off', his uncertain fate prompts Bagnold to describe these burial rituals:

> He was breathing heavily. They don't know yet whether he will live.
> When a man dies they fetch him with a stretcher, just as he came in; only he enters with a blanket over him, and a flag covers him as he goes out. When he came in he was one of a convoy, but every man who can stand rises to his feet as he goes out. Then they play him to his funeral, to a grass mound at the back of the hospital.[76]

This gentle and consolatory depiction suggests a peaceful death: the flag replacing the blanket giving the impression that the man is only sleeping. Bagnold describes the effort to mark the occasion of every separate death, despite their frequency. Still depicted as part of a convoy and surrounded by loyal comrades, the men perform ceremonial music to give appropriate occasion and to pay respect to the deceased. The description of his funeral suggests it is individual, when frequently funerals in the war zones were plural. The pastoral 'grass mound' is typically elegiac as the dead soldier is returned to the earth, and its proximity to the hospital suggests that he is not far removed from the living.[77] Bagnold writes later in more general terms about what happens when a man dies, imagining the death rituals happening out of sight:

> Orderlies come and go up and down the corridor. Often they carry stretchers – now and then a stretcher with the empty folds of a flag flung across it.
> Then I pause from laying my trays, and with a bunch of forks in my hand I stand still.
> They take the stretcher into a ward, and while I wait I know what they are doing behind the screens which stand around a bed against the wall. I hear the shuffle of feet as the men stand to attention, and the orderlies come out again, and the folds of the flag have ballooned up to receive and embrace a man's body.
> Where is he going?
> To the mortuary.
> Yes . . . but where else . . . ?
> Perhaps there is nothing better than the ecstasy and unappeasement of life?[78]

Similar to Dent's wish for a salute – 'What a pity we nurses have no kind of salute! I should dearly love to show the "boys going-up" some little respect, just as I always want to pay tribute when I attend a soldier's funeral' – Bagnold records her own private self-imposed code of respect, pausing in the midst of a chore in an attempt to pay homage to the dead.[79] Although she claims to 'know what they are doing', her imagined version of the burial rites happening behind the screen, with due codes of reverence, demonstrates the important role of imaginative compensation in the nurse narratives. The comforting image of the personified 'embrace' of the corpse by the flag suggests the man is cared for in death, perhaps mentally alleviating any guilt at the nurse's perceived failure in her role to cure the patient of his wound or illness. The concluding question shows Bagnold reconsidering the notion of an afterlife, to examine whether in these new wartime conditions an appreciation of ecstasy and unappeasement in *this* life, and not the next, may be more appropriate. What initially reads as a largely conservative imagining of ritual therefore becomes an interesting commentary on the changing attitudes towards death as a result of the war.

The nurses' shock at the treatment of the dead in some of the war zones is demonstrated by a set of unpublished diaries by Miss M. A. Brown, a VAD on board the Hospital Ship *Devanha* in the Mediterranean.[80] She writes in early 1916:

> Some Naval men have come on board & they tell us that the Serbians are suffering dreadfully from starvation from cold & hunger they are dying in hundreds, the roads for 5 miles out from this place are strewn with corpses.[81]

Brown found the lack of burial of these bodies 'too gruesome for anything':

> There is a small staff of 23 British soldiers & officers out here since 5 weeks they are trying to feed & clothe the Serbians who make their way here over the mountains, but it is [very?] hopeless work, The Italians wont [sic] lift a finger to assist the Serbians, of course they are a very useless & threftless [?] lot of people but one would think that for the sake of humanity they would feed the starving wretches, there were over 2000 expected here yesterday, but they did not arrive they are walking over the snow covered mountains goodness only knows how many miles, it takes them over 5 days to get down here, & they fall dead in dozens each day, there are trenches dug on each side of the road & they are just covered over in them, the Albanians come down from the hills in the night time & strip all the bodies of clothing etc. its [sic] too gruesome for anything. A British officer told us, that they sent out carts to pick up the dead for 5 miles out from the town & buried them, to try & keep down disease.

The passage is indicative of the nurse's horror at the way the dead are treated – that the Serbians are not properly buried and that their bodies are picked over by the Albanians – and a means for her to express national pride. She notes that the British are attempting to follow the usual peacetime procedures for the handling of corpses: an attempt to maintain hygiene and a mark of respect. In late January 1916, she writes: 'We had 4 more deaths today & as the French people suspect Cholera, we cannot send them ashore for burial, so we are to take them out to sea & bury them'.[82] The treatment of the dead becomes a marker of civility, where (unsurprisingly) it is the British soldiers and officers who treat the corpses in either a respectful or hygienic way.

Some burial rituals were more problematic than others, particularly descriptions of nurses' funerals. Like other funerals, these were related in largely consolatory modes, but there are moments when these depictions break down, probably because of the potential self-identification of nurses in these circumstances. Dent's account of a VAD funeral lapses into plain description, unusual for her otherwise propagandistic narrative.[83] The description of the fairly elaborate funeral cortège establishes the significance of the occasion:

> A cordon of R.A.M.C. lined the road, and down it passed the padre followed by the pipers wailing a dirge. Next came the coffin, a plain, unstained wooden one covered with the Union Jack. Then came the A.D.M.S., and some other staff officers, and then we nurses – Q.A.I.M.N.S., Territorial, Reserve, St. J.A.A., and B.R.C.

Dent describes the funeral scene in superlative terms: 'the padre read the address exquisitely and most impressively. It was a beautiful spring afternoon with a fleckless blue sky and floods of soft sunshine'. However, the patriotic rhetoric momentarily fails the nurse:

> The Union Jack is folded and laid aside, the pageantry and the impressive dignity of the scene loses its grip on one. Instead there comes to mind a picture of the dead girl, white and still, with closed eyes and crossed hands.

Here the diction of the flag and its accompanying 'pageantry', the propagandistic discourse which Dent subscribes to and maintains elsewhere, is momentarily undone by her vision of the corpse. However, the sorrow of the scene remains displaced: 'A French peasant woman with a tiny bunch of half-faded violets is sobbing loudly. The grave faces of the English nurses grow a little more set'. This uncharacteristically frank depiction of the realities of war is swiftly redressed by Dent, who re-establishes the discourse of sacrifice for one's country:

> No matter what consolation is proffered, death is always an irreparable loss. But surely it is better to have it come when doing work that counts, work of national and racial weight, than to live on until old and unwanted.
> And what a magnificent end to one's life, to lie there among those splendidly brave boys in the little strip of land which the French Government has given over in perpetuity to our dead. Thousands of the children that are to be, will come to such cemeteries, and will be hushed to reverence by the spirits of those who are not, by the spirits of the fallen that will for ever inhabit the scene.

Dent incorporates the death of the nurse into typically propagandistic discourse, suggesting the immortality and the gratitude of future generations.

The immediacy of the preceding description of the nurse's dead body has been counteracted by a consolatory narrative of shared sacrifice and the suggestion of the spirits of the fallen forever inhabiting the scene.

Brown's diary also includes a description of a VAD funeral, writing in mid-October 1915 from the Grand Hotel, Alexandria:

> To day Miss Crom [?] asked as many as could get away, to go to a V.A.D. Sister's funereal [sic]. The girl only arrived 2 weeks ago with over 100 Red Cross nurses she took dysentery immediately she [?] arrived & died this morning. The funereal was from the Hosp Schools at 19[.?] to the little Military Cemetery The Coffin was pure white covered with the Union Jack, & carried by relays of R.A.M.C. Orderlies. 100 V.A.D. followed, then the Territorials & las [sic] of all about 50 Reserves. We all walked to the little Cemetery, near the gates we walked between two rows of soldiers standing there.
>
> The Chaplain read the burial service & the Saluting party sounded the Last Post. There were several beautiful wreathes laid on the grave. As we left the Cemetrey [sic] we could not help nocticeing [sic], the numbers of graves newly made belonging to our men who had died in Hospital here. Outside the gates, there were 8 coffins waiting for burial. The V.A.D belonged to Whil[t?]by. she [sic] was 34 years of age.[84]

The amount of detail recorded by Brown indicates that this was a more elaborate funeral than most, involving representatives from multiple army branches, as well as several wreathes put on the grave. Brown's description is straightforward, not moving into the patriotic rhetoric of Dent's narrative. Her admission that they 'could not help noticing the numbers of graves newly made' perhaps suggests guilt that they have failed 'our men', or merely the nurses' ongoing shock at the numbers of dead. This is emphasised by Brown noting the further eight coffins to be buried, undermining this singular funeral. Two days later, Brown records another nurse death in minimal terms: 'Attended another V.A.D funereal to[-]day. This nurse was an only child. Nothing new'. Here, Brown doesn't go into detail, as the weary 'nothing new' shows the frequency of these deaths.

Cemetery Scenes and Early Attempts at Memorialisation

Despite the triumphant, propagandistic tone of many nurses' narratives, there was often an underlying fear that the dead would be forgotten or that their grave was not sufficiently commemorative. The nurses frequently described cemeteries, either in admiration or concern that they did not do justice to the dead. They also documented individual attempts to remember the dead and to give them a dignified burial.

One of the early images in Dent's *A V.A.D. in France* is a French cemetery that includes British graves. This conservative depiction adheres to idealised, prewar ideas of the dead:

> At Wimereux we climbed up to the cemetery, which has been extended to include a military section for the fallen British. Long lines of smoothed graves, each headed with a little wooden cross, – it is a picture of majestic simplicity, of infinite pathos, nothing tawdry, nothing trivial, nothing but the grandeur of simplicity. We think of the poor, maimed bodies, all that remain of that grace of English youth and comeliness, of the beauty that is consumed away, of man turned to destruction. We think of Time who unheedingly dims the proud stories of those valiant heroes. Each little, smoothed grave means a tragedy, a gap in some home across those dark waters. Our age has paid its price for the nation and the race. Those are the dead who won our freedom. May we cheat Time, and ever retain the thought. May it compel us to greater patience, greater fortitude, greater forbearance in the work that is to come.
>
> We turn from the graves and leave our dead to their bravely-earned rest on the little wind-swept hill. May they sleep in peace.

Dent's description suggests the 'smoothed' graves give order and individual position, counteracting the reality of the 'poor, maimed bodies' below. The propagandistic rhetoric ('those valiant heroes'), epigrammatic quality, and poetic, sermon-like language attempt to bestow dignity on the men. The emphasis on cheating 'Time' (capitalised and personified) instructs the reader to remember the dead, consoling the reader for personal loss through a suggestion of immortal glory: 'Our generation ended, these brave boys individually will be forgotten, but their deeds, dream-like in their amazing valour, have opened up a new day of freedom and independence which can never be forgotten. What a gift to posterity!'[85] In an earlier section of the narrative, entitled 'Extracts from the diary of a train sister', Dent presents a more individualised, less official type of commemoration:

> Aug. 15. In L– all day. Went for a walk, and passing through a cemetery, found there the grave of 'Jimmy Anzac' whom I had nursed in Malta. Poor, poor boy, and what a strange chance I should find his grave. [. . .]
>
> Sep. 7. Made arrangements for more permanent cross over Jimmy's grave.[86]

Dent clearly felt that the burden of Jimmy's adequate commemoration was her responsibility. Walker records her horror at the makeshift cemeteries she sees, which depersonalise the dead:

> On another day we walked to the nearest Soldiers' Cemetery – a square field full of wooden crosses with little aluminium plates on one side, and names painted on the other. They were so uniform and near together, that it was almost like rows of fencing. But one realised that for the time being, it was the best that could be done.[87]

The palpable horror that the men are being buried with little more than fencing for headstones is countered by the hope that these graves may be improved after the war. Other nurses registered the disparity between these new makeshift and older cemeteries. Smith notes 'the church where straggling iron crosses and wreaths of immortelles marked the peaceful graves of men who had died in the fullness of their days', where the lack of uniformity seems denotative of lives richly lived.[88]

Nurses frequently discussed memorials and remembrances at gravestones. Walker records the death of a patient known as 'The Spine Case', a New Zealander with a bullet embedded in his spine. When his death became inevitable and with no family nearby to visit him, Walker 'used to go in often, and buy him anything he fancied'.[89] When he dies after three weeks, she attempts to give his death meaning and occasion: 'we stood by, waiting for him to get his release. It seemed strange that the Australian Ward upstairs should have put on a hymn on their gramophone just then'. Walker then actively assumes the role of his mourner:

> Because he had volunteered to help England, and had died in her defence, I used to go up to the Cemetery where he was buried in a communal grave, and take flowers, until I left Tooting. Then the mother of another of our men who died, took over from me. 'He shall have flowers whenever I bring them for my son,' she said.

This communal effort to remember and commemorate the dead demonstrates that nurses did not easily forget their deceased patients and that grieving became a shared experience during and after the war. Walker's gesture is also a means of personalising the death of one of a number of soldiers buried in a communal grave. Walker writes similarly of a fellow nurse, Nurse Mitford:

> She was a Catholic, and had charge of the Catholic Mortuary, going down nightly to light the candles at the head and at the feet of the peaceful dead. I used to go with her, and before long felt that the Protestant dead, who had no candles, *must* have flowers, so I secured them. I did not believe either were *needed* to take our prayers to Heaven, or to guard the sleeping dead! But it made *me* feel they were *cared* for. When Nurse Mitford went on leave, I took over her job of looking after the Mortuary.

Walker explicitly states that this commemoration is an act more for the nurses themselves than for the men, demonstrating the nurses' longstanding concern for the dead and perhaps assuaging the feelings of impotence and powerlessness that many of them felt. This need to honour the dead may have been in part a reflection of the nurse's ongoing mourning. Walker continues: 'I found any sense of shrinking I might have had was overborne by reverence and pity. Pity because they seemed so lonely, though I knew they were not'.[90] It is hard not to read in this description the nurse's own loneliness as a war survivor.

Nurses' presence at the site of death gave them particular authority and responsibility when describing the deaths of patients. A number of texts consider the problem of consolation of relatives and friends at home, whether by letter or telegram, or in person. In a memorable scene in *A Diary without Dates*, a father has come to this home front hospital to ask Captain Matthew for information about his dead son, one of Matthew's subalterns.[91] Matthew's palpable reluctance to participate in, or even enter, the scene of mourning, implies an unwillingness both to talk about the boy (and possibly relive his death) and to play the role of knowledge-bearer of the deceased: 'he seemed in no hurry to go in [. . .] He waited almost three minutes, then he sighed and went in'. The father is presented as vulnerable and deferential – 'a little elderly man, his hat on his knees' – representative of any grieving relative. Bagnold notes 'his anxious, ordinary face' and plays on this concept of the man as everyman: 'A citizen . . . a baker or a brewer, tinker, tailor, or candlestick-maker . . .?' The description of the father's desire for information as '[t]he last hungry pickings from Captain Matthew's tired memory and nervous speech' suggests the man's overbearance on the Captain, portraying the burden of grief loaded onto those who were present at the death of their loved one. Although the man has come in the hope of consolation from someone who was present at his son's death, the 'great shrinking' of the nurse narrator looking in on the scene suggests the dearth of comfort available to the grieving father. Bagnold empathetically imagines the activities of his and many other families at home: 'There had been the buying of the uniform, the visits to the camp in England, the parcels to send out – always the parcels – week by week. And now nothing; no more parcels, no more letters, silence' (we will see this same linking of the wartime post with passing time and proof of survival in Chapter 3). This scene about a father's fruitless search for information and consolation ends ironically with his near encounter with a newly deceased corpse: 'At the end of the passage he almost collided with that stretcher which bears a flag. Of the two, the stretcher moved me least'. The nurse suggests that the grieving relative, rather than the dead young man, is the most pitiful element of the scene.

Tayler similarly acknowledges the nurse's burden of responsibility for the consolation of those at home, in her knowledge of their loved one's final hours. 'Many of them only expected to die, and gave one addresses in outlandish places to which to write to their parents. One always wondered if these letters arrived!', she writes of her patients. For another, a Parisian taxi-cab driver who eventually dies, she records:

> He reminded me a little of a Algerian officer I nursed at La Panne, who, in agonies with gas gangrene, seized my wrist and crushed it black and blue while shouting for 'Champagne et Suzanne.' Poor fellow! A very nice brother came afterwards and asked me what were his last words!

This tragicomic passage dispels notions of a heroic or romanticised death, instead portraying the reality as one of pain and longing. The added information that a relative sought comfort in the man's last words makes this tragedy ironic, as the nurse presumably had to provide a fictionalised account in line with the manner of death reported to those at home: quick, painless and honourable. The question of remembrance is highlighted by a patient who presumes he is dying and hopes to anticipate the consolatory note sent home:

> One Frenchman [. . .] who gave us a great deal of trouble, desired me to write to his father that he had died the death of a hero and, when I pointed out 'Nous ne sommes pas encore à ce point-là,' [We are not yet at that point'] was quite hurt. Him, I did manage to see again, being very noisy in another ward.[92]

This notion of the patient writing his own eulogy is quickly dismissed by Tayler's humorous comment. These scenes demonstrate that nurses were not only the people who cared for the men at their death bed, but also the knowledge-bearers and figures of consolation for many of the mourners at home.

In terms of self-consolation, Bagnold is increasingly explicit about the absolute lack of consolation for a death. Prompted by the sounds of guns outside, she writes of her preoccupation with death:

> I can only think of death to-night. I tried to think just now, 'What is it, after all! Death comes anyway; this only hastens it.' But that won't do; no philosophy helps the pain of death. It is pity, pity, pity, that I feel, and sometimes a sort of shame that I am here to write at all.

She documents her failed attempts to console herself, resolutely refusing to ameliorate or justify the deaths. This failure leaves her feeling a type of survivors' guilt, not dissimilar to her feeling of 'a sort of shame in such strength' in relation to men in pain earlier in the text. Bagnold suggests that no memorials can do justice to the dying men, again denying any type of consolation in traditional means of mourning, and shows her fear that the dead will be forgotten: 'everything is written in water', she writes, '[w]e talk of tablets to the dead. There can be none but in the heart, and the heart fades'. In a later section in the wake of an attack, Bagnold is clearly burdened by an intense awareness of the men they can't save: 'what about the Monks, Scutts, Gayners, whose wounds will never need a dressing or a tube – who lie along a front of two miles, one on his face, another on his back?' As she notes that 'Since 3.15 this morning a lot of men have died', her comment that 'Thank God one cannot go on realizing death' demonstrates the huge emotional burden placed on the nurses as primary mourners, as the only women present at the site of death to 'realize' it: to be the first to acknowledge it, and to provide consolation for those nearby and at home. Here, Bagnold does provide herself with a consolatory gesture, focusing on those who have survived: 'But one need not think of it. This is a ward; here are lucky ones. Even when I look at Rees, even when I look at the grocer, even when I look at the T.B. ward, I know that anything, *anything* is better than death'.[93]

In comparison with nurses' written memorials, we see similar commemorative gestures in contemporary material and visual culture. In the nursing album made by Patricia Young, a VAD nurse in a Red Cross Hospital in Dumfries, Scotland, she attempted to give the soldiers an individual space on the page, albeit in visual rather than written terms (see Figs 1.2 and 1.3).[94] Young noted

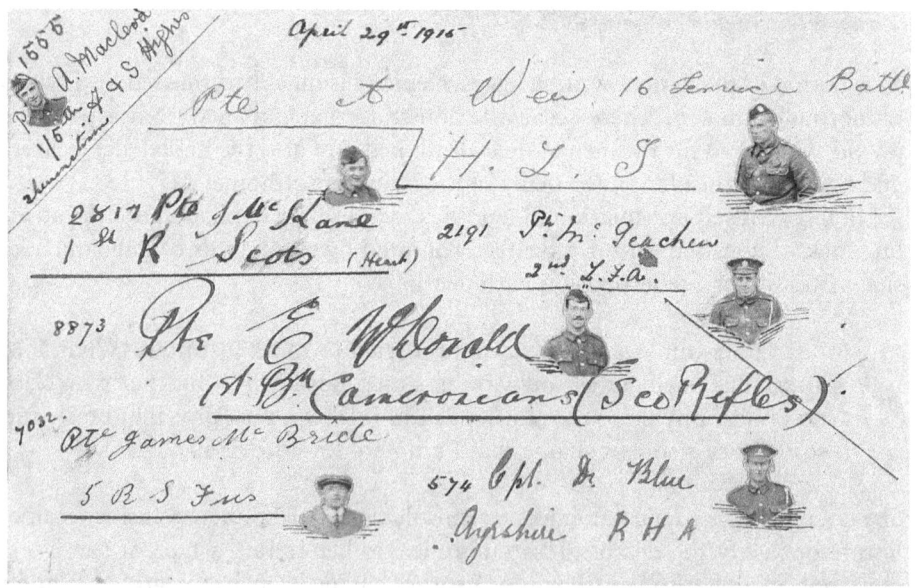

Figure 1.2 Two pages from Patricia Young, Album of photographs, autographs, and notes compiled by a nurse of the Volunteer Aid Detachment, Dumfries, Scotland, 1914–17. Yale Center for British Art, Friends of British Art Fund

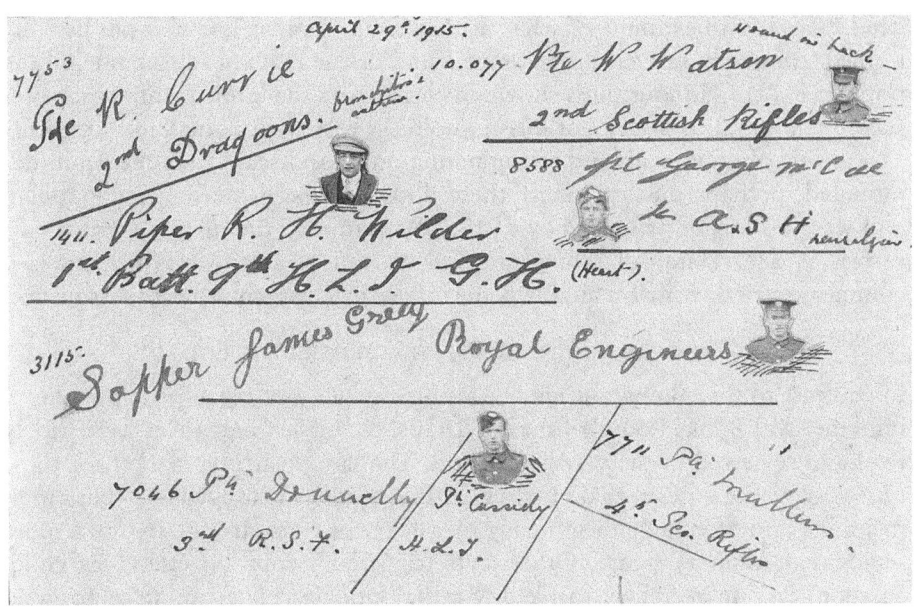

Figure 1.3 Two pages from Patricia Young, Album of photographs, autographs, and notes compiled by a nurse of the Volunteer Aid Detachment, Dumfries, Scotland, 1914–17. Yale Center for British Art, Friends of British Art Fund

the soldier's name and regiment next to a photograph she had cut out by hand from a group image to form an individual portrait. Florence Farmborough's *Russian Album, 1908–1918*, published posthumously in 1979, contains photographs taken during her time nursing on the Eastern Front, of burials, funerals, and cemeteries as well as graphic images of dead bodies on the ground, in open-air mortuaries, and 'side by side in pit-like graves [. . .] swarming with flies'. It documents the work of the orderlies with 'their melancholy task [. . .] of interring the dead'. There are also photographs which draw on the earlier commemorative tradition of the living posing with the dead, such as soldiers posing with the bodies of other soldiers who 'lie ready for interment, wrapped in sheets and strewn with flowers'. Another page which depicts 'routine' shows Farmborough and an orderly smiling at the camera while standing behind the beds of men who are dying. The caption reads like many of the written nursing memoirs: 'we stay in attendance on the dying when we can, trusting they will find comfort in our presence. A coffin, one of a small stock kept in readiness by our carpenters, stands ominously round the corner'. Another photograph shows a makeshift monument to the dead 'designed by some of the men in our Division', demonstrating an early attempt to formally commemorate the dead.⁹⁵ We see an example of what the historian Thomas Laqueur has usefully termed 'commemorative hyper-nominalism', or the mass need to name, in the popular Roll of Honour films shown in cinemas on the home front, which presented photographs of dead or missing soldiers with their names and regiments as a means of honouring and remembering on a local scale.⁹⁶ As the death toll mounted, perhaps unsurprisingly these films became increasingly unpopular, and were no longer produced by 1917.⁹⁷ We can read the nurses' written narratives as one version of a more general wartime urge towards personalised commemoration, which would become increasingly urgent after the Armistice.

Conclusion: Remembering before the End

In contrast to the combatant memoirs which would not reach peak popularity until the 'War Books Boom' of the late 1920s, the nurses' narratives were widely read and reviewed in the wartime period. The large wartime market for these nurses' narratives meant that nurses were frequently encouraged to publish their memoirs, and often given legitimacy by a foreword or introduction by a more senior male military figure. Other texts triggered a copy-cat effect: Sir Philip Sassoon, Private Secretary to Field Marshal Douglas Haig, wrote to Bagnold from the Front, 'I suppose there is not a VAD in France who has not now begun to keep a diary in emulation of you – and paper is so scarce'.⁹⁸ Although the publication figures haven't survived, anecdotal evidence demonstrates the prevalence of these texts. Grant Richards, writing about his firm's recent publications in *The Times Literary Supplement* in January 1918, noted of Olive Dent's *A V.A.D. in France* 'this book, although by a new writer, exists to the extent of thousands of copies in the bookshops and libraries of the country'.⁹⁹ Over a year later he noted: 'The booksellers seem to have had enough books about the V.A.D., but I notice that they still order Miss Olive Dent's "A V.A.D. in France" (6/- net) and the *Westminster Gazette* has just reviewed it'.¹⁰⁰ Although it was in his interest to stress the book's success, the lucrative market and demand for these nurses' books is evident, even after the war had ended. Marketing helped, as seen by the American nurse Shirley Millard's luridly titled 1936 memoir *I Saw Them Die*.¹⁰¹ This success did not always reach the nurses themselves, however: in 1918 Bagnold was paid threepence per copy of *A Diary without Dates* and wrote, 'So I shan't be opulent on it'.¹⁰²

Importantly, these nurses' texts were read, reviewed and imitated by the writers who would produce experimental literary work in the wartime and postwar period. Virginia Woolf anonymously reviewed E. M. Spearing's memoir *From Cambridge to Camiers under the Red Cross* in the *TLS* in May 1917.¹⁰³ We can imagine Woolf's interest being piqued by this Fellow of Newnham College who left her academic research to join the VAD, and whose book proofs, sent dutifully to Louvain University Press, were destroyed in the German devastation of the town. Her comments on the typicality of this narrative demonstrates her familiarity with this literary genre: 'As for the soldiers [. . .] Miss Spearing has the usual story to tell – so usual that we have almost forgotten how remarkable it is'. Woolf notes the 'concentration of life' evident in the text as one of the fascinations of the war for many people, but also quotes Spearing's own phrase, the 'community of suffering', to describe the 'deeper thoughts' experienced by the nurses and the soldiers. Woolf, however, wouldn't review Bagnold's *A Diary without Dates* the following year, and wrote very disparagingly about the book (and its author) to her sister Vanessa Bell.[104] Other writers recorded their interaction with nurses as future literary material: a letter from Katherine Mansfield to her later husband John Middleton Murry in December 1915 describes her encounter with a French nurse who 'has been nursing since the beginning of the war somewhere near Arles'. Mansfield made a mental note of what she had heard: 'She told me such good stories of the black soldiers – I must not forget them'.[105] Rebecca West, recognising the continuing popularity and profitability of the nurse's story, agreed to ghost-write a four-part fictional serial 'War Nurse' based on a volunteer American nurse's memoirs for *Cosmopolitan* Magazine in autumn 1926 and spring 1927 for $10,000. This was published anonymously in book form as *War Nurse: The True Story of a Woman Who Lived, Loved and Suffered on the Western Front* (1930), after West considered the text 'hack work'.[106]

This chapter demonstrates how nurses were implicitly positioned at the forefront of the contemporary preoccupation with death, burial and memorialisation, occurring as a result of the war. The nurses I have discussed were predominantly volunteers, who, because of the cultural expectations of women in nursing and death in peacetime, were offered little guidance on dealing with the dying and the dead in wartime. In seeking to come to terms with their experiences, I have argued here that most nurses' narratives used conservative literary tropes to represent their proximate encounters with the war dead, focusing on deathbeds, burial rites and cemeteries. The majority of nurses turned back to these conventional sites of mourning and commemoration as a means of putting their experience within traditional paradigms and as their most immediate commemorative framework, and because these literary modes – in the Victorian era and in the years preceding the war – were typically consolatory. The few exceptions to this, such as the graphic, modernist experiments of La Motte, were suppressed in the wartime and postwar years. However, the nurse narratives repeatedly demonstrate the inadequacy of these consolatory modes. It was impossible to imitate the Victorian deathbed scene in the wartime hospital, to give a man a traditional funeral or to bury him in a traditional cemetery. There were not yet new modes to take their place.

The nurse narratives simultaneously show the wartime renegotiation of death, and a very early version of what governments and individuals would be involved in for many years in the postwar period: the drive to commemorate and memorialise. These texts document the immediate reaction to the war, with frequently little revision before publication. Looking back to the first responses to mass mortality in mechanised warfare, the nurse narratives present us with the war's ideological assault on traditional modes of dying. They record the efforts of ordinary people to ensure dignity at the moment of death, rather than the retrospective, official attempts of the postwar period. Nurses were at the forefront of the enormous shock of the death of the war and their texts show their early attempts to renegotiate the representation of death, as civilians would do at a chronological and geographical distance a number of years later.

Notes

1. James Douglas, 'How a Nurse Sees the War' [review of Enid Bagnold's *A Diary without Dates*, 1918] (*Birmingham Gazette*, 19 March 1918), p. 2. *The British Newspaper Archive*, <https://www.britishnewspaperarchive.co.uk/viewer/BL/0000669/19180319/016/0002> (last accessed 19 July 2018).
2. Mary Borden, *The Forbidden Zone* (1929), p. 147.
3. Henrietta Tayler, *A Scottish Nurse at Work: Being a Record of What One Semi-Trained Nurse Has Been Privileged to See and Do during Four and a Half Years of War* (1920), p. 38.
4. Lyn Macdonald, *The Roses of No Man's Land* (1980; 1990), p. 3.
5. Higonnet, 'Authenticity and Art in Trauma Narratives of World War I,' *Modernism/Modernity*, 9.1 (2002), p. 104. I take for granted here that the nurses' narratives are trauma texts, as numerous critics have already demonstrated, particularly Carol Acton, '"Can't Face the Graves Today": Nurses Mourn on the Western Front', in *Grief in Wartime: Private Pain, Public Discourse* (2007), pp. 132–53. More recently, Carol Acton and Jane Potter's *Working in a World of Hurt: Trauma and Resilience in the Narratives of Medical Personnel in Warzones* (2015) traces trauma in the writings of medical personnel more broadly.
6. Sharon Ouditt, *Fighting Forces, Writing Women: Identity and Ideology in the First World War* (1994), p. 9.
7. Trained nurses served in Queen Alexandra's Imperial Military Nursing Service and Queen Alexandra's Royal Naval Nursing Service (both founded in 1902 at the end of the Boer War) and their Reserves, and the Territorial Force Nursing Service (founded in 1908). Volunteer nurses served in the VAD, the First Aid Nursing Yeomanry (founded in 1907) and Princess Mary's Royal Air Force Nursing Service (initially established as the Royal Air Force Temporary Nursing Service in 1918). The United States did not use volunteers, but instead started up an Army School of Nursing and used the probationer-nurses as a junior workforce during the war. American nurses served in the US Army Nurse Corps, American Red Cross and in the US Navy. Christine Hallett notes therefore that 'the Allied military nursing services were a curious amalgam of highly trained elite professionals, semi-trained volunteers, and confident but largely untrained lady-nurses', in *Veiled Warriors: Allied Nurses of the First World War* (2014), p. 18. For more on the history and

professionalisation of nursing during war, see Mary T. Sarnecky, *A History of the U.S. Army Nurse Corps* (1999), and Jane Brookes and Christine E. Hallett (eds), *One Hundred Years of Wartime Nursing Practices, 1854–1953* (2015).
8. Hallett, *Veiled Warriors* (2014), p. 19. Hallett notes that, 'While the powerful outputs of wealthy and well-connected volunteer nurses were published in several editions during the course of the twentieth century and are still current today, the work of professional nurses [. . .] is, for the most part, languishing, unpublished and largely unread, in archives throughout the world', p. 29.
9. See Hallett, *Veiled Warriors* (2014), pp. 19–20.
10. See Elizabeth Brown Pryor, *Clara Barton: Professional Angel* (1987) and Mark Bostridge, *Florence Nightingale: The Making of an Icon* (2008) for discussion of their legacies. The reputation of the British-Jamaican nurse Mary Seacole, a pioneer in the Crimean War, rivalled that of Nightingale and Barton in her lifetime, but her legacy has not been mythologised to the same extent, most likely due to racial prejudice. Jane Marcus has also suggested the importance of the suffrage campaign 'as the training ground for ambulance drivers and VAD nurses in World War I', in 'Corpus/Corps/Corpse: Writing the Body in/at War', Afterword to Helen Zenna Smith, *Not So Quiet . . . Stepdaughters of War* [1930] (1988), reprinted in Helen M. Cooper, Adrienne Auslander Munich and Susan Merrill Squier (eds), *Arms and the Woman: War, Gender, and Literary Representation* (1989), p. 135.
11. Higonnet, quoting from Borden, *The Forbidden Zone* [1929], in 'Women in the Forbidden Zone: War, Women, and Death', in Elisabeth Bronfen and Sarah Webster Goodwin (eds), *Death and Representation* (1993), p. 204.
12. Arthur G. McCoy, *If I Fail He Dies, Work for the Red Cross* (1918).
13. Porter Woodruff, Cover, British *Vogue* (1 May 1918). Although common propaganda images of nurses are regularly cited (for example, A. E. Foringer's *The Greatest Mother in the World*, 1917), and despite Pearl James's edited volume *Picture This: World War One Posters and Visual Culture* (2009) and Christine E. Hallett's *Celebrating Nurses: A Visual History* (2010), there is more analysis to be done of visual representations of nurses.
14. Higonnet, 'Authenticity and Art', p. 101.
15. The texts, often based on wartime diaries, were published up to the early 1930s, with one outlier published in 1970. Dent, *A V.A.D. in France* (1917); Bagnold, *A Diary without Dates* [1918] intro. by Monica Dickens (1978); Leake, *Letters of a V.A.D.* (1918); Beauchamp, *Fanny Goes to War* (1919); Tayler, *A Scottish Nurse at Work* (1920); Smith, *Four Years Out of Life* (1931); Walker, *With the Lost Generation, 1915–1919: From a V.A.D.'s Diary* (1970).
16. Christine E. Hallett is right to point out that some earlier critics tended to 'conflate the two [voluntary and trained nurses] as if they formed a homogenous group', in *Containing Trauma: Nursing Work in the First World War* (2009), p. 10.
17. Ellen N. La Motte, *The Backwash of War: The Human Wreckage of the Battlefield as Witnessed by an American Hospital Nurse* (1916).
18. Higonnet, 'Authenticity and Art', p. 92. See work by: Nicola Beauman, *A Very Great Profession: The Woman's Novel 1914–39* (1983); Sandra M. Gilbert and Susan Gubar, *No Man's Land: The Place of the Woman Writer in the Twentieth Century,*

Volume Two: Sexchanges (1989); Claire Tylee, *The Great War and Women's Consciousness: Images of Militarism and Womanhood in Women's Writing, 1914–64* (1990); Sharon Ouditt, *Fighting Forces, Writing Women* (1994); Santanu Das, *Touch and Intimacy in First World War Literature* (2005); Jane Potter, *Boys in Khaki, Girls in Print: Women's Literary Responses to the Great War, 1914–1918* (2005); Alison S. Fell and Christine E. Hallett (eds), *First World War Nursing: New Perspectives* (2013); Christine E. Hallett, *Nurse Writers of the Great War* (2016).

19. Smith, *The Second Battlefield: Women, Modernism and the First World War* (2000), p. 71. See also Ariela Freedman, 'Mary Borden's *Forbidden Zone*: Women's Writing from No-Man's-Land', *Modernism/Modernity*, 9.1 (2002), 109–24.
20. See Lyn Macdonald, *The Roses of No Man's Land*; Anne Summers, *Angels and Citizens: British Women as Military Nurses, 1854–1914* (1988); Janet Lee, *War Girls: The First Aid Nursing Yeomanry in the Great War* (2005); Yvonne McEwen, *It's a Long Way to Tipperary: British and Irish Nurses in the Great War* (2006); Kimberly Jensen, *Mobilizing Minerva: American Women in the First World War* (2008); Hallett, *Containing Trauma* (2009) and *Veiled Warriors* (2014); Brookes and Hallett (eds), *One Hundred Years of Wartime Nursing Practices* (2015). General medical studies include Jeffrey S. Reznick, *Healing the Nation: Soldiers and the Culture of Caregiving in Britain during the Great War* (2004), and Mark Harrison, *The Medical War: British Military Medicine in the First World War* (2010).
21. Smith, *The Second Battlefield*, p. 72.
22. Marcus, 'Corpus/Corps/Corpse: Writing the Body in/at War', p. 129. See also Smith, *The Second Battlefield*.
23. For example, Borden's *The Forbidden Zone* [1929], ed. Hazel Hutchison (2008), and La Motte's *The Backwash of War* [1916], ed. Cynthia Wachtell (2019), as well as a number of popular editions. For useful prefaces and afterwords, see Jane Marcus, 'Corpus/Corps/Corpse: Writing the Body In/At War', pp. 124–67, and 'Afterword: The Nurse's Text: Acting Out an Anaesthetic Aesthetic', in Irene Rathbone, *We that Were Young: A Novel* [1932] intro. by Lynn Knight (1989), pp. 467–98; Higonnet, 'Introduction', *Nurses at the Front* (2001), pp. vii–xxxviii.
24. Das, *Touch and Intimacy*, p. 10.
25. Bourke, *Dismembering the Male: Men's Bodies, Britain and the Great War* (1996); Carden-Coyne, *Reconstructing the Body: Classicism, Modernism, and the First World War* (2009).
26. Alison S. Fell, 'Nursing the Other: The Representation of Colonial Troops in French and British First World War Nursing Memoirs,' in Das (ed.), *Race, Empire and First World War Writing* (2011), pp. 158–74.
27. Acton and Potter, *Working in a World of Hurt* (2016).
28. Higonnet, 'Women in the Forbidden Zone' (1993); Acton, *Grief in Wartime* (2007).
29. Hallett, *Containing Trauma*, p. 65. The term seems to have been a colloquialism, as it does not appear in the contemporary handbooks and manuals.
30. Cantlie, *British Red Cross Society Nursing Manual, No. 2* (1912), pp. vii, 185.
31. Fitzwilliams, *A Nursing Manual for Nurses and Nursing Orderlies* (1914), pp. v, 267.
32. Young, *Outlines of Nursing* (1914).
33. Oxford, *Nursing in War Time: Lessons for the Inexperienced* (1914), pp. 52–3.

34. Richet, *War Nursing: What Every Woman Should Know, Red Cross Lectures*, trans. Helen De Vere Beauclerk (1918).
35. Fitzwilliams, *Nursing Manual*, p. 9.
36. Oxford, *Nursing in War Time*, pp. 1–2.
37. John Morley, *Death, Heaven and the Victorians* (1971); Michael Wheeler, *Heaven, Hell and the Victorians* (Cambridge: Cambridge University Press, 1994); Jalland, *Death in the Victorian Family* (1996); 'Victorian Death and Its Decline: 1850–1918', in Peter C. Jupp and Clare Gittings (eds), *Death in England: An Illustrated History* (1999), pp. 230–55; and *Death in War and Peace: Loss and Grief in England, 1914–1970* (2010).
38. Jalland, *Death in the Victorian Family*, p. 10.
39. Jalland. *Death in the Victorian Family*, p. 24.
40. Smith, *Four Years*, p. 3.
41. Smith, *Four Years*, pp. 93, 85–6, 90.
42. Smith, *Four Years*, pp. 124–6.
43. Walker, *With the Lost Generation*, p. 3.
44. Smith, *Four Years*, p. 127.
45. Acton, *Grief in Wartime*, p. 149.
46. Beauchamp, *Fanny Goes to War*, pp. 42–4.
47. In March 1918, Bagnold wrote to Frank Harris of the book's success: 'people even know who I am when I dine out. This sounds incredible on one little book but it has the good luck to be so as my reviews have been copious and very long and because people have talked about it a great deal', quoted in Anne Sebba, *Enid Bagnold: The Authorized Biography* (1986), p. 61. After an initial print run of 15,000 copies, by April 1918 the book was already in its third impression, 'Advertisement: Mr. Heinemann's List', *The Bookman*, April 1918, p. 29. *The Bookman* via ProQuest <https://ezproxy-prd.bodleian.ox.ac.uk:7316/docview/3065968?accountid=13042> (last accessed 2 May 2019). Although not appearing explicitly anti-patriotic, Claire Tylee argues that 'its careful restraint is better appreciated when set against the blaring war-time propaganda about devoted nurses and the heroic wounded, from which it detached itself', *The Great War and Women's Consciousness*, p. 190.
48. Bagnold, *Diary*, pp. 77–9.
49. Marcus, 'Corpus/Corps/Corpse: Writing the Body in/at War', p. 126.
50. Beauchamp, *Fanny Goes to War*, p. 48.
51. Smith, *Four Years*, pp. 93, 254, 123.
52. Hallett, *Containing Trauma*, pp. 184–5.
53. Leake, *Letters of a V.A.D.*, pp. 106–7.
54. Tayler, *Scottish Nurse*, pp. 97–8.
55. Bagnold, *Diary*, p. 267.
56. Tayler, *Scottish Nurse*, pp. 94–5, 42, 62.
57. Dent, *A V.A.D. in France*, pp. 335, 338.
58. Ellen N. La Motte, *The Backwash of War* (1916); Warner (published Anon.), *My Beloved Poilus* (1917); Mortimer, *A Green Tent in Flanders* (1917); Mary Borden, *The Forbidden Zone* (1929).

59. Hazel Hutchison has considered the similarities between Borden and La Motte's accounts in *The War that Used Up Words: American Writers and the First World War* (2015), pp. 141–60. Christine E. Hallett was the first to link and compare the four narratives that came out of this hospital in chapters 2 and 3 of *Nurse Writers of the Great War* (2016). I wrote about a series of previously unknown letters by Ellen N. La Motte now held in the Alan Mason Chesney Medical Archives of the Johns Hopkins Medical Institutions in 'The American Friends – Nurse, Suffragette, War Writer: Ellen N. La Motte's Life in Letters', *Times Literary Supplement*, 31 March 2017, pp. 17–19.
60. This is seen in (and in some cases, precedes) other contemporary British and American texts, including James Joyce's *Dubliners* (1914), Sherwood Anderson's *Winesburg, Ohio* (1919), Jean Toomer's *Cane* (1923), La Motte's friend and hospital director Mary Borden's *The Forbidden Zone* (1929), and William March's *Company K* (1933).
61. La Motte, *Backwash*, pp. 86–7.
62. La Motte, *Backwash*, p. 49.
63. La Motte, *Backwash*, pp. 55–9.
64. La Motte, *Backwash*, pp. 22–3.
65. La Motte, *Backwash*, pp. 30–2.
66. La Motte, *Backwash*, pp. 122–4.
67. La Motte, *Backwash*, p. 128.
68. La Motte, *Backwash*, pp. 159, 161–2.
69. See Kelly, 'The American Friends'.
70. La Motte, *Backwash*, pp. 163–4.
71. 'At the Telephone' is dated 26 June 1916. The only later dated vignette in the text is the final one, dated 27 June 1916.
72. Smith, *Four Years*, pp. 186, 126–7, 145.
73. Smith, *Four Years*, p. 90–1, 93.
74. Tayler, *Scottish Nurse*, pp. 40, 62–3.
75. Smith, *Four Years*, pp. 20–1.
76. Bagnold, *Diary*, p. 13.
77. See Peter M. Sacks, *The English Elegy: Studies in the Genre from Spenser to Yeats* (1985), for discussion of the conventions of elegy.
78. Bagnold, *Diary*, pp. 24–5.
79. Dent, *A V.A.D. in France*, p. 62.
80. Miss M. A. Brown (ARRC), 19 January 1916, *Diary*, Imperial War Museum Archives Documents.1001, 88/7/1 (only paginated to p. 22).
81. Brown, 20 January 1916, *Diary*, n.p.
82. Brown, 28 January 1916, *Diary*, n.p.
83. Dent, *A V.A.D. in France*, pp. 202–4.
84. Brown, 13 October 1915, *Diary*, pp. 16–18.
85. Dent, *A V.A.D. in France*, pp. 25–6, 70.
86. Dent, *A V.A.D. in France*, p. 128.
87. Walker, *With the Lost Generation*, pp. 32–3.
88. Smith, *Four Years*, pp. 52–3.
89. Walker, *With the Lost Generation*, p. 4.

90. Walker, *With the Lost Generation*, pp. 4, 11.
91. Bagnold, *Diary*, pp. 16–18.
92. Tayler, *Scottish Nurse*, pp. 99, 123–4, 39.
93. Bagnold, *Diary*, pp. 91, 22, 91, 114–15.
94. Patricia Young, Album of photographs, autographs, and notes compiled by a nurse of the Volunteer Aid Detachment, Dumfries, Scotland, 1914–17. Yale Center for British Art, Friends of British Art Fund.
95. Florence Farmborough, *Russian Album, 1908–1918*, ed. John Jolliffe (1979), pp. 68–77. This volume functions as a sequel to her earlier text *Nurse at the Russian Front: A Diary, 1914–18* (1974), which included forty-eight images. These images of the dead would not have passed the censor had the volume been published during the war.
96. Thomas W. Laqueur, 'Memory and Naming in the Great War', in John R. Gillis (ed.), *Commemorations: The Politics of National Identity* (1994), p. 160.
97. Michael Hammond has discussed these films in his chapter 'Anonymity and Recognition: The Roll of Honour Films', in *The Big Show: British Cinema Culture in the Great War, 1914–1918* (2006), pp. 70–97. Hammond notes that initially the films functioned as 'the cinematic expression of the common newspaper practice of publishing photographs and listing the names of local men who were serving' and only later 'shifted to include those who had been wounded, reported missing or killed', p. 72. He suggests that 'the series of static images in the Roll of Honour films take on the qualities of apparitions,' p. 93.
98. Quoted in Anne Sebba, *Enid Bagnold*, p. 62.
99. Grant Richards, *Times Literary Supplement*, 3 January 1918, p. 7. *The Times Literary Supplement Historical Archive,* <http://tinyurl.gale.com/tinyurl/BgwyfX> (last accessed 2 May 2019).
100. Grant Richards, *Times Literary Supplement*, 20 February 1919, p. 95. *The Times Literary Supplement Historical Archive,* <http://tinyurl.gale.com/tinyurl/Bgx282> (last accessed 2 May 2019).
101. Shirley Millard, *I Saw Them Die: Diary and Recollections of Shirley Millard*, ed. Adele Comandini (1936). Comandini was a screenwriter.
102. Quoted in Sebba, *Enid Bagnold*, p. 62.
103. Woolf, Virginia, 'A Cambridge VAD', *Times Literary Supplement*, 10 May 1917, p. 223. *The Times Literary Supplement Historical Archive,* <http://tinyurl.gale.com/tinyurl/Bgx5m1> (last accessed 2 May 2019).
104. Woolf told Bell in a letter on 29 January 1918: 'She has written a book, called, as you can imagine, "A Diary without Dates", all to prove that she's the most attractive, and popular and exquisite of creatures – all her patients fall in love with her – her feet are the smallest in Middlesex – one night she missed her bus and a soldier was rude to her in the dark – that sort of thing'. Quoted in Anne Sebba, *Enid Bagnold*, p. 61.
105. To John Middleton Murry [19–20 December 1915], in *The Collected Letters of Katherine Mansfield, Volume I: 1903–1917*, ed. Vincent O'Sullivan and Margaret Scott (1984), p. 220.

106. See Carl Rollyson, *Rebecca West: A Saga of the Century* (1995), pp. 89–90. Lorna Gibb similarly notes West's 'unwillingness to acknowledge the work which she regarded as little more than a financial necessity', in *West's World: The Extraordinary Life of Dame Rebecca West* (2013), p. 187. The text wasn't serialised until spring 1930. See 'War Nurse: An American Woman on the Western Front. A Vivid Record set down by Rebecca West,' serialised in *Hearst's International with Cosmopolitan* in February, March, April and May 1930, and published as a book later that year.

2

UNCOMFORTABLE PROPAGANDA: EDITH WHARTON'S WARTIME WRITINGS

In her 1934 autobiography *A Backward Glance*, the American novelist Edith Wharton recounts an anecdote of a dinner in Paris one summer evening during the 1920s. She was taken by surprise when one of the other diners, Félix Raugel, tells her that they have met before:

> I stared at him in wonder; and as he spoke the peaceful room vanished, and the twilight shadows of my suburban garden, and I saw myself, an eager grotesque figure, bestriding a mule in the long tight skirts of 1915, and suddenly appearing, a prosaic Walkyrie laden with cigarettes, in the heart of the mountain fastness held by the famous *Chasseurs Alpins*, already among the legendary troops of the French army. Seeing Félix Raugel again brought back to me with startling vividness the scenes of my repeated journeys to the front; the scarred torn land behind the trenches, the faces of the men who held it, the terrible and interminable epic of France's long defence.[1]

The encounter makes her vividly recall her wartime meeting with Raugel during a visit to the Vosges in August 1915. Her description of herself as 'an eager grotesque figure' suggests her retrospective embarrassment at her fervour to see the front, while her self-portrait as a 'prosaic Walkyrie' emphasises her awareness of her highly unusual position as a woman in the war zones. In this passage, Wharton returns to tropes from *Fighting France*, her 1915 text that came out of these trips to the front: her memory of 'the scarred torn land behind the trenches' repeats the text's substitution of landscape for bodies and reveals the landscape's lasting hold on her imagination.

At the outbreak of the Great War, Wharton was living in France. She quickly became a highly active participant in relief efforts and an advocate for American intervention in the war in her fiction and non-fiction. Wharton's explicit war writings consist of a series of non-fiction impressions published as articles in *Scribner's Magazine* and *The Saturday Evening Post*, and collected as *Fighting France* in 1915; three short stories 'Coming Home' (1915), 'Writing a War Story' (1919), and 'The Refugees' (1919); the 1916 fundraising anthology *The Book of the Homeless*; and the novels *The Marne* (1918) and *A Son at the Front* (1923), as well as a number of poems, newspaper articles and talks.[2] In the Wharton Collection at Yale, there is also an unfinished and previously unknown story from this period entitled 'The Field of Honour'.[3] This body of work demonstrates that Wharton did not remain 'pen-tied' as she had been at the beginning of the war, but that she engaged with the war in a variety of genres.[4] Despite her extensive war work, she produced a considerable amount of writing.

In 1914, Wharton was a celebrated author, having achieved critical and commercial success with *The House of Mirth* (1905). Her subsequent writing – including *Ethan Frome* (1911) and *The Custom of the Country* (1913) – had further cemented her reputation. She had moved permanently to Paris in 1910, and the final chapters of her autobiography, devoted to 'The War' and 'And After', give a sense of how much the periods of the war and its aftermath punctuated her life. Her work for her three main war charities – the American Hostels for Refugees, the Children of Flanders Rescue Committee, and Les Tuberculeux de la Guerre – was recognised by the award of the French Legion of Honour and the Belgian Queen Elizabeth's Medal, and she would still be raising money on their behalf until the late 1920s.[5] Aged fifty-two in 1914, Wharton represents an older generation of writers than the typically younger volunteer nurses I discussed in my first chapter. Wharton's position as American, pro-war, a professional writer and active participant provides a contrast to some of the other authors I examine, who were predominantly concerned with the commemoration and memorialisation of Allied soldiers. Wharton's writing instead raises questions over how writers justified the war deaths of Allied soldiers in order to validate the Allied war cause, and how they dealt with the difficult moral question of the wartime necessity of killing the enemy.

Wharton's war writing has frequently been discussed – and largely dismissed – as propaganda. Stanley Cooperman considered Wharton to have 'combined gentility with bloodthirst, the manners of the social novelist with the matter of the recruiting poster', and even Wharton's most steadfast advocates have been quick to dismiss her wartime writing.[6] Shari Benstock interprets '[t]hese slights to such a significant category of Wharton's canon' as resulting from 'the larger problems of categorizing women's contributions to war literature'.[7] Two book-length studies have focused exclusively on Wharton and the war. Alan Price's largely biographical study *The End of the Age of Innocence: Edith Wharton and the First World War* (1996) asks, 'How did a sophisticated social satirist turn so quickly into a partisan war propagandist?' and notes the 'shift in rhetorical registers' in Wharton's wartime writing, as she learned to 'hit and hold "the tremolo note" when its effects served her ends'.[8] Julie Olin-Ammentorp's recuperative 2004 study *Edith Wharton's Writings from the Great War* 'examines the wartime and war-related writings as a coherent and crucial part of Wharton's oeuvre'. She argues that Wharton's war writings, although not 'lost masterpieces', 'have not only intrinsic worth but biographical and historical value, and deserve far more study than they have received'.[9] The strength of this continuing reassessment of Wharton's wartime and postwar writing is further demonstrated by a number of recent readings of its feminism, links with genres such as travel literature, connections with modernist literature, and use of spatial tropes.[10] The most recent biography, by Hermione Lee, provides an extensive and detailed account of the war years.[11]

This chapter examines three texts by Wharton in different genres: *Fighting France* (1915), the wartime atrocity and revenge story 'Coming Home' (1915), and the unpublished and unfinished story 'The Field of Honour' (n.d.). Proximate to the war dead, Wharton turned to traditional sites of the dead (shrines, graveyards) to depict the dead, but, like the nurses, she demonstrates that these were frequently inadequate for wartime circumstances. Examining Wharton's manipulation of the difficult subject of the justification of war death demonstrates that she was a complex and accomplished propagandist, who expertly appropriated typical propaganda and literary tropes. However, her war writings contain a number of moments of distinct anxiety, apprehensiveness or unease concerning the dead, which undermine the straightforward propagandistic statements expressed elsewhere. These moments simultaneously demonstrate a deliberate literariness of one kind or another, and my close reading of what I consider to be an excess of figuration identifies and reveals Wharton's underlying anxiety concerning the war dead. In other words, the moments where we see Wharton at her most literary are often simultaneously those where we see her at her most anxious, demonstrating that even those who fully supported the war were simultaneously troubled by the mass deaths and new mourning customs that resulted.

More broadly, Wharton is a good example of many authors whose wartime writing articulated a particular sense of unease around the war and its casualties, which often manifested itself as a type of generic instability: a mixing of, and moving between, genres that indicates the writer was trying out different modes of representation for this new subject matter as they worked out how to respond to it. My chronological reading allows me to trace the trajectory of Wharton's war writings and suggest that these became more literary as the war proceeded and therefore ever more fully indicative of anxiety, even as Wharton became more outwardly propagandistic.

Fighting Words: Wartime Propaganda

During the First World War, governments, groups and individuals of every fighting nation produced a greater volume of propaganda than in any previous war, for 'the direction and control of public opinion towards certain ends'. Initially these ends were to generate support for the war and provoke men to enlist; as the war dragged on, they became more focused on maintaining morale at home and at the front. Not only was propaganda production 'rationalized and modernized' and conducted on 'a professional basis', but its distribution changed, supplying the popular mass daily newspapers with 'a more simplified and more sensational presentation of news'.[12] Towards the end of the war the relatively new technology of film provided a new image-focused mode of propaganda. In Britain, propaganda efforts were run through the War Propaganda Bureau – more commonly known as Wellington House – which began operating in early September 1914 under the direction of the Liberal MP Charles Masterman. In the United States the Committee on Public Information (CPI), created by President Woodrow Wilson and chaired by George Creel, was established on the US entry into war in April 1917 and lasted until June 1919. Both organisations used a wide range of media to promote their respective causes, including pamphlets, books, newspapers, posters, photographs, paintings, telegraphs, radio and films. Propaganda often took on new forms such as the Four Minute Men in the US, who gave four-minute patriotic speeches during the break between changing film reels in cinemas, as well as in other public spaces.

In the early stages of the war, American propaganda differed from European propaganda, because its predominant aim was to provoke intervention into what was seen as a European war. The sense of the geographical and metaphorical distance of the World War was captured in the enormously popular song 'Over There' (1917) by George M. Cohan, and this figuring of the relationship in spatial terms has since been appropriated as a structural metaphor in discussing America and the war.[13] John T. Matthews has argued that prior to America's entrance into the war in April 1917, 'America's distinctive relation to the Great War originated in its remoteness from the event itself':

> The American side of the Great War necessarily relied on institutions of representation – journalism, print propaganda, fiction, sermons – to make the war real in the place where it was not occurring. In important respects, American writing of the war *was* the war.[14]

The links between literature and propaganda were manifested in the public appetite for war stories and the recruitment of writers as propagandists. At Wellington House this included authors such as Sir Arthur Conan Doyle,

Rudyard Kipling, H. G. Wells, and Arnold Bennett. Peter Buitenhuis argues that 'the absence of hard news from the front' created demand for both war reportage and fantasy from writers:

> In most cases these fantasies were spontaneous; in others, it is clear that the fictions received official backing. The public appetite for stories about the war was very strong; people had a craving to know about the fighting and to see their faith in the moral and physical strength of the Allies reflected in an accessible form.[15]

Price notes that 'the appetite for atrocity stories was shared in 1916 by the American literary community' as well as Europe, and Buitenhuis argues that expatriate authors such as Henry James and Edith Wharton were 'influential catalysts of American opinion'.[16] Novelists could sway opinions.

Although Wharton wasn't officially recruited as a propagandist, her literary skills enabled her to present her reportage as a form of propaganda, and she later thematised the public need for war stories in her short story 'Coming Home'.[17] Wharton's role as public writer was increasingly bound up with her roles of reporter and witness, and the boundaries between fiction and reportage were frequently blurred: Lee argues that 'all Wharton's war writings up to 1917 were designed to rouse up America'.[18] She was paid twice the amount for her stories as for her war reportage, suggesting the material benefit of her war stories to her publishers.[19] The recruitment of writers as propagandists demonstrates the public appetite for war stories, which novelists such as Wharton were more than equipped to provide.

Avoiding the Wooden Crosses: *Fighting France*

> This afternoon, on the road to Gérbeviller, we were again in the track of the September invasion. Over all the slopes now cool with spring foliage the battle rocked backward and forward during those burning autumn days; and every mile of the struggle has left its ghastly traces. The fields are full of wooden crosses which the ploughshare makes a circuit to avoid; many of the villages have been partly wrecked, and here and there an isolated ruin marks the nucleus of a fiercer struggle. But the landscape, in its first sweet leafiness, is so alive with ploughing and sowing and all the natural tasks of spring, that the war scars seem like traces of a long-past woe; and it was not till a bend of the road brought us in sight of Gérbeviller that we breathed again the choking air of present horror.[20]

Between February and August 1915, Wharton made five 'expeditions' to the front lines, visiting Argonne and Verdun, Lorraine and the Vosges, Belgium and Alsace, 'some of which' she wrote, 'actually took me into the front-line trenches'.[21] She travelled with her American friend and later President of the American Chamber of Commerce in Paris, Walter Berry, and her chauffeur Charles Cook. Wharton was initially approached by the French Red Cross to report on the conditions in military hospitals near the front and to take supplies, but she proposed a number of further trips in order to report on the needs of hospitals to those who had the money to help. Four of the resulting five articles were published in the May, June, October and November 1915 issues of *Scribner's Magazine*, and the fifth in *The Saturday Evening Post* in November.[22] A further unpublished essay, 'The Tone of France', was added to the articles collected for book publication as *Fighting France* in November 1915, with thirteen photographs. Wharton's contacts and literary celebrity enabled her to gain access to war zones that were otherwise completely out of bounds to journalists and civilians, and she prided herself – perhaps with a knowledge of its improbability – on being the first civilian woman at the front, and how close she was able to get to the front lines.[23] 'We were given opportunities no one else has had of seeing things at the front. I was in the first line trenches, in 2 bombarded towns, &c &c – ', she told Robert Bridges, the editor of *Scribner's Magazine*, in May 1915 about her trip to the Vosges.[24] Wharton wrote the articles that became *Fighting France* for marked propagandistic purposes and with a distant American audience in mind, describing the physical conditions of the war zones to those far away in the States. We can read the passage above as an implicit explication of Wharton's own method, where she circuitously avoids the 'wooden crosses', relating 'the war scars' through imagery of the landscape and physical environs. In depicting war in a positive light, Wharton necessarily had to present death as a price worth paying for victory. Her depictions of death are therefore deflected into other modes of representation.

As with Wharton's other war writings, readings of *Fighting France* frequently dismiss the text as naïve propaganda, criticising her evasive presentation of the war dead through oblique modes or by not mentioning them at all. Clare Tylee argues that '[l]ike other members of the older generation, Wharton amply fulfilled the task of turning out pro-French propaganda designed to encourage American intervention in the war', referring to her as 'one of the literary tourists who produced a foreigners' guide to the Western Front'.[25] Matthews dismisses Wharton's obliquity as a type of wilful blindness to the war's horrors: '[i]n her fiction, as well as, even more oddly, in her journalism describing the front line itself, Wharton omits almost all mention of the actual wounding of people'. Her war scenes 'seem to have no casualties', and any accounts of casualties are 'strangely unrelated to human bodies'.[26] Contemporary reviews were more charitable: a 1915 *Bookman* review notes that although '[t]hese chapters, except for their occasional graphic descriptions of the havoc wrought in French fields and villages and cities, pay slight attention to the horrors of the conflict'; that instead 'Mrs. Wharton is more interested in the man behind the gun and the spirit that moves him than in the gun's achievement'.[27]

Despite being received as 'merely a simply told, realistic narrative of the things observed by a writer with the seeing eye in the daily life of the French people', Wharton's indirect mode constitutes an intensely literary sort of propaganda, such as her metaphoric substitution of shattered buildings for shattered bodies and her manipulation of point of view.[28] A large part of what makes her propaganda effective is her use of obliquity and deflection to downplay the deaths of Allied soldiers and provoke anger in her readers at the violence and destruction perpetrated by German soldiers. While agreeing with Matthews's description, I suggest instead that the omission of explicit death was a very conscious aesthetic decision for Wharton. Another contemporary review was therefore correct to note that 'Mrs Wharton's impressions of France in war time are imparted with her unfailing touch of literary distinction'.[29]

The French experience of 1915 would be characterised predominantly by an enormous loss of life in battles including Ypres, Neuve Chapelle and Loos, and little movement. Lee notes that 'over 50 per cent of the 1.3 million Frenchmen killed during the war died between August 1914 and December 1915', or more concretely 'two thousand young Frenchmen were killed in battle every day'.[30] The loss of three people Wharton knew during 1915 gives an indication of the ubiquity of the casualties: her friend Jean du Breuil de Saint-Germain in February, her translator Robert d'Humières in June, and her former footman Henri in September. The personal losses of her close friend Henry James in February 1916, and her friend and early mentor Egerton Winthrop and her former governess and literary secretary Anna Bahlmann in April 1916, further compounded this sense of loss. The loss of two young Americans in 1918 – her close friend Ronald Simmons in August as a result of the flu epidemic, and her cousin's son, the aviator Newbold Rhinelander, shot down and killed in France in September – contributed to her spirit being 'heavy with these losses'.[31]

In *Fighting France*, Wharton justifies and elides war death through the skilful use of stock propagandistic tropes: the suffering of innocent civilians and the ennobling and invigorating capacity of war experience. However, of most interest are the strange and unsettling encounters with the dead, which betray apprehension or even a marked anxiety about war death and the treatment of the dead, which undermine and disrupt this propagandistic text. Among these are moments of proleptic horror, where Wharton includes an imagined version of the horrors to come. Similarly, there are instances where the military victory gained is qualified – even disqualified – by the acknowledgement of the cost in human lives: 'But what it cost!' one character exclaims after the French have regained the small village of Vauquois (118). Olin-Ammentorp argues that although 'decidedly pro-French, it is not a doctrinaire work but a descriptive one', and in this way, it is 'very much a book without a thesis'.[32] The moments of anxiety evident in this propaganda text, written during the first fifteen months of the war, demonstrate that Wharton was still working out how to write about the war and its casualties.

Wharton uses death and mourning imagery throughout *Fighting France* as a means of obliquely discussing the war dead. In her first article charting the outbreak of war in August 1914, she writes of having the 'impression of suspended life': 'the shuttered streets were mute as catacombs, and the faintest pin-prick of noise seemed to tear a rent in a black pall of silence' (97). The word 'catacombs' would have obvious resonances for her contemporary audiences, and is written in retrospect with an awareness of the increasing death toll. Wharton notes later the 'orderly arrest of life' in an abandoned classroom in a convent (160). Considering the war as resulting in 'the senseless paralysis of a whole nation's activities', she uses a further metaphor of life ending: 'And in hundreds of such houses, in dozens, in hundreds of open towns [. . .] the heart of life had ceased to beat' (160). This language of death and mourning extends to the Parisians themselves: the women's faces look like 'memorial medals', moulded out of 'some dense commemorative substance', while the men's are like the classical bronzes of the Naples Museum, 'burnt and twisted from their baptism of fire' (104).

The most persistent example of Wharton's effective propaganda is the extended motif of buildings as substitutes for bodies. She repeatedly depicts land and buildings as having suffered the brunt of enemy aggression, rather than people: '[t]he country between Marne and Meuse is one of the regions on which German fury spent itself most bestially' (113). Towns and villages are 'victims' and leaving Sainte Menehould, '[e]very road branching away to our left was a finger touching a red wound' (129, 119). Wharton writes that, 'we have passed through streets and streets of such murdered houses, through town after town spread out in its last writhings' (129). Ypres is 'the dead city' which has been 'bombarded to death' and is explicitly compared to 'a disemboweled corpse', while the facades of the Cathedral and the Cloth Market are 'so proud in death' (158–9). In Dunkerque, 'a death-hush lay on the town [. . .] even more oppressive than the death-silence of Ypres' (168–9). Rheims has a 'look of deathlike desolation' (173). Passing through an unnamed town, Wharton writes:

> Oh, that poor town – when we reached it, along a road ploughed with fresh obus-holes, I didn't want to stop the motor; I wanted to hurry on and blot the picture from my memory! It was doubly sad to look at because of the fact that it wasn't *quite dead;* faint spasms of life still quivered through it. (143)

Wharton's metaphor of damage to buildings rather than bodies is most evident when she obliquely describes the mutilation of a girl's body:

> Between the clipped limes and formal borders the German shells had scooped out three or four 'dreadful hollows,' in one of which, only last

week, a little girl found her death; and the façade of the building is pockmarked by shot and disfigured with gaping holes. (138)

Occasionally Wharton brings her personification of houses and buildings full-circle by likening them to human victims: the village of Heiltz-le-Maurupt is 'so stripped and wounded and dishonoured that it lies there by the roadside like a human victim' (124). Passing through a frequently shelled woodland area, Wharton suggests that 'there was something humanly pitiful in the frail trunks of the Bois Triangulaire, lying there like slaughtered rows of immature troops' (164). These examples suggest the extent of Wharton's development of her metaphor as a means to mediate the violence and destruction of the war to civilians and soldiers, and thereby her conscious manipulation of her material for propagandistic purposes. By the time she wrote *The Marne* towards the end of the war, Wharton made this figurative language explicit:

> This was what war did! [. . .] it killed houses and lands as well as men. Out there, a few miles beyond the sunny vineyards and the low hills, men were dying at that very moment by hundreds, by thousands – and their motionless young bodies must have the same unnatural look as these warn ruins, these gutted houses and sterile fields . . . War meant Death, Death, Death – Death everywhere and to everything.[33]

Across all of her war writing, Wharton's choice of figurative language – buildings in place of bodies – is not surprising given her longstanding interest in architecture and home decoration.[34]

Occasionally the images of the personified houses that have been 'murdered' and the violent deaths of dying towns are tempered by the idea of cultivation and regrowth (see Fig. 2.1):

> before the black holes that were homes, along the edge of the chasms that were streets, everywhere we have seen flowers and vegetables springing up in freshly raked and watered gardens. My pink peonies were not introduced to point the stale allegory of unconscious Nature veiling Man's havoc: they are put on my first page as a symbol of conscious human energy coming back to replant and rebuild the wilderness . . . (129)

Wharton paradoxically notes of towns in the Argonne that '[e]ven in the most mortally stricken there were signs of returning life' (129). Her use of buildings and towns as metaphors for the human dead prevents the distressing direct presentation of the war dead, which was unlikely to prompt civilian readers to support American intervention or provoke them to enlist voluntarily. It simultaneously allows for the hopeful possibility of renewal and regeneration, which

Figure 2.1 Edith Wharton and Walter Berry among the ruins. Edith Wharton Collection. Yale Collection of American Literature, Beinecke Rare Book and Manuscript Library, Yale University

would be impossible if she had depicted corpses directly. The overall impression is of deliberate deflection and oblique representation. I turn now to three specific episodes in which this obliquity is undermined.

The first episode depicts Wharton's visit to a makeshift hospital in a church in the village of Blercourt (118–19):

> The church was without aisles, and down the nave stood four rows of wooden cots with brown blankets. In almost every one lay a soldier – the doctor's 'worse cases' – few of them wounded, the greater number stricken with fever, bronchitis, frost-bite, pleurisy, or some other form of trench-sickness too severe to permit of their being carried farther from the front. One or two heads turned on the pillows as we entered, but for the most part the men did not move.

The church, converted into a makeshift hospital, has become a strange wartime space at odds with its usual function; an incursion of the battlefield into sacred space. The wooden cots, like pews, hold soldiers who are close to death. Wharton notes the strange effect of a vespers service held in the church in the 'sunless afternoon' with 'the sick under their earth-coloured blankets', as though already dead and buried. Their 'livid faces' furthers this impression of their corpse-like nature, and the women present are engaged in a kind of proleptic mourning: Wharton observes 'the black dresses of the women (they seemed all to be in mourning)'. The figurative language adds to the sense of endings: the candle-gleams and their reflection 'were like a faint streak of sunset on the winter dusk'. The description of the service explicitly suggests a funeral ritual:

> presently the curé took up in French the Canticle of the Sacred Heart, composed during the war of 1870, and the little congregation joined their trembling voices in the refrain:
>
> 'Sauvez, sauvez la France,
> Ne l'abandonnez pas!'
>
> The reiterated appeal rose in a sob above the rows of bodies in the nave: '*Sauvez, sauvez la France*,' the women wailed it near the altar, the soldiers took it up from the door in stronger tones; but the bodies in the cots never stirred, and more and more, as the day faded, the church looked like a quiet grave-yard in a battle-field.

The juxtaposition of the patriotic hymn from the earlier Franco-Prussian war (1870–1) with the dying men of the present war makes for an odd scene. The refrain is sung 'in a sob' by the wailing women over the silent corpse-like 'bodies' in the nave: a manipulation of point of view which further encourages us to see them as already dead. The simile with which Wharton concludes is even stranger, acknowledging the death toll of the war to 'sauvez la France'. As the only depiction of dying Allied soldiers within the text, the bleakness of this scene makes it stand out, as does the lack of consolation provided by religion.

A further scene of uncomfortable propaganda presents a significant depiction of the enemy – the corpse of a German soldier seen from a peep-hole in the French trenches (147–9). The Captain giving Wharton's party a tour of a second-line trench offers to show her a first-line trench, and her excitement is evident: 'Here we were, then, actually and literally in the first lines! The knowledge made one's heart tick a little'. Taking 'a cautious peep round its corner', she finds the presence of the enemy difficult to comprehend: 'for a minute, I had the sense of an all-pervading, invisible power of evil, a saturation of the whole landscape with some hidden vitriol of hate'. Returning up the trench, Wharton is offered a further privileged viewpoint, which reveals the dead German soldier:

> we came again to the watcher at his peep-hole. He heard us, let the officer pass, and turned his head with a little sign of understanding.
> 'Do you want to look down?'
> He moved a step away from his window. The look-out projected over the ravine, raking its depths; and here, with one's eye to the leaf-lashed hole, one saw at last . . . saw, at the bottom of the harmless glen, half way between cliff and cliff, a grey uniform huddled in a dead heap. 'He's been there for days: they can't fetch him away,' said the watcher, regluing his eye to the hole; and it was almost a relief to find it was after all a tangible enemy hidden over there across the meadow.

The civilian temporarily gains a combatant's viewpoint: a perspective which reveals the war dead. The illicitness of the scene, conducted behind the Captain's back and negotiated in confidence between the watcher and Wharton, introduces an element of voyeurism: a suggestion that the civilian should not be allowed to view what she does. The civilian's momentary sharing of the combatant's viewpoint implies a temporary bridging of the gap between the two, and the transgression of the female viewer into an ideologically male sphere. It is important that the corpse that Wharton views metonymically is a German soldier, because the matter of fact description and the treatment of his body, left between both sides in a glen 'for days', would have been too distressing for an American readership, had he been an ally. Wharton's relief at finding this 'tangible enemy' is in contrast to prescribed and concrete characteristics of the German 'Hun' in stock Allied propaganda as primitive, savage and murderous barbarians, and seems almost sympathetic in acknowledging that they, too, want to collect their dead for proper burial. The inability to collect the body demonstrates the changed nature of death in wartime and the forced abandonment of previous codes and rituals of commemoration.

Perhaps the most disturbing scene describes an individual's unhealthy and fetishistic relationship with the war dead, in sharp contrast to two earlier scenes depicting more comforting, if idealised, treatment of the dead. In the first of these earlier scenes, Wharton describes the care for the dead shown by a reservist troop in the hills in Lorraine and the Vosges, in order to demonstrate the bonds forged between men in wartime and the dedication of the soldiers to their dead comrades:

> The care of this woodland cemetery is left entirely to the soldiers, and they have spent treasures of piety on the inscriptions and decorations of the graves. Fresh flowers are brought up from the valleys to cover them,

> and when some favourite comrade goes, the men scorning ephemeral tributes, club together to buy a monstrous indestructible wreath with emblazoned streamers. It was near the end of the afternoon, and many soldiers were strolling along the paths between the graves. 'It's their favourite walk at this hour,' the Colonel said. He stopped to look down on a grave smothered in beady tokens, the grave of the last pal to fall. 'He was mentioned in the Order of the Day,' the Colonel explained; and the group of soldiers standing near looked at us proudly, as if sharing their comrade's honour, and wanting to be sure that we understood the reason of their pride. (146)

The dead are superlatively and permanently commemorated with a 'monstrous indestructible wreath', and the effect is comforting and consolatory, reassuring the reader that traditional commemoration of the dead prevails in at least certain areas of the war zones. Wharton's choice to depict the woodland cemetery conforms to elegiac conventions of the return of the dead to nature and ensures a place of regular remembrance. The resilience of existing modes of remembrance is demonstrated in the accompanying photograph of an individual grave with a large wreath and flowers, marked and fenced off in an open wooded area. Wharton presents another positive portrayal in her description of Nieuport in Belgium, with an accompanying photograph of a decorated soldier's grave. The terrible destruction of the town has left a thirty-foot crater beside the cathedral graveyard, yet it remains 'the peacefullest spot in Nieuport, the grave-yard where the zouaves have buried their comrades':

> The dead are laid in rows under the flank of the cathedral, and on their carefully set grave-stones have been placed collections of pious images gathered from the ruined houses. Some of the most privileged are guarded by colonies of plaster saints and Virgins that cover the whole slab; and over the handsomest Virgins and the most gaily coloured saints the soldiers have placed the glass bells that once protected the parlour clocks and wedding-wreaths in the same houses. (164–5)[35]

Amid the surrounding apocalyptic scenes, this commemoration of the dead is intended to offer consolation through traditional modes of marking and remembering the dead: individual gravestones organised in orderly rows, which have been 'carefully set'. The multiple superlatives further suggest that the men are well cared for in death. As well as the return to traditional modes of mourning, the passage is consolatory in its return to religious modes of mourning, unlike the church scene.

In contrast to these idealised scenes, a third scene is highly disturbing in its depiction of obsessive commemoration (138–9). Wharton initially introduces this scene in positive terms: 'I have seen the happiest being on earth: a man who has found his job'. The town where he lives, Ménil-sur-Belvitte on the edge of the Vosges, is personified as 'badly battered', where 'a real above-ground battle of the old obsolete kind took place, and the French, driving the Germans back victoriously, fell by thousands in the trampled wheat'.[36] Wharton's description of the makeshift chapel that the local curé has created in the parsonage to commemorate the French deaths is increasingly disturbing:

> The chapel is also a war museum, and everything in it has something to do with the battle that took place among the wheat-fields. The candelabra on the altar are made of 'Seventy-five' shells, the Virgin's halo is composed of radiating bayonets, the walls are intricately adorned with German trophies and French relics, and on the ceiling the curé has had painted a kind of zodiacal chart of the whole region, in which Ménil-sur-Belvitte's handful of houses figures as the central orb of the system, and Verdun, Nancy, Metz, and Belfort as its humble satellites. But the chapel-museum is only a surplus expression of the curé's impassioned dedication to the dead. His real work has been done on the battle-field, where row after row of graves, marked and listed as soon as the struggle was over, have been fenced about, symmetrically disposed, planted with flowers and young firs, and marked by the name and death-dates of the fallen.

In this ersatz war museum religious iconography has been fastidiously reworked in military weaponry. The curé, Father Alphonse Colle, did exist: he was the pastor of Ménil-sur-Belvitte from 1908 until his death in 1943 and dedicated himself to commemorating the dead in the way Wharton describes. Photographs taken a few months after Wharton's visit show Colle standing in the ruins of the church; the altar and the interior of the war museum (where part of the zodiacal chart on the ceiling is visible); and the war cemetery he created on the battlefield, where Wharton describes his meticulousness in ordering, marking and naming the graves of fallen soldiers. The curé's collection and fetishisation of both bodies and military paraphernalia initially suggests a fantasy of participation, seen in the zodiacal chart placing Ménil-sur-Belvitte at the centre of the war. Rather than an urge to participate, however, the war has brought out in the curé the maniacal zeal of the collector: a transformation that Olin-Ammentorp suggests is 'more eerie than noble' (see Figs 2.2 and 2.3).[37]

Although this treatment of the dead could be lauded as admirable, Wharton emphasises its problematic nature:

> As he led us from one of these enclosures to another his face was lit with the flame of a gratified vocation. This particular man was made to do this particular thing: he is a born collector, classifier, and hero-worshipper. In

Figure 2.2 Edouard Brissy, Museum of the Battle of Ménil-sur-Belvitte, created by the priest present during the combat, 31 August 1915. © Ministère de la Culture – Médiathèque de l'architecture et du patrimoine, Dist. RMN-Grand Palais / Opérateur D

the hall of the 'presbytère' hangs a case of carefully-mounted butterflies, the result, no doubt, of an earlier passion for collecting. His 'specimens' have changed, that is all: he has passed from butterflies to men, from the actual to the visionary Psyche. (139)

The fanatacism of the collector is demonstrated in the illumination of the man in his increasingly perverted obsession. The very troubling analogy between collecting butterflies and collecting men suggests that there is little difference between these activities; that the curé's fastidiousness is simply transferred between 'specimens', from 'carefully-mounted butterflies' to carefully marked graves of soldiers. Despite being related in realist terms, Wharton's description of the curé through the modern figure of the collector – usually a collector of precious items, curios or antiques – and the motif of fetishism is markedly literary, one used by her close friend Henry James.[38] (As early as 1905, Wharton had written disparagingly of 'an impulse as sentimental as our modern habit of "collecting"'.[39]) Olin-Ammentorp suggests of this scene that 'the macabre details [. . .] depict the strangeness of the altered reality the war

Figure 2.3 Edouard Brissy, Museum of the Battle of Ménil-sur-Belvitte, created by the priest present during the combat, 31 August 1915. © Ministère de la Culture – Médiathèque de l'architecture et du patrimoine, Dist. RMN-Grand Palais / Opérateur D

had created'.[40] Wharton uses the extreme case of the collector to represent an unhealthy response to death that would have been recognisable to her reader in less obvious manifestations. Her mode of representation demonstrates both the literariness of her propaganda and her evident unease at the more uncomfortable aspects of the war. In this case, the authorities noticed it too, and the curé, repeatedly accused of stripping corpses after exhumation, was finally banned from exhuming and identifying the bodies of soldiers in December 1916.

What, then, do we make of these moments in a text aimed at encouraging American intervention in the war? Despite Wharton's appropriation of stock propaganda rhetoric and imagery, these strange moments of anxiety suggest that she was still working out how to respond to and represent some more unpalatable aspects of the war – particularly the enormous numbers of war dead – arising from the extraordinary and unprecedented conditions of its first fifteen months. Unlike some of Wharton's later war writing, *Fighting France* includes a range of genres, styles and formats. This mixing of genres, where, for example, she moves seamlessly between discussing the horrors of the experiences of the Belgian refugees and the shopping habits of Parisian women, makes the text difficult to classify. This is in part due to the text's origins in magazine publication, written during the busyness of relief work and to a tight deadline for publication. However, this is more likely because she was still working out how to respond to and write about the war and its dead. *Fighting France*, as the earliest and most generically unstable of all her war-related prose, therefore offers us an important insight into Wharton's early experimentation with genre, form and tone.

Imagining the Worst: 'Coming Home' and the Revenge Narrative

An important element of wartime propaganda was the atrocity story, which recounted the real or fabricated crimes of the enemy in exaggerated and sensationalist modes. Always claiming some element of veracity, atrocity stories were very common in both fictional form in magazines and novels, and non-fictional form in newspaper accounts and pamphlets. Trudi Tate notes that 'the most successful [Allied] propaganda campaigns were those based on fictions about German atrocities': the story of the Crucified Canadian, the German Corpse factory, and less specific, but widely reported accounts of bayoneted babies and raped nuns. These stories worked by exaggeration and caricature, were 'at once vague [. . .] and highly specific', and promoted a binary morality, where the atrocity was always committed by the enemy. Tate notes the irony that the 'many terrible and revolting acts which really did take place [. . .] were hardly ever used as propaganda', and that instead the 'most compelling and memorable stories to be taken up and circulated were almost always fictions'. These stories evolved from various literary traditions: 'recycled atrocity stories from earlier wars', horror stories, nineteenth-century sensational journalism, and pornography. It is clear that 'the element of sexual fantasy at work in much atrocity propaganda' was part of its popularity.[41] These atrocity stories were disturbing enough to justify the commissioning of the 1915 Bryce Report, as well as prompting a number of postwar studies highly critical of wartime propaganda.[42]

Early in the war, Wharton recounted multiple war rumours and atrocity stories in letters to friends and family in the States. In mid-August 1914, she told Anna Bahlmann, her German-born former governess, that there were 'German spies everywhere' in Paris and recounted stories of the many 'executions', such as at the Astoria hotel where 'a wireless plant had been found on the roof, & the manager, a German, shot immediately'. She repeatedly asserted the veracity of these tales:

> It is *a fact* that German towns, a week ago, were placarded with the announcement that the French Senate had rejected the war vote, that Poincaré had been assassinated & that Paris was in full commune?! Travellers coming back from Germany have seen these notices, & German prisoners have said they had been told so.[43]

97

In early September 1914, Wharton wrote to her friend Sara ('Sally') Norton: 'The "atrocities" one hears of *are true*. I know of many, alas, too well authenticated. Spread it abroad as much as you can [. . .] No civilized race can remain neutral in feeling now'.[44] In mid-September she wrote again to Bahlmann, telling her:

> I didn't believe the stories at first – but now they are too well authenticated. Belgian children arrived in Paris before I left with their hands cut off. Mme Forain [. . .] has in her care a man with his eyes put out & his ears cut off. Lady Gladstone [. . .] told R. Norton she had seen a Belgian woman with her ears cut off. Mrs. Cooper Hewitt had under her care in her Paris hospital a girl violated by six men under her parents' eyes.

Wharton acknowledges the problem of authenticity: 'It is a vast sadic orgy, which no judicial people could believe in at first, but which, now the wounded & refugees are pouring in, is written up in awful letters before us'.[45] Not all the stories were negative, however, such as the 'persistent rumours that Russian troops have been pouring through England for 8 days past, on their way to join the Allies [. . .] It seems the only hope!'.[46] Although we now know that some war atrocities did occur, Wharton's seemingly unquestioning belief in these stories demonstrates the war frenzy and anti-German sentiment of early wartime Paris, and her belief in the moral rightness of the war: that the German Empire should be 'exterminated'.[47] In mid-August, Wharton wrote to Bahlmann, the woman who had taught her German literature and philosophy, referring to the 'Teuton Savages': 'It is too horrible, isn't it, to think that Goethe & Nietzsche belonged to this race who have put themselves outside the ban of civilization?'[48]

A type of antidote to the atrocity tale, the revenge narrative developed as a particular genre of war writing, which enabled the textual enactment of readers' fantasies of, and desires for, retribution. Where the atrocity story was typically a non-fictional 'account' of the wrongdoings committed by German and enemy forces intended to incite hatred and pro-war sentiment in its reader, the revenge narrative was a fictionalised account of an atrocity which was then revenged, most frequently through the death of the (German) villain. The binary characterisation of these tales meant that the villain's death could always be justified as morally right, and could be violent and graphic in order to provide retribution for the opening atrocity. The violent impulses evident in these stories could be both exciting and sometimes disturbing for readers: Rudyard Kipling's 'Mary Postgate' (1915) is one of the most well-known and unsettling revenge narratives, in which the protagonist allows an injured German pilot to die slowly in her garden, denying him help after having witnessed a child being killed by the bomb he has seemingly dropped.[49] Kipling's story 'Sea Constables: A Tale of '15', written the same year, is similar in its presentation of a morally ambiguous death, where the protagonist refuses to help a neutral suspected of transporting fuel for the Germans through a naval blockade when he becomes ill and eventually dies.[50] Both stories are unusual revenge narratives, leaving the reader not knowing where their sympathy should lie.

In late March 1915 Wharton told Robert Bridges, the editor of *Scribner's Magazine*, that she had temporarily abandoned the 'sketch' she was working on, because '[t]he war has become too vast & terrible for such things'. She was, however, working on 'a longish story called "Coming Home"', her first war-related story, which she submitted at the end of May, and which was published in the December 1915 edition of *Scribner's Magazine*, and reprinted in *Xingu and Other Stories* (1916).[51] The narrator, H. Macy Greer, an American volunteer in the Relief Corps in Paris, relates his journey with a French invalided soldier, Jean de Réchamp, to his home in the Vosges to find out what has happened to his family during German occupation. It is insinuated that the Germans have refrained from destroying the house and its inhabitants because of a sexual relationship between Réchamp's fiancée Yvonne Malo and the German *Oberst*, Otto von Scharlach, a man renowned for his brutality. On their return to the front, Greer and Réchamp transport a German soldier with potentially fatal injuries to hospital. When their ambulance breaks down Greer sets out to find help, under the assumption that the German patient will survive in his absence, but with instructions for Réchamp to administer an injection if he worsens. On Greer's return, the German patient has died, and during his postmortem examination is revealed to be Scharlach.

Although 'Coming Home' appears to be a typical revenge narrative, the elliptical and ambiguous death scene makes it a fascinatingly uneasy one. I argue that Wharton uses the genre of the revenge narrative only to question its morality as she seems to endorse it. Wharton's focus on the narrative framing of events – a theme explicitly addressed in her later short story 'Writing a War Story' – provides a metafictional commentary on the composition of atrocity stories and revenge narratives, and the links between propaganda and narrative-making. Wartime culture was, as we have seen, saturated with war stories, and it was difficult to ascertain their reliability or truth. The narrative impetus arises from Réchamp's desire to find out 'the whole story' of what has happened to his family.[52] The revelation and concealment of knowledge motivates this story and the narrative ellipses presented to the narrator and characters are repeated metatextually in the gaps in the story for the reader. Here we see Wharton consciously experimenting with the motif of storytelling, because its wartime use and misuse was on her mind, repeatedly reminding the reader of the fictional construction of her tale through a range of literary devices, including the series of storytellers who structure the narrative and through commentary on modes of representation and genre. Wharton draws our attention to the distorting power of narrative: something that professional writers (including herself) were called upon to deliberately implement for propagandistic purposes during the war. Revenge stories such as 'Coming Home' demonstrate established writers tackling the uncomfortable emotions and ethical justifications surrounding wartime death.

'Coming Home' begins with a discussion of war stories, as soldiers are now able to construct narratives from their war experience:

> The young men of our American Relief Corps are beginning to come back from the front with stories.
> There was no time to pick them up during the first months – the whole business was too wild and grim. The horror has not decreased, but nerves and sight are beginning to be disciplined to it. In the earlier days, moreover, such fragments of experience as one got were torn from their setting like bits of flesh scattered by shrapnel. Now things that seemed disjointed are beginning to link themselves together, and the broken bones of history are rising from the battle-fields. (45)

The connection made between the inability to narrativise and the broken and mutilated body – the extended metaphor of the 'fragments of experience' as 'like bits of flesh scattered by shrapnel' – makes the notion of reconstruction physical. These war stories are a valuable commodity, and the narrator suggests it is an 'opportunity' for the men to collect them, some of whom have wasted their chance: 'Some are unobservant, or perhaps simply inarticulate; others [. . .] tend to drop into sentiment and cinema scenes' (45). Already we have a discussion of narrative framing and how genre can influence effect. H. Macy Greer, the man the unnamed framing narrator introduces, is held up as the only narrator who can make his subject 'seem as true as if one had seen it' (45). Despite his obfuscating physical characteristics – his 'voice like thick soup', 'slovenly drawl of the new generation', and lack of 'every shade of expression that intelligent intonation gives' – we are assured of his clear vision: 'his eyes see so much that they make one see even what his foggy voice obscures' (46). His name, an amalgam of familiar American names, similarly reassures us of his reliability, and his conversational tone encourages identification and shared unease with him at the story's conclusion. Wharton's publisher, Scribner, told her in June 1915: 'We need not elaborate on our liking for the way in which the story is told – the interposition of the American youth as the narrator gives it just the right touch for a story of these accumulating horrors'.[53] The framing narrator ends, however, with a statement of uncertainty about the story's genre, and coextensively its conclusive meaning: 'I am not sure how I ought to classify the one I have written down here' (46). As 'Coming Home' is only boxed by a narrative frame at its opening and not its conclusion, the ultimate meaning of the story is left to the reader.

'Coming Home' is structured by a chain of storytellers. This use of stacked narrators was popularised by Wharton's generation of writers, with Joseph Conrad's method discussed by Henry James in his 1914 essay, 'The New Novel', and Wharton finds a new lease of life for this narrative method in wartime.[54] We begin with the unnamed framing narrative, before transferring to Greer's narration and his encounter with Réchamp, who tells Greer 'he had had no word' of his family (47). Greer tells the story to a military chauffeur, who – in the first of the narrative's contrived fictional devices – already knows it and ensures that Réchamp travels with Greer to the Vosges, near to where Réchamp's family live. There they stay with another set of storytellers, some 'jolly Sisters of Charity' in a Hospice: 'what tales we heard around their kitchen-fire!' (53). Greer notes the atrocity stories feeding Réchamp's imagination:

> you know the stories we all refused to believe at first, and that we now prefer not to think about . . . Well, he'd been thinking about those stories pretty steadily for some months; and he kept repeating: 'My people say they're all right – but they give no details'. (54)

The next (unwitting) storytellers are revealed in retrospect. Passing through 'a particularly devastated little place', Greer and Réchamp had heard 'some more than usually abominable details of things done there', prompting Réchamp to remember the stories he overheard from wounded German soldiers while in hospital 'There was one name always coming back in their talk, von Scharlach, Oberst von Scharlach'. The stories move from being accounts of depersonalised evil deeds to that of a localised villain: from this point, 'whenever [Réchamp] saw a ruined village, or heard a tale of savagery, the Scharlach nerve began to quiver'. Greer, as the reader-surrogate within the text, depicts himself as more rational than Réchamp, reminding him that 'the Germans are not all alike' (55–6). Réchamp, however, is unmovable: 'He simply didn't listen . . . ' (56).

The next storyteller is Réchamp, recounting his engagement to Yvonne Malo. The analepsis that happens at this point presents another type of rumour-mongering: the sexual reputation of 'the new girl [. . .] who comes and goes as she pleases' (59). Réchamp's engagement was initially opposed by his family because of 'a heap of vague insinuations, baseless conjectures, village tattle' concerning Mlle Malo's character. His dismissal of these false stories further establishes him as a truth-seeker:

> He [. . .] hunted up the servant's record, proved her a liar and dishonest, cast grave doubts on the discretion of the curé's housekeeper, and poured such a flood of ridicule over the whole flimsy fable, and those who had believed in it, that [. . .] his grandmother gave way, and brought his parents toppling down with her. (62–3)

This desire for truth is also the primary quality noted of Mlle Malo, who is singled out as one who 'would despise any attempt at concealment', Réchamp tells Greer (55).

Elsewhere we see Wharton drawing on the conventions of the atrocity genre through the revelation and concealment of information. The next storyteller is another victim of the German depredations, but her story is withheld from the reader. Passing through the desolate country on their way to his home, Réchamp recognises an old woman wandering around in the ruins, where her 'unastonished eyes' foretell the horror of her story: 'Put together the worst of the typical horrors and you'll have a fair idea of it. Murder, outrage, torture: Scharlach's programme seemed to be fairly comprehensive' (69). Wharton, presuming knowledge of the genre from the reader, allows them to imaginatively construct a narrative from its typical generic characteristics. Rather than uncritically reproducing the genre therefore, she draws attention instead to its constructed nature. By contrast, other stories are more explicit in their violence. Greer recalls what he has heard from a doctor about a disturbed old lady: 'They're all like that where Scharlach's been – you've heard of him? She had only one boy – half-witted: he cocked a broom-handle at them, and they burnt him'. Réchamp attempts to recover more information, but the woman proves an unwilling storyteller: she 'relapsed into indifference', trailing off in an ellipsis (70–1).

Wharton experiments with different modes of representation to draw attention to framing devices. When Réchamp first arrives at his old home, Greer doesn't describe his reconciliation with his family, but asks the reader to imagine it:

> presently the lodge door opened, and an old man peered out. Well – I leave you to brush in the rest. Old family servant, tears and hugs and so on. I know you affect to scorn the cinema, and this was it, tremolo and all. Hang it! This war's going to teach us not to be afraid of the obvious. (72–3)

Disavowing the framing narrator's disdain for those members of the Relief Corps who 'tend to drop into sentiment and cinema scenes' in their war stories, Greer explicitly engages with cinematic representation (45). Although he notes the stock characters and the clichéd emotions, the conclusion is that these melodramatic scenes, 'tremolo and all', are not out of place in wartime (as Wharton herself wrote about her charity appeals, as we have seen). He suspends his disparagement and announces that 'the obvious' – the unsubtle and even excessive – is perhaps the only mode of representation appropriate to the war. His description continues to play on genre clichés. The long avenue to the house is

> Black as the grave, of course; but in another minute the door opened, and there, in the hall was another servant, screening a light – and then

more doors opened on another cinema-scene: fine old drawing-room with family portraits, shaded lamp, domestic group about the fire. (73)

The description of the family as stock characters demonstrates Greer's attempts to relate this war story in a particular mode, for particular effect, heightened by stock gestures: Mlle Malo 'went back to "prepare" the parents, as they say in melodrama' (74). The narrative playfulness with genre convention works as a commentary on the manipulation of information for propagandistic purposes in wartime writing.

The notion of unreliable or manipulated narration reaches its conclusion in the characters of Réchamp's family, relating how they survived the occupation of the Germans. Recalling the story's opening, it is clear that the role of storyteller carries some prestige, demonstrating the value of war stories as a type of cultural capital. A nominated figure recounts the tale: 'Grandmamma will tell you!', Réchamp's sister announces with excitement (75). Greer is aware of the importance of his participation as listener:

> The old lady paused for her effect, and I was conscious of giving her all she wanted.
> 'Well – ?'
> 'Will you believe it?'

However, it remains difficult for Greer to find out what has happened. Despite the grandmother's supposed honesty ('Well, I won't conceal from you'), it becomes apparent that her story is second-hand – '"Or so at least I was told," she added' – and Greer realises that Réchamp's sister 'had described the scene to her grandmother afterward'. Assuming incorrectly that Scharlach is French – 'The captain – what was his name? Yes, Charlot, Charlot' – the grandmother is proved, like many other storytellers in the text, to be an unreliable narrator (77–80). The final section at the family home concerns Réchamp's ultimately unsuccessful attempts to find out 'the whole story' (87). Mlle Malo maintains that there is no secret to reveal: 'But there isn't any story for him to hear!', arguing that legends 'grow up so quickly in these dreadful times' (87). When Greer and Réchamp leave the next morning, they are both preoccupied with the stories they have heard (and imagined): the 'little discrepancies of detail, and gaps in the narrative here and there' (89). The narrative secret is, of course, the possibility of sexual relations between Mlle Malo and Scharlach, which is never disproven or confirmed in the text.

The narrative preoccupation with hindrances to knowledge – the half-truths, rumours, and fables that cloud the narrative – is represented visually through the device of the blocked viewpoint. When Greer first describes the members of Réchamp's family, it is from a position without full perspective: 'I could see them all over Jean's shoulder' (73). Similarly, Greer witnesses Réchamp's and Mlle Malo's embrace through a partial view: 'I was behind him and could see her hands about his neck' (74). The lack of a full viewpoint replicates the position of not knowing the full story, where the withholding of narrative knowledge from both the reader and the narrator frustrates the reader's desire for information and illustrates the narrator's lack of omniscience. Wharton uses these devices as a means of making her manipulation of the story explicit, reminding the reader of the similar composition of atrocity tales.

The final section of 'Coming Home' establishes it as a revenge narrative through the death of Scharlach in a type of perverted deathbed scene. On their return to the hospital, Greer and Réchamp are told to transport the badly injured patient who 'might be saved by an operation if he could be got back to the base before midnight', meaning that a large part of the responsibility over the patient's survival rests with them (91). Greer is preoccupied with the man's appearance, whereas Réchamp avoids personalising him:

> In the shaky lantern gleam I caught a glimpse of a livid face and a torn uniform, and saw that he was an officer, and nearly done for. Réchamp had climbed to the box, and seemed not to be noticing what was going on at the back of the motor. I understood that he loathed the job, and wanted not to see the face of the man we were carrying. (92)

Greer's inability to read the man's face is an extension of the theme of the concealment and revelation of information. The motif of light suggests casting light on, or enlightening, but here 'the shaky lantern gleam' only allows a transitory, cinematic impression, recalling Wharton's experimentation with different narrative modes. Greer's second impression is more detailed, as he turns purposefully to look: 'Once I turned my pocket-lamp on him and saw that he was young – about thirty – with damp dark hair and a thin face' (92). Literally and metaphorically shining light on the patient, the description initially seems objective. However, the man's face preoccupies Greer: 'For half an hour or so I sat there in the dark, the sense of that face pressing close on me [. . .] a damnable face – meanly handsome, basely proud' (92–3). Although Greer tells us quite definitively that 'his look was inscrutable', he attempts to imaginatively fill out the patient's story, linking back to the thematic preoccupation with fictionalisation and the ability to construct narratives from only partial knowledge and few facts (92). The unreadability of the German patient is heightened by his silence, which Wharton has used as a fictional device throughout the story to represent the withholding of information. His only sound is 'a single moan' when the ambulance motor stops, but Greer's third impression shows that he has returned to a silent, almost corpse-like state: 'he lay perfectly still, lips and lids shut, making no sign' (93).

Scharlach's death occurs in the narrative ellipse while Greer is walking through a 'pitch-black forest' to fetch petrol for the broken-down ambulance, returning in the 'thinning darkness' (94). Although relatively simplistic, Wharton's use of light and dark imagery highlights the concerns of truth telling and deception that surround the death of the patient. Greer is very shocked by the death: '"Dead? Why – how? What happened? Did you give him the hypodermic?" I stammered' (94). He turns his pocket-lamp and scrutinising eye onto Réchamp: 'its light fell on Réchamp's face, which was perfectly composed, and seemed less gaunt and drawn than at any time since we had started on our trip' (94). The suggestion that the death has had a positive, rejuvenating effect on Réchamp will be repeated later in the narrative, and is a device we see in the later story 'The Field of Honour'. The implication is that there has been some wrongdoing, but because the death takes place offstage, this is concealed from the reader. Greer attempts to work out what happened to the man, in a preliminary postmortem:

> But I had been almost sure the man wasn't anywhere near death when I left him. [. . .] He didn't appear to have moved, but he was dead sure enough – had been for two or three hours, by the feel of him. It must have happened not long after I left . . . Well, I'm not a doctor, anyhow. (95)

His own self-questioning of his judgement alternates between statements of uncertainty and seemingly forced certainty – 'I had been almost sure [. . .] He didn't appear to have [. . .] It must have happened' – and concluding that perhaps his medical expertise is not sufficient to have correctly assessed the situation. However, his assessment of the time of the man's death will be proved accurate in the postmortem. The self-questioning coupled with the ellipses generates unease in this passage, indicating that there is no clear account of the patient's death. Greer makes it clear that the pair are very different in their response, and that some sort of role reversal has occurred: Réchamp 'had somehow got back [. . .] to a state of wholesome solidity, while I [. . .] was tingling all over with exposed nerves' (95).

Despite the elliptical death scene, the corpse is a visible and physical presence at the end of 'Coming Home'. The 'grim load' is taken into the base hospital for the postmortem, which Greer attends but Réchamp does not (95). Greer is very physically affected: 'I had a burning spot at the pit of my stomach while his clothes were ripped off him and the bandages undone' (95). When the identity of the corpse is revealed, Greer is at pains to assert his previous lack of knowledge, and thereby his own innocence: 'I handed over the leather note-case [. . .] and saw *for the first time* its silver-edged corners and the coronet in one of them' (96; my italics). The surgeon here acts as a foil to Greer, providing the congratulatory, triumphant response appropriate to the revenge narrative: '"A good riddance," said the surgeon over my shoulder' (96) (another blocked viewpoint). The functionary similarly exclaims, 'Ah – that's a haul!' (96). Although we could read the presence of the corpse as a type of visual gratification for the reader – a physical manifestation of revenge – this is not the typical celebratory death of the revenge narrative. The postmortem doesn't yield any conclusions, and the idea of only knowing one half of the story – of partial or incomplete vision – is further represented in 'the half-stripped body' (96). Despite the visible body in the text, the story behind the death remains unknown.

The possibility of wrongdoing and Greer's resultant unease is made explicit. Whereas Greer 'felt as old as Methusaleh', Réchamp seems to be positively cheered by the death: 'My friend greeted me with a smile. "Ready for breakfast?" he said, and a little chill ran down my spine' (96–7). This is the first time that Greer has noted him smiling, seemingly denoting his callousness. The final paragraphs show Greer attempting to rationalise the death:

> For, after all, I *knew* there wasn't a paper of any sort on that man when he was lifted into my ambulance the night before [. . .] And there wasn't the least shred of evidence to prove that he hadn't died of his wounds during the unlucky delay in the forest; or that Réchamp had known his tank was leaking when we started out from the lines.
>
> 'I could do with a *café complet*, couldn't you?' Réchamp suggested, looking straight at me with his good blue eyes; and arm in arm we started off to hunt for the inn. (97)

The italicised 'knew' returns the reader to the theme of knowledge and comprehension, and the problems of partial knowledge. Thinking in terms of 'evidence', Greer is assessing the case like a court case, where Réchamp is on trial. Unlike in 'Mary Postgate', where the reader is distanced by Mary's behaviour and there remains no other narrative figure with whom to identify, in 'Coming Home' the morally questionable action is removed from the reader-surrogate figure of Greer and focused instead on Réchamp. When the ambulance initially broke down, Greer had noted that Réchamp 'showed no particular surprise', but any suggestion of wrongdoing remains unproven (93). The final description of Réchamp 'looking straight at me with his good blue eyes' reads as an attempt by Greer to convince himself of his innocence (97). Greer conclusively re-allies himself with Réchamp and they leave, 'arm in arm'. If Réchamp did not know the patient to be Scharlach (despite having 'heard the men describing him at Moulins'), this lack of knowledge 'makes good' the death (69). The conditions of the death are left wholly ambiguous, meaning that the reader is effectively spared the uneasy moral question of whether this potential killing by negligence is permitted in the relativist morality of wartime.

Wharton's rejection of stark binary characterisation also contributes to the complex nature of this revenge narrative. She depicts German soldiers as not dissimilar from the Allies, contradicting their reputation as bestial and uncivilised. When an old woman walking around the ruins tells what Réchamp describes as 'one of the most damnable stories I've heard yet', even this report is immediately modified:

> She ended off by saying: 'His orderly showed me a silver-mounted flute he always travelled with, and a beautiful paint-box mounted in silver too [. . .] he sat down on my door-step and made a painting of the ruins . . . (69)

The Germans at Réchamp's house are cultured as well as having committed 'horrors' (85). Réchamp's grandmother tells Greer that 'Some of the brutes, it seems, are musical', and she is at pains to defend them : '"they were very decent – very decent," she almost snapped at me' (79, 76).

The interchangeability of terminology between German and Allied soldiers – seen by terms such as 'devil' and 'brute' – is also important in undermining 'Coming Home' as a straightforward revenge story. Réchamp 'had had a leg smashed, poor devil', and is later referred to as 'the poor devil left in the trenches' (46, 48). Greer refers to wounded soldiers as 'a couple of poor devils', and Réchamp repeatedly calls the German 'devils' (81, 55). Germans are similarly referred to as 'brutes', a term Greer later applies to himself: Réchamp's frown 'made me feel I had been a brute to speak in that way' (49, 81). Wharton's letters at the beginning of the war similarly demonstrate this interchangeability of terminology, referring to both the German as savages (the 'Teuton Savages') and the French war dead as devils, sometimes within the same sentence: 'Vandoyer has lost his brother, Mme Metman hers, Mme Scheikevitch hers – les devils se multiplient! [. . .] the savages are going to be beaten'.[55] The subtle but significant effect is the implied similarity, rather than difference, between the enemy nations, making the two characterisations less stark and determined. Greer's rational reminders to Réchamp that 'the Germans are not all alike' supports this more balanced representation (55).

Although using some obvious fictional devices, 'Coming Home' is far removed from the binary logic of typical propaganda. We have the form and conclusive effect of a revenge narrative, where the villain has been killed and good seemingly restored, but the intense uneasiness and ambiguity of the elliptical death scene undermine that effect. The motif of storytelling throughout works as a broader comment on Wharton's (voluntary) work for the Allied cause. This text performs its job as propaganda, but in so doing, raises questions about wartime morality and more broadly about the morality of propaganda itself: the ethics of how we frame narratives and the revelation and concealment of knowledge for particular purposes. Wharton was very aware of the art of manipulation through narrative, and despite her pro-war stance, this story demonstrates her unease with that knowledge.

Morbid Beauty: 'The Field of Honour'

Writing from Paris to Scribner in New York in late June 1915, Wharton confessed:

> Some months ago I told you that you could count on the completion of my novel by the spring of 1916; but I thought then that the war would be over by August. Now we are looking forward to a winter campaign and the whole situation is so overwhelming and unescapable that I feel less and less able to turn my mind from it. May I suggest, during the next six months, giving you instead four or five short stories, not precisely war stories, but on subjects suggested by the war? So many extraordinary and dramatic situations are springing out of the huge conflict that the temptation to use a few of them is irresistible. I have three in mind already and shall get to work on them as soon as I can finish my articles.

The unfinished novel would eventually become *Hudson River Bracketed* (1929), and the articles, Wharton's war reportage from the front line, were appearing in *Scribner's Magazine* and the *Saturday Evening Post* and would be published as *Fighting France* in November 1915. The previous month she had submitted 'Coming Home' to *Scribner's* for publication at Christmas 1915. However, it was only as the war was drawing to a close that she would write some of her proposed 'not precisely war stories', namely 'The Refugees' (published in January 1919 in the *Saturday Evening Post*) and 'Writing a War Story' (published in the *Woman's Home Companion* in September 1919). 'The Field of Honour' is an unfinished, unpublished nine-page war story. Six of the pages are in typescript, with annotations in pencil and black ink; the seventh is composed of six paper sections (two in typescript and the rest in manuscript) stuck together as one sheet. The eighth and ninth pages are made up of fragments, with earlier drafts on the versos. There are two fragments on the ninth page from separate stories: the first is a manuscript version of a discarded section from 'The Field of Honour'; the second, an unmarked fragment from 'The Refugees', suggesting that the stories were composed at roughly the same time (mid- to late 1918).[56]

Both stories concern the similar theme of the disconcerting transformation of women in wartime. The title, with 'honour' in the English rather than American spelling and meaning 'the battlefield; (also) the field where a duel is fought', was originally a phrase referring to the medieval battleground, which became part of commonplace Great War rhetoric, and eventually represented postwar memorialisation efforts.[57] Although unfinished, 'The Field of Honour' illustrates an important anxiety in Wharton's representations of the war – the fear that women were profiting from the war, specifically from the suffering and deaths of men – and provides insight into her literary preoccupations as the war ended.

The story begins, 'It is over a year since the war began', making the present presumably sometime between September and December 1915.[58] The plot concerns four key characters: the unnamed, ungendered (probably female) narrator, an American presumably living in Paris; the American woman Rose Belknap and her French Catholic nobleman husband 'Tom', the Marquis de La Varède, who have been (unhappily) married for several years; and Tom's male French friend, whom the narrator speaks to in the final scene about their shared concerns about Tom. The narrator tells us that since the war began, 'some life-histories have got themselves written': linking back to the war stories that open 'Coming Home'. The 'life-histories' in 'The Field of Honour' are presented in three scenes. The narrator recounts a dinner a week before the war with Rose and some of Tom's friends, and we learn that the marriage 'had been a mistake'. Two or three months later, the narrator meets Rose in the street in Paris and notices 'that she had never looked so pretty [. . .] in the universal gloom she was radiant'. Rose has been away working in a hospital in Brittany 'but her doctor had forbidden her to stay – the work was too exhausting', so she had returned to Paris and now nursed the wounded as part of a group called 'Les Consolatrices'. Rose explains to the shocked narrator that Tom (who has an unspecified addiction) has gone to the front, and, it is implied, to his death. A few days later, the narrator meets a friend of Tom's and asks 'how it was possible that a man in La Varède's condition could have been sent to the front'. The friend tells him that 'it's not so much a question of how fit a man is to go, but of how determined he is to go'. The draft ends with the friend's negative comments on Tom and Rose's marriage: 'You see, Tom ought never to have married an American – at least not one of your pretty ones'. The narrator tells him that, 'A good many of your compatriots seem delighted [to] keep them company', to which the man replies: 'In some ways we seem to be bad for each other'.

The characterisation promotes the story's moral ambiguity. The narrator and Rose have evidently had a close relationship in the past: 'I'd known her as Rose Belknap of New York and Rome and St Moritz, and I knew more about her than anyone', she says. But the narrator's dislike, even hatred, of Rose is obvious. Rose, representing America, is presented as crass and excessive in her tastes, with her vulgarity and shallowness emphasised: 'what was the use of having eyes like mountain-pools when all they had ever reflected was Fifth Avenue and the rue de la Paix?', the narrator asks. Similarly, the company she is with in the first scene is described as 'other like-minded idiots [. . .] the usual lot of plethoric asses and cackling clothes' pen-pegs', evidently with more money than sense: they are in a restaurant where 'it's no use fighting for one's purse when the bill comes round'. Wharton's characterisation of Tom, with whom the narrator has a similarly close relationship, is slightly more equivocal: 'good-looking, tired, disillusioned, without a conviction, and crammed full of prejudices', but with potential. Despite being 'a gambler, a dawdler, a purposeless disenchanted diner-out', Tom's character is predominantly based on tradition and stability, 'certain ancient and intrinsic facts for which a good many generations had fought and by which a good many more had lived'. In contrast, Rose is associated with transient spaces of (monied) modernity and consumption: her convictions picked up 'at the dressmaker's, the manicure's, the clairvoyant's, in the Sunday newspapers and the "all-story" magazines (she could never get to the end of a book), in tea-rooms and hotel lounges, and on the decks of steamers'. The narrator explicitly names her 'vanity' and her sense of entitlement (her belief that she 'was entitled to the first place everywhere') and from early in the story, her convictions are in question: 'As time went on I reluctantly decided that [. . .] all she was capable of caring for was noise and expensive hilarity'.

The concealed aspects of the characters further heightens the ambiguity of the narrative. Tom's unrevealed addiction – the fear of 'the old weakness' breaking out in relation to a 'drug' – is important to the plot, because it's not clear whether this condition will affect Tom's likelihood of being killed or not. The sex of the narrator, and her feelings towards Tom, is another prominent ambiguity. The narrator's particular irritation with Rose seems to be in large part because of her strong feelings for Tom: Rose 'seemed to take a perverse pleasure in not trying to see what I saw in her husband'. When Rose tells the narrator that she knows about 'the life Tom leads' (presumably his affairs), the narrator persists in instead seeing his potential: 'It's not the life he leads that counts; it's the life he was meant to lead'. The narrator dismisses Rose's seemingly legitimate question – 'But how about my happiness?' – instead 'turn[ing] the conversation to the Russian ballet'.[59] In one reading, the narrator is in love with Tom herself – a plot of triangulated desire similar to Rebecca West's 1918 novel *The Return of the Soldier* – which explains her particular horror at the idea of 'Tom – Tom at the front!' In response to Rose's argument that 'What could a poor little artless American girl do with a man like that?', the narrator's suggestion that some 'could have done a great deal', implies that she is talking about herself. However, the narrator kisses Rose's hand in the street, a traditionally male gesture, and speaks freely to one of Tom's male friends, suggesting the narrator could possibly be male. Like 'Coming Home', these ambiguous points are integral to this story of wartime morality, making the reader unsure of where their allegiances lie.

The meeting between the narrator and Rose in the street provides a commentary on the politics of women's war work. Wharton uses free indirect narration to satirise Rose's nursing as one of 'Les Consolatrices', using her own diction: 'It was awfully interesting and touching: she sat with the poor fellows, and took them fruit and flowers, and read aloud to them. (They had my sympathy; I'd heard her read aloud)'. This satire extends to Rose's design of a 'more becoming' version of the Red Cross uniform, which she is unfortunately forbidden to wear. Although this could be an attempt to legitimise her wartime activities, it is clear that Rose is only interested in her appearance. Rose's diction shows that her version and rhetoric of the war has come out of propaganda and popular representations, rather than real war work: 'she thought one ought to look one's best when one went on an errand of mercy'. Wharton, an extremely hard-working relief worker in Paris, observed with contempt the volunteer (particularly American) women workers who were only superficially interested in the war effort. In 'The Refugees', for example, we meet the 'refugee-raiders', society women who compete for Belgian refugees; and when we encounter a different Mrs Belknap in *The Marne*, we hear that '[she] donned a nurse's garb, poured tea once or twice at a fashionable hospital, and, on the strength of this effort, obtained permission to carry supplies (in her own motor) to the devastated regions'.[60]

What makes this story particularly interesting is its depiction of a common wartime fear: that women were profiting socially, professionally, even sexually from the wartime economy that privileged their lives over male lives.[61] The narrator's discovery that Rose's blooming is a direct result of her freedom from her husband going to the front provokes a violent impulse:

> 'The front – ?' I suppose I gaped at her, for she rejoined: 'Of course. Didn't you know he was contre-reformé? He left a week ago . . . ' Oh, the irresistible relief in her voice! Now I knew why she looked so pretty. I felt at that moment as if she were a venomous insect that one ought to smash under one's heel. Freedom from Tom! That was the only thing the war meant to her.

The implication is that Tom will probably die at the front: the narrator later asks Tom's friend 'And what if the old weakness broke out?', who answers, 'H'm . . . That might be the end of him, of course'. A similar trope is used in Kipling's story 'Mary Postgate', where the protagonist's quasi-orgasmic reaction as the pilot dies – an 'increasing rapture laid hold of her', followed by 'a luxurious hot bath' – means that she comes down to tea looking 'all relaxed' and '"quite handsome!"'[62] Although Kipling's story makes the link between the death of the man and the transformation of the woman more explicit, both stories use the beautification of women as a means of demonstrating contemporary concerns about the increasing potency of women in wartime.

The final scene provides a commentary on Tom and Rose's marriage, and, by extension, the relationship between France and America. This depiction of an unhappy marriage between an American women and a Frenchman was written during a period when Wharton was thinking about the French–American relationship more broadly. Her gladness at America's entry into the war in April 1917 may by this point have been tempered by anxiety on behalf of her adopted country. The story perhaps reflects Wharton's increasing estrangement from her home country; she would tell the Editor of the *American Magazine* in 1920, 'I no longer understand the new American'.[63] Wharton clearly spent time on the story: having had it typed, she then added revisions on two occasions, in both black ink and pencil. The more explicit nature of the story is likely the reason she did not finish and publish it, despite apparently revising it three times (from script to typescript, then annotated twice). However, in her correspondence with her main outlets for publication in this period – the *Saturday Evening Post*, *Scribner's Magazine* or *Woman's Home Companion* – there is no mention of the story. Perhaps it was difficult to place a war story after the war had ended and public interest had waned. Perhaps Wharton considered her harsh portrayal of volunteer women war workers too vitriolic, or abandoned the story in favour of writing what she knew would be a longer and more successful work, *The Age of Innocence*.

'The Field of Honour' provides a further example of uncomfortable war writing, as a story about inappropriate responses to actual and anticipated death in the war. Wharton's satire of women doing war work questions the politics of American women abroad during wartime, and asserts the legitimacy of only certain types of war work. She voices a common fear over women profiting from the war, using the motif of physical transformation – beautification – as a particularly gendered metaphor for gaining social potency. This undiscovered war fragment provides a further important response to the question of the appropriate response to the war dead, and the intense anxiety over inappropriate responses.

Conclusion

Through a close reading of three key war texts, I have demonstrated the literariness and complexity of Wharton's propaganda, and shown that a re-evaluation of her war-related writings is necessary. Her wartime writings self-consciously engage in various types of literariness – frequently demonstrated through an excess of figuration – and simultaneously reveal anxiety concerning the war dead. Her propagandistic writing is her most interesting when it betrays her anxieties about the justification for war death, and the treatment of the dead: what I have referred to as her 'uncomfortable propaganda'. At these moments the anxiety caused by the war dead and their treatment undermine and disrupt the propagandistic element of her writing. Grouping Wharton with the nurses suggests their similarities. Wharton was proximate to the war zone, having the unusual and privileged position of seeing the front lines, and with intensive contact with the wives, mothers and children, many of them refugees, in wartime Paris. Wharton's war writing is not formally innovative or modernist. Although in *Fighting France* I have chosen the moments where Wharton moves away from her usual mode and examines less typical sites, such as the ersatz war museum in the parsonage, she is typically realist in style and uses predominantly conservative motifs, such as the cemetery or the deathbed in 'Coming Home'. 'The Field of Honour' demonstrates her ongoing concerns as the war was ending, focused around the role of women in the war. In the immediate postwar years, as well as satirising women's work in stories like 'The Field of Honour' and 'The Refugees', she would turn her attention to civilian grief in her novel *A Son at the Front*, published in 1923. Wharton's wartime writing presents and examines difficult and complex themes such as the justification for killing and the unhealthy modes of mourning that developed in its wake. This means that her war writing is never as simplistic as has been assumed, and demands a closer look.

Notes

1. Wharton, *A Backward Glance* (1934), p. 351.
2. Wharton, *Fighting France: From Dunkerque to Belfort* [1915], ed. Alice Kelly (2015); 'Coming Home' was first published in *Scribner's Magazine*, 58 [December 1915], pp. 702–18, and republished in *Xingu and Other Stories* (1916), pp. 43–97; 'Writing a War Story' [1919], in *Edith Wharton: Collected Stories, 1911–1937*, ed. Maureen Howard (2001), pp. 247–60; 'The Refugees' [1919], in *Women, Men and the Great War: An Anthology of Stories*, ed. Trudi Tate (1995), pp. 174–98; Wharton (ed.), *The Book of the Homeless (Le livre des sans-foyer): Original Articles in Verse and Prose* (1916); *The Marne: A Tale of the War* (1918); *A Son at the Front* [1923], ed. Shari Benstock (1995). Some of Wharton's war poems and her newspaper articles 'My Work Among the Women Workers of Paris', *The New York Times Magazine* (28 November 1915) and 'Edith Wharton Tells of German Trail of Ruin', *The New York Sun* (6 April 1917), and her 'Talk to American Soldiers' (Lecture at the Soldiers and Sailors Club, Spring 1918) are reprinted in the Appendices in Julie Olin-Ammentorp, *Edith Wharton's Writings from the Great War* (2004). Some critics also include the novel *Summer* (1917) and the non-fiction *French Ways and Their Meaning* (1919) in this group. Further war writings are still being discovered or translated, such as articles and poems in the *Hyères Weekly News* and *Hyères and There Weekly News*, published by the American Red Cross in France, in Harriet B. Sanders World War I Scrapbook, Yale Collection of American Literature, Beinecke Library, YCAL MSS 995, Box 1, Folder 2, 1919.
3. 'The Field of Honour' (n.d.), Typescript (pp. 1–7 and 2 pp. holograph), Yale Collection of American Literature, Beinecke Library, YCAL MSS 42, Series I, Box 16, Folder 484. This story was critically unknown until I published it with an accompanying commentary: '"The Field of Honour": An Unknown First World War Story by Edith Wharton', *Times Literary Supplement* (6 November 2015), pp. 15–16.

4. Letter from Wharton to Charles Scribner, 30 January 1915. Correspondence between Wharton and Scribner's, 1914–15. Archives of Charles Scribner's Sons (C0101); 1786–2004 (mostly 1880s–1970s), Boxes 193–4, Folders 5 and 6. Manuscripts Division, Department of Rare Books and Special Collections, Princeton University Library, Princeton, NJ.
5. For a thorough and detailed account of Wharton's wartime relief efforts, see Alan Price, *The End of the Age of Innocence: Edith Wharton and the First World War* (1996). For more on the context of Wharton's war writings, as well as the publication history and reception of *Fighting France* in particular, see my introduction 'Wharton in Wartime' in *Fighting France*, pp. 1–73.
6. Cooperman, *World War I and the American Novel* (1967), p. 41.
7. Benstock, 'Introduction', in *A Son at the Front*, p. x.
8. Price, *The End of the Age of Innocence*, pp. xii, xiii. Price notes that the origin of this phrase 'tremolo note' is a letter from Wharton to Elisina Tyler, with whom she co-managed her war charities, from 12 April 1916: 'In the letter Wharton describes her struggle to overcome her longstanding reluctance to showcase pathetic individual cases of need to raise funds. "The Report [an annual report on the charities] is exactly the contrary of what I approve in that line, but I always get money by the 'tremolo' note, so I try to dwell on it as much as possible"', pp. xiv–xv.
9. Olin-Ammentorp, *Edith Wharton's Writings from the Great War* (2004), pp. 1, 5. See also Anne Marsh Fields's unpublished PhD dissertation, '"Writing a war story": Edith Wharton and World War I' (1992).
10. See criticism in the Bibliography by William Blazek, Geneviève Brassard, Peter Buitenhuis, Mary Carney, Mary Condé, Teresa Gómez Reus and Peter Lauber, Hazel Hutchison, Kate McLoughlin, Yolanda Morató Agrafojo, Alan Price, Sara Prieto, Mary R. Ryder, Mary Suzanne Schriber, Judith L. Sensibar and Claire Tylee.
11. Hermione Lee, *Edith Wharton* (2007), pp. 444–519.
12. Cate Haste, *Keep the Homes Fires Burning: Propaganda in the First World War* (1977), pp. 1–3.
13. See George M. Cohan, 'Over There' (1917); David M. Kennedy, *Over Here: The First World War and American Society* (1980; repr. 2004).
14. Matthews, 'American Writing of the Great War', in Vincent Sherry (ed.), *The Cambridge Companion to the Literature of the First World War* (2005), p. 217.
15. Buitenhuis, *The Great War of Words: Literature as Propaganda 1914–1918 and After* [1987] (1989), p. 102.
16. Price, 'Edith Wharton's War Story', *Tulsa Studies in Women's Literature, Toward a Gendered Modernity*, 8 (1989), p. 95. Buitenhuis, *The Great War of Words*, p. xvii.
17. Price notes that 'the phenomenon of American authors turning from fiction to propaganda to sway a neutral American reading public and to aid war charities was not uncommon between 1914 and 1917', citing Dorothy Canfield Fisher, Mary Roberts Rhinehart, Gertrude Atherton, Alice B. Toklas and Gertrude Stein, and Henry James as examples, in *The End of the Age of Innocence*, p. xii. He later notes: 'Occasionally [Wharton's] propaganda work extended into official government circles, as when she asked John Garrett at the American embassy to advise a

French inspector of propaganda about which American journalists could be used in support of the Allied cause', *The End of the Age of Innocence*, p. 46.
18. Lee, *Edith Wharton*, p. 457.
19. Price notes that Scribner's paid Wharton '$1000 in 1915 for each of her two stories, "Coming Home" and "Kerfol," but only $500 for each of the war articles', 'Edith Wharton's War Story', p. 97.
20. *Fighting France*, pp. 130–1. Further references will be included in the text.
21. Wharton, *A Backward Glance*, p. 352.
22. In *Scribner's Magazine*: 'The Look of Paris', 57.5 (May 1915), pp. 523–31; 'In Argonne', 57.6 (June 1915), pp. 651–60; 'In Lorraine and the Vosges', 58.4 (October 1915), pp. 430–42; 'In the North', 58.5 (November 1915), pp. 600–10. 'In Alsace', *The Saturday Evening Post*, 188.21 (20 November 1915), pp. 9–10, 32–3.
23. Although Wharton 'was not the only writer at the front', her letter to James notes that Henri de Jouvenel, the husband of the writer Colette, told her she was the first woman: 'He said: "Vous êtes la première femme qui soit venue à Verdun" – & at the Hospital [in Blercourt] they told me the same thing.' Letter to Henry James, 28 February 1915, in *The Letters of Edith Wharton*, ed. R. W. B. Lewis and Nancy Lewis (1988), p. 350. There were other American women writers working in various capacities in the war zones, including Mary Roberts Rhinehart, Mildred Aldrich and Nelly Bly, although Wharton was the most well-known writer among them.
24. Letter to Robert Bridges, 27 May 1915, Princeton University Library.
25. Tylee, 'Imagining Women at War: Feminist Strategies in Edith Wharton's War Writing', *Tulsa Studies in Women's Literature*, 16.2 (1997), pp. 327–8.
26. Matthews, 'American Writing of the Great War', pp. 226–30.
27. Florence Finch Kelly, 'Eye Witnesses of the War: *Fighting France*', *The Bookman*, 42 (December 1915), pp. 462–3, reproduced in James W. Tuttleton, Kristin O. Lauer and Margaret P. Murray (eds), *Edith Wharton: The Contemporary Reviews* (1992), pp. 222–3.
28. Kelly, 'Eye Witnesses of the War: *Fighting France*', p. 222.
29. Anon., 'Mrs. Wharton and Kipling on the War: Famous Writers Tell of Their Experiences at the Front – Recent Books on the European Conflict', *New York Times Book Review*, 5 December 1915, p. 490, in *Edith Wharton: The Contemporary Reviews*, p. 221.
30. Lee, *Edith Wharton*, p. 454.
31. Wharton, *A Backward Glance*, p. 368. Wharton was highly involved in attempts to find Newbold (who was reported missing before being confirmed dead) and mediating the news to her cousin Thomas N. Rhinelander and his wife. She eventually attended his funeral in their absence. See the unpublished letters sent by Wharton to Rhinelander in the Wharton Collection, YCAL MSS 42, Yale Collection of American Literature, Beinecke Library, YCAL MSS 42, Series XI: Louis Auchincloss Material, Oversize Box No. 64, Folder No. 1791.
32. Olin-Ammentorp, *Edith Wharton's Writings*, pp. 29, 40.
33. Wharton, *The Marne*, p. 28.

34. See *The Decoration of Houses*, co-written with the architect and interior decorator Ogden Codman Jr (1897), *Italian Villas and Their Gardens* (1904), and the travel narrative *Italian Backgrounds* (1905).
35. The Zouaves were light infantry regiments of the French Army originating in French North Africa.
36. The Col de la Chipotte Battle (25 August–9 September 1914) was strategically important for both the French and German sides. Over 4,000 French soldiers were killed.
37. Olin-Ammentorp, *Edith Wharton's Writings*, p. 40.
38. There are collector figures in a number of James's novels. For example, the titular 'spoils' of *The Spoils of Poynton* (1897) are Mrs Gereth's large collection of antiques, around which the plot revolves. There are collector characters in *The American* (1877) and *The Golden Bowl* (1904). The short stories 'The Aspern Papers' (1888), 'The Real Right Thing' (1899) and 'The Abasement of the Northmores' (1900) all concern collections of letters.
39. Wharton, *Italian Backgrounds*, p. 4
40. Olin-Ammentorp, *Edith Wharton's Writings*, p. 40.
41. Tate, *Modernism, History and the First World War* (1998), pp. 42–9.
42. Viscount James Bryce and the Committee on Alleged German Outrages, *Report of the Committee on Alleged German Outrages* [The Bryce Report] (1915). Post-war studies include: Harold D. Lasswell, *Propaganda Technique in the World War* (1927), and Arthur Ponsonby, *Falsehood in War-Time: Containing an Assortment of Lies Circulated throughout the Nations during the Great War* (1928).
43. To Anna Bahlmann, 15 August 1914, in *My Dear Governess: The Letters of Edith Wharton to Anna Bahlmann*, ed. Irene Goldman-Price (2012), p. 252.
44. To Sara Norton, 2 September 1914, *Letters*, p. 335.
45. To Bahlmann, 12 September 1914, *My Dear Governess*, p. 258. Wharton related the same stories with slightly varied details to Norton in late September: 'As to the horrors & outrages, I'm afraid they are too often true. – Lady Gladstone [. . .] told a friend of mine she had seen a Belgian woman with her ears cut off. And of course the deliberate slaughter of "hostages" in defenceless towns is proved over & over again', 27 September 1914, *Letters*, p. 340.
46. To Bahlmann, 4 September 1914, *My Dear Governess*, pp. 255–6.
47. See John Horne and Alan Kramer, *German Atrocities, 1914: A History of Denial* (2001). To Bahlmann, 12 September 1914, *My Dear Governess*, p. 258.
48. Letter to Anna Bahlmann, 15 August 1914, *My Dear Governess*, p. 251. Wharton's anti-German sentiment in this period brought her into conflict with some of her German-born friends. She told Bahlmann on 9 October 1914, 'I'm so glad you're *not* one of them!!', but didn't bring her over to Paris from the States, p. 261. Goldman-Price notes that Wharton told her niece Beatrix Farrand that she didn't send for Bahlmann because she was 'too ineradicably "Boche"!', 26 October 1914, quoted p. 261. Bahlmann eventually went to Paris in early 1915.
49. Kipling, 'Mary Postgate', published in *Nash's and Pall Mall Magazine* and *The Century* (September 1915), and subsequently in *A Diversity of Creatures* (1917), pp. 419–41.

50. Kipling, 'Sea Constables: A Tale of '15', published in *Metropolitan* (September 1915) and *Nash's Magazine*, October 1915, and subsequently in shortened form in *Debits and Credits* (1926), pp. 25–49.
51. Letter from Wharton to Bridges, 21 March 1915, Princeton University Library. Cable from Wharton to Scribner, 29 May 1915, Princeton University Library.
52. 'Coming Home', p. 87. Further references will be included in the text.
53. Letter from Scribner to Wharton, 18 June 1915, Princeton University Library.
54. James, 'The New Novel', published in *The Times Literary Supplement* in 1914 and republished in *Notes on Novelists, with Some Other Notes* (1914), pp. 314–61. Conrad is discussed on pp. 345–9.
55. Letters to Anna Bahlmann, 15 August 1914, *My Dear Governess*, p. 251, and 9 October 1914, p. 261.
56. There is a handwritten note on the front of the folder at the Beinecke Library stating 'Check holographs', but otherwise the inclusion of a different story in the same folder is unremarked.
57. The *Oxford English Dictionary* gives as an example of this phase in a quote from *The Times*, 19 July 1921: 'Paying solemn and patriotic tribute to the memory of our troops fallen on the field of honour', *OED Online*, <https://www.oed.com/view/Entry/69922?redirectedFrom=field+of+honour#eid183670029> (last accessed 3 June 2019). Wharton always used this English spelling. I am grateful to Irene Goldman-Price for verification of this.
58. All references to the story are from Kelly, 'The Field of Honour', p. 16. Here I have produced a 'clean' version of the text: I have corrected obvious spelling errors or incorrect punctuation, deleted words or phrases that are scored through, inserted Wharton's interlineal annotations and removed dashes from words that are not typically hyphenated.
59. There is a biographical dimension to this reference: R. W. B. Lewis notes that, 'At the end of May [1913], Edith went to the newly built Théâtre des Champs Elysées to see the Ballet Russe perform Igor Stravinsky's *The Rite of Spring*. It was the artistic event of the spring of 1913 in Paris, and Edith did not hesitate to call it "extraordinary"', in *Edith Wharton: A Biography* (1975), p. 346. In mid-July 1913, during a ten-day break in London, Wharton 'with Berenson and Lady Sybil Cutting had a second view of *The Rite of Spring*', p. 346.
60. Wharton, 'The Refugees', p. 176. Wharton, *The Marne*, pp. 26–7. There may be something tongue-in-cheek in this description: Wharton went in her own Mercedes (named 'Her'), with her chauffeur, to the war zones.
61. This argument builds on Sandra M. Gilbert and Susan Gubar's argument for the increased potency women seemed to gain in the war: whereas young men became 'increasingly abandoned by the civilization of which they had ostensibly been heirs, women seemed to become, as if by some uncanny swing of history's pendulum, ever more powerful', in *No Man's Land: The Place of the Woman Writers in the Twentieth Century, Vol. 2: Sexchanges*, pp. 262–3.
62. Kipling, 'Mary Postgate', pp. 440–1.
63. Correspondence with the *American Magazine*, Yale Collection of American Literature, Beinecke Library, YCAL MSS 42, Series III, Box 31, Folder 960.

Part Two

Grief at a Distance: Civilian Modernisms

3

MANSFIELD MOBILISED: KATHERINE MANSFIELD, THE GREAT WAR AND MILITARY DISCOURSE

Bulletin du Front:
   I advanced to the consul and gained a local success, taking the trench as far as Paris. I expect to advance again under cover of *gas* on Saturday. The enemy is in great strength but the morale of the Wig is excellent. Please explain this to Ribni & make him salute.[1]

Prefacing a letter to her partner and soon-to-be husband John Middleton Murry on her arrival in Paris in March 1918, Katherine Mansfield's mock '*Bulletin du Front*' demonstrates the permeation of her personal correspondence by military discourse. Having been in Bandol in the south of France since January 1918 for her health, Mansfield had become stranded in Paris during a three-week bombardment by the German *Superkanon* nicknamed 'Big Bertha' in March and April 1918, and she depicts her journey back to Murry in London in terms of military manoeuvre. Her explicit usage of war terminology and the mock bulletin heading demonstrate that Mansfield was very consciously parodying military reportage, while her comment about Ribni, one of her dolls, suggests the lighthearted tone of this text, intended solely for entertainment. The letter's conclusion – 'Now I must go back to the trenches & go over the top to the station – Goodbye – breathlessly with all my lovely heart' – demonstrates the combination of military rhetoric with the language of sentimentalism in Mansfield's war writing: a curious hybrid in which the noncombatant has made combatant language a means of modernist experimentation.[2]

My first two chapters examined proximate or intimate encounters with the war dead, which tended to use more traditional motifs and sites such as the deathbed and the graveyard in order to represent the dead, even if these were eventually proved inadequate. The second section of this book examines the more abstract modes used by civilian writers to depict the war and the war dead. These writers' metaphorical or physical distance from the war typically facilitated their literary experimentation with different modes of representation.

This chapter analyses how Mansfield appropriated military discourse at different stages in her personal correspondence, as a female civilian modernist writer, who – unusually – lived in France and Italy and travelled in the war zones, but remained at a distance from the war. She wrote: 'We are so near – really – Paris – London its nothing & yet between us there are swords & swords – '.[3] As a writer Mansfield recognised and embraced the potential for linguistic play that the war presented, and I am interested in the figurative language she employed to record and represent the effects of war. Three textual clusters in Mansfield's letters demonstrate the variety of her experimentation with war discourse: March 1915, when the first air raids in Paris provided a creative stimulus for her writing; March 1918, when she developed the motif of herself as combatant while under bombardment in Paris; and July to December 1919, when she used war-generated figurative language in order to depict her increasing illness. Despite her, at times intense, anxiety about the war, as her own death became more of a threat, flippant representation of the war became a counter-trope for her more personally serious battle with illness. This later half of 1919 was simultaneously the period when Mansfield began to assess the impact of the war on literature, in both her unpublished letters and her published critical reviews: assessments prompted in part by the many war books she reviewed that year. This chapter argues, then, that in her correspondence, Mansfield deliberately appropriated military discourse to describe her situation and her writing of the war and the war dead became increasingly bound up with her own potential death. More broadly, this chapter argues that the influence of the First World War was not marginal but key to Mansfield's literary development as a modernist writer.

The seriality of the letter genre makes it an especially useful means of marking time, measuring progress, and implying continuity. Examining Mansfield's letters in sequence allows us to trace the development of her rhetorical techniques, both within the individual letter – which Mansfield treats as a type of vignette with its own syntactical and rhetorical internal coherence – and across clusters of letters. Mansfield was a voluminous letter writer and her epistolary output outweighs her short stories, forming the bulk of her writing. Shifting the predominant critical focus from Mansfield's explicit war stories and her autobiographical response to her brother's death, this chapter suggests that whereas the Great War only enters Mansfield's fiction in largely oblique and elliptical modes, it explicitly permeates her personal writing.[4] It is in her private letters that we find 'political Mansfield', commenting on the public events of her time.⁵ Simultaneously Mansfield relished the performative aspect of letters, frequently appropriating the role of storyteller. Her revisions of the same wartime events in letters to different recipients demonstrate her experimentation with figurative language. There has previously been little critical interest in the letters in their own right, perhaps because the complete published collection has only recently become available.⁶ I include a brief description of Mansfield's letter conventions in lieu of an available critical discourse on women's wartime epistolary correspondence, before analysing the three letter clusters from 1915, 1918 and 1919.⁷

What were Mansfield's experiences during the war that she characterised as 'a terrible, tedious calamity', 'that dark place', and 'this bloody war'?⁸ Critical readings of Mansfield's writing have, until recently, underplayed the significance of her wartime context and the extent of her civilian war experience. Vincent O'Sullivan, by contrast, has asserted that, '[f]rom any perspective, the most important public event in Mansfield's lifetime was the First World War'.⁹ In February 1915, Mansfield travelled alone into the war zones to visit the French author and her then-lover Francis Carco, stationed in Gray, France, an event which provided the inspiration for one of her best-known war stories, 'An Indiscreet Journey' (written 1915), as well as being recounted in her *Journal* and two extant letters. On this trip, was Mansfield, as O'Sullivan suggests, 'perhaps the first to record the effects of gassing' on the men at the front, or did she, as Mary Burgan argues, move 'in the closed circle of her own sensibility in which the actual suffering of the wounded French soldiers seen along the way [intrude] only as so many touches of local color'?¹⁰ Mansfield's journey into the war zones gave her a privileged perspective on the effects of the war at first hand not usually afforded to civilians, particularly women. Similarly, her experience of the first air raids in Paris in March 1915 and the three-week bombardment of Paris in March and April 1918 provided her with a stimulus for her writing ahead of many of her contemporaries.¹¹ O'Sullivan therefore argues that '[f]or a civilian, Mansfield saw a good deal of the war'.¹² Moreover, she was in contact with a range of male and female figures both publicly and privately engaged in the war, including combatants, members of the War Cabinet and various ministries, medical personnel, conscientious objectors, and refugees, covering the spectrum of political responses.¹³ Of this network, Murry wrote that 'no single one of Katherine's friends who went to the war returned alive from it', a comment that, although not strictly true, gives an indication of the importance for Mansfield of those who did not return.¹⁴ The accidental death of her brother Leslie 'Chummie' Beauchamp in a hand-grenade accident during a training session in October 1915 caused her great suffering, exacerbated by the deaths of a number of her friends: the poet Rupert Brooke in April 1915, the artist Henri Gaudier-Brzeska in June 1915 and the writer Frederick Goodyear in May 1917. The inclusion of a quotation from Mansfield on the New Zealand War

Memorial in Hyde Park is therefore highly appropriate.[15] Despite this civilian war experience, there has been a surprising critical reluctance to view Mansfield as a war writer. This perception of Mansfield as curiously divorced from her sociohistorical context is reflected in the very limited number of stories included within collections of First World War writing: only 'An Indiscreet Journey' and 'The Fly' are regularly anthologised.[16]

'I HAVE A HORROR OF THE WAY THIS WAR CREEPS INTO WRITING': WAR DISCOURSE AND WRITING

In a letter to Murry from February 1918, Mansfield explicitly acknowledged the unintentional influence of the ongoing war on her own writing, using the metaphors of creeping, oozing and trickling to describe its pervading effects:

> I put all the unfinished MSS I had brought with me here in a row last night [. . .] & told them that none of them were really good enough – to march into the open (Ugh! No – I cant even in fun use these bloody comparisons. I have a horror of the way this war creeps into writing . . . oozes in – trickles in.)[17]

Her parenthetical distaste for these 'bloody comparisons' admits the disjunction between the situation she is recording (her evaluation of her literary manuscripts) and her descriptive mode. The question of being able to choose her words carefully would become increasingly important to Mansfield, and the unconscious inclusion of unwanted words caused her frustration, as she wrote in 1919: 'Even now, sometimes when I write to you a word shakes into the letter that I dont mean to be there'.[18]

Both Mansfield's deliberate and unintentional incorporation of military discourse – local to the Great War and more broadly – in her correspondence resulted in a hybridised figurative language – an example of what Allyson Booth has called elsewhere 'civilian modernism', which was significant for Mansfield's later literary development. Booth has examined some of the 'imaginative structures' and 'representational strategies' that writers used to represent their experience of the Great War, arguing that 'even at moments when the spaces of war seem most remote, the perceptual habits appropriate to war emerge plainly'. Despite Booth's rejection of these categories, her discussion of 'combatant and civilian modernism' is productive for my discussion, as I suggest that some of Mansfield's figurative language was chosen precisely because of her civilian status.[19] Civilian war writing contains the inherent difficulty of envisaging a war that the writer has not participated in any military or combative sense. Female war writing, unless written from the experience of nursing or war work, was for the most part written from the civilian experience, largely if not entirely based in the home country, and demonstrates different types of figurative language than that found in most male combatant novels. Less 'gory' and corporeally based, Mansfield's use of this figurative language is instead typically based on a civilian visual vocabulary – the frame of reference available for civilians on the home front (itself a curiously militarised metaphor for the civilian home space). In Mansfield's writing, we frequently see the war itself or people or objects related to the war depicted through everyday and household objects, or the changing seasons. A common trope of female writers was to use their body as a space for the inscription of the war, sometimes drawing on female-specific tropes such as pregnancy to depict their own personal war experience, as we will see in the case of H.D. in Chapter 4. Mansfield's particular version of this was to write the war through her increasingly debilitating illness, and to write her illness through the war. More broadly, my approach finds some precedent in the formal analysis of Mansfield's fiction undertaken by W. H. New, and further nuances the project undertaken by critics such as Booth and Vincent Sherry to draw out the specific impact of the First World War on modernist writing.[20]

This chapter therefore examines, as Kate McLoughlin has succinctly summarised, 'what happens when war and words are brought together'.[21] McLoughlin presents a range of possible reasons for the compulsion to write about war, some of which are particularly relevant in Mansfield's case. We may view Mansfield's insistent war-generated metaphor-making as a means of containing and controlling the war: 'imposing at least verbal order on the chaos makes it seem more comprehensible and therefore feel safer'. This is related to McLoughlin's later proposition that writing about war is 'cathartic, even curative', and Mansfield's persistent anxiety about the war was perhaps decreased by filtering it into contained rhetorical structures. There was also evidently an aspect of survivor guilt in relation to her brother, and the need to write about war was perhaps an attempt to make sense of it.[22]

'OH, WHAT IT MEANS TO GET LETTERS'[23]: MANSFIELD'S 'EPISTOLARIUM'

Although Mansfield and Murry's correspondence was not a typical combatant/civilian epistolary exchange, Mansfield's depiction of letters as a survival mechanism may well have been exacerbated by her wartime context. Despite the small but expanding critical discourse surrounding letters and what has been termed 'letterness', there has been limited criticism of war letters as a genre, with existing literature typically focused on romantic or maternal epistolary exchanges between the home front and the war zones.[24] Margaretta Jolly notes that '[u]nsurprisingly, war letters by professional writers tend to show heightened awareness of the function of writing in such situations', and an underlying assumption of this chapter is that Mansfield, as professional writer, identified the possibility for literary experimentation that the war offered.[25] She evidently recognised the value of letters, demonstrated by her work transcribing and editing Chekhov's letters with S. S. Koteliansky during 1919, and her prediction that her and Murry's letters 'will one day be published and people will read something in them [. . .] that "ought to have told us"'.[26] Although the putatively private space of the letter allowed Mansfield more political freedom than her published stories, she was highly aware of both the contemporary threat of censorship and the likelihood of her letters being published posthumously.

During the war, the authorities on all sides noted the importance of the continuance of the post in wartime in terms of morale, and civilians were encouraged to send regular letters to their loved ones in action, resulting in a new mass epistolary culture. Due in large part to the increase in prewar literacy rates, letter writing became a popular form of communication across all classes and age groups, with 12.5 million letters sent every week from Britain to the Western Front. This prompted various wartime epistolary innovations, including the establishment of mass censorship in Britain through the Defence of the Realm Act (introduced in August 1914), and the development of generic letter forms, such as the Field Service Postcard. Letters also took on a new commemorative value during and after the war, collected in popular memorial volumes for fallen soldiers, such as the book for Frederick Goodyear that Murry contributed to in 1918.[27] Although these volumes were not a new phenomenon, in wartime they came to stand in for the absent body of the soldier.

The sociologist Liz Stanley has popularised the term 'epistolarium' to refer to a writer's collection of letters. Despite the unnaturalness of this enterprise in terms of what Stanley refers to as the 'fragmentary and dispersed character' of an actual collection of letters, the epistolarium enables us to juxtapose revisions of letters and to trace the usage of different variants of war-generated figurative language. She argues that 'letters are definitely a very writerly form of communication':

> In their manuscript originals they are clearly a form in flight – they contain mistakes, crossings out, there are intimations of things there is no time or space to include, other responsibilities which make demands on the writer's time, as well as unconventional ways of filling the writing space, characteristic forms of punctuation (or its absence), distinctive turns of phrase, and particular forms of address or signature.

Stanley's discussion of the 'performance of self' in letter writing is clearly applicable to Mansfield with her skill at adopting and satirising different personae, underlined by the multiple names she used as signatures in letters to various recipients. Letter-writing practices 'often play with "other" genres or indeed shade into these', and Mansfield's parodies of other genres are present throughout her letters, demonstrated by the opening example in this chapter. The idea of letters as 'traces of this person in a particular representational epistolary guise' is evident in Mansfield's satirical letters, some of which are hard to characterise as her own.[28]

Considering the material conditions of writing, delivery and reading, Stanley's observation that 'letter writing is located *in*' and '*about* actual things', is clearly relevant for Mansfield's letters, which describe material objects and include everyday details, such as finances.[29] There are references to the material conditions of writing: Murry wrote in early October 1919 that Wingley, the cat, 'was sitting on my note-paper when I wrote, so I wrote my letter round him'.[30] Following two jealous letters to Murry, Mansfield suggested that the material conditions of letter-writing impinged on the contents of her previous letters:

> I have a feeling, Bogey my darling, that my letter yesterday did not *ring* properly. Please blame the insects – My hands feel as though they were on fire – all swollen and inflamed – They will be better in a day or two.[31]

Mansfield's letters fulfil Stanley's 'characteristics of metonymy and a simulacrum of presence', as her letters are frequently personified or take on human qualities: 'these letters take a shape which is *like* you – they are a minute manifestation of you. The A walks, the Y is a man waving his arms, the E is someone sitting down'.[32] She wished for her letter to be personified in the same way his letters were: 'I want this letter to warm you – to creep into your heart & blow – very gently – until all is tiny flames.[33] Stanley's notion that letters can 'construct, not just reflect, a relationship' is also made literal in Mansfield's case, where her initial relationship with Ottoline Morrell was entirely letter-based.[34]

One of the most important elements of the genre is seriality. Letters, Stanley argues, 'are characterised by temporal and spatial interruptions, are always "unfinished" in the sense of containing gaps, ellipses and mistakes, and also presume a response and thus an "after"'.[35] An 'epistolary ethics' develops between correspondents, with 'its own conventions and ethical dimensions'.[36] There also develops a 'processual dynamics', which changes over time:

> An economy of exchange and reciprocity is involved in long-term epistolary exchanges, with mutuality built in and giving rise to a processual dynamics in which there are distinctive (to the particular correspondence) interpretations of time and its passing ['by the time you receive this, I will . . . '] and space and its separations ['here I am . . . there you are . . . '].[37]

'By the time you have this letter I shall have heard from you and my present anxiety will – please Heaven – be over', Mansfield wrote to Murry from Italy in October 1919.[38] Stanley notes despite the 'temporal and spatial interruptions between the writing and the reading of a letter', arguing that 'when a letter is read [. . .] the present tense of the letter recurs – or rather occurs – not only in its first reading but subsequent ones too'.[39] The question of reciprocity frequently arose in Mansfield and Murry's particular epistolary ethics, often with accusations from Mansfield that Murry had neglected his letter-writing duties:

> I don't know what you think of yourself but *I* think youre a little pig of a sneak. Not a letter – not a sign – not a copy of the Saturday Westminster [Gazette] – plainly nothing. Why are you so horrid – or is it the post? Ill put it down to the post & forgive you, darling.[40]

Their letters were frequently disrupted by the wartime postal conditions, requiring the pair to send telegrams instead.[41] In March 1916, Mansfield wrote to her father that the newspaper he had sent from New Zealand had been opened by the censors.[42] Until Mansfield and Murry's marriage in May 1918, there was the added complication caused by Mansfield's use of the names of both Bowden (from her first marriage) and Mansfield. When she was in Italy in late 1919, the postal delays between England and Italy were further complicated by postal strikes. Murry devised a system for their correspondence, whereby each letter would begin with the number of days remaining until their reunion in May 1920.[43] Mansfield's letters in this period typically begin with the number of the letter(s) she has just received: 'Treasure brought to shore today: Monday nights letter. No. 3. No. 4.'.[44] However, letters frequently arrived in the wrong order, which meant that the seriality of the ongoing conversation was broken, causing some confusion between the pair.

The most prominent aspect in reading Mansfield's letters is the repeated expression of their importance for her, with increasing urgency when her illness worsened. In a letter of November 1919, she entreated Murry to 'throw them more quickly down the letterboxes, darling, *hurl* them, send them *flying*: tell them that if they come quickly there is nothing – nothing she wont give them'.[45] For Mansfield, a break in correspondence was perceived as a matter of life or death. In March 1915, she wrote to Murry from Paris:

> My heart dies in my breast with terror at the thought of a letter of yours being lost – I simply don't exist. I suppose I exaggerate – but Id plunge into the Seine – or lie on a railway line rather than lose a letter.[46]

This association of the non-arrival of a letter with death would prove to be a longstanding pattern.

1915: The War as Literary Experiment

From the beginning of the war, Mansfield was keen to translate her war experience into writing. She was aware that the war was of great interest to her readers, particularly her family members far away in New Zealand. In late September 1914 she wrote to Laura Kate Bright, her future stepmother:

> Here in London, we are in the throes of this frightful war. There are camps of soldiers in the parks and squares, in the streets there is always the sound and the sight of soldiers marching by. The big white trains painted with the red cross, swing into the railway stations carrying their sad burdens and often at the same time other trains leave crowded with boys in khaki, cheering and singing on their way to the front.[47]

In the letter as a whole, Mansfield deliberately appropriated the register of newspaper reportage through common affective tropes and superlative descriptions, producing what Stanley calls 'a particular representational epistolary guise'.[48] Despite Mansfield's understanding of the human cost of war seen in the 'sad burdens' returning 'at the same time' as the enthusiastic soldiers leaving for the war zones, the letter becomes increasingly propagandistic as she applauds 'the display of real and splendid courage on the part of all the people' and notes 'the poor Belgian refugees arriving in London, one an old lady of 93, who had walked miles to escape the soldiers', and whose 'house had been burned down and all her possessions were gone'. Similarly her description of 'a small boy, whose parents had both been shot' lends eyewitness authority to the contemporary propagandistic newspaper rhetoric of the 'rape of Belgium'. The effect is heightened by alliteration: 'streets [...] sound [...] sight of soldiers'. However, rather than having swallowed the propagandistic tone she appropriated here, Mansfield was experimenting with conventional wartime rhetoric, common in this cultural moment. It is not clear whether the 'unacknowledged excerpt' in the Wellington *Evening Post* as a 'letter' from London was published with or without Mansfield's consent (or whether she had suspected it might be published), but the performative nature of her war writings was apparent from the war's outset.[49] She was perhaps playing on this new role a few months later in December 1914 and early 1915, when she told her father and brother that she was going to France to report on the war, when she was in fact going to visit Carco.[50] She even donned a military style jacket for a portrait taken in a London studio in 1915 (see Fig. 3.1).

Mansfield's representations of air raids in 1915 in letters to multiple recipients demonstrates her increasing awareness of the war's potential for literary experimentation, and how letters were 'tailored for particular correspondents'.[51] Following her visit to Carco in February 1915, Mansfield stayed in his Paris flat in March and May, where she experienced some of the first air raids. On 21 March Mansfield wrote to Murry of the fervour that the first raid had excited: 'Every soul carried a newspaper – L'Information came out on orange sails – La Patrie lifted up its voice at the metro stations. Nothing was talked of but the raid last night'. Mansfield herself clearly participated in the mass excitement, continuing in a seemingly breathless aside, '(Im dying to tell you about this raid but Im sure I shant be able to.)'. Despite Mansfield's reservations about her

Figure 3.1 Alfred Hughes (1870–1933), Portrait of Katherine Mansfield wearing a military style jacket in 1915, probably taken in Hughes's London studio. Ref: PAColl-10046-07. Alexander Turnbull Library, Wellington, New Zealand

ability to tell the story, her initial series of simple descriptive clauses without adjectival embellishment soon develops into an intensely literary description of the air raid:

> I came in, made some tea – put out the lamp and opened the shutters for a while to watch the river. Then I worked until about one. I had just got into bed and was reading Kipling's 'Simple Contes des Collines,' Bogey, when there was a sharp quick sound of running and then the trumpets from all sides flaring 'garde à vous'. This went on – accompanied by the heavy groaning noise of the shutters opening and then a chirrup of voices. I jumped up & did likewise. In a minute every light went out except one point on the bridges. The night was bright with stars. If you had seen the house stretching up & the people leaning out – & then there came a loud noise like doo-da-doo-da repeated hundreds of times. I never thought of zeppelins until I saw the rush of heads & bodies turned upwards as the Ultimate Fish (see *The Critic in Judgement*) passed by, flying high with fins of silky grey. It is absurd to say that romance is dead when things like this happen – & the noise it made – almost soothing you know – steady –

and clear doo-da-doo-da – like a horn. I longed to go out & follow it but instead I waited and still the trumpets blared – and finally when it was over I made some more tea & felt that a great danger was past – & longed to throw my arms round someone – it gave one a feeling of boundless physical relief like the aftermath of an earthquake.[52]

Mansfield was trying simultaneously to explain the event objectively for Murry ('Bogey', who is directly addressed) and to embellish it, allowing herself more creative licence as the scene progressed. She makes use of internal rhyme ('light [. . .] bright'), and repetition of phrasing ('the house stretching up & the people leaning out'). The imagery of elongation is mirrored in the repeated long vowel sounds: 'a loud noise like doo-da-doo-da' and 'flying high'. The syntax becomes increasingly disrupted through the multiple ellipses, reproducing the nervous excitement generated by the air raid. Mansfield depicts the mass response to the unfamiliar object in synecdochal, almost futurist terms, in 'the rush of heads & bodies turned upwards' – a familiar modernist response. She belies her stated unfamiliarity with the Zeppelin by constructing it into a metaphor by means of a literary allusion to Byron's *The Vision in Judgement* (1822).[53] Mansfield – who was clearly thrilled by the experience – attempted to express the intense emotion provoked by the air raid through the simile of the experience of an earthquake.[54]

Her reworking of this same event in letters to Carco and Koteliansky demonstrates her deliberate and skilful use of different literary modes. In a letter written in French to Carco the same day, Mansfield seems more aware of the simultaneous attraction and danger of the Zeppelins, writing that the sound of the motors was 'as if at once to reassure you and to deceive you'. The rest of the description is more fantastical:

> But what pleased me most was the darkness in all the houses when they opened the shades and the sight of all the people at the windows. It was like a dream. I thought that everyone, quite suddenly, was going to fly.[55]

Mansfield moves away from direct description into fantasy, as the actual danger posed by the Zeppelins is underplayed in favour of the pleasurable aesthetics of the scene they prompt. Her letter to Koteliansky the next day is written in a further different register, the mock-pastoral mode: 'here the very fact of walking about in the air makes one feel that flowers and leaves are dropping from your hair and from your fingers'. The deliberately democratic syntax suggests the playful, childlike nature of this letter, and removes the danger posed by the artificial Zeppelins through juxtaposition with natural beings in the sky: 'The nights are full of stars and little moons and big zeppelins – very exciting. But England feels far far away – just a little island with a cloud resting on it. Is it still there?'

This fanciful mode is reinforced by the simple diction, use of polysyndeton, and the repetition of conjunctions and words ('little' and 'far'). The whimsical nature of the letter – complete with Mansfield's flirtatious sign-off, 'With love to you / Kissienka' – suggests that she immediately recognised the possibility for literary experimentation presented by the war, as is demonstrated by her three contrasting descriptions of the same air raids for different readers.[56]

Mansfield's own excitement and fear is explicit in a letter to Murry written later the same day, telling him that she was 'really rather thrilled' when another alert began. She initially aestheticises the raid – 'search lights sweep the sky. They are very lovely, lighting up one by one the white clouds' – but depicts it in more negative and frightening terms as the letter continues. The external environment both stimulated and disturbed Mansfield's writing process, producing a syntactically and thematically disrupted narrative. 'As I wrote that more bugles sounded', she wrote, punctuating the rest of the letter with parenthetical updates and an unsettling combination of tenses:

> These raids after all are *not* funny. They are extremely terrifying and one feels such a horror of the whole idea of the thing. It seems so cruel and senseless – and then, to glide over the sky like that and hurl a bomb – n'importe où – is diabolic – and doesn't bear thinking about. (There go the trumpets again & the sirens and the whistles. Another scare!) All over again. At B's [Beatrice Hastings's] this afternoon there arrived 'du monde' including a very lovely young woman – married & *curious* – blonde – passionate – We danced together. I was still so angry about the horrid state of things.
>
> (Oh God – its all off again!) I opened the shutters – the motors flew by sounding the alarm – I cant talk about the tea party tonight. At any rate it isn't worth it really. It ended in a great row. [. . .] It seemed *so* utter rubbish in the face of all this – now. A very decent and pleasant man saw me home happily. Otherwise I think I might have been sitting in a Y.M.C.A. until this moment – it was so very dark.'

The fragmented syntax and short disconnected sentences, as well as the juxtaposition of the sombre discussion of aerial bombardment with a more frivolous discussion of her attraction to a woman she met at the party that afternoon, seems demonstrative of Mansfield's disturbed thinking. This juxtaposition may have been an attempt to distract herself from her immediate environment, which she only allows to intrude as parenthetical statements with exclamation marks, or perhaps an unconscious linking of the fearful excitement of the air raids and the sexual stimulation of the young woman. The next day, however, Mansfield's description of the dangers of the air raid were seemingly negated: 'I felt very flat when I bought La Patrie at midday & found that no zeppelins had arrived after all'. However, she was explicit about the inspiration the event gave her: 'This afternoon Im going to write about last night. [. . .] Send it somewhere – will you please?'[57] Mansfield clearly considered that the air raids would be of interest to British readers and intended for her story to be published.

Although she didn't eventually write the story, these passages demonstrate the creative stimulus the war initially gave Mansfield and her early attempts to represent her war experiences in writing.[58] In this period – all in the first year of the war – she was experimenting with different literary modes, drawing on the conventions of war reportage in September 1914, and trying out modes of writing about air raids through different genres in March 1915. Mansfield was therefore highly aware of her own literary construction of events. The war at this stage was a new subject matter for her, one which came with its own rhetorical conventions and terminology, but which simultaneously offered an opportunity – even a challenge – for experimentation and playfulness which Mansfield seemed to relish. Conversely, the letter to Murry written during an air raid demonstrates the war's unanticipated impact on her writing, seen in the syntactically and thematically disrupted narrative. By the end of 1915, Mansfield's personal experience of the war and her own personal loss had jarred her out of its accompanying rhetoric.

The death of Mansfield's beloved brother Chummie in October 1915 generated a period of intense grief. Chummie had stayed with her in London for a week in August 1915 and her last letter to him (in the *Collected Letters*, at least) speaks of her desire for more time with him: 'It meant a tremendous lot seeing you and being with you again [. . .] but the worst of it is I want always to be far *more* with you', she writes. 'This is not a letter', the letter ends, 'It is only my arms round you for a quick minute'.[59] The news that he had been killed only six weeks later, soon after his arrival in France, was devastating to Mansfield.[60] She and Murry left for Bandol in mid-November: 'VERY MUCH REGRET THAT I CANNOT DINE WITH YOU TONIGHT LEAVING ENGLAND SUDDENLY A DAY EARLIER AND SIMPLY IN CHAOS PLEASE FORGIVE ME', she telegrammed to Mary Hutchinson, giving an indication of her emotional state.[61] Mansfield the modernist writer moves from creative joy in the new linguistic possibilities offered by the war to another bereaved civilian woman, anxiously trying to find out information about her relative's final moments. In a letter which begins with Mansfield asking Koteliansky to find and keep safe one of Leslie's caps that she left behind, she tells him:

> I had a letter from his friend again. He told me that after it happened he said over and over – 'God forgive me for all I have done' and just before he died he said 'Lift my head, Katy I can't breathe – '
>
> To tell you the truth these things that I have heard about him blind me to all that is happening here – All this is like a long uneasy ripple – nothing else – and below – in the still pool there is my little brother.[62]

Over the next few months, Mansfield dreamt of him repeatedly and saw apparitions: 'It was my brother who sat on the verandah step stroking a kitten that curled on his knee', she wrote about the hotel where she was staying.[63] This is not surprising given that she told Murry, who had returned to England, that '[s]ince I have been alone here the loss of my little brother has become quite real to me. I have entered into my loss'.[64] In one of her frequent dreams, Mansfield and her brother are in the war zones, and she unwittingly puts them in danger:

> I had a very vivid dream last night that I and my brother were in Berlin without passports – We were having lunch in the waiting room of a railway station at a long table – with several german soldiers just back from the front with their equipment etc. I see now the proud wives carrying the men's coats for them etc. Suddenly in a dreadful pause I began to speak English. [. . .] In a flash I knew we were done for. Brother said 'make for the telephone box' but as we got in a soldier smashed his helmet through the glass door. Crash! I woke to a violent peal of thunder.[65]

We see here how military discourse has affected Mansfield's dreams, in a letter which presages the ways she will depict herself as an active participant in the war in the future. We also see Mansfield the big sister working through the ways she perceives herself to have not protected her brother, here figured as the wartime fear of revealing something to the enemy. Her journal over this period reveals her intense grief about Chummie:

> I think I have known for a long time that life was over for me [. . .] though he is lying in the middle of a little wood in France and I am still walking upright, and feeling the sun and the wind from the sea, I am just as much dead as he is.

The reason she doesn't commit suicide, she writes, is because of her 'duty to perform to the lovely time when we were both alive', but her future work will be a memorial: 'I will just put on the front page: To my brother – Leslie Heron Beauchamp. Very well: it shall be done'.[66] The death of her brother led Mansfield to remember their shared childhood and to a desire to 'write recollections of my own country [. . .] I long to renew them in writing'. In February 1916 Mansfield turned to a conventional memorial form, the elegy, but sought to write 'almost certainly in a kind of special *prose*'.[67] In some of her fiction she moved towards New Zealand settings, first in *The Aloe*, revised as *Prelude*, but in her private correspondence she continued to write frequently about the war.[68] The very real impact of the war, the loss of her brother, is the context for this personal writing.

In the Thick of the Bombardment: Mansfield and Combat in 1918

In comparison with her description of the 1915 air raids where the attacks, or alerts, provided a creative impetus, Mansfield's depiction of her experience of the bombardment of Paris in March 1918 strikes a very different note. From the beginning of 1918, Mansfield's letters repeatedly expressed anxiety about the war and how long it would continue. We may then return to McLoughlin's suggestion that writing about the war – in Mansfield's case in unusual and purposefully casual figurative language – can be understood as a means of containing it.[69] Despite this, there is a sense that Mansfield was increasingly frivolous in her inclusion of war diction in her own writing, because the war was ostensibly decreasingly dangerous to her in comparison to her own illness. It is in this period that Mansfield began to adopt war diction in relation to herself, particularly the metaphor of combatant in her self-descriptions, implicitly linking the war with her own battle for health.

In early March 1918, when Mansfield was in Bandol for her health (following her formal diagnosis with tuberculosis in late 1917), she returned to her earlier experimentation with the creative possibilities opened up by the war. Whereas Murry had previously been the 'valiant little warrior' of the pair, Mansfield now depicted herself in the role of active (at least in civilian terms) participant in the war.[70] She wrote of being 'mobilised':

> Now about the Food cards. I am so glad you have got bacon because it means fat. I had already decided to try & persuade you to let us feed at home le soir while the war is on. Ill go out with a bastick and buy things and make scrumbuncktious little dinners for us. It will be 100 times as cheap and awfully good for I have gleaned many hints here – and essen *muss* der Mensch & I should always be black with fury if I gave up a cowpong and did not get what I thought *a fair cooked return*. The sugar of course I will save too for jam. Saxin just as good in coffee – That kitchen is so 'to hand' that we must make use of it while the war is on and save save save. See, Ill be mobilised too. I wont do it after the war but I will while the war is on.[71]

Combining domestic with military imagery, this passage demonstrates the hybridised figurative language or 'civilian modernism' Mansfield developed during the war.[72] She appropriates the persona of the wartime housewife – a further 'epistolary guise' – mimicking her determination to make do with the rationed provisions she has.[73] The repetition of 'save save save' echoes the contemporary wartime rhetoric of rationing, first introduced in Britain in January 1918, and the repetition of 'while the war is on' further mimics contemporary war talk. The playful and lighthearted tone (seen in the pun of *'fair cooked return'*), the casual inclusion of French and German phrases, the colloquial language ('scrumbuncktious little dinners'), and the exaggerated similes and metaphors ('100 times as cheap') suggest that this is another of Mansfield's experiments with military discourse, intended solely for her reader's amusement.

Developing her new participatory role, Mansfield wholly adopted this metaphor of herself as combatant during the next few weeks when she became stranded in Paris and depicted her attempts to return home to Murry in military language. Her journey back from Bandol had already been very difficult because of a 'new "strictness"' with regards to the reasons civilians could use for travelling between the countries.[74] It became clear in mid-March that she would be unable to travel home until granted permission by the authorities in Bedford Square.[75] She sent her long-suffering companion L.M. (Ida Baker, nicknamed Leslie Moore by Mansfield) ahead of her to Marseilles to 'spy out the land', and she wrote of her wish to '*break though*', asking Murry to 'keep calm and keep *confident* & know how I am fighting'. She signed the letter from '[y]our small but fighting Wig'.[76]

A letter from mid-March 1918 from Marseilles demonstrates Mansfield incorporating the feminine 'weapon' of sexuality into this military diction. She writes of the previous calm of Bandol 'compared to this violent battle' of Marseilles, telling Murry, 'I must bring you up to date with this Battle of the Wig'. Mansfield's battle becomes feminised, with her 'weapon' being the extended metaphor of her own female sexuality, as she attempted to speed up the process of gaining permission to travel by flirting with the local doctor, whom Mansfield refers to as 'Doctor Poached Eyes': 'I determined to get him by the only weapon I could'. Although this method seems to have worked and she gained the 'chit' she needed to travel, Mansfield was disgusted by the experience: 'I sit here in this café – [. . .] thinking how utterly corrupt life is – hideous human beings are – how loathsome it was to catch this toad as I did – with such a weapon – '. She then returns to her original combatant metaphor, writing of Marseilles as a war zone and of herself as male combatant:

> Marseilles is so hot and loud – They scream the newspapers and all the shops seem full of caged birds – parrots & canaries – shrieking too – And old hags sell nuts & oranges - & I run up and down *on fire* – Anything – anything to get home! – It all spins like a feverish dream. I am not *un*happy or happy. I am just as it were in the thick of a bombardment – writing you, here, from a *front* line trench.

Mansfield's parody, where she writes of being '*on fire*' and suggests that she is actually in the war zone, demonstrates her increasingly offhand appropriation of military idiom. The caged birds, rather than representing others, suggest her own feelings of entrapment. Through her negative phrasing, halting syntax, and use of dashes, her writing itself imitates the fragmented experience of bombardment.

The internal echo-chamber of this passage, characterised by polysyndeton and dualisms, 'hot and loud [. . .] parrots & canaries [. . .] nuts & oranges [. . .] up and down [. . .] Anything – anything [. . .] not *un*happy or happy', further demonstrates its construction for effect, rather than veracity. Her sign-off combines her masculine militaristic diction with her typical romantic language: 'fighting & tired but yours for ever'.[77] The next letter, written the following day and quoted at the beginning of this chapter, takes Mansfield's appropriation of war diction again into the realm of parody through the mock *Bulletin du Front*. Mansfield extends her parody to suggest that in assuming the traditionally male combatant role herself, she has prevented Murry from participating: 'I have fallen into this old war – I felt that one of us would – but Bogey – oh – God – I thank Thee that it is I and not my beloved who am here – '.[78] Although she presented it in romantic terms (and drawing on religious rhetoric), Mansfield's sense that she was the one suffering came from an understanding that her deteriorating personal health was her own battle to fight.

Mansfield's playful parody would not last long. By the time she arrived in Paris in late March 1918, she was already highly fatigued and anxious to return to Murry in time for their imminent marriage. She recorded the physical impact of the air raids on her worsening health:

> This place is in a queer frame of mind. I came out of the restaurant last night into plein noir. All the cafés shut – all the houses – couldn't understand it. Looked up & saw a very lovely aeroplane with blue lights – 'couleur d'espoir' said an old man pointing at it. And at the door of the hotel was met by the manager & made to descend to the caves. There had been an alerte. About 50 people came & there we stayed more than long enough. It was a cold place & I was tired. At eight this morning as I lay in bed – bang, whizz – off they went again. I washed & dressed & just had time to get downstairs before the cannons started. Well *that* alerte n'est past encore fini. Its now *3.45.*[79]

In stark contrast to her playful depictions in March 1915 and even earlier the same month in March 1918, Mansfield's unusually plain diction here reveals her physical and syntactic fatigue, as well as her state of resignation and weariness concerning the war. Her initial sense of pleasure in the aeroplane in the 'colour of hope' – presumably a French plane that she thinks will protect them – is eliminated by the 'alerte' in which she then had to participate. Her depiction of the shells ('bang, whizz') is a deflated version of her previous efforts to record the auditory scene and is a typical piece of onomatopoeia that she appropriates. Her sense of exhaustion was not without foundation. The second alert, which had been going on for nearly the past eight hours, continued as she wrote. The alert caused the city to stop functioning, and most importantly to Mansfield, the closure of the post offices: 'All I care is that it holds up all communication with England – no telegrams get through & letters are delayed'.[80] Later in March, she pessimistically noted that, 'as those letters were practically thrown into the Cannons mouth God knows if they will ever get there – '.[81] Perhaps it is in this respect that Mansfield could be accused of moving 'in the closed circle of her own sensibility', as Burgan suggests.[82]

Mansfield's letters from this period are punctuated with expressions of her unhappiness and cynicism. The physical stress the raids put on her is evident. She was by this stage suffering from the debilitating illness that would ultimately kill her. On her return to England she wrote to L.M. that she had lost a stone and that the Doctor had told her there was no doubt that she had tuberculosis.[83] A few weeks earlier she had written to Murry: 'The spring this year seems to me *hateful* – cruel – cruel – [. . .] The world is *hideous*'.[84] She repeatedly wrote of her physical discomfort:

> At one oclock this morning, I got up & wrapped up in shawlets & went down to the cave & sitting there in a heap of coal on an old upturned box – listening to the bloody Poles & Russians – it all seemed a sort of endless dream – Oh so tiring – so utterly fatiguing. I've caught a cold, too – and that makes the life in the caves so beastly – They are like tombs.[85]

The air raids had ceased to be an impetus for her writing, only an impediment: '"writing" is rather difficult because of the bombardments', she wrote to Murry.[86] However, there are still some instances of Mansfield finding inspiration in the air raids. Discussing the times when 'the gunfire is violent', she wrote, 'I am keeping notes of the kind of things people say about it – some *terribly* good things'.[87] Even when she did not feel imaginatively stimulated by the raids, she continued to record her experiences. 'As I write, I can hear the patrol planes booming away – and out on the boulevard all the shops are being protected with strips of paper over the windows – in all sorts of patterns –', she wrote in late March, 'But this is not Paris: this is Hell'.[88]

Mansfield's letters from March 1918 therefore move from parodic and flippant representations of the war – seen in the imaginative sequences of herself as the 'mobilised' wartime housewife sorting out the rationed foodstuffs, and as combatant writing 'from a *front* line trench' – to descriptions of air raids in which anxiety and fatigue predominate. The physical impact of the air raids on her increasingly debilitating illness is evident. Mansfield's increasingly flippant incorporation of war language and discourse perhaps suggests that the war was, for her, becoming a counter-trope to her more personally serious battle with illness. The rhetorical strategies Mansfield used to represent the war in this period were both a means of expressing her anxiety and depression, and of managing it through containment of the war in humorous and offhand modes.

Becoming 'battle stained': Mansfield and Illness in 1919

After the war ended in November 1918, the war became, as with many of her fatigued contemporaries, conspicuously absent from Mansfield's letters. Instead, her worsening illness dominated her letters and, for the first time, shaped the rhythm of her correspondence. Despite Mansfield's enthusiasm at the beginning of the year for her new doctor and treatments, her letters were increasingly punctuated by expressions of her physical suffering, and frequently she could not write for some time because of an intervening bad bout or her experimentation with a new treatment. Although the letters chart the fits and starts of her condition, however, her condition was getting steadily worse, which can be seen in her 1919 passport photo (see Fig. 3.2). The second half

Figure 3.2 Photograph from Katherine Mansfield's passport and her signature (as Kathleen Mansfield Murry), issued in 1919. Ref: MS-Papers-11326-070-02. Alexander Turnbull Library, Wellington, New Zealand

of 1919, July to December, was a period in which Mansfield was increasingly preoccupied with her own mortality. In the last three months of the year in particular, her letters demonstrate her deliberate return to the use of military discourse to describe her own illness, at the same time as she was engaged in critical discussions with Murry about the effect of the war on language and literature. Her assertion of the significance of the war for the arts therefore coincided with her own renewed use of its diction and tropes.

In spring 1919, Mansfield implicitly linked her illness during the winter of 1918 with the war, and her repeated expressions of her joy in the natural world and the spring suggest a reinvigorated enjoyment of life after the four years of the war. The spring was recorded as being cold, wet and rather dull, so it seems that her reactions were unduly positive.[89] She wrote to Dorothy Brett on 1 January that at a party given by herself and Murry she was pleasantly surprised at their own vitality: 'It made me realise all over again how thrilling & enchanting life can be – & that we are not old – the blood still flows in our veins. We still laugh – '. We can read this joyous celebration of new life and creativity – in what she terms 'a very New Year indeed' – as an implicit celebration of peacetime, where the change of season works as a larger metaphor for the end of the war.[90] In April she described the (temporary) relief of her illness to Ottoline Morrell as 'the lifting of that appalling cold, dark wing that has hidden everything for what feels to me – an eternity', a description which seems to simultaneously refer to the war. She used a seasonal metaphor: 'We have all been wintry far too long'.[91] This typically literary motif of expressing renewal and rebirth through the changing of the seasons provided Mansfield with a means of writing about the new world of peacetime, without mentioning the old wartime one. She wrote a week later to her friend, the artist Anne Estelle Drey: 'I simply died this winter; retired underground and was not'.[92] The metaphor of rebirth fits in with Mansfield's deliberate exclusion of the war from her letters from January to April 1919, and perhaps a more general wartime urge to forget the previous four years. Mansfield's joyful depictions of her natural surroundings after her serious illness in winter 1918 is a trope frequently seen in writings by those who are close to, or in danger of, death. David Cannadine has noted of soldiers' writing that 'the prospect that this day, this hour, this minute might be the last resulted in a heighted perception of the world around them'.[93] Mansfield's use of this typical wartime trope may then be an unconscious extension of herself as combatant.

In contrast to her exhilaration in nature and life during the first half of 1919, Mansfield had a vehemently negative response to Peace Day, the public celebration of the Peace Treaty in July 1919, telling Ottoline Morrell:

> These preparations for Festivity are too odious. In addition to my money complex I have a food complex. When I read of the preparations that are

being made in all the workhouses throughout the land – when I think of all those toothless old jaws guzzling for the day – and then of all that beautiful youth feeding the fields of France – Life is almost too ignoble to be borne. Truly one must hate humankind in the mass – hate them as passionately as one loves the few – the very few.[94]

Her extended metaphor of consumption and feeding draws on fairly conventional anti-war rhetoric ('all that beautiful youth') and the trope of the sacrifice and slaughter of the younger generation in favour of the older one. (Osbert Sitwell used the same metaphors in his poem 'Corpse-Day, July 19th, 1919': 'Old, fat men leant out to cheer / From bone-built palaces [. . .] Crowds became drunk / On liquor distilled from corpses.').[95] Mansfield's loathing of this conservative celebration of military power, which she notes will include 'portraits eight times as large as life of Lloyd George & Beatty blazing against the sky – and drunkenness and brawling & destruction', leads her, unsurprisingly, to the loss of her brother: 'I keep seeing all these horrors [. . .] and then my mind fills with the wretched little picture I have of my brother's grave – '.[96] Mansfield, who rarely wrote about her brother in her letters after 1915, confronts the problem that many civilian women were facing in the immediate postwar period; the tension between relief at the ending of the war and the necessary painful mourning of brothers, husbands and sons. The passage moves between highly literary construction through extended metaphor and allusion ('Life might be so wonderful – There's the unforgettable rub!') to the very basic questions of a civilian attempting to comprehend the significance and purpose of the recent war: 'What is the meaning of it all? One ought to harden one's heart until it is all over'. Mansfield, who wishes she could 'believe in immortality', perhaps unsurprisingly turns from the question of the war dead to her own imagined death from tuberculosis in humorous terms:

> To arrive at the gates of Heaven – to hear some grim old angel cry 'Consumptives to the right – up the airy mountain, past the flower fields and the boronia trees – sufferers from gravel, stone & fatty degeneration to the left to the Eternal Restaurant smelling of Beef Eternal.' How one would skip through! But I see nothing but black men, black boxes, black holes, and poor darling Murry splitting a very expensive black kid glove his Mama had made him buy . . . One must get out of this country.[97]

Her dislike of the traditional paraphernalia of death, summarised as 'black men, black boxes, black holes' and Murry's 'very expensive black kid glove', is similar to Virginia Woolf's 1917 description of 'generalizations' (she notes the 'military sound of the word') which 'bring back somehow Sunday in London,

Sunday afternoon walks, Sunday luncheons, and also ways of speaking of the dead, clothes, and habits'.[98] Mansfield's questioning of traditional death rituals was steeped in this mid-1919 moment, when new forms of ritual and remembrance were being widely considered.

Mansfield did get out of the country, going to Ospedaletti in northern Italy from September 1919 for her health. Here she became preoccupied with her own mortality as the potentially fatal nature of her illness was increasingly apparent. Her illness initially seemed to improve: in mid-October she told Murry that she was 'getting *absolutely well*', and contrasted this with her condition the previous year: 'Think of last October 14th [. . .] at night I had fever in that North room & felt I was going to die'.[99] However, she quickly became ill again, writing in late October: 'Nothing on earth to worry about, Im sure. One cant have a disease & be O.K. all the time'.[100] Her insistence on her own health, asserting in early November that 'Im not ill' (underlined three times), alternated with her intense 'fear of death'.[101] In late November she was preoccupied with her own body: 'I cant forget my body for a moment. I think of Death – the melancholy fit seizes me'. This preoccupation extended even to her surroundings: 'Ospedaletti itself is quite the most beautiful little place Ive ever seen [. . .] The cemetery bulks in my vision but then Im an abnormal creature'.[102]

Mansfield's repeated fears about her illness and potentially imminent death coincide with her renewed use of figurative military language, perhaps because of the similarity between her illness and the long war that had lasted for years without hope of a positive resolution. In mid-October, she noted that '[i]t is my illness which has made me so bad-tempered at times. Alas! one cant fight without getting battle stained'.[103] Later that month, her acquisition of six packets of 'black soldiers cigarettes [. . .] made to be distributed to dying Zouaves in hospital' aligned her rhetorically with those dying soldiers. Perhaps not coincidentally, in the same letter Mansfield was writing about her own mortality: 'If the Lord will give me 30 years with my Bogey [. . .] he can do what he likes with whats left of my bones and feathers after that'.[104] Mansfield's particular focus on the metaphor of fighting demonstrates that she had again returned to the motif of herself as combatant. At the end of October, she was 'fighting all the time the most *overwhelming depression*'.[105] In early November, she begged Murry for letters, telling him '*I can fight through all this* if I am in touch with you,' and reassuring him a few days later that, 'We are winning, but the fight has been so long'.[106] 'Let us *fight* now & then lay down our arms & love', signing the letter, 'You own own [*sic*] / Wig the warrior'.[107] Even the weather was militarised in this period: 'The storm [. . .] has withdrawn to await reinforcements', while the wind was 'blowing great huge guns'.[108]

Although sometimes her metaphor referred to a joint cause she was fighting with Murry or to their fight to be together, Mansfield's combatant language largely referred to her own battle with illness. Her frame of reference now extended beyond the most recent war to war more generally, suggesting her very conscious inclusion of military language. At the end of October, her lung wasn't 'exactly painful but it creaks like a Sam Browne belt'.[109] In December, she described her heart in the terms of an American Civil War song: 'It *bangs throbs beats* out "tramp tramp tramp the boys are marching" double quick time with very fine double rolls for the kettle drum. How it keeps it up I dont know. I always feel its going to give out'.[110] The war worked as a counter-trope to her own battle with illness, providing a framework for her depiction of her illness and a less immediate means of discussing the possibility of death.

Running alongside Mansfield's preoccupation with her mortality and her renewed use of military language was her dependence on letters, because of what she depicted as their restorative qualities. Mansfield came to see letters in almost superstitious terms as a means of protection against her worsening illness, where the continuance of letters meant a continuance of life. In early October she was eagerly awaiting Murry's next letter – 'I live for letters when I am away from you – *for* them – *on* them – *with* them' – and told him that she would be 'made new again when your letter comes'.[111] Her joy when she received a postcard the next day is evident, joking that letters would even bring her back from the dead: 'I feel quite different with this postcard. When I die, just before the coffin is screwed up, pop a letter in. I shall jump up and out'.[112] In early October she wrote that Murry's latest letter '*was breath of life to me*', and in November his 'marvellous letter [. . .] *breathes* joy and life'.[113] Letters even induced a form of physical ecstasy: 'Your letters are [. . .] almost too much for me: they make me feel breathless'.[114] In late October, she rhetorically linked the lack of letters with death: 'I was simply *dying* for letters today, none yesterday or the day before'.[115] In early November Mansfield implored Murry, 'TRY to send me letters often or cards or papers from the office – anything', threatening that a lack of correspondence could be dangerous for her health: 'HELP ME HELP ME! If I veep I getta de fever and I am veeping strong!!', warning him again, 'But write me AT LENGTH' [underlined three times].[116]

Underlying Mansfield's fixation on letters was her concern over continuity, where the seriality of letters acted as indicators of survival. In early November she told Murry: 'If only one could rid oneself of this *feeling of finality* – if there were a *continuity*. [. . .] The feeling that one goes on [. . .] but *its really all over*'.[117] In late November, she feared that they would never meet again: 'I get overwhelmed at times that it *is* all over, that we've seen each other for the last time', and that later readers would read a 'queer finality in their letters'.[118]

Mansfield's concern with her own mortality and renewed use of military figurative language coincides with the period (the second half of 1919) when she began to consider the long-term effects of the war on literature and aesthetics.

The day before the first anniversary of the Armistice, she wrote to Murry about Woolf's new novel *Night and Day*, which she was reviewing:

> I don't like it, Boge. My private opinion is that it is a lie in the soul. The war never has been, that is what its message is. I dont want G. forbid mobilisation and the violation of Belgium – but the novel cant just leave the war out. There *must* have been a change of heart. It is really fearful to me the 'settling down' of human beings. I feel in the *profoundest* sense that nothing can ever be the same that as artists we are traitors if we feel otherwise: we have to take it into account and find new expressions new moulds for our new thoughts & feelings. Is this exaggeration? What *has* been – stands – but Jane Austen could not write Northanger Abbey now – or if she did Id have none of her.[119]

Expanding outwards from Woolf's novel, Mansfield twice asserts that the war had fundamentally changed art and argues for the necessity of 'new expressions new moulds' after the war, suggesting that the war had stimulated the (ongoing) development of literary modernism. Her assertion that the novel ignores the war is a reworking of the same sentiment from the previous day, when Mansfield had been angry about 'the *disgraceful* dishonesty' in the newspapers, including a review of the book in *The Times*: 'there has been no war – all is as before – What a crew!'[120] Mansfield stressed the idea of facing the war: 'it positively frightens me – to realise this *utter coldness* & indifference. [. . .] Inwardly I despise them all for a set of *cowards*. We have to face our war – they wont'. She presented herself as a soldier or warrior in comparison to the 'cowards' Woolf and the 'Blooms Berries', as she disparagingly referred to them in a letter to Ottoline Morrell.[121] Mansfield then links this idea of facing the war with facing her illness: 'I fail because I don't face things. I feel almost I have been ill so long for that reason'.[122] It is perhaps this linking of the war with her illness which contributed to the language of suffering that both Murry and Mansfield used. He told her on 11 November that 'you and I have suffered the war more than anyone, that we have really known, do really know, what sorrow and pain are'.[123] Mansfield's response is similarly couched in the language of involvement: 'I share it all – your knowledge of how we have suffered, how we seem of all our generation to have been to the war'.[124]

The question of the effects of the war on literature continued to preoccupy Mansfield throughout November 1919. Her dissatisfaction with the contemporary novel led her to explicate her own aesthetic method, an unofficial modernist manifesto, which outlines the conditions of postwar writing:

> the more I read the more I feel all these novels will not do. After them Im a swollen sheep looking up who is not fed. And yet I feel one can lay

> down no rules: Its not in the least a question of material or style or plot. I can only think in terms like 'a change of heart'. I cant imagine how after the war these men can pick up the old threads as tho' it never had been. Speaking to *you* Id say we have died and live again. How can that be the same life? It doesn't mean that Life is the less precious of [*sic*] that the 'common things of light and day' are gone. They are not gone, they are intensified, they are illumined. Now we know ourselves for what we are. In a way its a tragic knowledge. Its as though, even while we live again we face death. But *through Life*: thats the point.[125]

It is important to situate this well-known passage in context. During the period when Mansfield was preoccupied with her worsening illness, she suggested that the war also provided a knowledge of mortality; that after the war, death was omnipresent as an inherent part of life. Her suggestion that the knowledge gained from the war is a 'tragic knowledge' both refers to the idea of original sin – the knowledge of mortality gained through a terrible act – and is simultaneously redemptive. Mansfield again returns to the language of 'facing' death, linking this with her own need to face her illness, implicitly presenting her illness as a mode of war experience. She described her own aesthetic method as follows:

> But of course you dont imagine I mean by this knowledge 'let us eat and drink-ism'. No, I mean 'deserts of vast eternity'. But the difference between you and me is (perhaps Im wrong) I couldn't tell anybody *bang out* about those deserts. They are my secret. I might write about a boy eating strawberries or a woman combing her hair on a windy morning & that is the only way I can ever mention them. But they *must* be there. Nothing less will do. They can advance & retreat, curtsey, caper to the most delicate airs they like but I am bored to Hell by it all. Virginia – par exemple.[126]

In late 1919, Mansfield's intense anxiety concerning her illness and mortality, her renewed use of military diction, and her preoccupation with the effects of the war were mutually reinforcing. Mansfield's assertion of the significance of the war for the arts coincided with her own renewed use of its diction and tropes: even her 'deserts' 'advance & retreat'. This is the central paradox in Mansfield's late work: her repeated calls to 'face' the war and her seemingly contradictory method of indirection, only explicitly referring to the war in a handful of her stories.[127] I examine this further in Chapter 5.

For Mansfield, 1919 was therefore simultaneously a period of increasingly debilitating illness and preoccupation with her own potential death, and simultaneously a time of asserting the impact of the war on literature. The reintroduction of militaristic discourse into Mansfield's letters in the second half of

1919, following the seemingly deliberate exclusion of it in the first half of the year, was not coincidental, but indicative of her linking the war dead with her own potential death. Reading Mansfield's statements about postwar literary form in November 1919 in their broader epistolary context therefore gives her remarks about the necessity of facing and representing the war – and by extension, death – a different resonance.

Conclusion: Mansfield as Civilian Modernist

Contrary to the idea that the war had 'used up words' as Henry James claimed in 1915, Mansfield was interested in the possibilities for aesthetic experimentation and new figurative language that the war offered.[128] This chapter has examined the ways that Mansfield appropriated war language in three clusters of letters from 1915, 1918 and 1919. Mansfield's initial attempts to render her civilian war experience in the 1915 cluster demonstrate her pleasure experimenting with different modes of writing her new subject. The combination of expressions of anxiety and depression with playful and flippant uses of military discourse in her 1918 letters from Paris suggests that the war had become – to Mansfield, at least – a less serious subject than her own illness. Here, Mansfield used war-generated figurative language in relation to her own body, developing the motif of herself as combatant and the war as a counter-trope to her own battle with illness. After Mansfield's deliberate exclusion of military diction in the first half of 1919, her letters from July to December 1919 demonstrate her renewed use of this figurative language at a time when her illness was becoming increasingly debilitating and she was preoccupied with her own mortality, at the same time as she was considering the impact of the war on the arts. These overlapping discourses of the war, illness and mortality were not coincidental, but mutually reinforcing.

Rather than being ancillary writings then, letters may actually be where modernist experimentation took place. For Mansfield, letters were an importance space for innovation, allowing her to try out military tropes and figurative language in various contexts, as well as providing a space to exercise her thoughts on postwar literary form. Although Mansfield's comments on the 'new expressions new moulds' necessitated by the war are regularly quoted, this chapter has situated them in their broader epistolary context, tied up contextually with Mansfield's preoccupations with illness and mortality and her deliberate and renewed use of military figurative language. Reading her letters in this context, as well as the new mass epistolary culture of wartime, allows us to read this modernist manifesto afresh.

This chapter forms the first half of the second part of this book, examining representations of the war dead at a distance. Although the war did not make Mansfield into a modernist writer – she was already an experimental writer before the war began – her writing was clearly highly stimulated and developed by this new subject matter. Mansfield is an unusual case, as a female civilian who lived near and travelled to the war zones, and wrote letters back to her noncombatant husband on the home front. The hybrid literary idiom developed in Mansfield's letters – a type of civilian modernism – would in turn influence her creative development and her fiction. In her stories which explicitly mention the war, we see the war's influence through the ways it was experienced and understood on the home front by civilians. The war is contained, domesticated and commodified into 'toy cannons and soldiers and zeppelins' or represented through a crying woman ('Spring Pictures', 1915); depicted as causing changes to civilian life through the satire of upper-class callousness of 'Two Tuppenny Ones, Please' (1917); experienced through the interior monologue of a civilian woman in response to a letter from a soldier in the war zones ('Late at Night', 1917); depicted as something which impedes leisure travel ('A Dill Pickle', 1917); presented through sentimental souvenirs brought home to sweethearts and through references to 'my poor dear lad in France' ('Pictures', 1919); seen through the 'men in khaki' and '"hospital boys" in blue' in a crowd on a public holiday ('Bank Holiday', 1920); and depicted through a parent's grief at the loss of his son ('The Fly', 1922).[129] Even 'An Indiscreet Journey' (1915), the only story written directly from Mansfield's experience in the war zones, depicts the violence of war through a smashed bottle and spilt wine in a French cafe.[130] The war and its distinctive discourse provoked Mansfield into a mode of civilian modernism, which became the style of (some of) her later stories, and it turned her, through her response to contemporary literature, into the theorist of modernism which she might not otherwise have become.

Notes

1. To J. M. Murry, 19 [March] 1918, in *The Collected Letters of Katherine Mansfield, Volume II: 1918–1919*, ed. Vincent O'Sullivan with Margaret Scott (1987), p. 130. All letters are to J. M. Murry, unless otherwise noted. I have retained Mansfield's irregular punctuation and spelling and her use of italics.
2. 19 [March] 1918, CLVII, p. 131. Con Coroneos has noted this combination of military and sentimental language in 'Flies and Violets in Katherine Mansfield', in Suzanne Raitt and Trudi Tate (eds), *Women's Fiction and the Great War* (1997), pp. 197–218.
3. [24 March 1918], CLVII, p. 138.
4. Only one chapter addresses Mansfield's letters: Anna Jackson, '"Not Always Swift and Breathless": Katherine Mansfield and the Familiar Letter', in Gerri Kimber and Janet Wilson (eds), *Celebrating Katherine Mansfield: A Centenary Volume of Essays* (2011), pp. 202–13. For the field of criticism on Mansfield and the First World War, see Claire Tylee, '"The Magic of Adventure" – The Western Front and Women's Tales About the War-Zone, 1915–16 (May Cannan, Katherine Mansfield, Ellen La Motte, Mary Borden)', in *The Great War and Women's Consciousness: Images of Militarism and Womanhood in Women's Writing, 1914–64* (1990), pp. 75–102; Christiane Mortelier, 'The French Connection: Francis Carco', in Roger Robinson

(ed.), *Katherine Mansfield: In from the Margin* (1994), pp. 137–57; Con Coroneos, 'Flies and Violets in Katherine Mansfield' (1997); Christine Darrohn, '"Blown to Bits!": Katherine Mansfield's "The Garden-Party" and the Great War', *Modern Fiction Studies*, 44.3 (1998), pp. 513–39; Angela K. Smith, '"I have broken the silence": Katherine Mansfield's War', in *The Second Battlefield: Women, Modernism and the First World War* (2000), pp. 162–9; Ariela Freedman, 'After the Party: Woolf, Mansfield, and World War I', in *Death, Men, and Modernism: Trauma and Narrative in British Fiction from Hardy to Woolf* (2003), pp. 81–102; Angela Smith, 'Katherine Mansfield at the Front', *First World War Studies*, 2.1 (2011), pp. 65–73; Alice Kelly, 'Katherine Mansfield, War Writer', Introduction to Kelly and Isobel Maddison (eds), *Katherine Mansfield Studies, 6, Special Issue on Katherine Mansfield and World War One* (2014), pp. 1–10 and the essays within this volume. Anne Fernihough and Lee Garver have examined Mansfield's prewar political engagement: Fernihough, 'Introduction', in Kathleen Murry [Katherine Mansfield], *In a German Pension* [1911], ed. Fernihough (1999), pp. ix–xxxi; Lee Garver: 'The Political Katherine Mansfield', *Modernism/Modernity*, 8.2 (2001), pp. 225–43.
5. I take the term from Lee Garver, 'The Political Katherine Mansfield'.
6. Completed with the publication of *The Collected Letters of Katherine Mansfield, Volume V: 1922–1923*, ed. Vincent O'Sullivan and Margaret Scott (2008).
7. A term popularised by Liz Stanley in 'The Epistolarium: On Theorizing Letters and Correspondences', *Auto/Biography*, 12 (2004), 201–35.
8. To Harold Beauchamp, 6 March 1916, in *The Collected Letters of Katherine Mansfield, Volume I: 1903–1917*, ed. Vincent O'Sullivan and Margaret Scott (1984), p. 252. To Ottoline Morrell, [16 June 1917], *CLVI*, p. 311. To Ottoline Morrell, [11 August 1917], *CLVI*, p. 324.
9. O'Sullivan, '"Finding the Pattern, Solving the Problem": Katherine Mansfield the New Zealand European', in Roger Robinson (ed.), *Katherine Mansfield: In from the Margin* (1994), p. 14.
10. O'Sullivan, p. 18; Burgan, *Illness, Gender, and Writing: The Case of Katherine Mansfield* (1994), p. 37.
11. The first air raids on the UK occurred in January 1915 on Great Yarmouth and King's Lynn on the East Coast. London was not raided until May 1915, making Mansfield's experience in Paris novel to her British metropolitan readers.
12. O'Sullivan, '"Finding the Pattern"', p. 18.
13. These acquaintances included Rupert Brooke, Frederick Goodyear, Henri Gaudier-Brzeska, Robert Graves and Siegfried Sassoon (whom Murry helped draft his 'Declaration' in 1917), who served as combatants; Gordon Campbell (Assistant Controller at the Ministry of Munitions), and John Maynard Keynes, who worked in the Treasury during the war (and whose house Mansfield and Murry rented from Dorothy Brett from late 1916 to early 1917); George Nathaniel Curzon, a member of the War Cabinet; Georges Duhamel, who had written about his experiences as an army surgeon in *Vie des Martyrs: 1914–1916* (1917); Ottoline and Philip Morrell at Garsington, and her brother Henry Cavendish Bentinck, opposed to the war; Muirhead Bone, the Scottish war artist; the conscientious objectors Bertrand Russell and Clive Bell; and the Belgian refugee Maria Nys, who stayed at Garsington. Mansfield also

writes about her lengthy conversation with a war nurse in a letter to J. M. Murry, [19–20 December 1915], *CLVI*, pp. 220–1.
14. Mansfield, *Journal of Katherine Mansfield: Definitive Edition*, ed. J. Middleton Murry (1954), p. 104.
15. The quotation – unrelated to war – is from Mansfield, *The Urewera Notebook*, ed. Ian A. Gordon (1978), p. 39. The memorial, dedicated on 11 November 2006, is entitled *Southern Stand* and 'commemorates the enduring bonds between New Zealand and the United Kingdom, and our shared sacrifice during times of war' ('Design for NZ Memorial in Hyde Park, London', Press Release, New Zealand Government, 2005). <https://www.beehive.govt.nz/release/design-nz-memorial-hyde-park-london> (last accessed 1 June 2019). I am grateful to Hanna Smyth for alerting me to this memorial.
16. 'The Fly' is included in *Women, Men and the Great War: An Anthology of Stories*, ed. Trudi Tate (1995), pp. 68–72; and *Lines of Fire: Women Writers of World War I*, ed. Margaret R. Higonnet (1999), pp. 412–16. 'An Indiscreet Journey' and 'The Fly' are also included in *The Penguin Book of First World War Stories*, ed. Barbara Korte and Ann-Marie Einhaus (2007), pp. 77–92, 297–302.
17. [12 and 13 February 1918], *CLVII*, p. 70.
18. [15 October 1919], in *The Collected Letters of Katherine Mansfield, Volume III: 1919–1920*, ed. Vincent O'Sullivan and Margaret Scott (1993), p. 26.
19. Booth, *Postcards from the Trenches: Negotiating the Space between Modernism and the First World War* (1996), pp. 4–5. Booth does not offer a definition for this term.
20. New, *Reading Mansfield and Metaphors of Form* (1999); Booth, *Postcards from the Trenches*; Sherry, *The Great War and the Language of Modernism* (2003).
21. McLoughlin, 'War and Words', in McLoughlin (ed.), *The Cambridge Companion to War Writing* (2009), p. 15.
22. McLoughlin, 'War and Words', pp. 19–20.
23. [17 November 1919], *CLVIII*, p. 100.
24. For letters and 'letterness', see Liz Stanley, 'The Epistolarium: On Theorizing Letters and Correspondences', *Auto/Biography*, 12 (2004), 201–35; Margaretta Jolly and Liz Stanley, 'Letters As / Not a Genre', *Life Writing*, 2.2 (2005), 91–118; Sarah Poustie, 'Re-Theorising Letters and "Letterness"', *Olive Schreiner Letters Project: Working Papers on Letters, Letterness & Epistolary Networks*, 1 (2010), 1–50. For war letters, see Alice Kelly, 'Letters from Home: Wartime Correspondences', which considers the First World War letter genre, in Ann-Marie Einhaus and Katherine Baxter (eds), *The Edinburgh Companion to the First World War and the Arts* (2017), pp. 77–94.
25. Jolly, 'War Letters', in Jolly (ed.), *Encyclopedia of Life Writing: Autobiographical and Biographical Forms* (2001), pp. 927, 928.
26. [21 November 1919], *CLVIII*, p. 106.
27. See Mansfield's letter to Murry concerning Goodyear's memorialisation book, 12 March [1918], *CLVII*, p. 119. This was published as *Frederick Goodyear, Letters and Remains, 1887–1917* (1920).
28. Stanley 'The Epistolarium', pp. 204, 213, 212, 217, 223.
29. Stanley, 'The Epistolarium', p. 212.

30. O'Sullivan and Scott, Footnote 3, *CLVIII*, p. 14.
31. [21 October 1919], *CLVIII*, p. 38.
32. [16 November 1919], *CLVIII*, pp. 98–9.
33. [1 November 1919], *CLVIII*, p. 62.
34. Stanley, p. 211. Mansfield writes to Ottoline Morrell, 'I long to know you. I love you in your letters', [17 May 1916], *CLVI*, p. 268.
35. Stanley, 'The Epistolarium', p. 221.
36. Stanley, 'The Epistolarium', p. 210.
37. Stanley, 'The Epistolarium', p. 214.
38. [5 October 1919], *CLVIII*, p. 8.
39. Stanley, 'The Epistolarium', pp. 213, 208.
40. [22–24 March 1915], *CLVI*, p. 165.
41. [21 December 1915], *CLVI*, p. 222.
42. To Harold Beauchamp, 6 March 1916, *CLVI*, p. 251.
43. O'Sullivan and Scott, Footnote 1, *CLVIII*, p. 31.
44. [11 October 1919], *CLVIII*, p. 16.
45. [1 November 1919], *CLVIII*, p. 62.
46. [26 March 1915], *CLVI*, p. 169.
47. To [Laura Kate Bright], [21 September 1914], *CLVI*, pp. 139–40. Mansfield's father married Bright in 1920 after the death of Mansfield's mother Annie Burnell Beauchamp (née Dyer) in 1918.
48. Stanley, 'The Epistolarium', p. 223.
49. O'Sullivan and Scott, Footnote 1, *CLVI*, p. 140.
50. To Harold Beauchamp, 15 December 1914, *CLV1*, p. 142. O'Sullivan and Scott discuss the letter from Leslie Beauchamp to Harold Beauchamp of 11 February 1915 which mentions this, Footnote 5, p. 143.
51. Stanley, 'The Epistolarium', p. 211.
52. [21 March 1915], *CLVI*, pp. 158–9.
53. The title is confused with Murry's 1913 poem *The Critic in Judgement*. O'Sullivan and Scott, Footnote 6, *CLVI*, p. 160.
54. Alex Moffett also offers an interesting reading of Mansfield's accounts of the 1915 air raids in 'Katherine Mansfield's Home Front: Submerging the Martial Metaphors of "The Aloe"', in *Katherine Mansfield Studies, 6, Katherine Mansfield and the First World War* (2014), pp. 69–83.
55. To Francis Carco, [c. 21 March 1915], *CLVI*, p. 161. The letter is recounted in Carco's *Montmartre à vingt ans* (1938) and the original manuscript has been lost, meaning that, as O'Sullivan and Scott state in their Editorial Note, 'one must be wary of accepting what he quotes as completely authentic', p. xxiii.
56. To S. S. Koteliansky, 22 March 1915, *CLVI*, p. 163.
57. [22–24 March 1915], *CLVI*, p. 166.
58. She wrote the next day within the same letter: 'After all I never wrote a thing', [22–24 March 1915], *CLVI*, p. 166.
59. To Leslie Beauchamp, [25 August 1915], *CLVI*, pp. 197, 198.
60. Leslie Beauchamp 'crossed to France in late September, and was killed in a hand-grenade accident at Ploegsteert Wood, near Armentières, on 7 Oct. 1915', O'Sullivan and Scott, Footnote 1, *CLVI*, p. 198.

61. Telegram to Mary Hutchinson, [15 November 1915], *CLVI*, p. 199.
62. To S. S. Koteliansky, 19 November 1915, *CLVI*, pp. 199, 200.
63. [9 December 1915], *CLVI*, p. 204.
64. [16 December 1915], *CLVI*, p. 215.
65. To J. M. Murry, [17–18 December 1915], *CLVI*, p. 216.
66. 20 October 1915, in *The Diaries of Katherine Mansfield*, ed. Gerri Kimber and Claire Davison (2016), pp. 171–2.
67. 22 February 1916, *Diaries*, pp. 191–2.
68. *The Aloe* was first published by Virginia and Leonard Woolf at the Hogarth Press in 1918, and then revised and included as *Prelude* in *Bliss and Other Stories* (1920).
69. McLoughlin, 'War and Words', p. 19.
70. [Early January 1917], *CLVI*, p. 290. 'Warrior' was figurative for Murry, who had been declared medically unfit for active service and instead worked in the War Office as editor of the *Daily Review of the Foreign Press*.
71. 4 March [1918], *CLVII*, pp. 105–6. Saxin, a brand name for saccharine, was a sugar substitute used due to wartime shortages.
72. Booth, *Postcards*, p. 5.
73. Stanley, 'The Epistolarium', p. 223.
74. [16 March 1918], *CLVII*, p. 125.
75. [16 March 1918], *CLVII*, p. 125.
76. [14 and 15 March (1918)], *CLVII*, pp. 123. [17 March 1918], *CLVII*, pp. 127–8. Mansfield was 'Wig' and Murry was 'Tig'.
77. [18 March 1918], *CLVII*, pp. 129–30.
78. [30 March 1918], *CLVII*, pp. 146–7.
79. [23 March 1918], *CLVII*, pp. 136–7.
80. [24 March 1918], *CLVII*, p. 138.
81. [26 March 1918], *CLVII*, p. 141.
82. Burgan, *Illness, Gender, and Writing*, p. 37.
83. To Ida Baker, [12 April 1918], *CLVII*, p. 164; [18 April 1918], *CLVII*, p. 166.
84. [24 March 1918], *CLVII*, p. 138.
85. [25 March 1918], *CLVII*, pp. 139.
86. [25 March 1918], *CLVII*, p. 139.
87. [31 March 1918], *CLVII*, p. 147.
88. [26 March 1918], *CLVII*, p. 140.
89. For 1919 weather in London, see <http://www.london-weather.eu/article.59.html> (last accessed 1 June 2019).
90. To Dorothy Brett, [1 January 1919], *CLVII*, pp. 298–9.
91. To Ottoline Morrell, [c. 20 April 1919], *CLVII*, p. 313.
92. To Anne Estelle Drey, [c. 28 April 1919], CLVII, p. 315.
93. Cannadine, 'War and Death, Grief and Mourning in Modern Britain', in Joachim Whaley (ed.), *Mirrors of Mortality: Studies in the Social History of Death* (1981), p. 209.
94. To Ottoline Morrell, [c. 13 July 1919], *CLVII*, p. 339.
95. Sitwell, 'Corpse-Day, July 19th, 1919', in *Wheels, 1919: Fourth Cycle*, ed. Edith Sitwell (1919), pp. 9–11.

96. To Ottoline Morrell, [c. 13 July 1919], *CLVII*, p. 339. The celebrations were to include a fireworks display with 'portraits of Royalty, of the Prime Minister Lloyd George, and a group representation of Sir David Beatty, Admiral of the Fleet, with other military leaders', O'Sullivan and Scott, Footnote 3, *CLVII*, p. 340.
97. To Ottoline Morrell, [c. 13 July 1919], *CLVII*, p. 339.
98. Woolf, 'The Mark on the Wall', *Monday or Tuesday* [1917] (1973), p. 47.
99. [15 October 1919], *CLVIII*, p. 27. [13 and 14 October 1919], *CLVIII*, p. 25. Mansfield refers to this again to Murry the following day: [15 October 1919], *CLVIII*, pp. 26–7.
100. [22 October 1919], *CLVIII*, p. 41.
101. [3 November 1919], *CLVIII*, p. 66. [23 November 1919], *CLVIII*, p. 113.
102. [4 December 1919], *CLVIII*, p. 133.
103. [15 October 1919], *CLVIII*, p. 26.
104. [23 October 1919], *CLVIII*, pp. 45–6.
105. [31 October 1919], *CLVIII*, p. 61.
106. [2 November 1919], *CLVIII*, p. 65. [5 November 1919], *CLVIII*, p. 73.
107. [9 November 1919], *CLVIII*, pp. 81.
108. [3 November 1919], *CLVIII*, p. 66. [26 November 1919], *CLVIII*, p. 122.
109. [31 October 1919], *CLVIII*, p. 61. A Sam Browne belt is a 'leather belt for dress uniform, with a strap passing over the right shoulder,' in common usage from the Boer War onwards, O'Sullivan and Scott, Footnote 3, *CLVIII*, p. 61.
110. [4 December 1919], *CLVIII*, p. 135. This is '[t]he first line of the chorus from "Tramp! Tramp! Tramp!", the well-known song of the Northern armies in the American Civil War, the words and music by G. F. Root.', O'Sullivan and Scott, Footnote 5, *CLVIII*, p. 139. I am grateful to Ali Smith for alerting me to this letter and the previous one cited.
111. [5 October 1919], *CLVIII*, p. 9.
112. [6 October 1919], *CLVIII*, p. 9.
113. [8 October 1919], *CLVIII*, p. 13; [22 November 1919], *CLVIII*, p. 109.
114. [22 October 1919], *CLVIII*, p. 42.
115. [26 October 1919], *CLVIII*, p. 48.
116. [2 November 1919], *CLVIII*, p. 65.
117. [8 November 1919], *CLVIII*, p. 65.
118. [21 November 1919], *CLVIII*, p. 106.
119. [10 November 1919], *CLVIII*, p. 82. The review was published as 'A Ship Comes into the Harbour' in the *Athenaeum*, 21 November 1919, O'Sullivan and Scott, Footnote 1, *CLVIII*, p. 83.
120. [9 November 1919], *CLVIII*, pp. 80–1.
121. To Ottoline Morrell, 15 August 1917, *CLVI*, p. 326.
122. [10 November 1919], *CLVIII*, pp. 82–3.
123. O'Sullivan and Scott, Footnote 1, *CLVIII*, p. 99.
124. [16 November 1919], *CLVIII*, p. 98.
125. [16 November 1919], *CLVIII*, p. 97.
126. [16 November 1919], *CLVIII*, pp. 97–8.
127. These stories are 'Spring Pictures' [1915], 'An Indiscreet Journey' [1915], 'Two Tuppenny Ones, Please' [1917], 'Late at Night' [1917], 'A Dill Pickle' [1917],

'Pictures' [1919], 'Bank Holiday' [1920], and 'The Fly' [1922]. 'Spring Pictures' and 'An Indiscreet Journey' are included in *The Collected Fiction of Katherine Mansfield, Volume 1: 1898–1915*, ed. Gerri Kimber and Vincent O'Sullivan (2012), pp. 435–8, 439–51. The other stories are included in *The Collected Fiction of Katherine Mansfield, Volume 2: 1916–1922*, ed. Gerri Kimber and Vincent O'Sullivan (2014), pp. 22–4, 24–6, 97–103, 178–85, 223–6, 476–80.
128. Quoted in Preston Lockwood, 'Henry James's First Interview', *New York Times* [Magazine Section], 21 March 1915, p. 4. <https://ezproxy-prd.bodleian.ox.ac.uk:7316/docview/97753617?accountid=13042> (last accessed 2 May 2019).
129. Quotes from 'Spring Pictures', *CFVI*, p. 435. Quotes from 'Pictures' and 'Bank Holiday', both *CFVII*, pp. 179, 223.
130. 'An Indiscreet Journey', *CFVII*, p. 447.

4

THE CIVILIAN WAR NOVEL: H.D.'S AVANT-GARDE WAR DEAD

The American imagist poet and novelist H.D. (Hilda Doolittle) was profoundly affected by the Great War, suffering the wartime stillbirth of her and her husband Richard Aldington's 'own sweet dead baby' in May 1915, the death of her brother Gilbert in combat in France in October 1918, and the subsequent death of her father from a grief-related stroke in March 1919.[1] Originally from Bethlehem, Pennsylvania, she had lived in London since 1911 where she was active in the imagist circle of writers and poets. H.D. was not formally involved in the war in any capacity, but experienced air raids in London and the breakdown of her marriage as a result of her husband's presence at the front. H.D.'s belief that the stillbirth of her daughter was a direct result of 'shock and repercussions of war news broken to [her] in a rather brutal fashion', that '[k]haki killed it', became her mode of identification with, and participation in, the scene of mass death around her.[2]

H.D. was the furthest removed from the war of the writers I examine, both spatially and temporally. Already an experimental writer before the war, H.D. – removed from the war in both spatial and temporal terms – provides the most abstract fictional representation of the war dead. In *Bid Me to Live (A Madrigal)* (begun 1918, but not published until 1960), her novel focusing on the wartime period, H.D. represents the civilian war experience: the ways the war permeated home front life, changed perceptions of time and death, and placed heavy emotional burdens on the women at home. There is no death scene or war corpse in this text. The primary death depicted is of a civilian: the death of her child, presented in a fragmentary, disjointed narrative. The depiction of the war dead in non-realist and mediated forms, through her own body and the use of new technologies such as the cinema, presents us with a view of the war dead by a civilian who had never seen them. This chapter examines the formally and thematically avant-garde modes that H.D., the civilian, female, professional writer, chose to write about the war dead, through a close reading of *Bid Me to Live*.[3]

H.D.'s highly experimental and oblique writings on war and war death fit into what Allyson Booth has referred to as 'civilian modernism'.[4] More broadly, the particular literary strategies that characterise H.D.'s modernism include a chronologically disrupted narrative and preoccupation with time; the use of repetition and refrains; the vocabulary of new bodies of knowledge, including psychoanalysis and sexology; and the mixing of highbrow classical, literary and artistic allusion with fragments of British and American popular war culture (poetry, songs, propaganda).[5] An acknowledgement of the newness and novelty of the era is also present: 'Times liberated, set whirling out-moded romanticism [. . .] It was a time of isms. And the Ballet' begins *Bid Me to Live*.[6] Many of these characteristics feature throughout H.D.'s work, but the particular inflection of these in relation to the war makes this a mode of civilian modernism.

Bid Me to Live is one of the texts in H.D.'s self-proclaimed 'Madrigal trilogy', a series of autobiographical novels which chart the Great War years and its aftermath: the others are *Asphodel* (written 1921–2) and *Paint It Today* (1921).[7] My discussion of *Bid Me to Live* is informed by my study of the two undated typescript drafts at the Beinecke Library, Yale University, which are a significant yet neglected resource for the development of the novel.[8] This explicitly autobiographical *roman à clef* retells the story of the First World War years, charting the retrospective stillbirth of Julia (H.D.) and Rafe's (Richard Aldington's) child and the breakdown of their marriage, Rafe's affair with Bella (Dorothy [Arabella] Yorke), and Julia's affair with Cyril Vane (Cecil Gray).[9] It represents what H.D. considered 'the War I story' that she 'had been writing or trying to write [. . .] since 1921', a conclusive version of the trauma story.[10] The multiple, palimpsest-like and contested sites of composition and revision demonstrate that H.D. repeatedly reworked the text over an extended period. H.D. wrote in December 1949 that *BML* (then *Madrigal*) was 'roughed out' in summer 1939, revised after the Second World War in the late 1940s and finished in 1949, but not then published until 1960.[11] Once she had 'corrected and typed out *Madrigal*, last winter [1948]', she was 'able conscientiously to destroy these earlier versions'.[12] This personal wartime story means that the text is concerned with both individual and collective trauma, and works as an avant-garde example of what I term the civilian war novel.

Like many other modernist women writers, H.D. is only now being recognised in her political context.[13] Although critics have noted the profound impact of the war on H.D., there has been insufficient analysis of the literary modes she used to depict her grief in the wake of the Great War, particularly the significance of her repeated attempts to represent the First World War period. There has been some interest in recent years of H.D.'s fictional representations of her wartime stillbirth.[14] Much of the criticism surrounding H.D. and war focuses on her writings from the Second World War: critics such as Ariela Freedman and Julia Goodspeed-Chadwick have focused on texts such as *Tribute to Freud* (1956), *The Gift* (published 1982), and H.D.'s Second World War poetry, primarily *Trilogy* (1946).[15] Previous readings of *Bid Me to Live* have focused on its autobiographical content, such as Caroline Zilboorg's edition of the text, which considers its autobiographical and historical context, or its status as a trauma text: both reading the text as a case study of a traumatised subject (Suzette A. Henke; Freedman) and within a historicised framework of the culture of war trauma (Trudi Tate).[16] My own earlier work traces H.D.'s working through of her wartime trauma in the Madrigal cycle.[17] Goodspeed-Chadwick places H.D. alongside Djuna Barnes and Gertrude Stein as American modernist women writers examining war trauma and the female body, focused predominantly on the Second World War.[18] Critics such as Bryony Randall, Rachel Connor and Laura Marcus have discussed H.D. and war in relation to particular contexts, including time and temporality, and the visual image and cinema (particularly her involvement with the magazine *Close-Up*).[19]

Here, I develop these readings to explore the avant-garde modes that H.D. used to write about the war dead, focusing on three themes: wartime civilian experience; the war and the female body; and mediating the war (specifically, the war and cinema). I suggest that H.D. turned to abstract modes of representation of the war dead in the absence of direct war experience. In this sense, like Katherine Mansfield, she provides an example of civilian modernism, and her writings demonstrate how later modernist writers would depict the war dead.

'It was always the last time': Wartime Civilian Experience and Proleptic Mourning

The civilian or home front novel presents the war and the war dead from the civilian's perspective, either without scenes from the war zones or solely imagined versions of those scenes.[20] In contrast to combatant narratives, typically concerned with representing explicitly war-related experiences and scenes, civilian war novels focus on the domestic, the everyday and the mundane, and the alteration of these things in wartime, as well as the lack of knowledge about the war zones and the continual waiting for news. The frequent use of war diction by civilians to describe home front situations shows the strange combination of military and domestic rhetoric, as we have already seen in Mansfield's correspondence. In *Bid Me to Live*, these rhetorical incongruities occur when Rafe is on leave, as military imagery is written into the domestic setting. The first page of the novel provides a description of the wartime civilian generation as already 'dead':

> Were they extrovert? Introvert? They had no names for these things. True, the late war-intellectuals gabbled of Oedipus across tea-cups or Soho café tables; it was not Vimy or Loos they talked of. What was left of them was the war-generation, not the lost generation, but lost actually in fact, doomed by the stars in their courses, an actuality, holocaust to Mars, not blighted, not anaemic, but wounded, but dying, but dead. (1)

The contemporary discourse of psychoanalysis informs the civilians' talk, rather than the war. However, it is these civilians, away from the battles they refer to, who are named as the 'war-generation', distinguished from those who had died ('the lost generation'). Like Mansfield's self-representation as combatant, civilians, here represented by intellectuals in bohemian Soho, are the ones depicted as wounded and dying combatants, playing on the double meaning of 'late' and suggesting that the civilians are, in fact, the lost generation. The mixed diction of the passage, both of the domestic setting of tea-cups and café tables and of war wounding and death, exemplifies the idea of civilian modernism: a type of rhetorical experimentation that juxtaposes war idioms and imagery with domestic ones.

The war permeates everything in wartime London: 'as the war crept closer [. . .] it absorbed everything' (40). It even enters into and reshapes language, attaching itself as a prefix to the most ordinary of nouns. H.D. writes of 'a war-Sunday morning in a war-ridden city', and Bella is in the 'ultra-fashion of last war-spring' (21, 60). Rico's 'little house of life' had been 'swept away in the war-tornado' and 'the worse war-tide of Paris had washed up Bella' (51, 60). The rhetoric of catastrophe embellishes the mundanity of the civilian war, what H.D. calls elsewhere 'the dreariness of this present' (35). However, the vast mortality did in fact create a wartime atmosphere 'surcharged with death', as H.D. wrote in a 1917 letter to the poet Marianne Moore.[21] In *Asphodel*, H.D. writes of 'the ruin of London' (A 148), and in *Palimpsest* of '[t]his new and empty city, a ghost replica'.[22] In *Bid Me to Live*, wartime London is 'a dead city':

> City of dreadful night, city of dreadful night. She saw the railed-in square, the desolation of the empty street. It was a city of the dead. [. . .] A volcano was erupting. Along streets empty of life, there were pathetic evidences of life that had once been, an ash-bin, a fluttering scrap of newspaper, a cat creeping stealthily, seeking for stray provender. Ashes and death; it was the city of dreadful night, it was a dead city. (65)

The non-human landscape is depicted as a wartime wasteland, its apocalyptic overtones made explicit by allusions to James Thomson's 1874 long poem *The*

City of Dreadful Night and the Bible: 'another spurt of fire and brimstone told them that the war was not yet over' (66).[23] H.D. demonstrates her awareness of the randomness of death 'at any moment' (2), what she refers to later as the 'constant reminder' and 'imminent possibility' of death in wartime London.[24] In 1915 Freud (with whom H.D. would undertake two periods of psychoanalysis in 1933 and 1934) similarly argued: 'it still seems a matter of chance whether a particular bullet hits this man or that; but the survivor may easily be hit by another bullet'.[25] London after an air raid is 'a grave-yard', H.D. asserts, where 'any stone might have been our tomb-stone, a slice of a wall falling, this ceiling over our heads' (6). The multiple air-raid scenes remind the reader of the omnipresent possibility of attack on the home front – Julia 'groped for the matches and the candle that she kept in readiness by her bed, in case of sudden air-alarm' – what H.D. represents as 'the curtains that might at any moment part on carnage in Queen's Square', where she lives (33, 2).

Bid Me to Live is structured around the cycle of Rafe's leaves from the front, greatly contributing to the novel's distorted sense of time. The duration of the war is uncertain and the novel is punctuated by the refrain, 'The war will never be over' (36, 41, 54). Although there is an idealised sense of a prewar period – Julia speaks to Bella 'in the old pre-war style', and Elsa (Rico's German wife) is 'a pre-war Prussian' with 'pre-war German distinction' (54, 42, 51–2) – this past is itself depicted as a war casualty:

> The past had been blasted to hell, you might say; already, in 1917, the past was gone. It had been blasted and blighted, the old order was dead, was dying, was being bombed to bits, was no more. But that was not true. Reality lived in the minds of those who had lived before that August. They had lived then. (11–12)

The metaphor used to describe the effect of the ongoing war is again a military one: 'underneath, she was shot to bits – they all were – waiting for the end. The war will never be over' (41). This background of ongoing conflict and increasing war fatigue results in a type of paralysis, as many situations cannot be resolved until the end of the war: particularly the love triangle between Julia, Rafe and Bella. Julia and Bella decide to leave the decision to Rafe, waiting 'till he comes back', begging the question that implicitly structures the novel: 'Would he come back?' (62).

When he leaves in the novel's opening scene, Rafe gives Julia his service wristwatch in case he does not return. The modernist preoccupation with time is here coupled with new military paraphernalia. Although wristwatches had been used to synchronise troop movement in colonial wars in the late nineteenth century, they were first issued on a mass scale during the First World War, and gradually became popular with civilians. The War Office began to issue wristwatches to soldiers from 1917 onwards, although officers were expected to purchase theirs using their allowance.[26] Wristwatches were necessary for new modes of warfare led by remote command but reliant on the coordination of manoeuvres. A 1916 British War Office handbook of instructions includes a section on the 'Synchronisation of watches', which notes: 'All Officers must acquire the habit of checking their watches daily with the official time', warning that 'any delay at this moment [zero time] may be disastrous'.[27] Considering 'affective encounters with time', Cedric Van Dijick has argued that the wristwatch 'informed an understanding of temporality in corporeal terms'. The wristwatch symbolises 'one's individual relationship to time', but also meant 'public time was now [. . .] literally worn *on* the body'. In the wartime context, it enacted a corporeal imposition of military time', symbolising 'the way in which oppressive systems of time were lived and internalized'. As Van Dijick notes, 'since the Somme an almost obsessive reliance on accuracy and punctuality had heralded a new kind of warfare: precise, timed, synchronized', meaning that 'the wristwatch emerged out of a moment in modern history when temporality [. . .] turned into an oppressive system of control'.[28] This state control of time extended into postwar memorialisation, when the new Two Minutes' Silence presented a temporally limited period of remembrance.[29]

Rafe's officer's watch symbolises 'war-time', the military control of time. Giving the watch to Julia, Rafe puts her under this controlled time, metaphorically making the unwilling civilian into a soldier. H.D. uses this object as a physical embodiment of the strange war-time, as a metaphor of entrapped time, literally behind bars: 'Its disc was covered with round woven wire, like a tiny basket, bottom side up, or a fencer's mask. Time in prison, that time. It ticked merrily away, inside its little steel cage' (8). (Rafe's watch has a shrapnel guard, then called a mesh guard or watch protector, added if the watch didn't have unbreakable glass.) Personified as 'the little demon', the watch is a reminder of the intense pressure during leaves (9).[30] Julia's suggestion that the watch has stopped demonstrates her wish to break out of this military ownership of their time, and the wartime cycle in which they are trapped (9).

H.D devotes much narrative space to exploring the complex emotions produced by this strange set of temporal circumstances. The ritual of Rafe's leaves is established in the opening scene, 'the night before he was going back to France', which follows the pattern of previous leaves: 'He would be going back to France. To-morrow, to-day. They would brew tea (all this had happened before)' (8, 6). The ritual of tea-making reinforces the sense of repetition:

> He was swishing tea-leaves round, he would dump them expertly on a bit of newspaper, spread open on the carpet, and rinse out the tea-pot [. . .] before he poured the preliminary boiling water in the brown pot. Then he would rinse that out again, measure in the tea. (8)

The deliberate, seemingly enforced continuity of the scene provides us with an example of a repeated action as an attempt to defy death, akin to Mansfield's letter-writing. Letter-writing is here depicted similarly as a life-giving ritual: 'As if he (so he said) was kept alive [. . .] by the letters that she sent him' (23). Carrying out a recurring action is an attempt to ensure that Rafe will keep returning:

> Every cigarette, if you came to think of it, was continuity. Chain-smoking. Smoking now, to-night, this evening (this morning) was ritual in sequence; the narcotic incense, the dried crumbled leaf, was actually a leaf, grown with a white flower. Actually, the symbol of this incense was white, narcotic, a white flower. (7)

As Rafe kisses her, Julia is concerned that he will put out her cigarette, symbolically breaking the ritual. The metaphor of incense heightens the cigarette's ritualistic connotations: 'She was holding onto something, the small spark of fire, the smoldering at the end of an incense stick, her cigarette' (10). Despite these repeated attempts at forging continuity, however, it is clear that this is impossible due to the confusion of war-time: 'The watch was the same watch, but time was different. Months, days were smashed. There was no continuity. She had given up pretending' (28).

In the strange war-time punctuated by leaves and returns – and the emotional burdens of both of these states – civilians frequently engaged in a type of proleptic mourning: for their loved ones at the front, and for their generation as a whole. The continual fear throughout the novel that this might be 'the last time' makes for a strange continuous dying in the present tense (17). Rafe repeatedly speaks of the possibility of his own death, which Julia attempts to deny: 'Death? It was not possible. He was going to say it. He did say it' (10). H.D. depicts death as something both imminent and yet continuously ongoing. Julia thinks after one of Rafe's visits:

> She would be alone now to recover from this last leave, till the next leave, if there was a next leave. He was dead already, already he had died a half-dozen times, he was always dying.
> 'I won't come back,' he had said the last time but he came back. (16)

Rafe is in the liminal process of 'always dying', causing Julia to be in a perpetual pseudo-mourning state: 'It was always the last time' (17). This sentiment is repeated: 'The mood, maybe for the last time, was on them' (11); 'the same scene [. . .] herself and Rafe Ashton, for the last time' (40). The banality of the comic expression, 'he was always dying', and the use of present tense, indicates the strange situation of the home front. As Randall argues, 'mimicking the tone of a wife complaining about an irritating yet endearing habit of her husband, poignantly indicates the domesticity of war experience – death in battle is assimilated to the experience of married life'.[31] The sentiment, 'if I don't come back', is variously phrased throughout the text, forming a further refrain (10, 25, 39). Similarly in *Asphodel*, the H.D. character Hermione Gart highlights the oddly temporal status of a husband in the process of dying, discussing someone whose 'husband was *being killed* in Flanders' (*A* 108). Julia refers to Rafe's 'death-fixation' and his various proto-memorial gestures, giving her his watch and 'the last batch of letters that you sent me' (51, 15, 14). H.D. summarises the paradoxical situation of wartime absence experienced by civilian women: 'She had lived with him, absent, so intensely. He would be almost nearer, once he had gone, than he was now' (11).

However, Rafe's fears of not returning are justified. Julia hears stories of other soldiers who have been killed before their next trip home, such as 'Paulette in the *quartier*; she had a child, its father was killed before the next *permission*' (60). The lack of control over one's own time means:

> They were all marking time. Rafe was simply another lover, young officer on leave, *permission* Bella called it, and *I have a rendez-vous with death* was the singular leit-motif of what Bella was saying; she was not living, any more than the rest of them were, in any known dimension. [. . .] Rico made neat pictures, put Bella on a band-box, painted her on a fan. But opening the fan, there were other dimensions, layers of poison-gas, the sound of shrapnel, the motto that ran across the top of the fan when it was spread open was *I have a rendez-vous with death*. Bella had known that boy, too, in Paris. He had gone, and the other in horizon-blue, who came here to see her, would go, probably; what other still? Bella was seeing this, in those terms. Rafe was just another officer on leave, *permission* she called it. (60–1)

Bella, Julia's rival, is already a type of war widow: her lover in Paris has been killed earlier. Like Julia who 'was shot to bits', Bella, revealed as a mourner, is 'shot to pieces' (41, 62). H.D.'s representation of this element of Bella's character and narrative is characteristically oblique. The theatrical imagery associated elsewhere with Bella is combined with military imagery here, producing a complex extended metaphor. H.D. makes two references to the American soldier poet Alan Seeger's 'I Have a Rendezvous with Death', published posthumously in the 1917 collection *Poems* and anonymously reviewed in *The Egoist* by T. S. Eliot, who had taken over the assistant editorship from H.D. and Aldington in June 1917.[32] The poem, conservative stylistically and in terms of content, suggests the soldier's acceptance of death for his country. H.D.'s inclusion of this patriotic fragment, like her later inclusion of lines from war songs, uses popular representations of soldiers as a point of comparison with real soldiers. This passage indicates the uncertainty of the wartime situation for women: the unnatural condition of constant, yet anticipatory, mourning. It is through this revelation that Julia identifies with her rival: 'facing Bella, Julia felt that she was looking at herself in a mirror, another self' (61).

An important element of the civilian experience was the lack of available representation of the war zones. Michael Paris notes:

> the British had been spared any direct experience of the realities of war for well over a hundred years. What most people knew of war came through the reminiscences of veterans, and what they heard in the popular soldiers' ballads, saw in theatricals and read in popular accounts, and that image of war was softened, sanitised and often wildly romantic.[33]

Consequently civilians found it difficult to picture what their loved ones were experiencing and frequently used other modes to write about the war and the war dead. H.D. repeatedly addresses this problem in *Bid Me to Live*, referring to popular representations of soldiers, and civilians' attempts to visualise the war zones. Julia references these popular imaginings as she pictures Rafe:

> She had her allowance from America to live on, and she sent back her separation allowance so that he and some of the other Tommies (before he had his commission) would have the price of coffee or beer or whatever it was they got in those dug-out estaminets, where they crowded in the rain. Was it always raining? (16)

War songs and popular poems are woven throughout the narrative, creating a modernist collage. Writing Rafe a letter after he has left for the front, Julia turns again to sentimentalised representations of soldiers, referencing a war song that is explicitly referred to in the later cinema scene: 'Well, where will you be now with your overcoat collar turned up, asleep? Or have you fumbled in your fabulous old kit-bag for your pipe yet?' (24).[34] In the cinema scene, H.D. also includes misremembered lines of the popular war song 'It's a Long Way to Tipperary', writing '*Good-bye Piccadilly, good-bye Leicester Square*' instead of the lyrics, 'Good-bye Piccadilly, farewell Leicester Square' (75).[35] This suggests that she was remembering the words by heart, and the effect is impressionistic, rather than accurate. The repeated phrases from the song that punctuate the scene represent the polyglot impressions of the war for the civilian: the barrage of war information in written, verbal and visual forms, and the difficulty of validating one form of information over another.

H.D. draws attention to the strange disparity between her prewar experiences of France and its current status as a war zone:

> He was going back to France. France? But France was asphalt melting under a downtrodden, scuffed heel, 'I ought to get these mended.' They walked back to the *Île de France* and sat in the shade on the cobblestones by the river [. . .] (18)

The incongruity of these two differing significations for France (Julia's idealised memories of her and Rafe's prewar time in Paris versus wartime France) demonstrates the civilian difficulty in comprehending the situation in the war zones, where she is only able to visualise the points of departure and return: 'Out there? The train would be moving off, she was spared the horror of that. She had seen so many trains in, off, inevitably running into rows of returned invalids' (21–2). H.D. explicitly refers to the inadequacy of visual (propagandistic) representations at home:

> They had shouted of honour and sacrifice for two years, three years now [. . .] the posters that screamed at one at street-corners had no more reality, not as much, as the remembered Flemish gallery of the Louvre and the abstract painted horror of a flayed saint – they were past feeling anything; she was. (20)

The question of imagination versus reality is shown by Martha, another civilian woman in mourning, who presents a further foil for Julia (after Bella): 'Martha's husband had lately been reported lost, swept off a raft in a river, Mesopotamia (Mespot, Rafe called it). Things like that were so utterly fantastic' (20).

Martha's mourning has been forestalled: her husband, like many others, has been reported 'lost' but not killed. Julia signals her disbelief in the 'utterly fantastic' story that Martha has been told, and dislikes Martha's imaginings of the front because they heroicise and romanticise her husband's fate: 'This morning would be the worst [. . .] Julia would be forced to listen to a story again that was Robinson Crusoe fantasy, a raft in a river. Mespot, out of the Bible, Euphrates?' (20). The scene demonstrates the ultimate lack of knowledge of civilians about the conditions of the war zones, and their recourse to other modes to attempt to comprehend them.

'I HAVE DONE MY BIT, I HAD MY CHILD': THE WAR AND THE FEMALE BODY

The most striking of H.D.'s avant-garde modes is her depiction of the war dead through a turn inwards, using her own body as a mode of representation. Her portrayal of the stillbirth she suffered in 1915 as her war trauma (and as Julia's war trauma) is a particularly female mode of writing about war death, using her body and experience as a means of writing about mass death, similar to Mansfield's depiction of her illness in militarised diction.

The first explicit mention of the child's death in the midst of an air raid immediately posits it as a war death. The air raid, recounted in the past tense in the first chapter, is anticipated by the description of Rafe and Julia's married life in militaristic terms: 'They crawled under *Mercure de France*, barricaded themselves with yellow-backed French novels [. . .] Superficially entrenched, they were routed out by the sound of air-craft' (3). The war has intruded onto the home front, literally and rhetorically, and the pair of writers have unsurprisingly hidden themselves under a mountain of text. Significantly, it is the female civilian Julia, not Rafe, who is injured in the attack:

> she stumbled down the iron stairs (that was the Hampstead flat) and bruised her knee. Just in time to see the tip-tilted object in a dim near sky that even then was sliding sideways and even then was about to drop. Such a long way to come. It drifted from their sight and the small collection of gaping individuals dispersed. Leviathan, a whale swam in city dusk, above suburban forests. My knee. It was a black gash, she might have broken her leg. (3–4)

Julia's wound seemingly gets worse – her knee is initially 'bruised', then becomes 'a black gash' – like the soldier who doesn't initially realise the severity of his wound, and like a traumatic event which is latent in the damage it causes. There is an element of irony too: the suggestion that she has been lucky in that 'she might have broken her leg'. The air raid demonstrates the civilian writer's incorporation of militarised imagery to describe non-war related objects (the novels which become barricades) and the use of literary imagery to describe new war objects (the Zeppelin). The fascination with the spectacle of the Zeppelin is seen in the 'gaping individuals', depicted in similar terms to the 'the rush of heads & bodies turned upwards' in Mansfield's descriptions of air raids in Paris in 1915. H.D. similarly uses imagistic description and literary allusion to aestheticise the experience: Mansfield's 'Ultimate Fish [. . .] flying high with fins of silky grey' is here depicted as Leviathan, a great whale.[36] The new subject matter stimulates literariness, suggesting that H.D.'s modernism, like Mansfield's, is provoked by her wartime civilian context. Mansfield's exhilarated reaction, however, is distinct from the character Julia's pained response. In depicting the war as affecting the female, not the male, body, the scene presents a synecdochal representation of one of the novel's key themes: the assertion of female suffering in wartime. The physical injury pre-empts and represents the larger wound of Julia's stillbirth, but also stands in for the psychological injuries of home front trauma. This highly stylised representation demonstrates H.D.'s avant-garde mode of writing the war dead.

Most importantly, the air-raid scene links the loss of Julia and Rafe's child with the war. The story is introduced in the text obliquely. Attending to her wound leads Julia to think about the child she lost earlier:

> Suddenly, as he filled a basin from the bathroom, her mind, which did not really think in canalized precise images, realized or might have realized that if she had had the child in her arms at that moment, stumbling as she had stumbled, she might have . . . No. She did not think this. She had lost the child only a short time before. But she never thought of that. A door had shuttered it in, shuttering her in, something had died that was going to die. Or because something had died, something would die. But she did not think that. (4)

What has happened to the child is not immediately obvious. There are various layers of retrospective knowledge here: the interesting moderation that 'her mind [. . .] realized or might have realized' implies the explicit presence of a 'present I' narrator suggesting what the 'past I' may have subconsciously thought. The strange fatalism is perhaps an attempt at self-consolation in the imagined scenario: the ellipsis suggests that, even if the child had survived, Julia may have lost it later in the air raid. The passage is seemingly disingenuous in its ironical self-referentiality: Julia apparently 'did not really think in canalized precise images', whereas H.D. was the nominal imagist poet (and the word 'canalized' itself seems to allude to the birth canal). The passage is highly stylised through the repetition of verbs: realise, stumble, think, shutter, die. Comparing the published version with the first typescript draft, we see that in the first draft, the fact the child was stillborn is made explicit:

> Suddenly, as he filled a basin from the bath-room, her mind, which did not really think in canalized precise images, realized or might have realized that if she had had the child in her arms at that moment, stumbling as she had stumbled, she would have bashed its head against the dark wall – it – would – have – been – killed – anyway. No. She did not think this. The child had been still-born and only a short time before. (First draft, pp. 7–8)

The imagined loss of the child in the air raid provides a further example of the strange condition of mourning somehow out of place in wartime, akin to Julia's proleptic mourning for Rafe. In the second typescript draft – the same as the published version – the graphic depiction of the fate of the child and the explicit mention of the stillbirth have been elided, with the child more ambiguously 'lost'. H.D.'s revisions from graphic to elliptical, more moderate imagery suggest her perhaps coming to terms with the events she describes as she reworked the text, or deliberately deciding to make her writing more abstract. This turn towards more moderate and carefully constructed imagery is continued throughout H.D.'s revisions of the text, making the published version less explicit than the typescript drafts, instead allowing narrative juxtaposition to convey the meanings that may previously have been conveyed by explicit description. Significantly, at the end of this sequence Rafe decides to enlist, linking the air-raid scene and the death of the child with his choice to participate and his potential death.

Throughout the novel, Julia's stillbirth is depicted as her war trauma and her mode of participation in the war effort. In the first draft, H.D. writes, 'I have done my bit, I had my child' (first draft, p. 8.). This military phrase draws on the contemporary war language of 'doing one's bit', a phrase typically used to recruit male soldiers but also women war workers, as seen in multiple propaganda posters which depicted women in war industries (see Fig. 4.1). By the second draft and in the published text, this explicit statement linking female participation in the war effort with producing a child

Figure 4.1 Septimus E. Scott, *These Women are Doing Their Bit* (London: Johnson, Riddle & Co., 1916). Sponsored by the Ministry of Munitions. © IWM (Art.IWM PST 3283)

has been deleted. However, H.D. explicitly makes Julia's trauma coterminous with the war throughout the later text, syntactically aligning them: 'The war was not yet a week old and the child that she was just bearing only a few weeks old [. . .] It happened actually almost identically with the breaking out of the war' (32).

H.D. explicitly depicts Julia's stillbirth as a metaphorical death. Julia refers to the stillbirth as 'her near-death' (6), her 'crucification' (first draft, p. 50), changed to her 'crucifixion' (second draft, p. 44), and states she cannot 'go back, step over my own corpse and sweat blood' (26). The only corpse in the text, then, is that of Julia's own imagined body. In the later versions, mentally addressing her husband, Julia compares herself with Christ in the Garden of Gethsemane as a means of asserting the extent of her suffering: 'I spared you what I went through, you do not spare me. I did not tell you; my agony in the Garden had no words' (second draft, p. 50). In the first draft, H.D. represents the stillbirth in graphic and violent imagery of a prolonged and intensely painful metaphorical death. Two extra sentences were deleted in later versions: 'I was paralysed at the prolonged agony of my own death. But I had to go on, had to go on being killed piecemeal' (first draft, p. 50). In *Palimpsest*, H.D. uses the metaphor of stillbirth to more generally express the failed promise of the war generation, intertwining her personal suffering with national trauma: 'They were a still-born generation' of the war (*P* 117).[37]

The scene of Rafe's nightmare demonstrates a different type of intrusion by the war onto the home front and onto the female body. Nightmares allow the graphic descriptions of the horrors of war (or imagination of those horrors) without euphemism or concealment. The scene shows Rafe, as Tate notes, to be 'suffering from a mild form of war neurosis'.[38] In the published version, Julia recounts a night when Rafe 'had muttered incoherently of [. . .] some horses that got caught in their traces or reins and something that happened to someone pulling on the reins, and then something that had happened to the horses' (19). The passage continues:

> Maybe he was making it up, and lying tense and cold beside him she thought that it might be better for him to go on; she did not know if he were awake or asleep. She did not know whether it was better to pretend to be there, to fling arms about a stranger. Now she wondered if he were making it up or was he dreaming? Did he want to make this up, to ruin what she had so carefully preserved, the fact of this room, the continuity of this bed, the presence of herself, the same self beside him? No, he was not making it up. (19–20)

Again we have a focus on preservation, continuity, and the civilian need to maintain the semblance of prewar life; an exercise that H.D. demonstrates required effort. The first draft contains a more graphic and extended version of this section, which was subsequently excised:

> she did not know if he were awake or asleep, but whatever it was he was talking about, he was explicit about the horses and the insides of the horses and the way the cart or ammunition carriage had jammed against a block of concrete; trench? She did not know whether it was better to pretend to be there, to fling arms about a stranger. Now she wondered if he were making it up or was he dreaming? Did he want to make this up, to ruin what she had so carefully preserved, the fact of this room, the continuity of this bed, the presence of herself, the same self beside him[?]
>   She could babble, too, incoherent things, mutter of death and blood. That had happened to her, bleeding to death, almost, but she did not know that[,] She had scarcely known it, not recognized its danger, but it was blood anyhow, and splashed entrails[,] hers. It was her own entrails she thought, torn out like one of those Flemish tortures that we used to gape at in the Louvre and pretend were funny. They were funny. It was all funny. The horses had shouted or screamed, they were not the horses in the bull-ring where they cut out their tongues. She didn't say anything, had not. It was better for the one who talked[,] who shouted and grunted like a stuck-pig. It was better for him, he could talk, [a]wake or asleep or delirious or just faking something. She hoped he were not faking it, acting, for that would be worse, even [than] if it were true. (First draft, pp. 38–9)

Here the content of Rafe's dreams is described with unequivocal bluntness. Julia interprets the intrusion of Rafe's war nightmares onto the home front as an attack on her female civilian role: to preserve the home front and to ensure continuity for the combatant, and her own efforts at preservation. At the same time, Rafe's nightmares make Julia 'present' in combat in ways she couldn't otherwise be: the graphic description of the dream gives her something to abstract herself from, in H.D.'s civilian modernist terms.

The nightmare sequence provokes memories of Julia's own traumatic experience. Like the sections deleted from the first typescript draft, the deleted passage demonstrates the perceived lack of acknowledgement of her simultaneous wartime suffering. The excised passage begins with her assertion of her similarly traumatic experience, implicitly comparing her experience with Rafe's through explicit imagery, and her belief that the birth is her version of the war trauma the men were suffering: 'She could babble, too [. . .]'. The passage is notably one of the most graphic scenes in the text, violently depicting the experience and dangers of her stillbirth. H.D. claims and asserts female suffering in wartime through the motif of physical suffering, and the corporeal experience of the war is transposed onto the female body. H.D. resents the silencing of the civilian trauma in favour of the war victim, claiming, 'It was better for him, he could talk'. The 'Flemish tortures' mentioned are more graphic in the first version of the text: 'his skin in small red painted pieces, a painting, important like that Rembrandt (was it,) or Ruebens' [*sic*] carefully painted slab of raw beef with its veins and fat and the very stench of meat coming from a carefully painted slab of grained marble that it lay on' (first draft, pp. 39–40). The version in the second draft is much more muted: 'the abstract painted horror of a flayed saint' (second draft, p. 34). Working from the published version, Tate argues that when Julia wakes later with a 'muddle of poisonous gas and flayed carcasses' in her head (21), this demonstrates 'Rafe's nightmares which have spilled into her unconscious', signifying that '[r]igid distinctions between woman and man, civilian and soldier, are broken down even as they are invoked'.[39] It seems more likely that H.D. is re-emphasising the differences in these categories, and asserting her own wartime suffering away from the battlefield. Tate notes that Julia cannot voice her trauma, because of the different natures of their war suffering: Rafe's is legitimate, hers is not. H.D.'s deletion of this section in the second draft suggests that she either revised this view or considered it too controversial for publication.

The war is represented, then, through literal and metaphorical incursions onto the home front and the female body: through physical objects such as Rafe's watch; through an air raid; Julia's stillbirth; and via Rafe's nightmare and its effect on Julia. As Julia lies in bed the morning after Rafe has left for the front, this physical incursion of the front onto the female body becomes again apparent:

> The blaze and flame of chemicals was in the room, in the back of her head, her forehead was cooler. She might manage it somehow that the whole head calmed down and the muddle of poisonous gas and flayed carcasses be dispersed somehow. It was actually a taste in her lungs, though while he was here, she had not recognised it, said it was some sort of vague idea, but she knew it was true. He had breathed a taint of poison-gas in her lungs, the first time he kissed her. (21)

Through the metaphor of poison-gas entering her lungs, H.D. uses the new war rhetoric to show the intensely negative effect of the war on the civilian, providing a further example of civilian modernism. The male combatant brings the war back with him when he returns from the war, a type of pollution which contaminates both the female body and the home front: a physical expression of the war affecting all aspects of life. Other examples of Julia's encounters with objects and experiences from the front are accompanied by a sense of being coerced into sharing something against one's will. When Rafe puts his watch on her wrist, the action is violent: he 'tightened it with a hard twist, he bent over her hand, secured the strap in the fresh-cut eye-hole' (15). Rafe tells her he gives it the watch 'to give you some idea – ' presumably of the male combatant experience of war at the front, but this knowledge is unwanted by Julia (15). She instead seems distressed to be physically associated with this military object, resulting in a sense of disorientation: she is 'tugging at the strap to pull off the officer's wrist-watch that had been last time in Loos, Lenz? Where was it? Where is this?' (15). Similarly H.D. describes the female body being involuntarily brought into physical contact with the military: 'Now there was nothing but the rough khaki under her throat. Her chin brushed buttons, her thin-clad chest felt buttons, he was holding her too tight. She didn't say anything' (15). This visceral, corporeal contact with the militaristic is violent and invasive.

Other civilian war novels demonstrate the same unwanted incursion of the war onto the home front. From the beginning of Rose Macaulay's pacifist novel *Non-Combatants and Others* (1916), the war has entered the home front: the drawing-room the protagonist Alix observes from outside seems to be 'full of intelligence and war and softly shaded electric light'.[40] The implicit violence concealed by this democratic syntax and unexpected juxtaposition reminds us of Mansfield's descriptions of air raid nights as 'full of stars and little moons and big zeppelins'.[41] Attempts to imagine the war zones have a physical impact on female characters, as we see when Alix lies awake in the night:

> Her forehead was hot and her feet were cold. She was tense, and on the brink of shivering. Staring into the dark she saw things happening across the seas: dreadful things, ugly, jarring horrifying things. War – war – war. It pressed round her; there was no escape from it.

The war in this scenario, oppressive and claustrophobic, has completely overtaken the home front: 'Every one talked it, breathed it, lived in it'. The letters she receives from those in the war zones are depicted in military metaphors and considered to be potentially lethal: 'They seemed to Alix like bullets and bits of shrapnel crashing into her world [. . .] She might, from her nervous frown, have been afraid of "stopping one"'. Even hearing war songs has a physical effect: leaving the room, she was 'shivering, as if she was cold or very tired, or frightened . . . '. When the other women come in and talk about the 'ripping stories' they have heard about the war, she puts the book she is reading under her pillow 'as a protection against something'.[42]

Like *Bid Me to Live*, *Non-Combatants and Others* includes a scene where the female civilian Alix overhears the nightmares of her soldier brother, an experience that makes her physically ill:

> Outside his own window, John, barefooted, in pink pyjamas, stood, gripping with both hands on to the iron balustrade, his face turned up to the moon, crying, sobbing, moaning, like a little child, like a man on the rack. He was saying things from time to time . . . muttering them . . . Alix

heard. Things quite different from the things he had said at dinner. [. . .] His eyes were now wide and wet, and full of a horror beyond speech. [. . .] Alix, to hear no more, put her hands over her ears and turned and ran into the bedroom. [. . .] Alix was most suddenly and violently sick.

The nightmare continues to affect Alix as she imagines the trenches:

> Whizz-bangs, pom-poms, trench-mortars spinning along and bouncing off the wire trench roof . . . Minnie coming along to blow the whole trench inside out . . . legs and arms and bits of men flying in the air . . . the rest of them buried deep in choking earth . . . perhaps to be dug out alive, perhaps dead . . . What was it John had said on the balcony – something about a leg . . . the leg of a friend. . . pulling it out of the chaos of earth and mud and stones which had been a trench . . . thinking it led on to the entire friend, finding it didn't, was a detached bit . . .

In comparison with Julia's response which asserts her own past wartime suffering, the effect on Alix is again physical: 'Alix, seeing her friends in scattered bits, seeing worse than that [. . .] turned the greenish pallor of pale, ageing cheese'. In both cases, the war and war knowledge are unwanted intrusions, which threaten the female civilian both mentally and physically. Alix's response is to go and live with people who 'probably know nothing about the war, except that there is one'.[43]

Film was also used to examine the same problem of unwanted war images for civilians. Rebecca West's (unacknowledged) inclusion of the 1916 film *The Battle of the Somme* in *The Return of the Soldier* (1918) demonstrates the impact of watching war films on civilians, where the staged 'over the top' scene provides additional imagery for the civilian protagonist Jenny's 'bad dreams' about her soldier cousin away at war:

> By night I saw Chris running across the brown rottenness of No Man's Land, starting back here because he trod upon a hand, not even looking there because of the awfulness of an unburied head, and not till my dream was packed full of horror did I see him pitch forward on his knees as he reached safety – if it was that. For on the war-films I have seen men slip down as softly from the trench-parapet, and none but the grimmer philosophers would say that they had reached safety by their fall. And when I escaped into wakefulness it was only to lie stiff and think of stories I had heard in the boyish voice [. . .] of the modern subaltern.[44]

Whereas Julia and Alix's dreams are interrupted by the nightmares of men home on leave, here the civilian woman's own nightmares are bolstered by images she has seen in the cinema. Again, the impact of these war images on the female civilian is clear: Jenny argues that these troubled dreams 'are the dreams of Englishwomen today'.[45]

In her study of war and the female body, Goodspeed-Chadwick suggests that '[i]n order to protest war and draw attention to trauma suffered by female subjects, the authors evoke corporeal representations', which are 'often grounded in the author's personal experience'. She asserts the radical nature of H.D.'s representations of her trauma, arguing that 'female presence and sometimes female corporeal suffering during wartime are transgressive literary and sociohistorical acts'.[46] H.D.'s depiction of her stillbirth as war trauma is an avant-garde literary strategy, as the direct comparison of female suffering with male suffering in the war remains controversial. Although she wasn't the only writer to link war death with childbearing, representing the war dead through this mode demonstrates her experimental and avant-garde method, and the aesthetic distance between her work and the work of other writers that I have discussed.[47]

'The dead were watching destruction': Mediating the War Dead

The cinema scene is the culmination of a chapter which depicts another air raid and its aftermath. H.D. depicts the war dead by describing a group of soldiers in a cinema on the home front, watching a non-war-related film set in Italy which includes a possibly fatal car crash. The cinema scene is the key scene in the text to depict soldiers *en masse*, symbolically 'all the soldiers in the world', where the use of the relatively new medium of cinema provides a particularly modern mode of representation, and one of the only cinema scenes in a First World War novel to use the medium to write about the war dead (74).

Going to the pictures was a relatively new experience in wartime England. The industry had been established in the two decades prior to 1914, with the first cinema showings in Britain and in the US in the 1890s. Enthralment with the new technology is evident in H.D.'s description, even when writing about the dead. During the war years, the cinema was a popular entertainment in Britain for showing war films and other films, frequently comedies. As critics such as Andrew Kelly and Michael Hammond have suggested, the cinema changed and developed in wartime.[48] Michael Paris notes that although initially viewed by the British government as 'simply frivolous entertainment; a crude indulgence for the pleasure of the lower classes', the cinema was increasingly harnessed for propagandistic purposes.[49] Marcus notes that in the three years in which official films were produced, 240 were released, alongside 152 issues of official newsreel.[50] Early newsreels 'were full of scenes of marching men, laughing as they accepted cigarettes and flowers from the crowds of onlookers who cheered them on their way to France'.[51] War films offered civilian audiences one of the few visual representations of the war zones, providing images to help them imagine what their loved ones were experiencing. As documentaries, they frequently included recreations or representations of battles: the most famous is *The Battle of the Somme* (1916), a film which over 20 million people saw in the first six weeks of its release: incredibly, an estimated 80 per cent of the British adult population.[52] Other fictional wartime films were frequently highly propagandistic in purpose.[53] On the other hand, non-war-related films remained highly popular, offering audiences a means of escapism. This was true both on the home front and in the war zones. There were twenty makeshift cinemas set up within the British sector of the Front by mid-1916, which showed predominantly comedies (soldiers preferred American comedies and Charlie Chaplin was a favourite).[54] A cover of the *Illustrated London News* from August 1918 shows bedridden soldiers convalescing in an American base hospital in France watching a Chaplin film projected onto the ceiling (see Fig. 4.2).[55]

The connections between modernity, modernism and cinema have been explored at length by critics, frequently interested to trace the similar perspectives, techniques and narrative experimentation in cinematic representation and modernist writing.[56] As Marcus notes, modern war and film, developing contemporaneously, have 'a complex and profound interconnection, as twin technologies of modernity'.[57] It is not my intention here to trace how H.D.'s modernist techniques are analogous with cinematic narrative, or to examine how her interest in cinema influenced or inflected her writing. My reading of this scene focuses on its dramatisation of the difficulty of civilian engagement with the war, and the links between cinema and memorialisation, which H.D. consciously draws on in this scene. Representing the war dead before they had died constitutes a type of proto-memorialisation of the men. Using the new technology of cinema represents a particularly modern, secular mode of memorialisation.

H.D.'s choice of the cinema as a mediation of the war dead is particularly fitting, because of cinema's very nature as itself already past: the production of film necessitates a lapse of time. Laura Mulvey notes 'the resonance of death that culture and the human imagination have associated with photographic images'.[58] H.D.'s use of the link between photography and death recalls and reimagines Victorian memorial photography, which simultaneously draws on the role of wartime cinema in proto-commemoration. Hammond has analysed the phenomenon of the 'Roll of Honour' films, which presented photographs of dead or missing soldiers as a means of honouring and remembering on a local scale: 'the cinematic expression of the common newspaper practice of publishing photographs and listing the names of local men who were serving'.[59] The initial popularity of these explicit acts of commemoration demonstrates the power of cinema in this period, even when the images being shown were still ones: 'the photographs, paradoxically still images projected by an animating machine, arrest for a brief moment the momentum of modernity'.[60] Hammond links these films to the slide shows and phantasmagoria of the nineteenth century, suggesting that

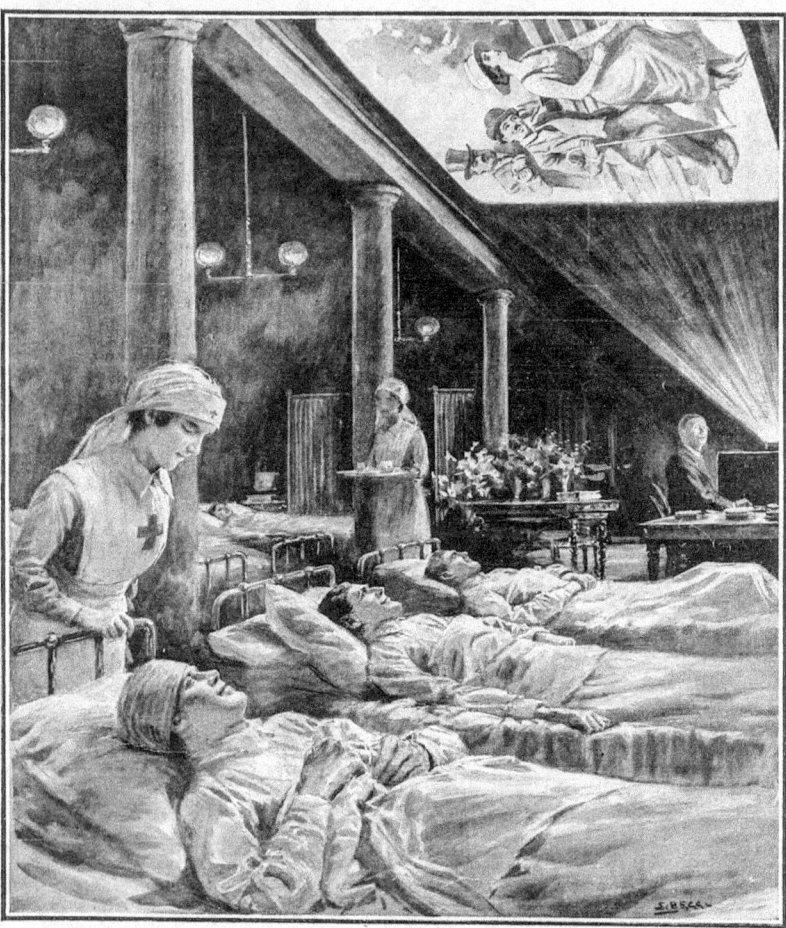

Figure 4.2 Samuel Begg, 'A Hospital-Ceiling as a Screen for Moving Pictures: A Cinema for Bedridden Wounded Soldiers at a Base in France', Cover of *Illustrated London News*, 10 August 1918. © Illustrated London News Ltd/Mary Evans

'[g]iven this older continuum of visual engagement and the cinema's associations with the showmanship of the carnival, the series of static images in the Roll of Honour films take on the qualities of apparitions'.[61] Marcus writes of the impression of cinema as a 'ghost-world':

> This perception of the spectrality of cinematic, and photographic, images reemerged with striking force for many viewers of the war films, in a context in which the soldiers pictured on the screen were very likely to be corpses by the time the films were viewed, granted a ghostly posthumous existence on the screen.[62]

Hammond suggests similarly that 'from the outset the cinematic image had been associated with the spirit world':

> The official war film *Battle of the Somme* provided an example of re-animated soldiers in a faked attack that was undoubtedly the main attraction of the film. By late 1917 it had circulated throughout the country and the depiction of these soldiers going over the top had taken on the texture of ghosts.[63]

Andrew Shail has noted H.D.'s linking of soldiers with the cinema, and I argue that this is primarily because of the association of photography and cinema with the dead.[64] As Roland Barthes notes of photography, equally applicable to cinema: 'that rather terrible thing which is there in every photograph: the return of the dead'.[65]

The air raid which occurs before Julia and Vane go to the cinema establishes the carnivalesque and later hallucinogenic quality of the chapter: an extension of the ongoing theme that '[t]hings were all out of shape' (63). The scene is punctuated by the sounds of the ongoing raid: 'There would be this pause, then there would be the tic-tic-tic again' (63). Vane, having come over to take Julia out for dinner, successfully encourages her to leave the house to go to a restaurant, defying air raid regulations and linking illicit sexual and war participation. In contrast to the dangerous reality of the ongoing air raid – 'A sudden clang very near, then swift diminuendo, an ambulance' – the atmosphere in the restaurant is of shared relief and escapism (66). The air raid has brought people, including 'many officers', into an intimacy through a sense of survival, suggesting civilian and military experience as analogous to some extent: 'This was a party [. . .] It was the aftermath of another air-raid, they were all safe' (68). However, unlike other scenes where Julia asserts her own war participation, this moment demonstrates her desire to escape the war. Julia blames her evasive behaviour on the wine, which Vane notes she has hardly drunk. She finds comfort in the wine being prewar – 'These grapes were grown on another continent, another world, before there had been war' – and this escapism is part of her attraction to Vane 'who did not talk of war' (69).

H.D. uses the motif of intoxication to suggest that the civilian, outside of her normal state, is unable to prevent thoughts of the war and war dead occurring. Julia's thoughts, shifting between remembered scenes and the present one, move on to soldiers and the problem of civilian culpability in the war deaths:

> Now the room was this room and her room dissolved into the smoke of countless cigarettes of other officers on leave. All the other officers were the same, they were the same shape. They all wore brown belts. They wore, she supposed wrist-watches. They all thought alike. They were so many paper-dolls, a string of paper-dolls, a hundred, a thousand officers on leave. (71)

The depersonalising effect of the war has resulted in the generic appearance of the men, all exact replicas who even think in the same way. The 'smoke of countless cigarettes' generates the hallucinatory nature of the scene where the unquantifiable soldiers move from a hundred to seemingly a thousand present.

> The palms of her hands cupped the crystal goblet. She held solid crystal in her hand. A shifting plane of gold that had been Rhineland grapes steadied her, concentrated her, held her to her centre. Cyclone-centre, she had thought. But to achieve the very centre, it had been necessary for a million young men to die. It had been necessary. . . but don't think. There they all are, shouting, and now that group swaying to Tipperary.
>
> 'It's getting very hot, don't you think we better go now?' For she could not endure the thought of even the very least of these young men going back . . . going back . . . But this was madness. This was touch of fever. Impossible to live so intensely, keyed-in to all this. They're happy, aren't they? Well, let me be happy with the same sort of desperation.
>
> She placed the goblet carefully back on the table. Yes, the room was going round. No, she was not drunk. Or was . . . two glasses . . . yes, it was obvious that she had a touch of fever.
>
> Yes, she must get out. Yes, she must go home. (71)

Although the 'solid crystal' goblet provides something definitive to hold onto, like the cigarette that Julia holds earlier, the idea of powerlessness dominates. Julia's thoughts demonstrate the civilian's sense of culpability and impotence in imagining the war. The image of Julia being '[c]yclone-centre', held in place by the prewar wine, suggests that the war continues around her but does not harm her, the calm at the centre of the storm. Here we see the civilian breaking down at the thought of the numbers of men dying in the war: Julia, in her intoxicated, even feverish, state, explicitly acknowledges to herself that her secure position on the home front is the result of these deaths of 'a million young men'. The repetition of 'it had been necessary', as though to convince herself, suggests the problematic nature of this justification. Her civilian guilt is evident: 'They're happy, aren't they?', she attempts to reassure herself. She is faced with a visual, almost cinematic image of the soldiers ('There they all are'), shouting both to each other and of their presence, and the move into the present tense at the end of the first paragraph heightens their sense of immediacy. The image of the soldiers 'swaying to Tipperary' combines Julia's war-generated tipsiness with the civilian difficulty in picturing the war, turning instead to stock tropes and popular representations, as we have seen before. Here again a war song is referenced to represent the men's experiences, immediately recognisable to the reader without quotation marks.[66] The war dead, the scene suggests, are the repressed of the text, and their appearance – or real men recalling the war dead – makes the narrator feverish and almost incoherent.

Julia's repeated assertion that she has participated in the war is extended here to the suggestion that she has already died in the war. Vane's description of his cottage in Cornwall provokes her to imagine the imminent deaths of the men:

> It was haunted, he said. But haunted with something different, far ghosts, not real near ghosts, men who might be ghosts to-morrow, the latest vintage (1917) grapes to be crushed. . . There they all were. But she was already cast out, trodden under foot, she already had died. Already she was out of her body, she patronised them in her tolerance. She had escaped, was dead, they had that yet to do.
>
> They would be going back to-morrow, this morning. She would be going back. . . back to a room that was tomb. . . or womb that had ejected her. There she was standing against the door she had just closed. (72)

Here we see H.D. drawing on discourses of both the spectral and the religious, as well as popular American war culture. This is the mass version of the individual proleptic mourning that Julia is engaged in with Rafe, where Julia is anticipating the inevitable future deaths of the men. Here she aligns herself with the soldiers, even suggesting that her knowledge of death is superior to them. Death is presented as liberation – she had 'escaped', whereas the men still 'had that yet to do'. The time sequence is fatalistic: 'They would be going back to-morrow'. The linking of the images of the men and the wine exemplifies H.D.'s unconventional mode of writing the war dead. She draws on the lyrics of the American Civil War song *The Battle Hymn of the Republic* in describing the men as being 'trodden under foot', presenting the violent deaths of the soldiers through the metaphor of grape-pressing: 'He is trampling out the vintage where the grapes of wrath are stored'.[67] The reference to blood as wine also clearly links the soldiers to Christ and the tradition of communion, comparing their sacrifice with his death on the cross: a religious allusion that is not surprising given H.D.'s Moravian background. The first draft is more graphic in its description of these soldiers: 'men who might be ghosts to-morrow, the latest vintage 1918 grapes to be crushed, red blood to pour' (first draft, p. 133). The reference to 'red blood' is elided in subsequent versions, consistent with H.D's attempts to reduce the more violent and graphic descriptions in the text. The further imagery she uses links the idea of her having already died – the return to the tomb – with the imagery of stillbirth, in an inverted image of the 'womb that had ejected her'.

The cinema offers a means of escapism from the images Julia has created for herself: 'Pictures? [Vane] was offering her pictures, he was offering another dimension' (72). Inside the cinema, the theme of participation continues. Julia detaches herself from the outside world, 'the hectic aftermath' of the air raid and by extension the war: 'It was all very clear now. What was going on outside, was going on outside. It had nothing to do with her. There they sat centralised, the Tree and the Angel, *revenants*' (72–3).[68] Their spatial positioning – centralised – contradicts Julia's disavowal of her part in what is going on outside. Julia and Vane are both central to the action and removed from it. This tension occurs throughout the text as a whole, representing the problem of the civilian's participation in the war. Like the wine before it, here the intoxicant is cigarette smoke: 'The pit beneath them was filled with smoke of countless cigarettes that wafted a cosmic brew, a sort of narcotic dope of forgetfulness' (73). The smoke prevents Julia thinking about what she doesn't want to remember: both her intolerable home situation and the 'million young men' who have died in the war (71). Despite its ameliorating effect, the smoke comes from 'countless cigarettes' of soldiers in the pit below them: another reminder of the numbers of men involved in the war effort.

Julia and Vane's position in the cinema – and in relation to the men in the pit – has now shifted. Previously 'centralised', they are now awkwardly, uncomfortably placed, on the periphery: 'seated at an awkward angle in the corner of a box, the only seats left in the house' (73–4). This motif of being liminally positioned is significant, and recalls Edith Wharton peering through the peephole in *Fighting France* as we saw in Chapter 2: the question of civilian engagement with the war depicted through the motif of sight and perspective. Julia and Vane's position gives a distorted viewpoint, 'too near and too high', meaning they are not seeing the image as they should: 'They peered over the edge of the box and a foreshortened car dashed round a sunlit cliff' (74). The idea of gaining perspective on the war situation is very important:

> They were not good seats, but the last in the house and it had been necessary for some reason to come here. To-night, something was decided. As

> she peered over the edge of a box, she was looking down on the screen. She had been summoned or invited or propelled toward this box, this seat in the circle.

The passive tense and vagueness of the decision made ('something was decided') heightens the sense of a lack of agency and fatalism in the language. Positioning is again significant, although not immediately straightforward. Julia has been propelled toward a seat 'in the circle', suggesting inclusion and participation, but she remains in the position of an outsider, with a disadvantaged perspective: the car on the screen is described as 'slanting, gigantic, foreshortened below her line of vision' (75).

> Below her, below them, were the thousands; it seemed that all the soldiers in the world, symbolically, were packed into this theatre. There was music, too near, pouring at them from an organ, playing the usual sentimental ditties, and the voices of the thousand thousands of all the soldiers in the world were joining in to swell this chorus, this Day of Judgement; how many of them would come back? (74)

The soldiers, who represent 'all the soldiers in the world', are participating in, and endorsing, contemporary representations of themselves in the 'sentimental ditties' to which they sing along. H.D. employs this stereotype of the happy and naïve soldier to heighten the pathos of the question of how many would return. Here we see an updated version of the scene set in a church converted into a makeshift hospital in *Fighting France*, where Wharton watches the convalescing soldiers singing a hymn, discussed in Chapter 2. Rather than a church, H.D.'s soldiers are in the modern secular space of a cinema, but there are clear religious overtones seen in the organ and the reference to this 'Day of Judgement'. The music Julia and Vane hear – like the images they see – is 'too near', suggesting a broader difficulty in gaining perspective on the contemporary war situation. This positioning is reminiscent of Freud's consideration of the war in 1915:

> Swept as we are into the vortex of this war-time, our information one-sided, ourselves too near to focus on the mighty transformations which have already taken place or are beginning to take place, and without a glimmering of the inchoate future, we are incapable of apprehending the significance of the thronging impressions, and know not what value to attach to the judgements we form.[69]

Freud suggested that comprehension of the war and its meaning at the present moment was impossible: a sense that is apparent in H.D.'s text begun and set in wartime.

H.D. creates the commemorative aspect of the scene through traditional motifs of memorialisation. Watching from her limited viewpoint, Julia 'realised that the silver wavering [of the film projection] was the very shape and texture of olive-leaves, flickering in the wind' (74). Olive leaves, representing both peace and victory, were traditionally used to crown victorious warriors. As the first of many classical allusions within this section, H.D. evokes earlier modes of war memorialisation and the glorification of heroes slain in battle. The olive leaves are only indirectly linked with the men here – even the image of olive leaves is 'flickering' and uncertain – but H.D.'s use of modern technology to recall classical war commemoration is a particularly modernist means of presenting the war dead, or soon-to-be war dead. The scene offers a proleptic memorialisation of the soldiers, which links into the choice of the medium of film as an inherently historical medium: that what we see on the screen must, by necessity, already be past.

Expecting a Hollywood film, Julia notes that the setting of the film is unusual: 'Oddly, it was not America [. . .] but it was Italy' (74). However, this is not a war film, but a dramatic narrative including a love triangle and a fast-moving car:

> The car swept on. She was dragged forward with the car and the voices rose up in rhythm to the inevitable. The car would swerve, would turn, it swerved, it turned, they swerved, they turned with it, it was dashing to destruction along the edge of a narrow cliff, they were dashing with it. But no, *good-bye Leicester Square*, the car swept on. She edged forward further, her eyes were adjusting, focussing to this scene of danger without. It was danger without. Inside she was clear, the old Greek katharsis was at work here, as in the stone-ledged theatre benches of fifth-century Greece; so here, a thousand doomed, the dead were watching destruction, Oedipus or Orestes in a slim car, dashing to destruction. (74)

The mode of description mimics the action on screen, with the short clauses imitating the rapid progress of the car. The audience, in their involvement with the film, move with the car, and thereby share the car's fate – with the men. The destruction of the car stands in for the men, made explicit through a further fragment of 'It's a Long Way to Tipperary'. Danger is displaced, depicted as outside the cinema and on the screen in the scene of destruction they watch. The description of 'the dead [. . .] watching destruction' provides us with the epitome of H.D.'s avant-garde representations: representing war death by describing a group of soldiers watching a film of a car speeding to destruction in a cinema. Describing the soldiers while still alive, innocently enjoying light, escapist entertainment, singing along to wartime ditties and enjoying the adventure story unfolding on the screen, heightens the poignancy of the scene and adds to its pathos. At the same time, H.D. explicitly links the soldiers to Greek tragic heroes, 'Oedipus or Orestes', suggesting their deaths are inevitable and the war itself to be a tragedy. The deliberate anachronism of Greek tragic figures travelling in the car demonstrates the mixture of the modern and classical, which is a key element of H.D.'s modernism.

Julia and Vane's awkwardly situated position in the cinema with a number of soldiers highlights the tension between soldier participation and civilian observation. Julia is enthralled by the moving images, moving herself closer to see better, and explicitly considers herself to be experiencing the film – and the fate – with the men:

> *Good-bye Piccadilly.* No, it swerved, it bent, they swerved, they bent with it. The multitude, herself, Vanio, all of them swerved and turned. She was part of this. She swerved and veered with a thousand men in khaki, toward destruction, to *the sweetest girl I know.* (74–5)

Julia's repeated assertions of being 'part of this' claim her own participation in the war through her stillbirth. However, H.D.'s awareness of the incongruity of this female war participant is demonstrated in her particular choice of lyrics about the sweetheart waiting on the home front. The female war participant has no place in this song.

The question of fatalism underpins this section. There is a recurrent rhetoric of the inevitable: the soldiers' voices 'rose up in rhythm to the inevitable'; in following the car, they were 'all rushing toward some known goal'; and the enemy in the film 'projects himself forward toward the same inevitable screen-destruction' (74–5). Similarly, there is a narrative certainty or fatalism in the film on the screen. The story follows a typical narrative plot and H.D.'s description suggests its typicality: 'there was the usual mountain slope, hairpin bend' (74). The film's protagonist demonstrates this sense of narrative convention:

> Striding with hero-boots toward a door at the end of a seemingly endless corridor, he was yet striding toward some known goal, some known objective. It was not yet. But soon there would be some unravelling of this mystery, *it's a long way to go.* (75)

Despite various narrative and visual clichés, however, the audience do not necessarily know the ending to the film. H.D. here represents the wartime lack of knowledge of how long the war would go on (represented in the 'seemingly endless corridor'). The need for the narrative 'unravelling of this mystery' is also arguably a desire for some larger understanding of the war's purpose and its duration, seen in the reference to the war song. Read in conjunction with the assertions of inevitability, the unravelling represents the implied narrative conclusion: the death of the soldiers. The repeated allusions to tragic heroes compound the sense of fatalism.

The scene ends with a possible solution to the 'mystery', which comes in the guise of a woman: 'This was the answer to everything, then, Beauty, for surprisingly, a goddess-woman stepped forward' (75). We see, through Julia's perspective, the ability of the viewer to impose their own imaginative desires onto the actress on the screen: a topic H.D. addressed in the first section on 'Beauty' in her contribution 'The Cinema and the Classics' in *Close-Up* in 1927.[70] In the process of imaginative imposition H.D. describes here, her particular choice of classical mythology is significant. The woman is characterised initially as the Greek 'Persephone in Enna' (75), the maiden abducted by Hades and taken to the underworld where she becomes queen, associated with both the spring and the dead. Her association with Enna, in Sicily, Italy, fits the film being set in Italy and the frequent motif of Italy, the place of H.D. and Aldington's prewar courtship, and by extension Julia and Rafe's. Next she is characterised as 'a hooded woman, Demeter, looking out': Persephone's mother, demonstrating the woman's capacity as mourner, as she searched and grieved endlessly for her child. Finally she is characterised as 'watching from the rocks (Primavera with her flowers) the flight of another car, rounding the same bends, in tangible perspective' (75). 'Primavera with her flowers' refers both to the Greek myth and perhaps to the fifteenth-century painting *Primavera* by Sandro Botticelli, which H.D. and Aldington most likely saw together in the Galleria dell'Accademia in Florence in May 1913, during their travels in Italy.[71] These classical allusions therefore draw together the themes of death, mourning and birth. The woman on the screen is described as 'Venus and the looking-glass, Persephone in Enna, Primavera': here H.D. expands her metaphor to liken the woman to the Roman myth of Venus and her mirror, representing beauty and fertility (76).[72] The subsequent statement – 'There are violets in the air' – reminds us both of Persephone's association with violets, and violets as a symbol of mortality and immortality, appropriate for a scene concerning the war dead (76).[73]

Again we see the invocation of conventional narrative tropes. The heroine's role becomes clear, as the love interest in the typical triadic plot structure:

> Love-motive. She is watching for the first young man – the hero? – while another – the enemy? – rounds the same curves, projects himself forward toward the same inevitable screen-destruction. This time, surely, this unknown but exactly apprehended 'other' must dash off, rounding the last terrific hairpin bend, to inevitable destruction. But not yet.
>
> The Greek messenger will convey all that, presently, entering with ghost-gesture, indicating with ghost-gesture, the solution of the mystery. Not yet. (75)

The wartime context becomes explicit in the binary, yet uncertain categorising of the two men as 'hero' and 'enemy'. It is impossible to distinguish which is which, and both seem prey to 'the same inevitable screen-destruction'. Again, classical allusion enhances the modern: the woman is now characterised as the Greek messenger Hermes, responsible for conducting souls into the underworld and providing 'the solution of the mystery'. What has been a scene of leisured entertainment has become a memorial one.

The female actress comes to represent Beauty itself; a redeeming figure in the ugliness of wartime, and one interestingly not finally gendered:

> There she was exactly incorporated, no screen-image. Here was Beauty, a ghost but Beauty. Beauty was not dead. It emerged unexpectedly in the midst of this frantic maelstrom. The Spirit moved, gestured. The smoke from the thousand cigarettes was incense, breathed by ghosts-to-be, toward Beauty. Julia was part of this, part of the teeming crowded theatre, one of the audience, one with them, *goodbye Leicester Square. It's a long, long way.*
>
> But not too long, not unattainable. (76)

The motif of smoke becomes incense in the worship of beauty, which has survived despite the times. The closing feeling seems hopeful in that Beauty still exists, and the 'not too long' suggests that the war will soon be over and soldiers will be able to return home. Unfortunately, however, the redeeming illusion of Beauty is broken when the lights go up:

> The theatre light switched on at the interval, showed the thousand uncovered heads, all alike, smoothed back, here and there a white arm in a sling. For the most part, the arms in slings wore khaki bandages. That is what she saw.
>
> She was gazing into a charnel-house, into the pit of inferno. 'Our languid lily of virtue nods perilously near the pit.' The old-fashioned theatre curtain now mercifully swept to the floor. Heavy dusty maroon velvet had mercifully slid across the veil of the temple, where just a moment since, a miracle of light and shadow had embroidered in luminous threads the garment of a goddess. (76)

The men are either already injured, hence their being on the home front, or are soon to be killed. The potential manner of their deaths is represented in their synecdochal representation in body parts, seen in terms of heads and arms. Julia has already asked Vane to 'Take me away', and she is next seen standing on 'unsteady cramped legs, her back to the pit of inferno', seeming to turn away from it (76). Is there something ameliorating in the mention of the 'old-fashioned theatre curtain' or the 'dusty box-curtain with looped tasselled cords, like a curtain in a Victorian doll's house' (76)? The modern film and the experience of watching it are concealed by something antiquated, with the adjective 'mercifully' used twice in this context. At the close of this chapter, and for the first time directly, the word 'heroic' is used for the men: 'The voices rose again from the pit, voices of heroic angels, surging on toward their destruction, *pack all your troubles in your old kit bag and smile, smile, smile*' (76). The 'heroic angels' are glorified and pitied for their inevitable fate, and the inclusion of a war song represents both their stoicism and naïveté. The conclusive feeling of this avant-garde scene of proleptic memorialisation is pity.

Conclusion

It is clear that H.D. wrote about the war in part to understand her traumatic experiences better, even many years later. I have argued that *Bid Me to Live* presents an example of the civilian war novel, by examining three different areas of representation within the text. First, the depiction of wartime civilian experience, where I discussed the environment of wartime London, the strange war-time presented in the novel and the condition of continual proleptic mourning, and the attempts by civilians to imagine the front in the absence of experience or reliable representation. Second, I examined the war in relation to the female body, discussing the air-raid scene where Julia is injured, Julia's stillbirth as her war trauma, and the scene of Rafe's nightmare. H.D.'s deliberately provocative assertion of female suffering during wartime, demonstrated by her decision to portray her stillbirth as a mode of war participation, constitutes a necessarily female mode of writing about the war dead. The novel's significant depiction of parallel suffering to that of the men makes it a political text which implicitly protests the effects of the war on women.

Finally I discussed the air raid and cinema scene, particularly the motif of the cinema as a means of addressing the problem of civilian representation of the war dead. H.D.'s use of the new technology of film provides an avant-garde mode of proleptically representing the war dead and attempting memorialisation, as she presents the soldiers before their death. The new medium of cinema was fascinating for contemporaries and a frequent subject for literary representation. Simultaneously, feelings about soldiers, the war and the war dead were difficult to represent in writing. Using the cinema as a type of mediation of the war dead was both aesthetically innovative and allowed H.D. some distance from a painful subject. The film's status as past event made it a particularly useful tool for writing about the war dead, from the postwar position of H.D. writing the text. The ending of the scene has already been determined, accounting for the motif throughout of the fatalistic, the inevitable. The scene therefore enacts a type of proleptic mourning for, and memorialisation of, the men.

More generally, H.D.'s writings demonstrate the immediate and longstanding destructive and psychologically damaging effects of the war on the home front. Her civilian modernism draws together a variety of allusions and references, including British and American popular war culture, new bodies of knowledge, such as psychoanalysis and sexology, and classical and religious allusion. These non-traditional modes of representation suggest that H.D. considered traditional commemorative forms to be no longer appropriate or useful, and her avant-garde war novel provides an early example of how war commemoration and literary innovation would become intertwined in the postwar period.

NOTES

1. Letter from Aldington to H.D., 4 August 1918, in *Richard Aldington and H.D.: The Early Years in Letters*, ed. Caroline Zilboorg (1992), p. 120.
2. H.D., *Tribute to Freud* [1956], intro. Peter Jones (1971), p. 46. H.D., *Asphodel* [1921–2], ed. Robert Spoo (1992), p. 108. Further references will be included in the text, preceded by *A*. The war news was the sinking of the *Lusitania* in May 1915, causing the deaths of 1,198 passengers and crew, and precipitating America's entry into the war in April 1917.
3. I use avant-garde to refer to 'new and experimental ideas and methods in art, music, or literature', *Lexico*, <https://www.lexico.com/en/definition/avant-garde> (last accessed 4 April 2019). For further explication, see Renato Poggioli, *The Theory of the Avant-Garde* [1962], trans. by Gerald Fitzgerald (1968); Peter Bürger, *Theory of the Avant-Garde* [1974], trans. by Michael Shaw (1984).
4. Booth, *Postcards from the Trenches: Negotiating the Space between Modernism and the First World War* (1996), p. 5.
5. For a reading of H.D.'s modernism including how it 'engages with the major theories or knowledges, such as psychoanalysis and sexology', see Polina Mackay, 'H.D.'s Modernism', in Nephie J. Christodoulides and Polina Mackay (eds), *The Cambridge Companion to H.D.* (2012), p. 52.
6. H.D., *Bid Me to Live* [1960], ed. Caroline Zilboorg (2011), p. 1. Further references will be included in the text.
7. H.D., *Asphodel* [1921–2] (1992); H.D., *Paint It Today* [1921], ed. Cassandra Laity (1992). The trilogy is sometimes extended to become the 'Madrigal cycle', including the novel *HERmione* [1927], intro. Perdita Shaffner (1981). Stanford Friedman has suggested that H.D. perhaps echoes Aldington's war poem 'Madrigal' in naming her trilogy, noting that the term 'madrigal' is ironic, 'evoking in the midst of war the image of a lyric form associated with Elizabethan love songs in timeless pastoral settings', in 'Return of the Repressed in H.D.'s Madrigal Cycle', in Susan Stanford Friedman and Rachel Blau DuPlessis (eds), *Signets: Reading H.D.* (1990), pp. 233–4. Claire Tylee notes that '[a]n echo, a slightly varying repetition, is fundamental to the madrigal-form', which is relevant to my discussion of these similar but variant texts, in *The Great War and Women's Consciousness* (1990), p. 238. She notes the significance that 'the word "madrigal" (that H.D. insisted on, despite her publishers) is supposed to have derived from the Latin, meaning "of the womb"', p. 238.

8. H.D. Papers, Yale Collection of American Literature, Beinecke Rare Book and Manuscript Library, *Bid Me to Live*, First typescript draft. Parts I–IX with corrections by H.D. Not dated. YCAL MSS 24, Series II, Box 20, Folders 630–2; and Second typescript draft. Parts I–XI with corrections by H.D., used as typesetting copy. Not dated. YCAL MSS 24, Series II, Box. 20, Folders 633–8.
9. In a *Newsweek* interview in May 1960, H.D. said of *BML* 'I am Julia', cited by Janice Robinson, *H.D.: The Life and Work of an American Poet* (1982), p. xiv. A number of the group wrote their own *romans à clef* about this period, and their texts include D. H. Lawrence's *Aaron's Rod* (1922), John Cournos's *Miranda Masters* (1926), and Richard Aldington's autobiographical novel *Death of a Hero* (1929). Helen McNeil suggests that Ezra Pound depicted H.D. 'as the war-wounded Dido of Canto 7' in *The Cantos*, 'Introduction' in *Bid Me to Live* (1984), p. xiii.
10. H.D., 'H.D. by Delia Alton' [1949–50], in Adalaide Morris (ed.), *The Iowa Review, H.D. Centennial Issue*, 16.3 (1986), p. 180.
11. H.D., 'H.D. by Delia Alton'. On the title page of the undated first draft, pencilled brackets have been drawn around the typed title 'BID ME TO LIVE by DELIA ALTON', and 'Madrigal' written above, suggesting the title be changed from *BML* to *Madrigal*, H.D.'s original novel. On the title page of the undated second draft, the title is 'MADRIGAL (BID ME TO LIVE) by DELIA ALTON'. 'Madrigal', however, has been crossed out, as have the typescript brackets around 'Bid Me to Live' crossed out, as *BML* was the publisher's choice. 'Delia Alton' has been crossed out and 'H.D.' written instead. Janice S. Robinson notes that '[a]t H.D.'s insistence the book was subtitled *A Madrigal*, but she usually refers to *Bid Me to Live* as *Madrigal*', in *H.D.*, p. 119.
12. H.D., 'H.D. by Delia Alton', p. 180. Robinson notes that '[o]nly a few of the early versions of the story were destroyed', with the surviving versions held in the Beinecke Library, Yale, p. 119. There remains contention over the novel's dating. Claire Tylee argues that '[t]he first draft seems to have been composed in 1927', *The Great War and Women's Consciousness*, p. 231. Stanford Friedman contends that *BML* was 'first drafted in 1939 after her divorce from Aldington became final', *Psyche Reborn: The Emergence of H.D.* (1981), p. 31. Zilboorg dates the novel even earlier, arguing that *BML* was 'probably begun as early as the summer of 1918', *Richard Aldington and H.D.: The Early Years*, p. 47, as does Barbara Guest in *Herself Defined: The Poet H.D. and Her World* (1985), p. 88.
13. The prominent critical approaches to H.D. are feminist, psychoanalytical, biographical or queer. See, for example, Susan Stanford Friedman, *Psyche Reborn* (1981), and *Penelope's Web: Gender, Modernity, H.D.'s Fiction* (1990); Rachel Blau DuPlessis, *H.D.: The Career of that Struggle* (1986); Diana Collecott, *H.D. and Sapphic Modernism, 1910–1950* (1999). The field of H.D. studies has grown very quickly during the past fifteen years, in part due to a number of new editions published by University of Florida Press and the publication of *The Cambridge Companion to H.D.* (2012).
14. Matt Kibble, 'The "Still-Born Generation": Decadence and the Great War in H.D.'s Fiction', *Modern Fiction Studies* 44.3 (1998), pp. 540–67; Alice Kelly, 'Revising Trauma: Death, Stillbirth and the Great War in H.D.'s Fiction', in Maria Stadter Fox (ed.), *H.D.'s Web*, 4 (2009), pp. 27–67; Aliki Sophia Caloyeras, 'H.D.: The Politics

and Poetics of the Maternal Body' (unpublished PhD dissertation, University of Pennsylvania, 2012); Elizabeth Brunton, '"I had a Baby, I Mean I didn't, in an Air Raid": War and Stillbirth in H. D.'s *Asphodel*', *Women's Writing*, 24.1 (2017), pp. 66–79.
15. Ariela Freedman, *Death, Men and Modernism: Trauma and Narrative in British Fiction from Hardy to Woolf* (2003); Julia Goodspeed-Chadwick, *Modernist Women Writers and War: Trauma and the Female Body in Djuna Barnes, H.D., and Gertrude Stein* (2011).
16. Suzette A. Henke, *Shattered Subjects: Trauma and Testimony in Women's Life-Writing* (1998); Trudi Tate, 'H.D.'s War Neurotics', in Suzanne Raitt and Trudi Tate (eds), *Women's Fiction and the Great War* (1997), pp. 241–62.
17. Kelly, 'Revising Trauma'.
18. Julia Goodspeed-Chadwick, *Modernist Women Writers and War*, p. 7.
19. Randall, *Modernism, Daily Time and Everyday Life* (2007); Connor, *H.D. and the Image* (2004); Marcus, *The Tenth Muse: Writing about Cinema in the Modernist Period* (2007). H.D. was interested in film during the extended period of the composition of *Bid Me to Live*, and some of her writings on cinema have been collected in James Donald, Anne Friedberg and Laura Marcus (eds), *Close Up, 1927–1933: Cinema and Modernism* (1998).
20. Other examples of the civilian war novel, both wartime and postwar, include H. G. Wells, *Mr. Britling Sees It Through* (1916); Rose Macaulay, *Non-Combatants and Others* (1916); Rose Allatini [A. T. Fitzroy], *Despised and Rejected* (1918); Rebecca West, *The Return of the Soldier* (1918); D. H. Lawrence, *Aaron's Rod* (1922); Virginia Woolf, *Jacob's Room* (1922) and *Mrs. Dalloway* (1925). Although begun in the same period, *Bid Me to Live* was published much later and can be considered a late civilian war novel.
21. H.D., letter to Marianne Moore, 29 August 1917, in Stanford Friedman (ed.), 'H.D. (1886–1961)', in Bonnie Kime Scott (ed.), *The Gender of Modernism: A Critical Anthology* (1990), p. 138.
22. H.D., *Palimpsest* [1926], pref. Harry T. Moore (1968), p. 143.
23. Zilboorg, Note in *Bid Me to Live*, p. 130.
24. H.D., 'H.D. by Delia Alton', pp. 192, 204.
25. Freud, 'Thoughts for the Times on War and Death' [1915], in *Sigmund Freud: Collected Papers, Volume 4*, trans. under supervision of Joan Riviere (1959), p. 307.
26. A list of 'Officer's Kit for the Front' in a 1916 handbook listed a 'Luminous wristwatch with unbreakable glass' as the first item. Captain B. C. Lake, *Knowledge for War: Every Officer's Handbook for the Front* (1916), p. 173, quoted by David Boettcher, <http://www.vintagewatchstraps.com/trenchwatches.php> (last accessed 30 March 2019).
27. *Instructions for the Training of Divisions for Offensive Action* (40/W.O./3591), issued by the War Office General Staff Great Britain (London: Harrison, 1916), pp. 54, 13, quoted by David Boettcher, <http://www.vintagewatchstraps.com/trenchwatches.php> (last accessed 30 March 2019).
28. Van Dijick, 'Time on the Pulse: Affective Encounters with the Wristwatch in the Literature of Modernism and the First World War', *Modernist Cultures*, 11.2 (2016), pp. 161–8.

29. Although, as Randall Stevenson has suggested in *Reading the Times: Temporality and History in Twentieth-Century Fiction* (2018), this 'unusually absolute civic order' coincided with simultaneous changes in perceptions of 'the non-homogeneous time and space proposed by Einstein's Theories of Relativity', prompted by study of a solar eclipse in May 1919, pp. 92–3.
30. H.D.'s epithet may nod to John Cournos and Aldington's 1916 translation of Fyodor Sologrub's novel *The Little Demon*, which was reviewed by Alec W. G. Randall, '"The Little Demon"', *The Egoist*, 1 April 1916, p. 52. The front page of the next issue (1 May 1916) featured a front-page article by Aldington with the same title, pp. 65–6. All pages from *The Egoist* accessed via the *Modernist Journals Project*, <http://modjourn.org/render.php?view=mjp_object&id=EgoistCollection> (last accessed 2 April 2019).
31. Randall, *Modernism, Daily Time and Everyday Life*, p. 137.
32. H.D. was the assistant editor with Aldington from June 1916 (Vol. 3, No. 6) to May 1917 (Vol. 4, No. 4), although H.D. did the majority of the work after he left for France in December 1916 (also see Zilboorg, 'Introduction', pp. xxiv–xxv). Aldington had been the Assistant Editor with Leonard A. Compton-Rickett from the first issue in January to June 1914, before becoming sole Assistant Editor from July 1914. Seeger, *Poems* (1916; 1917). Eliot found Seeger charmingly old-fashioned: 'The work is well done, and so much out of date as to be almost a positive quantity. [. . .] Seeger is certainly not Georgian, hardly even Victorian; he goes back to the early Keats; and what is still more extraordinary, to the Coleridge of the "Ode to France," with a touch of the eighteenth century, the odes of Colins and Grey [sic]. It is a strange and pleasant literary sensation', 'Short Reviews', *The Egoist*, Vol. 4, No. 11 (December 1917), p. 172.
33. Paris, 'The Great War and the Moving Image: Cinema and Memory', in Adam Piette and Mark Rawlinson (eds), *The Edinburgh Companion to Twentieth-Century British and American War Literature* (2012), p. 58.
34. George Asaf [George Henry Powell], music by Felix Powell, 'Pack Up Your Troubles in Your Old Kit-Bag and Smile, Smile, Smile!' (c. 1915).
35. Jack Judge and Harry Williams, 'The Immortal "It's a Long Way to Tipperary": The Marching Anthem on the Battlefields of Europe' (1912).
36. Mansfield to J. M. Murry, [21 March 1915], in *The Collected Letters of Katherine Mansfield, Volume I: 1903–1917*, ed. Vincent O'Sullivan and Margaret Scott (1984), pp. 158–9.
37. Matthew Kibble suggests that this 'self-defeating metaphor [. . .] restores a literal meaning to the word "generation" (the act of begetting), only to undermine this act of origin with the image of stillbirth'. The 'ideas of descent and genealogy' that accompany H.D.'s metaphor are thus shown to have stalled as soon as they are invoked, 'The "Still-Born Generation"', p. 541.
38. Tate, 'H.D.'s War Neurotics', p. 255.
39. Tate, 'H.D.'s War Neurotics', p. 255.
40. Macaulay, *Non-Combatants*, p. 5.
41. Mansfield to S. S. Koteliansky, 22 March 1915, *CLVI*, p. 163.
42. Macaulay, *Non-Combatants*, p. 17, 9, 16, 17.

43. Macaulay, *Non-Combatants*, pp. 18, 20–1, 23.
44. West, *Return of the Soldier*, p. 5. Marcus notes that this scene links dreams and war films, 'The Great War in Twentieth-Century Cinema', in Vincent Sherry (ed.), *The Cambridge Companion to Literature of the First World War* (2005), p. 282. Paris writes of the scene: 'This twenty-one second sequence had tremendous effect on audiences – here was the real war at last', p. 60. Although the scene was actually filmed in Britain, other scenes in the film did include 'unprecedented footage of the pain and trauma on the faces of the troops, and a longer sequence that presents graphic images of the dead – German, of course – a slow pan across a heap of bodies at the bottom of a crater and later the unceremonious mass burials of the enemy dead', 'The Great War and the Moving Image', p. 60.
45. West, *Return of the Soldier*, p. 5.
46. Goodspeed-Chadwick, *Modernist Women Writers and War*, pp. 5–8.
47. See work in the Bibliography by Jennifer A. Haytock and Aimee L. Pozorski on Ernest Hemingway.
48. Kelly, *Cinema and the Great War* (1997); Hammond, *The Big Show: British Cinema Culture in the Great War, 1914–1918* (2006).
49. Paris, 'The Great War and the Moving Image', p. 59.
50. Marcus, 'The Great War in Twentieth-Century Cinema', p. 281.
51. Paris, 'The Great War and the Moving Image', p. 59.
52. *The Battle of the Somme*, dir. Geoffrey Malins and J. B. McDowell (1916). Marcus, 'The Great War in Twentieth-Century Cinema', p. 281.
53. For example, *Hearts of the World – The Story of a Village*, dir. D. W. Griffiths (1917).
54. Marcus, 'The Great War in Twentieth-Century Cinema', p. 285.
55. Samuel Begg, 'A Hospital-Ceiling as a Screen for Moving Pictures: A Cinema for Bedridden Wounded Soldiers at a Base in France', Cover of *Illustrated London News*, 10 August 1918. Accessed via the *British Newspaper Archive*, <https://www.britishnewspaperarchive.co.uk/viewer/bl/0001578/19180810/001/0001> (last accessed 2 May 2019).
56. For example, Susan McCabe, *Cinematic Modernism: Modernist Poetry and Film* (2005); David Trotter, *Cinema and Modernism* (2007); Andrew Shail, *The Cinema and the Origins of Literary Modernism* (2012).
57. Marcus, 'The Great War in Twentieth-Century Cinema', p. 280.
58. Mulvey, *Death 24x a Second: Stillness and the Moving Image* (2006), p. 58.
59. Hammond, *The Big Show*, p. 72.
60. Hammond, *The Big Show*, p. 73. Hammond notes that as the war progressed and the death toll mounted, these films lost their popularity and were 'generally discontinued' by 1917, p. 72.
61. Hammond, *The Big Show*, pp. 92–3.
62. Marcus, 'The Great War in Twentieth-Century Cinema', p. 287.
63. Hammond, *The Big Show*, p. 92.
64. Shail, *The Cinema and the Origins of Literary Modernism*, p. 186.
65. Barthes, *Camera Lucida: Reflections on Photography* [1981] trans. by Richard Howard (2000), p. 9.

66. Judge and Williams, 'The Immortal "It's a Long Way to Tipperary"' (1912).
67. Julia Ward Howe [Mrs Dr S. G. Howe], 'The Battle Hymn of the Republic: Adapted to the Favorite Melody of "Glory Hallelujah"', originally written for the *Atlantic Monthly* (Boston, MA: Oliver Ditson & Co., c. 1862). H.D. uses the same metaphor of grapes that run throughout the novel to describe the long period of its composition: '*Madrigal*, left simmering or fermenting, is run through a vintner's sieve, the dregs are thrown out. [. . .] The War I novel has been fermenting away during War II', 'H.D. by *Delia Alton*', p. 212.
68. H.D.'s mention of 'the Tree and the Angel' appears to be an allusion to the medieval Legend of the Rood, which relates the story of Adam's son Seth seeking an elixir from the Tree of Life to make his father immortal. The angel at the gate will not admit Seth, but will allow him to collect a seed from the tree, which he buries with his dead father's body. The seed grows into a tree which eventually becomes the cross on which Christ is crucified, linking back to H.D.'s comparison of the soldiers with Christ. H.D.'s allusion here is characteristically oblique, but in general terms recalls men's struggles against mortality. The mention of 'revenants' refers to the ghosts of the men we see proleptically invoked here.
69. Freud, 'Thoughts for the Times', p. 288.
70. 'The Cinema and the Classics, Part I. Beauty', in *Close-Up*, 1.1 (July 1927), collected in *Close Up, 1927–1933: Cinema and Modernism*, pp. 105–9. H.D. in particular discusses Greta Garbo: 'This is beauty, and this is a beautiful and young woman not exaggerated in any particular, stepping, frail yet secure across a wasted city [. . .] The screen has been touched by beauty, and the screen, in spite of all the totems, must finally respond, Polyphemus of our latest day, to the mermaid enchantment', pp. 107, 109.
71. Sandro Botticelli, *Primavera* (late 1470s or early 1480s), Uffizi Gallery, Florence.
72. H.D. may have also seen the *Rokeby Venus* by Diego Rodríguez de Silva y Velázquez, c. 1647–51, depicting Venus and her looking-glass, in the National Gallery in London. The painting had become more well known after having been attacked and damaged by the suffragette Mary Richardson in 1914, as a means of protesting the lack of women's suffrage.
73. The flower had been linked since 1915 with remembrance of the dead through 'Violet Day', a forerunner of the poppy as the 'symbol of perpetual remembrance'. See <http://adelaidia.sa.gov.au/events/violet-day> (last accessed 24 April 2019). Virginia Woolf also uses the motif of violets in terms of war remembrance, as I discuss in Chapter 5.

Part Three

Modernist Death: Postwar Remembrance

5

MODERNIST MEMORIALS: VIRGINIA WOOLF AND KATHERINE MANSFIELD IN THE POSTWAR WORLD

> I forget my first view of Molly, going down the Strand the night of the Cenotaph; such a lurid scene, like one in Hell. A soundless street; no traffic; but people marching. Clear, cold, & windless. A bright light in the Strand; women crying Remember the Glorious Dead, & holding out chrysanthemums. Always the sound of feet on the pavement. Faces bright & lurid – poor M.'s worn enough by that illumination. I touched her arm; whereupon she jumped, like some one woken. A ghastly procession of people in their sleep.[1]

In a diary entry from mid-December 1920 Woolf recorded meeting the young writer Mary (Molly) Agnes Hamilton as a means of 'enlarging her sphere'.[2] After noting her thoughts about their conversation, Woolf ends her account with a memory of her last meeting with Molly: the evening of 11 November 1920, the day the Cenotaph had been unveiled by King George V in Whitehall at 11am, followed by the interment of the Unknown Warrior in Westminster Abbey.[3] The enormous popularity of the temporary wood-and-plaster Cenotaph, designed by Sir Edwin Lutyens and erected on Whitehall on 18 July 1919, the day before the Victory Parade, had led to the Cabinet agreeing a permanent version on 30 July 1919, and construction began in January 1920 (see Fig. 5.1). The unveiling was part of the funeral procession of the Unknown Warrior, where the King first placed a wreath on the coffin on the gun carriage, before releasing the Union Jack flag that had been draped over the Cenotaph,

Figure 5.1 Crane Arthur, Unveiling of the Cenotaph and the funeral of the Unknown Warrior, Armistice Day, 1920. © IWM (Q 14966)

followed by the Two Minutes' Silence (for only the second time, after its introduction in 1919). The funeral cortege then processed to Westminster Abbey, where the Unknown Warrior was interred. Over the course of the week after the ceremony, an estimated 1.25 million mourners filed past the new permanent memorial, leaving flowers that reached 3 metres deep at its base.

Woolf's depiction of the scene, 'like one in Hell', is characteristically not focused on the Cenotaph itself. Woolf, walking down the Strand, would have met the mourners head-on, as they were encouraged to walk up the Mall and right on Whitehall to the Abbey, as they had at the Ceremony, but the numbers would have made it very busy in both directions (see Fig. 5.2). Woolf records the lack of traffic – Whitehall and a number of other streets had been closed to traffic for a number of days to accommodate the mourners – instead focusing on the people 'marching' and the sound of their feet: a motif that reappears in her later fiction. She depicts the women mourners holding out their traditional funerary flowers and invoking 'the glorious dead', the inscription on the side of the Cenotaph, but this may be Woolf imaginatively conflating personal grief with state slogans of public remembrance. Both the scene and

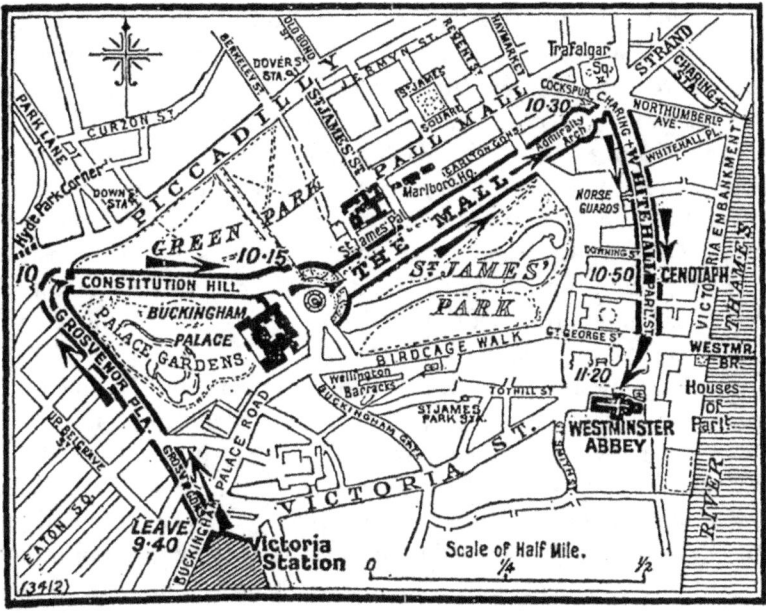

Figure 5.2 'The Last Journey', *The Times*, 10 November 1920, p. 12. © The Times/News Licensing

the people's faces are described as 'lurid', the faces lit by artificial light on the Strand. What Woolf sees here is the 'special illumination' arranged, as *The Times* reported, 'so that the Cenotaph and wreaths may be seen by the public until midnight'.[4] This was to ensure that as many mourners as possible could visit the Cenotaph and the Tomb, without being hurried: 'We wish to emphasize that it is in no way a spectacular show, but an act of homage to the dead and their relatives [. . .] none of those who wish to visit either the grave or the Cenotaph will be hustled'.[5] We don't know what Hamilton, the author of the pacifist wartime text *Dead Yesterday*, made of the event.[6] Woolf's reaction, however, is clear: the 'ghastly procession' of mourners (with its resonances of 'ghostly') are sleepwalkers: fatigued, grieving, worn down. There is no comfort to be had in this scene. In mid-April the following year (1921) Woolf recorded a formal scene of remembrance: 'I walked past Downing St yesterday & saw a few men in cabs, a few men with despatch boxes, orderly public watching, wreaths being laid on the Cenotaph'. This time she doesn't record any response whatsoever, moving on swiftly: 'Lytton's book [*Queen Victoria*] already selling 5 thousand copies, & the weather perfect'.[7]

This chapter considers the intersection of memorialisation and modernism, analysing the literary representation of the new public memorial culture in the postwar world. I consider how writers responded to the new public memorial landscape around them, how they drew on memorials at home and war cemeteries abroad as new narrative sites, and how this commemorative culture affected modernist representations of death. My focus is predominantly the postwar writings of Virginia Woolf and Katherine Mansfield, two civilian modernist writers whose work depicts a postwar culture of commemoration that was still very much in the process of formation. I also draw on work by E. M. Forster, Rudyard Kipling and Christopher Isherwood, to demonstrate how other contemporary, not necessarily modernist, writers were dealing with the same topic, bringing into relief the particular tropes and techniques of Mansfield and Woolf.

The ongoing question of how and where to bury and commemorate the war dead – debated in Parliament, homes, church halls and pubs – provided the context for these works. The immediate postwar period from about 1919 to 1923 was both the era of 'high modernism' and of what Samuel Hynes calls 'monument-making': a crucial simultaneity that has gone surprisingly neglected by critics.[8] As I discussed in the Introduction, the temporary and then permanent Cenotaphs were only one of a number of national government-led gestures of remembrance, including a number of public structures and rituals of remembrance: the Two Minutes' Silence (begun on 11 November 1919) and the Poppy Appeal (begun in 1921), the construction of formalised cemeteries in the former war zones, and thousands of local memorials at home. These memorials and rituals – attempts to fix meaning as Samuel Hynes suggests – were being erected and established while there was still an ongoing search for the missing and confirmation of the numbers killed, and while the negotiations for the terms of the postwar settlements were still underway.[9] This chapter considers the literary response to the key questions of the immediate postwar period: the ongoing identification and burial of bodies; the question of locating and visiting the dead; and the building of local and national memorials.

This culture of memorialisation was a hugely important context for the development of literary modernism, that has previously been overlooked.[10] This is an interesting oversight given the critical fixation with texts published in 1922 – the year that Willa Cather claimed 'the world broke in two' – most of which were written during this period of mass public memorialisation.[11] This context wasn't only reflected in modernist texts: the golden age of detective fiction, written mostly by women, was unsurprisingly this same period. The titles of some of Dorothy L. Sayers's popular mystery novels – as just one example – *Whose Body?* (begun in 1921, published in 1923), *Unnatural Death* (1927),

The Unpleasantness at the Bellona Club (1928, about a body that has been hidden during the Two Minutes' Silence), and the short story collection, *Lord Peter Views the Body* (1928) – share this focus on absent and present corpses, although present it in different ways.[12]

Of the two writers, more has been written about Woolf and the war than Mansfield, reflecting both Woolf's explicit war writings and the much broader body of scholarship on Woolf. Critics such as Mark Hussey (and the essays within his edited volume), Helen Wussow, Karen Levenback and Christina Froula have considered Woolf as a war writer; shorter readings by Allyson Booth, Vincent Sherry and David Sherman complement this scholarship in relation specifically to war death.[13] Hussey suggests, in line with many of these critics, that '*all* Woolf's work is deeply concerned with war'[14]. Mansfield, as we saw in Chapter 3, has had less written about her as a war writer, despite arguably being more personally affected by the war through the death of her brother, killed in an accident while training in October 1915.[15] She wrote much less explicitly than Woolf about the war in her fiction, and her life was cut short at the height of her powers, dying of tuberculosis aged thirty-four in January 1923. Reading the two writers in juxtaposition has been, and continues to be, productive for critics, especially as they shared a relationship of both intense admiration and rivalry.[16] Mansfield told Woolf in a letter of August 1917 that, 'We have got the same job, Virginia & it is really very curious & thrilling that we should both, quite apart from each other, be after so very nearly the same thing'; Woolf, in May 1920, recorded in her diary 'a common certain understanding' between the two writers – a queer sense of being "like"'.[17] Both writers shared a preoccupation with death. In Mansfield's case, this was predominantly fear in relation to her own death; for Woolf, it was more abstract: 'I like [. . .] to question people about death'.[18] Woolf's immediate response to Mansfield's death in January 1923 demonstrates the significance of her role in Woolf's writing life: 'it seemed to me there was no point in writing. Katherine wont read it'.[19] However, the pair had some clear differences, including class, nationality and attitudes towards sexuality, which sometimes caused conflict.[20]

Each writer influenced the other in the context of their war writing. Mansfield's November 1919 review of *Night and Day* heavily criticised Woolf for omitting the war, discussed in Chapter 3: a review that deeply affected Woolf and may have precipitated her choosing an explicit war subject for her next novel, *Jacob's Room*. It would be Mansfield, by contrast, who largely sublimated the war in her postwar writing. In early June 1920 Woolf recorded the '2 hours priceless talk [. . .] about books, writing of course' the pair shared over lunch, where they discussed Mansfield's negative review of *Night and Day*: 'a first rate novel, she said. The suppression in it puzzling, but accounted for by circumstances'.[21] Whether or not Mansfield was appeasing Woolf's hurt pride about the review is unclear, but these two authors discussing the effects of the war on their work ranks as one of the great unrecorded meetings of modernism.

This chapter does not read the relationship between the two writers in the postwar years, but rather considers the means by which they both wrote about the war dead and the new postwar culture of mass, official commemoration. In the first section, I discuss the question of absent and consolatory bodies through readings of Woolf's *Jacob's Room* and Mansfield's 'The Garden Party' (both 1922). The second section considers the question of locating and burying the dead, seen through the depiction of new war cemeteries and battlefield pilgrimage in Mansfield's 'The Fly' (1922), Forster's story 'Our Graves in Gallipoli' (1922), and Kipling's 'The Gardener' (1925). The final section considers new public memorial culture and ritual through the representation of memorials on the home front as new narrative sites in Woolf's *Mrs. Dalloway* (1925) and Isherwood's *The Memorial* (1932). The chapter ends with some thoughts on modernist death in Woolf's *To the Lighthouse* (1927), and the broader implications for later fictional representations of death. What the majority of these texts share, regardless of the sex of the author, is a focus on the responses of civilians, usually women, to their deaths of their men as the postwar world settled down into a new reality; a period when wartime civilian modernism became, more simply, modernism.

Absent and Consolatory Bodies

After the war – with the ongoing search for the missing and confirmation of the numbers killed, the construction of war cemeteries and the development of battlefield tourism, and the construction of war memorials and remembrance rituals – it was impossible to represent death without invoking the recent experience of mass mortality. As Christine Darrohn has argued, '[a]fter the Great War, to imagine a beautiful corpse might seem either a grotesque act of escapism or a courageous feat of imagination': we might say the same of a good or beautiful death.[22] After the First World War, it was very difficult to depict death through traditional sites and tropes without a sense of irony, parody or scepticism.[23] This change started to come into effect from the first mass casualties in late August 1914 and continued into the postwar era of high modernism.

Although *Jacob's Room* (1922) is the only one of her novels usually described as a 'war-novel', much of Woolf's postwar work in fact explores the civilian response to the war dead, demonstrating her engagement in the contemporary debate concerning the correct way to bury, commemorate and mourn the dead.[24] Woolf makes the change in civilian society after the war explicit: in *Mrs. Dalloway* (published in 1925, set in 1923), Peter Walsh, returning after an absence of five years, observes that those years (1918–23) had been 'somehow very important', that 'a change of some sort had undoubtedly taken place'.[25] This change is sometimes represented as potentially liberating: already in the 1917 story 'The Mark on the Wall', the narrator discusses 'generalizations' (noting 'the military sound of the word') which 'bring back [. . .] Sunday in London, Sunday afternoon walks, Sundays luncheons, *and also ways of speaking of the dead* [. . .] There was a rule for everything'.[26] But the dismay and incomprehension within contemporary British society at the unprecedented number of war dead also led to uncertainty and disarray. 'Such confusion everywhere!' Betty Flanders proclaims at the end of *Jacob's Room*, the text that counts its protagonist among the war dead at its conclusion.[27] Woolf explicitly rejected conventional modes of writing fiction, theorising her ideas on fiction and character-drawing in 'Modern Novels', a 1919 essay for *The Times Literary Supplement*, revised in 1925 as 'Modern Fiction'.[28] Although Woolf doesn't suggest that the war is responsible for this change, it is clear that it posed an unanticipated break in modes of acceptable representation: it was, as she wrote years later in 1940, 'like a chasm in a smooth road'.[29] Changed reality necessitated changed representation, as Mansfield had noted in 1919 in her review of *Night and Day*, and Woolf asserted this need for a postwar mode when 'elegy' became a more appropriate term for her fiction.[30]

Begun in 1920 and published in 1922, *Jacob's Room* is Woolf's most explicit attempt to write a civilian war novel, documenting the responses of those on the home front to the death of the protagonist, Jacob Flanders. Judith Hattaway notes that *Jacob's Room* is 'written *out of* the War years: it looks back at what had been lost in that conflict but also searches for a form in which to convey it'. The novel 'shows an order cracking to create the possibility of new formations'.[31] William R. Handley has argued that its form resists 'the epic closedness and the kind of militaristic authority in this world that will eventually destroy [Jacob]'.[32] The prolepsis of Jacob's patronym 'Flanders' reveals his narrative trajectory from the beginning: it signifies 'a name, a place, and a way of dying' which 'both grants identity and cancels it out', as Laura Marcus argues.[33] Following the shock of Jacob's death, his mother's closing question about Jacob's shoes – 'What am I to do with these, Mr. Bonamy?' – reflects the lack of an appropriate mode of memorialisation (155). The text resolutely refuses to idealise Jacob or his generation, or to provide a conventional biography or obituary. Instead, it focuses on what Hattaway refers to as the war's 'points of contact with the "ordinary" life left behind', suggesting that traditional statues and monuments for the war dead are redundant in the postwar world.[34]

In a period preoccupied with the question of how to commemorate the war dead, it is not surprising that Woolf was considering how, in narrative terms, to 'sum up' a person. When she came up with 'some idea of a new form for a new novel' in late January 1920, she was seeking to write something consciously different:

> the approach will be entirely different this time: no scaffolding; scarcely a brick to be seen [. . .] the theme is a blank to me; but I see

immense possibilities in the form I hit upon more or less by chance 2 weeks ago [. . .] I must still grope & experiment but this afternoon I had a gleam of light.[35]

Woolf's existing interest in literary characterisation during this period soon found a viable theme in the narrative of a soldier killed in the war. The postwar cult of both individual and mass commemoration provided a useful means for Woolf to explore 'character-mongering', and more broadly the question of posthumous biography and memorialisation (135). Woolf and Leonard were familiar with the wartime and postwar popularity of memorial volumes, having produced a version of their own as the second publication of the Hogarth Press in 1918 for Leonard's youngest brother Cecil, killed in November 1917 during the Battle of Cambrai.[36] It again demonstrates the imbrication of modernist and memorial culture that they paused publication of Mansfield's *Prelude* to publish Cecil's memorial volume. Unlike other memorial volumes which included impressions from army captains, friends, school teachers, and others, this was simply a volume of Cecil's poetry. In July 1918, Woolf reviewed the memorial volume produced for Rupert Brooke, writing privately that it was 'a disgraceful sloppy sentimental rhapsody, leaving Rupert rather tarnished'.[37] Her published review was slightly more positive, but drew attention to the impossibility of complete biography, particularly for one who had died so young. One is left, as Woolf writes, 'not with a sense of completeness and finality, but rather to wonder and to question still: what would he have been, what would he have done?'[38]

Appropriately for a novel describing the civilian experience of war, the text is structured around Jacob's absence, proleptically invoked from the beginning: 'Where *is* that tiresome little boy?' asks his mother Betty Flanders (3). The unanswered calls of his name ('Ja-cob! Ja-cob!') that begin and end the narrative emphasise his absence. Woolf describes Jacob through the objects in his empty room: both a deliberate mockery of the Edwardian novelists' mode of constructing character that she critiques in her 1924 essay 'Mr. Bennett and Mrs. Brown' and another means of demonstrating Jacob's fundamental emptiness as a character: he 'looked extraordinarily vacant' (25). This empty space of his room, which comes to represent loss, also functions as a cenotaph of sorts, an empty tomb. These 'exquisite outlines enclosing vacancy', a phrase Woolf uses later in the text, will be a recurrent motif (136).

A key mode of Woolf's modernist experimentation was to structure her text around a protagonist with little actual characterisation, focalised instead through the impressions of others. Here we see Woolf's narrative version of the Unknown Warrior – a central, depersonalised, silent figure, on whom others can project their own impressions and observations – demonstrating contemporary commemorative culture meeting modernist narrative technique. *Jacob's Room* explicitly rejects redundant Victorian modes of memorialisation and biography – caricatured in Jacob's undergraduate essay, 'Does History consist of the Biographies of Great Men?' – and traditionalists in the text such as Mr Floyd, 'the editor of a well-known series of ecclesiastical Biographies' (16). Woolf instead represents Jacob incompletely and inconclusively through passing impressions and fragments, a method commented on reflexively by the text's refrain: 'It is no use trying to sum people up' (24). The reader sees Jacob through a series of other people's impressions of him, and he is described by a number of characters through various epithets, often superlatives and frequently contradictory statements: 'a powerfully built young man' (23), 'the silent young man' (49, 59), 'extraordinarily awkward [. . .] Yet so distinguished-looking' (50), 'too good – too good' (52), 'the most beautiful man we have ever seen' (63), 'a military gentleman' (64), 'like one of those statues' (67), 'a little regal and pompous' (92). Sometimes Jacob's lack of individual character is portrayed as a statue-like stillness, again enabling others to project their impressions onto him: 'Not a muscle of his face moved' (50); 'He looked at them without moving' (52). These impressions of Jacob are accompanied by acknowledgements that these characterisations are subjective and external:

> Nobody sees any one as he is [. . .] They see a whole – they see all sorts of things – they see themselves . . . (23)
>
> But something is always impelling one to hum vibrating, like the hawk moth, at the mouth of the cavern of mystery, endowing Jacob Flanders with all sorts of qualities he had not at all [. . .] (61)

The narrative repeatedly draws attention to the fallibility of its observers – one character repeatedly refers to Jacob as 'Mr. Sanders' and relates a conversation heard through a wall – highlighting the role of subjectivity, memory and impression involved in trying to summarise another person (87). Even the text's dominant sentiment – 'It seems that a profound, impartial, and absolutely just opinion of our fellow-creatures is utterly unknown' (60) – is qualified by being itself an impression of how life 'seems'. 'Unknown' in the period Woolf was writing was a term with heavy resonance. Woolf's deliberately vague characterisation of Jacob links him to both the new memorial idea of the Unknown Warrior (known as 'the Unknown' in the papers) and the grave designation for unidentified bodies: 'Known Unto God', a phrase chosen by Kipling.

The necessity of imaginative imposition in characterising Jacob draws directly on contemporary rhetoric surrounding the Unknown Warrior, the new memorial site whose meaning rested on this same possibility of imaginative imposition by others. Contemporary newspaper accounts repeatedly drew attention to this multiplicitous quality of the memorial. When Woolf was reading the papers on nearly any day in the autumn of 1920, especially around Armistice Day in November, she would have seen this quality being discussed:

> Cavalry, Infantry, Artillery, Engineers: he was all. [. . .] He who comes to-day was, and is, one and all of these. And he was more; for it was not only on land that he fought. But where he died at sea he lies too deep to be brought home, even by a nation's longing. So – for it is understood that this coffin of his comes from France – when he died far off, in Gallipoli, in Mesopotamia, in Africa, or wherever the outermost wash of the Great War broke on the margins of the world, whether he lies in a grave scraped in the dry sand among sun-baked rocks or in the dark tangle of forest undergrowth. Everywhere it is he, the Unknown Dead, who marks the farthest outposts of the Empire that he saved.[39]

Like the Unknown Warrior, Jacob appears classless – 'one would have found it difficult to say which seat in the opera house was his, stalls, gallery, or dress circle' – and is of unknown origin: 'descended [. . .] from a family of the greatest antiquity and deepest obscurity' (59). The new memorial gesture of the Unknown Warrior therefore provides a perfect outlet for Woolf's contemporary preoccupation with the challenges of characterisation, and her play with the imaginative imposition of others onto Jacob almost directly reflects the immediate postwar memorial context of her text.

Jacob's lack of individualisation allows him to stand in for his generation in the same way as the Unknown Warrior. He is typically presented as like many of the young men around him, albeit those of a particular educated class: the 'distinction' which is considered 'one of the words to use naturally' in relation to Jacob is therefore ironic (59). His accoutrements fail to distinguish him in any way: even 'Jacob's walking stick was like all the others' (93).[40] His peers at Cambridge are described *en masse*:

> so many young men, some undoubtedly reading, magazines, shilling shockers, no doubt; legs, perhaps, over the arms of chairs; smoking; sprawling over tables, and writing while their heads went round in a circle as the pen moved – simple young men, these, who would – but there is no need to think of them grown old. (34)[41]

Although Jacob is distinguished superficially by the fact that he 'ate dates' and 'burst out laughing', he is, in fact, indistinguishable from this group of young men and completely depersonalised when he returns to his rooms: 'as if the old stone echoed [. . .]: "The young man – the young man – the young man – back to his rooms"' (35, 37).[42]

The description of the young men in the common room through body parts emphasises the corporeality of their bodies, bodies described through synecdoche: 'legs [. . .] heads [. . .] hands [. . .] legs issuing here, one there crumpled in a corner of the sofa', leaving 'only gestures of arms, movements of bodies [. . .] arms and bodies moving in the twilight room' (34–6). This reminds us that these bodies would, within a short space of time, be broken into parts or disappear, eviscerated by shells or buried far from home.[43] The disappearance of these young men is anticipated from the beginning of this section: 'Look, as they pass into service, how airily the gowns blow out, as though nothing dense and corporeal were within' (24).[44] The pathos of the scenes of the young men at Cambridge is heightened by the allusion to Binyon's 'They shall grow not old', Jacob's laughter which 'died in the air', and the muffled 'stroke of the clock [. . .] as if generations of learned men heard the last hour go rolling through their ranks and issued it [. . .] for the use of the living' (34–6). We know that Jacob is mistaken in finding 'the sound of the clock conveying [. . .] a sense of old buildings and time; and himself the inheritor' (36). Jacob is synecdochal of an entire generation of young men who won't inherit: he becomes, in costume later in the text, appropriately 'like the figure-head of a wrecked ship' (63). His surname (and fate) isn't unique, but stands for his generation.

The only war scene in the novel comes within a metafictional passage on 'character-mongering', where we again hear the refrain: 'It is no use trying to sum people up' (135). However, in a passage where the narrator initially opposes the 'character-mongers', she seems to eventually side with them in comparison to their alternative: 'the men in clubs and Cabinets [who] say that character-drawing is a frivolous fireside art, a matter of pins and needles, exquisite outlines enclosing vacancy, flourishes, and mere scrawls' (135–6). The narrative then moves into the only description of the war zones:

> The battleships ray out over the North Sea, keeping their stations accurately apart. At a given signal all the guns are trained on a target which (the master gunner counts the seconds, watch in hand – at the sixth he looks up) flames into splinters. With equal nonchalance a dozen young men in the prime of life descend with composed faces into the depths of the sea; and there impassively (though with perfect mastery of machinery) suffocate uncomplainingly together. Like blocks of tin soldiers the army covers the cornfield, moves up the hillside, stops, reels slightly this way and that, and falls flat, save that, through field-glasses, it can be seen that one or two pieces still agitate up and down like fragments of broken match-stick. (136)

Anticipating the mass death we see depicted in *To the Lighthouse* (Andrew and his comrades), the passage is concerned with the question of the collective versus the individual. The young men here are grouped, not individualised: 'a dozen young men', like 'blocks of tin soldiers'. The army acts, and even dies, as a unit: 'the army [. . .] reels slightly this way and that, and falls flat'. The new precisely timed and mechanised modern warfare has the ability to obliterate entire groups simultaneously, and the men with their 'composed faces' who 'suffocate uncomplainingly' represent a particular English educated class (we think of Jacob's companions at Cambridge). The few soldiers who survive are dehumanised, described instead through a domestic image, another version of the civilian modernism we have seen elsewhere: 'like fragments of broken matchstick'. Modern warfare, Woolf suggests, is entirely dependent on the devaluing of the individual and his character. This makes the Unknown Warrior – a war corpse devoid of defining features – the perfect symbol.

Jacob's Room, like the postwar culture in which it was written, is suffused, explicitly, with death: what the text calls 'mourning emblems', female mourners ('women with veiled hair'), memento moris, and hints of violence, as John Mepham has noted (69).[45] These memento moris prefigure Jacob and his generation's fate from the beginning, from the sheep's skull the child Jacob finds on the beach (where the encroachment of nature onto the skull prefigures the 'Time Passes' section of *To the Lighthouse*), the dead butterflies and the death's-head moth, to the ram's skull carved in the wood above the door of one of Jacob's lodgings (6, 17, 59). The text has the smell of violets – associated since 1915 with remembrance of the war dead – from the violets on board the boat near the Scilly Isles ('Strangely enough, you could smell violets'), the 'violent scents, and mourning emblems' of Cornwall, to lower-class 'Moll Pratt on the pavement, offering violets for sale' (39, 40, 86).[46] The narrative is frequently interrupted by unspecified sounds of grief: we hear 'a wavering, quavering, doleful lamentation' (64) and 'a mournful cry' (85). The novel begins and ends with a female mourner: a grieving widow, who has simultaneously lost her son. As the reader sees things through her (frequent) tears – 'The entire bay quivered; the lighthouse wobbled' (3) – they, too, become one of the text's mourners.

Woolf's destabilisation and parodying of these mourning emblems, as well as conventional sites and means of commemoration, suggest they are no longer appropriate. The novel was written while arrangements for the war dead were still being made, hence the moveable signifiers of death. There is particular difficulty in the text in locating and visualising the dead, in a period when finding the dead was paramount. Betty attempts, unsuccessfully, to locate her dead husband in geographical terms: 'Captain Barfoot is in Scarborough: Seabrook is dead' (3). Graves are transferred into other less stable representations: 'the cottage smoke droops, had the look of a mourning emblem, a flag floating its caress over a grave. The gulls [. . .] seem to mark the grave' (39). Tombstones are unreadable: 'Then, perhaps, a mason's van with newly lettered tombstones recording how some one loved some one who is buried in Putney. Then the motor-car in front jerks forward, and the tombstones pass too quick for you to read more' (97).

Fanny Elmer in 'the disused graveyard in the parish of St. Pancras [. . .] strayed between the white tombs which lean against the wall, crossing the grass to read a name, hurrying on when the grave-keeper approached' (99). Tombstones also fail to signify, as the false epitaph Betty Flanders put on her husband Seabrook's tombstone shows: '"Merchant of this city," the tombstone said [. . .] well, she had to call him something' (11). Her unsuccessful mourning of her husband is partly due to the fact that although correctly sited (he is imagined in the grave), her mental version of him is completely false, as she is unable to accept the decomposition that his body would have undergone in the intervening two years: 'Seabrook lay six foot beneath [. . .] doubtless his very face lay visible beneath, the face of a young man whiskered' (10). Jacob's lover Florinda 'for parents had only the photograph of a tombstone beneath which, she said, her father lay buried', much like the photographs of graves sent to grieving families by the Imperial War Graves Commission. Even this seemingly normal grave is satirised, exaggerated as a potentially monstrous grave: 'Sometimes she would dwell upon the size of it and rumour had it that Florinda's father had died from the growth of his bones which nothing could stop' (65). The deaths of other characters in *Jacob's Room* – Betty's brother Morty 'lost all these years – had the natives got him, was his ship sunk – would the Admiralty tell her?' – clearly relate directly to the civilian experience of their war dead, with no body and only uncertain facts as to the conditions of death (78). These deaths continue to preoccupy the female characters: Betty is seen 'musing about Morty' (78); while Florinda 'prattles', the 'tomb of her father was mentioned' (66). Traditional monuments have become meaningless:

> Mrs. Lidgett took her seat beneath the great Duke's tomb [. . .] A magnificent place for an old woman to rest in by the very side of the great Duke's bones, *whose victories mean nothing to her, whose name she knows not*, though she never fails to greet the little angels opposite, as she passes out, wishing the like on her own tomb. (54; my italics)

Although Jacob is linked with traditional modes of statuary – at the opera, 'Clara Durrant said farewell to Jacob Flanders, and tasted the sweetness of death in effigy' (57), and Florinda tells him, 'You're like one of those statues' (67) – the proleptic narrative of the minor character of Jimmy, who now 'feeds crows in Flanders', provides a more probable trajectory (83). It is not only traditional modes of memorialisation that fail to function: even the new war cemeteries and graves are made to seem comic, seen in Betty's letter announcing the demise of a pointedly named old friend: 'Do you remember Old Miss Wargrave [. . .] She's dead at last, poor thing' (77). Despite Woolf's humour, there is always 'the overpowering sorrow [. . .] brewed by the earth itself' (40). In August 1920, Woolf asked in her diary – ostensibly in relation to what she saw as 'the sadness, the satire' of *Don Quixote* – if sadness is 'essential to the modern view?'.[47] In late October, she referred to 'our generation so tragic'.[48] The impact of the war on the whole postwar world, including civilians, is clear.

Despite Jacob's name and the frequent allusions to death throughout the text, Jacob's death remains sudden and unexpected at the end of the text, characteristically 'off-stage', and mediated by his friend Bonamy, 'He left everything just as it was' (155). There is no death scene or body over which to mourn. Roger Fry's response to the text draws attention to this lack of a body: 'I was praised whole-heartedly by him [. . .] only he wishes that a bronze body might somehow solidify beneath the gleams & lights – with which I agree', Woolf noted in her diary in November 1922.[49] The narrative compensates for this lack of a body by using domestic imagery and the synecdochal use of belongings to stand in for the absent dead, seen in the descriptions of Jacob's room and the 'pair of Jacob's old shoes' as his memorial (155). Woolf's choice of a personal and domestic object rather than one of grand, national importance prioritises a civilian, rather than an official, national approach to memorialisation. With Jacob's death occurring at the end of the text, the narrative ends as mourning begins with, as John Mepham notes, 'the wound of grief wide open', denying a sense of closure.[50] Woolf's war novel demonstrates how the lack of an appropriate response to the dead continued into the 1920s, even while new official forms were being established.

Woolf was writing *Jacob's Room* from April 1920 to November 1921, when the postwar world was beginning to settle down again into normal life, and the long-term effects of the war were beginning to be experienced. She was thinking explicitly about autobiography and life-writing, and she was part of the newly formed Memoir Club where a dozen or so members each read an autobiographical chapter at the meetings.[51] In February 1921 where John Maynard Keynes read a long piece on the negotiations for the second renewal of the Armistice, Woolf was characteristically 'a little bored by the politics, & a good deal impressed by the method of character drawing'.[52] Woolf was also thinking about memorialisation. In Easter 1920 she reviewed Henry James's letters, collected after his death in 1916.[53] Her note on the death of 'poor Mrs Humphry Ward' the same month demonstrates her own fears about literary immortality: 'it appears that she was merely a woman of straw after all – shovelled into the grave & already forgotten'.[54] In mid-April, Woolf went into Chelsea Church – in a version of Mrs Lidgett – and 'saw the tablet to H.J. [. . .] spindly letters, & Jamesian phrases'.[55] The solidity of James's memorial must have contrasted with Mrs Humphry Ward's perceived ephemerality. Woolf also read Lytton Strachey's new biography of Queen Victoria (which was dedicated to her), noting: 'I doubt whether these portraits are true – whether thats not too much the conventional way of making history – But I think I'm coloured by my own wishes, & experimental mood'.[56] The question of how to write a life (her own or someone else's), and how to draw a character – particularly posthumously – was foremost in Woolf's mind throughout this period.

It wasn't just the deaths of people Woolf knew, but strangers too. In May 1920 Woolf wrote of being asked by the 'Women's Times' – *The Times's* new bi-monthly *Woman's Supplement* – for a 'light article [. . .] on Psychology of War Widows'.[57] Woolf didn't write the piece, noting that she wanted to 'get on with Jacob' (itself arguably a fictionalised version of the same topic). Returning from a meeting with her sister Vanessa Bell in London the next month, Woolf wrote that she often thought 'of the dead who have walked in the city'.[58] In late June the death of a young man, who had fallen off a roof at a party held at 50 Gordon Square, where Vanessa lived, caused some shock: 'He crossed, perhaps to light a cigarette, stepped over the edge, & fell 30 feet onto flagstones [. . .] He died in the ambulance that fetched him. The dance was stopped.'

It is the perceived coldheartedness of the younger generation that seems to be the most shocking for Woolf: 'Nessa says the younger generation is callous. No one was upset; some telephoned for news of other dances'.[59] This reaction is contrasted with Woolf's sense of the abnormality of this death: 'A strange event – to come to a dance among strangers & die – to come dressed in evening clothes, & then for it all to be over, instantly, so senselessly'. Rishona Zimring refers to this as 'shock in the aftermath of war, the lingering senselessness of the recent past haunting scenes of a precarious restored order', linking it to Clarissa's response in *Mrs. Dalloway*: 'in the middle of my party, here's death'.[60] In the same letter, Woolf noted: 'Our generation is daily scourged by the bloody war. Even I scribble reviews instead of novels because of the thick skulls at Westminster & Berlin'.[61]

In contrast to Woolf's absent Jacob, Katherine Mansfield's 'The Garden Party' is an unusual modernist text in its depiction of a corpse.[62] However, this sublimation of the war dead was entirely in keeping with Mansfield's method. Completed in October 1921 and published in February 1922, the story was written while Woolf was finishing *Jacob's Room*. Its earlier publication made Woolf jealous: 'K.M. bursts upon the world in glory next week; I have to hold over Jacob's Room till October'.[63] Mansfield's story opens with the preparations for a party held by the upper-class Sheridan family, temporarily interrupted by the news of the accidental death of Scott, a lower-class workman down in the village who has been thrown off his horse, leaving a wife and five children. This arrival of the news of an accidental civilian death stands in for a war death. Laura, the adolescent protagonist, immediately presumes the garden party will be called off due to the news – 'But we can't possibly have a garden party with a man dead just outside the front gate', protests Laura – but her siblings and mother consider this an 'extravagant' notion (407, 408). Although ostensibly a story about class-consciousness and Laura's potential transcendence of her class through encounters with various lower-class figures, the story is primarily a *Bildungsroman*, where the protagonist will learn about the presence of death in life. It implicitly concerns the appropriate civilian response to the war dead and offers a fantasy of the peaceful war dead.

The difference between civilians and combatants is figured through class distinctions, with the upper-class representing civilians and the lower-class combatants. This distinction is enacted through the two spheres in the story: the Sheridans live in a large house with a number of servants, whereas 'the little cottages [where the workman lived] were in a lane to themselves at the very bottom of a steep rise that led up to the house' (408). This lane was 'forbidden' to the Sheridan children when they were little 'because of the revolting language and of what they might catch' (408). Following the party, Mrs Sheridan sends Laura with a basket of leftover food to the widow and her children. Christine Darrohn has noted the similarities of these cottages to trenches, arguing that the 'description of Laura's journey to the Scotts' home, with its emphasis on descent and darkness [. . .] suggests the more recent imagery of modern trench warfare'.[64] Although the cottages 'were far too near' for the Sheridans' liking, the two spheres are demarcated by a broad road, metaphorically distancing the war dead from the civilian space of the garden party. It is the troubling transgression between these spheres that drives the story.

Entering the poverty-stricken home, Laura encounters first a community of female mourners (the 'old, old woman', the widow's sister and the grieving widow) and then the body of the dead man. The widow is figured in realistic terms, but appears almost monstrous to the young girl: 'Her face, puffed up, red, with swollen eyes and swollen lips, looked terrible' (412). It is hard not to see in this grieving woman the war widow, a familiar figure in the immediate postwar landscape. In contrast, Mansfield presents Laura's encounter with the dead man as a positive, consolatory experience: 'There lay a young man, fast asleep – sleeping so soundly, so deeply, that he was far, far away from them both. Oh, so remote, so peaceful. He was dreaming. Never wake him up again' (413). Laura imagines his thoughts: 'All is well, said that sleeping face [. . .] I am content' (413). In what Darrohn considers 'the most radical revision of the corpse', she notes that 'the metaphor of sleep creates the impression that death is a choice voluntarily selected over life [. . .] as though it were possible for him to be revived'.[65] The corpse is both near – tangible and intimate to the viewer – and at a distance: 'What did garden parties and baskets and lace frocks matter to him? He was far from all those things' (413). Unlike the absent body of Jacob, Mansfield presents us with a physical manifestation of mortality and the consolatory intimacy of the Victorian deathbed.

This inaccessible but 'content' and whole male corpse is a civilian fantasy of the war dead: a consolatory and idealised impression of so many men who died away from home, 'blown to bits' like Mansfield's brother Leslie 'Chummie' Beauchamp. The fantasy of the whole aestheticised male corpse attempts to return to traditional sites of the dead and the Victorian good death.

Darrohn notes that this story 'depends on a man's violent death even as it erases the traces of injury from his body', that Mansfield 'restores a remarkable, emphatic wholeness to the male corpse'.[66] The image of the man sleeping arguably refers directly to Mansfield's diary entries in February 1916 where she sees her brother 'lying fast asleep' next to her. The next evening she imagines her brother calling her and looks out of the window: 'I seemed to see my brother dotted all over the field – now on his back, now on his face, now huddled up, now half pressed into the earth'.[67] Mansfield, like many civilian women grieving their absent men, imagines her brother's body in troubling terms – not traditionally buried, but moving, restless and unlocated.

For two writers who were 'after [. . .] the same thing', Woolf and Mansfield's method here is effectively opposite: Woolf creates an absent soldier, created almost entirely through other people's impressions and who dies offstage; Mansfield presents a seemingly peaceful civilian death, with a present, whole and visible corpse. In part Mansfield's story is about a consolatory corpse – her own version of the Unknown Warrior – but it is also a story about the impact of the war on perceptions of life and death. To understand this, we have to go back to her letters to her husband John Middleton Murry in November 1919 on the effects of war, prompted by her negative review of *Night and Day*, discussed in Chapter 3. Mansfield suggested:

> I cant imagine how after the war these men can pick up the old threads as tho' it never had been. Speaking to *you* Id say we have died and live again. How can that be the same life? It doesn't mean that Life is the less precious of [*sic*] that the 'common things of light and day' are gone. They are not gone, they are intensified, they are illumined. Now we know ourselves for what we are. In a way its a tragic knowledge. Its as though, even while we live again we face death. But *through Life*: thats the point. We see death in life as we see death in a flower that is fresh unfolded. Our hymn is to the flower's beauty – we would make that beauty immortal because we *know*.[68]

Mansfield asserts that the war has fundamentally changed reality, that it has given people a 'tragic knowledge' of death. Both life and death are fundamentally changed by it – one cannot be seen without the other. In one way, this was a personal philosophy for Mansfield, as the war and a knowledge of her own mortality developed simultaneously, as we saw in Chapter 3. But here she talks in universal terms. Mansfield went on to qualify what this meant for literature through two literary references:

> But of course you dont imagine I mean by this knowledge 'let us eat and drink-ism'. No, I mean 'deserts of vast eternity'. [. . .] I couldn't

tell anybody *bang out* about those deserts. They are my secret. I might write about a boy eating strawberries or a woman combing her hair on a windy morning & that is the only way I can ever mention them. But they *must* be there. Nothing less will do.[69]

Mansfield doesn't mean that this knowledge should result in a hedonistic enjoyment of life (her reference to the Bible: 'Let us eat and drink / for tomorrow we die'), but instead a continual awareness of death (Andrew Marvell's poem 'To His Coy Mistress': 'But at my back I alwaies hear / Times winged chariot hurrying near: / And yonder all before us lye / Deserts of vast Eternity.').[70] Mansfield makes explicit her method of indirection and obliquity, that she would not reference this new knowledge of death caused by the war directly, instead only doing it through other implicit means.

Reading this passage from 1919 – Mansfield's unofficial modernist manifesto – illuminates 'The Garden Party' as an oblique depiction of the war dead: displaced into a civilian setting and focalised through the perspective of an adolescent. The child protagonist gains a knowledge of mortality through an encounter with a corpse, standing in for the 'tragic knowledge' gained by people through the war: effectively the *Bildungsroman* of a generation. The experience of everyday life is 'intensified [. . .] illumined', from the superlatively 'perfect day' for the party ('They could not have had a more perfect day for a garden party if they had ordered it', 401), to the roses which have bloomed especially ('Hundreds, yes, literally hundreds, had come out in a single night') and the endless 'canna lilies, big pink flowers, wide open, radiant, almost frighteningly alive on bright crimson stems' (404). The guests' comments, which reach us only in fragments, support this notion of intensified experience, even before Laura has gained her new knowledge: '"Never a more delightful garden party . . . " "The greatest success . . . " "Quite the most . . . "' (410). The garden is, of course, an appropriate setting for the gaining of new knowledge – we think of the Garden of Eden – but Mansfield also linked garden parties (with their accompanying marquees) with the war, referring to the war in a 1919 review as 'the greatest of all garden-parties'.[71] The superlative language of the garden party also recalls the language used to describe the prewar summer of 1914: it was remembered by contemporaries as 'the most idyllic for many years [. . .] warm and sunny, eminently pastoral', which became in retrospect 'a permanent symbol for anything innocently but irrecoverably lost'.[72]

Whereas Woolf's method was by comparison 'bang out' through her explicit references to Jacob's death in the war, Mansfield's story is not immediately recognizable as being about the war until we read it closely, despite the traditional sites and tropes of the dead – the corpse, the mourning woman and mourning emblems such as the lilies. However, reading the story with Mansfield's 1919 comments in mind, including her metaphor 'We see death in life as we see death in a flower that is fresh unfolded', makes explicit that this story concerns the new knowledge of death brought about by the war: 'And the perfect afternoon slowly ripened, slowly faded, slowly its petals closed' (410).

GRAVE FINDING IN FRANCE: LOCATING AND BURYING THE DEAD

Woolf didn't mention the first anniversary of the Armistice in her diary, although she noted the next day that she had seen her old friend Violet Dickinson:

> I think Violet Dickinson must be skipped, save that I may note how she has been grave finding in France & planting Lady Horner's rosemarys upon German tombs. All this she enjoyed highly, in her humorous sporting way, & had been most touched by an inscription she found telling how Ainsworth of the hussars had loved his life & loved his horse & dog.[73]

Dickinson lived near to Lady Frances Horner, who had lost her son and son-in-law (Raymond Asquith, son of the former Prime Minister) in the war, and who counted Lutyens and Asquith as friends. Dickinson had presumably offered to take plants from Lady Horner's garden to the cemeteries then being constructed in France. Dickinson's jubilant tone, at least as Woolf records it, is at odds with the events she describes, although in keeping with her personality. Woolf's inclusion of the detail of the inscription perhaps returns us to Leonard's brother Cecil, who, like Horner's son, had been in the Hussars. This brief diary entry is, to my knowledge, Woolf's only explicit comment on these new war cemeteries and the new tradition of battlefield pilgrimage, which enabled the bereaved to visit the graves of their dead, as discussed in the Introduction.

While Mansfield's 'The Garden Party' was being published in the *Saturday Westminster Gazette* in three parts in February 1922, she was completing her most explicit war story, 'The Fly'.[74] The story concerns two civilian fathers, Woodifield, a retired man, and the unnamed boss of a successful London firm, who have both lost sons in the war. Here a reference to the new war cemeteries, which neither has visited, has the effect of provoking enormous grief. The text presents two contrasting models of mourning: Woodifield is described as 'on his last pins', and we learn that 'since his . . . stroke, the wife and the girls kept him boxed up in the house every day of the week except Tuesday', with the ellipsis suggesting that it may have been provoked by his grief (476). His life is controlled by his family, who, for example, won't let him drink: 'they won't let me touch it at home' (478). The older boss by comparison seems to have processed his grief more healthily: he boasts of his smart office to Woodifield ('New carpet [. . .] New furniture [. . .] Electric heating!') and enjoys a position of masculine privilege. His war loss is a silent presence: he 'did not draw old Woodifield's attention to the photograph [. . .] of a grave-looking boy in uniform standing in one of those spectral photographers' parks' which 'had been there for over six years' (476).⁷⁵ There is a clear link between photography and the dead, discussed in Chapter 4, but here the photograph does not represent the dead: 'the expression was unnatural [. . .] The boy had never looked like that' (479). Woodifield can't initially remember what it is he wants to tell the boss, but the whisky that the boss supplies makes him remember that his two daughters have recently visited the grave of his son in Belgium, and had come across the grave of the boss's son:

> 'The girls were delighted with the way the place is kept,' piped the old voice. 'Beautifully looked after. Couldn't be better if they were at home [. . .] it's all as neat as a garden. Flowers growing on all the graves. Nice broad paths.' (477)

Despite Woodifield's more lighthearted discussion of the price of jam in the hotels for war tourists ('They think because we're over there having a look round we're ready to pay anything'), the reminder of their loss physically affects both men. Woodifield's hands had already begun 'to tremble' and once he has left, the boss cancels his appointments and 'covered his face with his hands. He wanted, he intended, he had arranged to weep. . .' (476, 488). He cannot cry, precisely because of the 'terrible shock [. . .] when old Woodifield sprang that remark upon him about the boy's grave' (488). The image of the cemetery disturbs the boss's memory of his son: 'the boss never thought of the boy except as lying unchanged, unblemished in his uniform, asleep for ever', much like Betty Flanders' imagined version of Seabrook or the dead man in 'The Garden Party' (478). The vision makes the boss relive the trauma of his son's death: 'when Macey had handed him the telegram that brought the whole place crashing about his head. "Deeply regret to inform you . . ."' (478). The knowledge of the cemetery has also frustrated the boss's previous coping mechanisms: 'he was puzzled' that he 'wasn't feeling as he wanted to feel'. His response is to slowly kill a fly for pleasure: a minor act of vengeance not unlike that seen in Kipling's revenge story 'Mary Postgate' (1915), discussed in Chapter 2. The fly suggests the helplessness of war death: the nurse Henrietta Tayler suggested men were 'dying like flies' in the hospital where she worked.⁷⁶ Mansfield's depiction of the man repeatedly dropping blots of ink on the fly – a substitute for tears, and a reversal of Betty Flanders' ink becoming tears in Jacob's room – gives him a perverse pleasure: 'What would it make of that! What indeed!' (480). Although his killing of the fly makes him temporarily forget his grief – as he 'lifted the corpse on the end of the paper-knife and flung it into the waste-paper basket' – it is clear that his grief remains open. Rather than bringing comfort, the new war cemeteries offered no consolation to bereaved civilians and could in fact provoke intensely unhealthy responses.

Another example illuminates the extent to which writers used the new sites of war death and commemoration in satirical terms. E. M. Forster's 'Our

Graves in Gallipoli' written in the same month that *Jacob's Room* came out (October 1922) is a dialogue between two war graves on the hillside on 'the summit of Achi Baba', one 'killed' in Gallipoli in 1915.[77] The piece is a direct response to the Chanak Crisis, a war scare between the United Kingdom and Turkey in September 1922. '*Punch* [. . .] showed a picture lately in which the Prime Minister of England, Lloyd George [. . .] is urged to go to war to protect "the sanctity of our graves in Gallipoli"', the First Grave tells the Second. The picture the grave refers to was published in *Punch* in late September 1922.[78] The pacifist writer A. A. Milne wrote a *Daily News* article in early October referring to the cartoon which ridiculed the suggestion of 'a debt owed to the British war dead at Gallipoli', as Ann Thwaite notes. Forster responded to the article in a letter to the paper a few days later:

> Sir, – Mr A. A. Milne's brilliant article deserves special thanks for its scathing analysis of 'the sanctity of our graves in Gallipoli'. [. . .] The bodies of the young men who are buried out there have no quarrel with one another now, no part in our quarrels or interest in our patronage, no craving for holocausts of more young men. Anyone who has himself entered, however feebly, into the life of the spirit, can realize this.
>
> It is only the elderly ghouls of Whitehall who exhume the dead for the purpose of party propaganda and employ them as a bait to catch the living.[79]

The use of the dead for political purposes was not new, but Forster's response to the debate over the use of the dead is to have the dead speak for themselves, personifying the graves and by extension, the dead. This new site of the dead is not represented in any traditional or consolatory way, instead showing the unquiet, even chattering, dead. The graves discuss the reasons that wars are fought, the means by which (poor) men are made to fight, and the ways the men are commemorated after death. The First Grave tells the Second Grave, 'We are important again upon earth. Each morning men mention us', but it becomes clear that the graves have, in fact, been forgotten: 'No monument marks them, for they escaped notice during the official survey'. The dialogue highlights the distance between politicians and the men who fight, with one grave asking: 'Why do the eminent men speak of "our" graves, as if they were themselves dead?'. This is a satire on the use of war deaths to justify further war, accusing politicians of wanting more graves as a sign of imperial power:

> SECOND GRAVE: If they go to war, there will be more graves.
> FIRST GRAVE: This is what they desire. [. . .]
> SECOND GRAVE: But where will they dig them?

> FIRST GRAVE: There is still room over in Chanak. Also, it is well for a nation that would be great to scatter its graves all over the world. Graves in Ireland, graves in Irak, Russia, Persia, India, each with its inscription from the Bible or Rupert Brooke. When England thinks fit, she can launch an expedition to protect the sanctity of her graves, and can follow that by another expedition to protect the sanctity of the additional graves.

The perceived emptiness of new memorial language is evident in the satirical reference to the graves' inscriptions. The article attacks war profiteers: the artist who 'hopes to illustrate this war as he did the last, for a sufficient salary', the politicians who only invoke the dead 'in order to touch the great heart of the nation more quickly' and who wage war indiscriminately, and the 'rich men' who wage war in their 'desire to be richer' and 'must persuade poor men [. . .] to go there for him'. Winston Churchill, largely responsible for the failed Gallipoli offensive, is 'Churchill the Fortunate, ever in office, and clouds of dead heroes attend him'. The article condemns the rhetoric of the dead by politicians:

> A phrase must be thought of, and 'the Gallipoli graves' is the handiest. The clergy must wave their Bibles, the old men their newspapers, the old women their knitting, the unmarried girls must wave white feathers, and all must shout, 'Gallipoli graves, Gallipoli graves, Gallipoli, Gally Polly, Gally Polly,' until the young men are ashamed and think, What sound can that be but my country's call? and Chanak receives them.

Allyson Booth suggests that 'the lapsing of "Gallipoli" into "Gally Polly" suggests both the ease with which language can be twisted to support petty causes and the resistance of the dead to *any* cause'.[80] When the First Grave notes that the deaths of further men at Chanak 'will make our heap of stones for ever England, apparently', a flippant reference to Brooke, the Second Grave reveals that he was, in fact, a Turk in life. He preaches unity: 'All graves are one. It is their unity that sanctifies them, and some day even the living will learn this'. The First Grave retorts: 'Ah, but why can they not learn it while they are still alive?'. Having the graves make the argument that Forster himself made in the newspaper ('The bodies of the young men [. . .] have no quarrel with one another now') – is a satirical means of considering manipulation of the dead for political gains. As the dialogue ends with 'warlike preparations [. . .] on the opposite coast', there is a sense of endless war, where the two graves discuss where the future burials will be located and where war can always be waged in the name of past sacrifices.

Forster's talking war graves demonstrate another version of how this new site of remembrance was used in the early 1920s for the purposes of satire and political protest. Forster worked as a Red Cross 'searcher' in Alexandria, Egypt from November 1915 in the Wounded and Missing Bureau of the Red Cross, and was discharged in January 1919, by that time 'Searcher-in-Chief'. His job was to 'go round the Hospitals and question the wounded soldiers for news of their missing comrades', a job that Nicola Beauman notes he did 'with admirable tenacity and tact'.[81] A pacifist, Forster wrote in October 1916 that war 'entails an inward death': 'It has taken the place of all the old healthy growths – love, joy, thought, despair – deluding men by its semblance of vitality'.[82]

'The Gardener', a story written very rapidly by Rudyard Kipling in March 1925 following one of his numerous visits to war cemeteries, presents a conclusively more consolatory version of these new sites of the dead and battlefield pilgrimage, while simultaneously demonstrating a surprising unease.[83] Ostensibly a story about locating the dead as Helen Turrell goes for the first time to visit the grave of her nephew Michael in one of the new war cemeteries, more importantly it is about the question of legitimate grief. Most critics read Michael as Helen's illegitimate child and this seems to have been Kipling's intention, writing in his diary on 14 March 1925: 'Have begun a few lines on the story of Helen Turrell and her 'nephew' and the gardner [sic] in the great 20,000 cemetery'.[84] Like Jacob, the death of Michael is prefigured from the start of the story, anticipating the position of Helen as inevitable mourner. He threatens as a child, 'Lots of little boys die quite soon. So'll I. *Then* you'll see!', an outburst that results in tears for both (402). Michael's death is depicted within the narrative in ironic terms: 'just after Michael had written Helen that there was nothing special doing and therefore no need to worry, a shell-splinter dropping out of a wet dawn killed him at once'. In characteristically modernist terms, his body is concealed at once: 'The next shell [. . .] laid down over the body what had been the foundation of a barn wall, so neatly that none but an expert would have guessed that anything unpleasant had happened' (405).

For an author who played a key role in the process of official public memorialisation, as the literary advisor to the then Imperial War Graves Commission and heavily involved with the war cemeteries, Kipling's depiction here is surprisingly satirical about the rapid state interpellation of the civilian into a mourner.[85] This story doesn't conceal the frequency of this kind of death – 'By this time the village was old in experience of war, and, English fashion, had evolved a ritual to meet it' – and Helen's grief follows a well-trodden path:

> Helen, presently, found herself pulling down the house-blinds one after one with great care, and saying earnestly to each: 'Missing *always* means dead." Then she took her place in the dreary procession that was impelled to go through an inevitable series of unprofitable emotions. (405)

If the war made men into mechanised 'blocks of tin soldiers' as we read in *Jacob's Room*, this story suggests a similar mechanisation of female mourners: '"I'm being manufactured into a bereaved next of kin", she told herself, as she prepared her documents' (406). Institutional rhetoric is depicted as unexpectedly empty and formulaic: 'when all the organizations had deeply or sincerely regretted their inability to trace, etc, something gave way within her and all sensations [. . .] came to an end in blessed passivity' (406). Here distance is figured as the isolation of the mourner in her grief: despite having 'no interest in any aftermath, national or personal, of the war', Helen 'moving at an immense distance [. . .] sat on various relief committees and held strong views – she heard herself delivering them – about the site of the proposed village War Memorial' (407).

As Helen moves 'on to another process of the manufacture' into a war mourner, she goes to visit Michael's grave in France (407). The narrative highlights the strange language of leisure tourism that accompanied battlefield pilgrimage: the cemetery 'could be comfortably reached by an afternoon train which fitted in with the morning boat, and that there was a comfortable little hotel [. . .] where one could spend quite a comfortable night and see one's grave next morning' (407–8). This reiterated comfort is in stark contrast to what is described as 'the nightmare' of the trip (409). The two women that Helen meets, both models of unhealthy mourning, act as foils for her own grief. The first, a hysterical 'large Lancashire woman', cannot remember the details needed to locate the grave of her son (408). Her sobbing and enforced restraint is a sad case of private grief clashing with official bureaucracy, a situation that seems too frequent: '"They are often like this", said the officer's wife' (408). The mothers, already grieving the loss of their sons away from home, are doubly distanced by the bureaucratic rhetoric of the war graves: the 'new world of abbreviated titles' that denotes location, that Helen notes (407). The second woman, Mrs Scarsworth, is herself an illegitimate mourner, obtaining commissions to photograph graves in order to visit the grave of her lover. Already on her ninth pilgrimage to the graves, she has to confess to someone:

> '*You* don't know what that means. He was everything to me that he oughtn't to have been – the one real thing – the only thing that ever happened to me in all my life; and I've had to pretend he wasn't. I've had to watch every word I said, and think out what lie I'd tell next, for years and years!' (411–12)

Helen, of course, does understand, although there is no response from her in the narrative to the woman's breakdown: 'I can't keep it up any longer. Oh, I can't!' (412). The woman's need to confess prefigures Helen's acknowledgement by the gardener.

The cemetery is, like many of the war cemeteries in 1925, still under construction. 'The place was still in the making [. . .] Culverts across a deep ditch served for entrances through the unfinished boundary wall' (412–13). Helen's initial impression of the cemetery is confused:

> She did not know that Hagenzeele Third counted twenty-one thousand dead already. All she saw was a merciless sea of black crosses, bearing little strips of stamped tin at all angles across their faces. She could distinguish no order or arrangement in their mass; nothing but a waist-high wilderness as of weeds stricken dead, rushing at her. (413)

Despite the temporary attempts at burial and individual memorialisation in the crosses with naming strips, there is nothing comforting in this account for the grieving mother: the dead are a 'mass', a 'wilderness'. Kipling increased the number of dead from the number he saw on his visit to a cemetery: 'Went off to Rouen Cemetery (11,000 graves) and collogued [sic] with the Head Gardener and the contractors. One never gets over the shock of this Dead Sea of arrested lives'.[86] The 'Dead Sea' of Kipling's initial impression becomes 'merciless' in its fictional rewriting. Helen goes to the finished area of the cemetery, 'a block of some two or three hundred graves whose headstones had already been set, whose flowers were planted out, and whose new-sown grass showed green' (413). The man tending the graves asks who she is looking for and Helen tells him the name, 'my nephew' (413): 'The man lifted his eyes and looked at her with infinite compassion before he turned from the fresh-sown grass toward the naked black crosses. "Come with me", he said, "and I will show you where your son lies"' (414).

The man, presumably for the first time, acknowledges Helen as Michael's mother. Here the war cemetery, despite its lack of order, offers some redemption: a site of acknowledgement of both her loss and herself as a grieving mother. The clear Christ-like characteristics of the man – his 'infinitive compassion' and the Biblical allusion to John 20:15 evoked by Helen 'supposing him to be the gardener' – gives a broader resonance to the story (414). In suggesting a parallel between Mary Magdalene looking for the absent body of Christ in the tomb with Helen's search for her missing son's grave, Kipling implicitly compares Michael, and by extension all of his dead comrades, with Christ: a common wartime trope we saw earlier in the nurses' narratives. Although Michael is buried in the unfinished area of the cemetery, there is a sense that order will be restored, that the dead will be arranged and put in their correct places with proper headstones. The gardener will care for these graves with the 'infinite compassion' he showed Helen, and the 'young plants' he puts in the earth signal regrowth and renewal, both for the land and for Helen (414).

Kipling, a writer publicly involved with giving meaning to the mass death of the war, here presents us with a story of very private and intimate grief, using the new site of the war cemetery. In a public discourse which privileged the mother as the mourner, we wonder if the depiction of illegitimate grief here relates to his own experience as a bereaved father. Much like Mansfield's whole, sleeping corpse in 'The Garden Party' as an implicit response to the news of her brother 'blown to bits!', Kipling's narrative fantasy of having definite news of a child (moving from the ambiguous status of 'missing' to dead) and finally locating a body and visiting a grave arguably provided a narrative compensation for an experience that was denied to him in relation to his own son John, whose body was never found within Kipling's lifetime.

Modernist Death

In contrast to the domestic, private mourning of *Jacob's Room*, *Mrs. Dalloway* (1925) examines public, collective mourning and the grand, national process of monument-making. Woolf's two contrasting protagonists explore the social response to 'this terrible war': the civilian society hostess Clarissa Dalloway and the shell-shocked war veteran Septimus Warren Smith who 'could not feel' (191, 113). Set in mid-June 1923, four years after the Treaty of Versailles, the famous scene documenting the collective response to the passing car indicates the contemporary collective state of grief, a cultural malaise: 'for in all the hat shops and tailors' shops strangers looked at each other and thought of the dead; of the flag; of Empire [. . .] For the surface agitation of the passing car as it sunk grazed something very profound' (22). The effects of the war are obviously still very present: 'The War was over, except for some one like Mrs Foxcroft eating her heart out because that nice boy was killed and now the old Manor House might go to a cousin; or Lady Bexborough who opened a bazaar, they said, with the telegram in her hand, John, her favourite, killed' (5). The presentation of Mrs Foxcroft and Lady Bexborough juxtaposes two contrasting models of mourning, and Clarissa inwardly praises Lady Bexborough's public suppression of her grief:

> This late age of world's experience had bred in them all, all men and women, a well of tears. Tears and sorrows; courage and endurance; a perfectly upright and stoical bearing. Think, for example, of the woman she admired most, Lady Bexborough, opening the bazaar. (11)

In linking the terms valorised in warfare ('courage' and 'endurance') with a particular class-based model of repression and uprightness concerning war grief – what Karen Levenback terms 'the "normal" activity of repression' that Septimus lacks – Woolf critiques one contemporary response to the war dead.[87] Unlike the earlier uncertain world of *Jacob's Room*, the 1923 society of *Mrs. Dalloway* seemingly has a respected, *correct* way to mourn: what Sigmund Freud considered the conventional attitude towards death – 'to hush it up'.[88]

The text suggests that this model cannot be upheld: Peter Walsh reflects that 'in privacy one may do as one chooses. One may weep if no one saw' (198). Tears are often unintentionally public, as the model of stoic repression (the 'wax seal' over societal grief) cannot contain 'the well of tears' caused by the enormous death toll. This is demonstrated by Mr Bowley, last seen discussing the fate of Jimmy in *Jacob's Room*:

> Little Mr Bowley, who had rooms in the Albany and was sealed with wax over the deeper sources of life, but could be unsealed suddenly, inappropriately, sentimentally, by this sort of thing – poor women waiting to see the Queen go past – poor women, nice little children, orphans, widows, the War–tut-tut – actually had tears in his eyes. (25)

The question of the appropriate way to respond to the war dead as opposed to the 'inappropriate' and 'sentimental' way is arguably the central preoccupation of *Mrs. Dalloway*.

The novel draws attention to new public monuments and ceremonies, questioning the appropriateness of these new symbols. At Whitehall, Peter Walsh sees a memorial ceremony with marching boys: 'on their faces an expression like the letters of a legend written round the base of a statue praising duty, gratitude, fidelity, love of England' (65–6). The narrative compares the boys' patriotism to the 'Big Words' that to many had been exposed as fraudulent and meaningless. The ceremony is accompanied by a public code of reverence: they carry 'the wreath which they had fetched from Finsbury Pavement to the empty tomb. They had taken their vow. The traffic respected it; vans were stopped' (66). The Unknown Warrior remained a new feature of London public ideology: a memorial site that another war victim, Miss Kilman, will later shield her eyes against (174). Building on the mechanised 'blocks of tin soldiers' we saw in *Jacob's Room*, here Woolf develops the militarisation and discipline of the boys into a proleptic complex metaphor of the memorialised dead, 'on they marched [. . .] as if one will worked legs and arms uniformly, and life, with its varieties, its irreticences, had been laid under a pavement of monuments and wreaths and drugged into a stiff yet staring corpse by discipline' (66). The reference to legs and arms reminds us of the synecdochal male body parts seen in the Cambridge common rooms seen of *Jacob's Room*. Life itself here, seen in the individual characters and 'varieties' of the boys in training Woolf suggests, has been turned into a figurative war corpse, buried beneath the pavements of the city landscape and the new public memorial culture (the use of 'monuments', rather than memorials, suggesting a celebratory rather than commemorative tone).

Other writers were engaging with new memorials as literary sites. A key scene in Christopher Isherwood's 1932 novel *The Memorial* is set at the service for the new village war memorial, where new modes and rituals for remembering the dead are inaugurated. The war widow Lily (a version of Isherwood's widowed mother) reacts strongly to the way that 'the Vicar read the names of the Fallen':

> The reading of the names, so crudely recorded, alphabetically, without any preface or title, seemed ugly and brutal to her. She had been similarly struck, though not so strongly, by a call-over she had heard on a Speech Day at Eric's school. It had seemed to her that this was a glimpse of the real man's world, so hard and formal and cold. She had hardly thought of Richard, as one had to think of him, of course, turned forth over there, on the Other Side, with Frank Prewitt, Harold Stanley Peck, George Henry Swindells – all so naked and lost, clinging together, learning the new rules and ways, dazed and unfamiliar.[89]

Isherwood, like Woolf, draws attention to the specifically masculine militarisation and discipline: the ways that the soldiers remain to some extent under orders even in death. Lily explicitly links this to the masculine public school culture of which her son is now part, an institutional version of Woolf's marching boys that will similarly interpellate the boys into future warriors. Isherwood uses Lily to voice the anger and unhappiness many civilian women felt about the new rituals of democratic death: 'Why couldn't they have read out the officers' names first? She'd heard that the names on the Memorial were put in the same way. That was really disgraceful, because, in fifty years' time, nobody would know who anybody was' (82). However, Lily still considers the memorial 'in very good taste compared to the granite atrocities they were putting up in the neighbouring villages' (84).

Alongside Woolf's parodying of particular societal responses and official means of remembrance, there is clearly an experimental attempt to rework some of these modes in less official terms. David Bradshaw has argued that despite Woolf's depiction of these new monuments as 'anti-monuments', the novel does reflect some elegiac conventions in its imagery. He notes that the paragraph following Walsh's encounter with the boy soldiers begins 'A patter like the patter of leaves in a wood', where 'falling or fallen leaves' recall 'an ancient literary topos for the dead'. In using this trope, 'Woolf not only problematizes the boy soldiers' presence in Whitehall by presaging their deaths in battle, but also, in a sense, like Walsh, joins in their act of remembrance'. Bradshaw draws attention to moments where Woolf re-imagines these monuments and ceremonies in less official forms, noting the 'novel's statuary moments, in which characters bring to mind (or are themselves described as) monumental figures cast in attitudes of grief or lamentation'.[90] Woolf's recreation of the Two Minutes' Silence in the aeroplane scene functions as one of these moments, implicitly invoking this new public ritual of remembrance: 'As they looked the whole world became perfectly silent [. . .] and in this extraordinary silence and peace, in this pallor, in this purity, bells struck eleven times, the sound fading up there among the gulls' (26).

In contrast to, and excluded from, the public monuments and ritual that claim to memorialise the war dead, Septimus Warren Smith proclaims himself to be the sole commemorator of the dead, 'the giant mourner' (91). Septimus's suicide, unlike any of the other deaths being discussed, is represented within the narrative. The reader is given access to his thoughts through free indirect narration as he considers 'Mrs Filmer's nice clean bread-knife [. . .] Ah, but one mustn't spoil that' (195). The domestic, banal setting and flippant tone make Septimus's actual suicide a shock: he 'flung himself vigorously, violently down on to Mrs Filmer's area railings' (195). Interestingly, although this death unusually occurs within the narrative, the 'horribly mangled' remains of Septimus are immediately hidden from view and he becomes, belatedly, one of the concealed war dead: Mrs Filmer 'made [Rezia] hide her eyes in the bedroom' as 'she must not see him' (195–6). The death is distanced through the lack of a deathbed scene and the absence of a visible corpse. Like Mrs Sheridan's concern about whether the man's death happened in her garden in 'The Garden Party', Mrs Filmer is very concerned to keep Septimus's body (and co-extensively the war dead) out of the domestic space: '(they wouldn't bring the body in here, would they?)' (196). This lack of confrontation coincides with a civilian exculpation from blame: 'A sudden impulse, no one was in the least to blame ([Dr Holmes] told Mrs Filmer)' (196). This belated death of a combatant remains at a distance: Clarissa learns of the death of 'a young man' through Lady Bradshaw, who has learnt of it via her husband, who received a phone call (240).

Written nearly ten years after the end of the war, Woolf's 1927 novel *To the Lighthouse* presents the reader with the quintessential modernist death: '[Mr Ramsay stumbling along a passage stretched his arms out one dark morning, but, Mrs Ramsay having died rather suddenly the night before, he stretched his arms out. They remained empty.]'[91] This parenthetical death-knell announcement is a hyperbolic version of postwar representations of death. In a death sentence that suddenly and violently interrupts the narrative, Mrs Ramsay is brusquely and bluntly disposed of. There is no body or funeral service. The matter-of-fact, emotionless tone, the lack of information concerning the conditions or cause of Mrs Ramsay's death and the fact that the events are related, as Marcus notes, 'in double retrospect' alienate the reader from the death.[92] The death is further mediated through third-hand information, mirroring the wartime confusion and misinformation over who had died: 'Some said he was dead; some said she was dead. Which was it?' (159). The fact that all the deaths of the novel occur in 'Time Passes', the section which charts the war years, is indicative of the mass deaths of that short period, and Prue's and Andrew's deaths are related in a similar parenthetical mode. Andrew's war death, which 'mercifully was instantaneous', is related in what Vincent Sherry notes is euphemistic and conventional idiom, giving 'some sense of the typicality – the immensity – of the incident [Woolf] depicts', and simultaneously representing the civilian experience of a war death, distanced through language.[93]

Similar to the use of one figure to signify a generation in *Jacob's Room*, Woolf bases *To the Lighthouse* around one family but allegorically relates a national war narrative through the disintegration and renewal of their family home. The benefit of retrospection means that the war can now be, as Sherry notes, 'parenthesized, contained as an interlude' within a larger narrative.[94] Woolf's choice to portray the chaos, disruption and decay of the war years through the encroachment of nature onto the family home demonstrates a retrospective ability to place the war within a natural cycle, suggesting inevitable renewal after disintegration. The returning Ramsays therefore 'expected to find things as they had left them' (159). Significantly, it is women who come in to restore the house, a process which itself seems both funereal and potentially renewing; we learn that 'twined about [Mrs McNab's] dirge' there was 'some incorrigible hope' (149). The restoration of the house by the servants is described in female terms as 'some rusty laborious birth seemed to be taking place', suggesting reparation, healing, rebirth (159).

Conclusion

This chapter demonstrates some of the ways that writers responded to, and depicted, the new public memorial landscape in the postwar period. The question of absent and consolatory bodies was key in the immediate postwar years. *Jacob's Room* shows Woolf parodying traditional means of commemoration, biography or obituary in the postwar decade. New modes of official commemoration are similarly rejected in favour of representation of the dead through non-traditional sites (Jacob's room, his shoes). Woolf's use of the new memorial trope of the Unknown Warrior seen in the imaginative imposition of others onto Jacob, in conjunction with her new modes of writing character, functions as an example of memorial culture meeting modernist literary experiment. Mansfield's 'The Garden Party', by contrast, offers a consolatory narrative of the peaceful and content dead, through a fantasy of a present and whole corpse. This story is not ostensibly about the war dead, but it demonstrates Mansfield's postwar method of seeing 'death in life', and functions as a bildungsroman where Laura gains the 'tragic knowledge' people gained during the war.[95] The section on locating and burying the dead suggests that 'The Fly' depicts the disturbing effects of the repression of war grief and demonstrates the lack of consolation offered by the new war cemeteries. Forster's satirical 'Our Graves in Gallipoli' makes his talking graves themselves question the absurd rhetoric of men fighting to protect these new sites of the dead. Kipling's 'The Gardener', although satirical in its depiction of the bureaucracy administering the new war sites, is ultimately consolatory in its location of a corpse and the legitimation of a mourning mother. The final section on modernist death shows how *Mrs. Dalloway* parodies and playfully reworks new memorial sites and commemorative practices, such as the Two Minutes' Silence, to demonstrate their inadequacy for the 'well of tears' created by the war. Septimus's suicide, as a belated war death, is depicted satirically as uncomfortable for those on the home front, and therefore is immediately concealed from public view. *To the Lighthouse* presents a key version of modernist death, showing the representational distance of the modernist death from the Victorian lengthy deathbed scene. The restoration of the Ramsay house in the third section is not a typical memorial to the dead, but suggests some hope of renewal and moving forward after a trauma. Ultimately this collection of both modernist and other texts demonstrate the explicit preoccupation of literature in the immediate postwar period with the war dead – a preoccupation that would continue, in more muted and often more abstract tones, into the 1930s.

Notes

1. Woolf, 12 December 1920, in *The Diary of Virginia Woolf, Volume II: 1920–24*, ed. Anne Olivier Bell, assisted by Andrew McNeillie [1978] (1981), pp. 79–80.
2. 12 December 1920, *DVWII*, p. 79.
3. 12 December 1920, *DVWII*, p. 79.
4. 'Unknown Warrior', *The Times*, 4 November 1920, p. 13. *The Times Digital Archive*, <http://tinyurl.galegroup.com/tinyurl/9fCeh9> (last accessed 3 April 2019).
5. 'Unknown Warrior', *The Times*, 4 November 1920, p. 13. *The Times Digital Archive*.
6. Hamilton, *Dead Yesterday* (1916). The book had been published by Woolf's half-brother Gerald Duckworth's press. It doesn't appear that Woolf had read the novel.
7. Woolf, 12 April 1920, *DVWII*, p. 109. Lytton Strachey, *Queen Victoria* (1921).
8. Hynes, 'Monument-Making', chapter 14 in *A War Imagined: The First World War and English Culture* [1990] (1992), pp. 269–82.
9. Hynes, *A War Imagined*, pp. 269–70.
10. Joanna Scutts has begun to trace the importance of this context in 'Battlefield Cemeteries, Pilgrimage, and Literature after the First World War: The Burial of the Dead', *English Literature in Transition, 1880–1920*, 52.4 (2009), pp. 387–416. None of the major modernist surveys from the past thirty years – of which there are too many to include here – consider in any detail the influence of the new culture of war commemoration on postwar literature.
11. Cather, *Not Under Forty* (1936), Prefatory Note. See, for example, Michael North, *Reading 1922: A Return to the Scene of the Modern* (1999); Kevin Jackson, *Constellation of Genius, 1922: Modernism Year One* (2012); and Jean-Michel Rabaté, *1922: Literature, Culture, Politics* (2015).
12. For further discussion, see Stacy Gillis, 'Consoling Fictions: Mourning, World War One, and Dorothy L. Sayers', in Patricia Rae (ed.), *Modernism and Mourning* (2007), pp. 185–97, and Victoria Stewart, *Crime Writing in Interwar Britain: Fact and Fiction in the Golden Age* (2017).

13. Mark Hussey (ed.), *Virginia Woolf and War: Fiction, Reality and Myth* (1991); Helen Wussow, *The Nightmare of History: The Fictions of Virginia Woolf and D. H. Lawrence* (1998); Karen Levenback, *Virginia Woolf and the Great War* (1999); Christina Froula, *Virginia Woolf and the Bloomsbury Avant-Garde: War, Civilization, Modernity* (2005); Booth, *Postcards from the Trenches: Negotiating the Space between Modernism and the First World War* (1996), especially the first two chapters on 'Corpselessness' and 'Corpses', pp. 21–63; Sherry, *The Great War and the Language of Modernism* (2003), especially 'Woolf, Among the Modernists', pp. 235–97; Sherman, *In a Strange Room: Modernism's Corpses and Mortal Obligation* (2014), especially 'The State's Unending Vigil: Owen's and Woolf's Unknown Warrior', pp. 44–107.
14. Hussey, 'Living in a War Zone: An Introduction to Virginia Woolf as a War Novelist', in *Virginia Woolf and War*, p. 3.
15. See Chapter 3 for a summary of this scholarship.
16. The key text on the relationship between the two writers is Angela Smith, *Katherine Mansfield and Virginia Woolf: A Public of Two* (1999). For a more recent assessment, see Christine Froula, Gerri Kimber and Todd Martin (eds), *Katherine Mansfield Studies*, 10, Special Issue on *Virginia Woolf and Katherine Mansfield* (2018).
17. Letter to Woolf, [c. 23 August 1917], in *The Collected Letters of Katherine Mansfield, Volume I: 1903–1917*, ed. Vincent O'Sullivan and Margaret Scott (1984), p. 327; Woolf, 31 May 1920, *DVWII*, p. 45.
18. Woolf, 17 February 1922, *DVWII*, p. 167.
19. Woolf, 16 January 1923, *DVWII*, p. 226.
20. For discussion of this, see Smith, 'A Common Certain Understanding' in *Katherine Mansfield and Virginia Woolf*, pp. 30–62.
21. Woolf, 5 June, *DVWII*, p. 45. The lunch was on 2 June, Derby Day, when the sun 'burnt', p. 45.
22. Darrohn, '"Blown to Bits!": Katherine Mansfield's "The Garden Party" and the Great War', *Modern Fiction Studies*, 44.3 (1998), p. 514.
23. This line of argument – that the dominant mode of interpretation of the war was ironic – is, of course, put forward by Paul Fussell in *The Great War and Modern Memory* (1975; repr. 2000).
24. Although not termed 'a war book' until Winifred Holtby's 1932 study, *Virginia Woolf* (1932), cited in Karen L. Levenback, *Virginia Woolf and the Great War*, p. 44.
25. Woolf, *Mrs. Dalloway* [1925], ed. Claire Tomalin (1992), p. 93. Further references will be included in the text.
26. Woolf, 'The Mark on the Wall' [1917], in *A Haunted House and Other Stories* (1973), p. 47. It was first published in *Two Stories*, written and printed by Virginia Woolf and L. S. Woolf at the Hogarth Press (1917), and then republished in *Monday or Tuesday* (1921). The first story in *Two Stories*, 'Three Jews' by Leonard Woolf, concerns the Jewish protagonist's visits to a cemetery to the grave of his first wife and his conversations with the Jewish cemetery keeper. The first woodcut to accompany Leonard's story, of four by Dora Carrington, is of a cemetery with a mourner and a gravedigger.

27. Woolf, *Jacob's Room* [1922], ed. Sue Roe (1992), p. 155. Further references will be included in the text.
28. Unsigned essay, 'Modern Novels', *Times Literary Supplement*, 10 April 1919, pp. 189–90. *The Times Literary Supplement Historical Archive*, <http://tinyurl.galegroup.com/tinyurl/9ptez7> (last accessed 22 April 2019). Woolf, 'Modern Fiction' [1925], in *The Essays of Virginia Woolf, Volume 4: 1925–28*, ed. Andrew McNeille (1994), pp. 157–65.
29. Woolf, 'The Leaning Tower' [1940], in *The Essays of Virginia Woolf, Volume 6: 1933–1941, and Additional Essays 1906–1924*, ed. Stuart N. Clarke (2011), p. 269.
30. 'I have an idea that I will invent a new name for my books to supplant "novel". A new – by Virginia Woolf. But what? Elegy?', 27 June 1925, in *The Diary of Virginia Woolf, Volume III: 1925–30*, ed. Anne Olivier Bell [1980] (1982), p. 34.
31. Hattaway, 'Virginia Woolf's *Jacob's Room*: History and Memory' in Dorothy Goldman (ed.), *Women and World War I: The Written Response* (1993), pp. 19, 24.
32. Handley, 'War and the Politics of Narration in *Jacob's Room*', in Hussey (ed.), *Virginia Woolf and War* (1991), p. 115.
33. Marcus, *Writers and Their Work: Virginia Woolf* (1997), p. 86.
34. Hattaway, 'Virginia Woolf's *Jacob's Room*', p. 14.
35. Woolf, 26 January 1920, *DVWII*, pp. 13–14.
36. C. N. S. Woolf, *Poems*, ed. P. S. Woolf (1918). For description of the volume, see Joanna Scutts, 'Virginia and Leonard Woolf Remember Their War Dead', <https://lithub.com/virginia-and-leonard-woolf-remember-their-war-dead/> (last accessed 3 June 2019).
37. Woolf, 23 July 1918, in *The Diary of Virginia Woolf, Volume I: 1915–19*, ed. Anne Olivier Bell, intro. by Quentin Bell [1977] (1979), p. 171.
38. Woolf, 'Rupert Brooke', *The Times Literary Supplement*, 8 August 1918, p. 371. *The Times Literary Supplement Historical Archive*, <http://tinyurl.galegroup.com/tinyurl/9qurhX> (last accessed 24 April 2019).
39. 'Armistice Day, 1920,' *The Times*, 11 November 1920, p. 16. *The Times Digital Archive*, <http://tinyurl.galegroup.com/tinyurl/9fENQ2> (last accessed 3 April 2019).
40. Very occasionally Jacob is differentiated from other characters: 'Only Jacob [. . .] looked a little different' distinguished by the 'book he would at nine-thirty precisely [. . .] open and study, as no one else of all these multitudes would do' (55).
41. The line 'there is no need to think of them grown old' appears to be an allusion to the line 'They shall grow not old' in Lawrence Binyon's poem 'For the Fallen', first published in *The Times* (21 September 1914), and included in the anthology *The Winnowing Fan: Poems on the Great War* (1914).
42. In her diary on 13 August 1921, Woolf quotes *The Autobiography of Leigh Hunt*, noting that going home from Shelley's funeral, Hunt & Byron 'laughed till they split'. Later in the text we see Jacob 'laughing so much that he could not speak' (41), and arguably his ability to laugh personalises and humanises him, to some extent. Woolf's comments on Hunt's passage provide commentary on her preferences for writing narrative and biography: 'This is human nature, & [Hunt] doesn't mind owning to it [. . .] history so dull because of its battles & laws; & sea voyages in books so dull because the traveller will describe beauties instead of going into the

cabins & saying what the sailors looked like, wore, eat, said; how they behaved', *DVWII*, p. 130.
43. While writing the novel, Woolf similarly wrote of the disabled soldiers she saw in London in bodily terms: 'stiff legs, single legs, sticks shod with rubber, & empty sleeves are common enough. [. . .] I sometimes see dreadful looking spiders propelling themselves along the platform – men all body – legs trimmed off close to the body', 18 February 1921, *DVWII*, p. 93.
44. This image is subsequently militarised: 'although great boots march under the gowns' (24). The real Trinity College, Cambridge – one of the largest colleges in the university – lost 619 men in the Great War, including students, Fellows and staff, giving a sense of the scale of loss for college and university communities. See <http://trinitycollegechapel.com/about/memorials/war-memorials/> (last accessed 20 April 2019).
45. Mepham, 'Mourning and Modernism', in Patricia Clements and Isobel Grundy (eds), *Virginia Woolf: New Critical Essays* (1983), p. 152.
46. The flower had been linked since 1915 with remembrance of the dead through 'Violet Day', a forerunner of the poppy as the 'symbol of perpetual remembrance'. The first Violet Day was in July 1915, the last was in August 1970. The event was predominantly held in South Australia, but also in other places across Australia. See <http://adelaidia.sa.gov.au/events/violet-day> (last accessed 24 April 2019). Violets and the dead were also associated in more personal terms for Woolf: Tom Eliot apparently 'uses violet powder to make him look cadaverous', she noted on 12 March 1922, *DVWII*, p. 171.
47. 5 August 1920, *DVWII*, pp. 55–6.
48. 25 October, *DVWII*, p. 72–3. Woolf refers explicitly to ongoing unrest in Ireland and the coal strike in England, but the language of their 'generation' refers back to the longstanding impact of the war.
49. 27 November 1922, *DVWII*, p. 214.
50. Mepham, 'Mourning and Modernism', p. 152.
51. Olivier Bell and McNeillie, Footnote 9, 3 March 1920, *DVWII*, p. 23.
52. 5 February 1921, *DVWII*, p. 89.
53. 10 April 1920, *DVWII*, p. 27.
54. 10 April 1920, *DVWII*, p. 29. Woolf, in fact, wasn't correct about this at all: Ward, who had died in late March, 'had a tremendous send-off, with condolences from Royalty and the eminent, a Times leader, a two-column obituary, and a country funeral at Aldbury', Olivier Bell and McNeillie, Footnote 7, *DVWII*, p. 29.
55. 15 April, p. 30. Olivier Bell and McNeillie note that James's funeral 'took place in Chelsea Old Church in March 1916', Footnote 10, *DVWII*, p. 30.
56. 15 September 1920, *DVWII*, p. 65.
57. Woolf, 20 May 1920, *DVWII*, p. 40. It seems that this article never appeared. The first issue of 'The Woman's Supplement' was on 23 June 1920, the announcement appearing the day before in *The Times*, 22 June 1920, p. 17. *The Times Digital Archive*, <http://tinyurl.galegroup. com/tinyurl/9d8Ea8> (last accessed 29 March 2019).
58. Woolf, 8 June, *DVWII*, p. 47.
59. Woolf, 29 June 1920, *DVWII*, p. 51.

60. Zimring, *Social Dance and the Modernist Imagination in Interwar Britain* (2013), p. 202.
61. Woolf, 29 June, *DVWII*, p. 51. Two weeks later, she complained that she hadn't written *Jacob's Room* for three weeks because of her reviewing duties, 13 July, *DVWII*, p. 53.
62. First published in an edited form as 'The Garden-Party' in three parts in the *Saturday Westminster Gazette* on 4 February 1922, pp. 9–10, and 11 February 1922, p. 10, and the *Weekly Westminster Gazette* on 18 February 1922, pp. 16–17, and then published in the collection *The Garden Party: and Other Stories* (1922). Mansfield, 'The Garden Party', in *The Collected Fiction of Katherine Mansfield, Volume 2: 1916–1922*, ed. Gerri Kimber and Vincent O'Sullivan (2014), p. 407. Further references will be included in the text.
63. Woolf, 14 February, *DVWII*, p. 161. Woolf was talking about the publication of *The Garden Party: and Other Stories*.
64. Darrohn, '"Blown to Bits!"', p. 531.
65. Darrohn, '"Blown to Bits!"', p. 521.
66. Darrohn, '"Blown to Bits!"', pp. 514, 520.
67. Mansfield, 13 February 1916, in *The Diaries of Katherine Mansfield*, ed. Gerri Kimber and Claire Davison (2016), p. 203.
68. To J. M. Murry, [16 November 1919], in *The Collected Letters of Katherine Mansfield, Volume III: 1919–1920*, ed. Vincent O'Sullivan and Margaret Scott (1993), p. 97.
69. To J. M. Murry, [16 November 1919], *CLVIII*, pp. 97–8.
70. The Biblical reference is Paul's letter to the Corinthians (1 Corinthians 15:32; cf. Isaiah 22:13). Marvell, 'To His Coy Mistress', *The Poems of Andrew Marvell*, ed. Nigel Smith (2015), pp. 76–8.
71. Mansfield, 'Dea Ex Machina', review of W. B. Maxwell's *A Man and His Lesson*, *The Athanaeum*, 26 September 1919, in *The Poetry and Critical Writings of Katherine Mansfield*, ed. Gerri Kimber and Angela Smith (2014), p. 511.
72. Fussell, *The Great War and Modern Memory* (1975; repr. 2000), pp. 23–4.
73. Woolf, 12 November 1919, *DVWI*, p. 312.
74. Mansfield, 'The Fly' (1922), in *CFVII*, p. 476. Further references will be included in the text.
75. Mansfield wrote to S. S. Koteliansky after the death of her brother: 'On the mantelpiece in my room stands my brother's photograph', 19 November 1915, *CLVI*, p. 200. In her diary, she noted there were 'times that your photograph "looks sad"', *Diaries*, p. 192.
76. Tayler, *A Scottish Nurse at Work* (1920), p. 95.
77. Forster, 'Our Graves in Gallipoli' in *Abinger Harvest* (1936), pp. 33–5. All quotes included in the text are from these pages. The article was published in the first section, 'A commentary on passing events'.
78. The picture, drawn by the magazine's chief cartoonist Bernard Partridge, depicts John Bull pointing to the newspaper that Lloyd George is reading and telling him 'if you are resolved to defend the freedom of the straits and the sanctity of our graves in Gallipoli you will have the country and the empire with you', 'A Non-Party

Statement', *Punch*, 27 September 1922, <https://punch.photoshelter.com/image/I0000_GIoPKeXiRQ> (last accessed 25 April 2019).
79. Milne, 'Another Little War', *Daily News*, 4 October 1922, and Forster, 'Another Little War', *Daily News*, 9 October 1922, quoted in Ann Thwaite, *A. A. Milne: His Life* (1990), pp. 229–30.
80. Booth notes that this also prefigures the manipulation of words by the masses that we see in the chanting of 'Esmiss Esmoor' in the trial scene of *A Passage to India* (1924), *Postcards from the Trenches*, p. 53.
81. To S. R. Masood, 29 December 1915, in *Selected Letters of E. M. Forster, Volume One: 1979–1920*, ed. Mary Lago and P. N. Furbank (1985), p. 232. Nicola Beauman, *Morgan: A Biography of E. M. Forster* (1993), pp. 295, 307.
82. Letter from Forster to Goldsworthy Lowes Dickinson, quoted by Beauman, *Morgan*, p. 295.
83. 'The Gardener', *McCall's Magazine*, April 1925, illustrated by Arthur E. Becher; *Strand Magazine*, May 1925, with eight-line epigraph, illustrated by J. Dewar Mills. Collected as the final story in *Debits and Credits* (1926), followed by the poem 'The Burden' (with two verses included as an epigraph), pp. 399–416. Further references will be included in the text.
84. 14 March 1925, TS, 'Rudyard Kipling's Motor Tours', Wimpole Papers 25/8, Special Collections, University of Sussex Library, quoted by Lisa Lewis, <http://www.kiplingsociety.co.uk/rg_gardener1.htm> (last accessed 1 June 2019).
85. In May 1922, King George V and a group including Field Marshal Earl Haig and Sir Fabian Ware undertook a tour of the cemeteries in Flanders and Northern France, many of which were still under construction. Kipling joined them for parts of the tour. He drafted the speech that the King delivered on the final day of his tour, which assured listeners that the King was satisfied that the Commission's principles of equality of treatment in death, including for those with no known grave, were being carried out. Kipling wrote a poem about the tour, 'The King's Pilgrimage', published in *The Times* and *The World* (New York) on 15 May 1922, which supported the points made in the King's speech (which was also published), and was later used as the epigraph to Sidney C. Hurst, *The Silent Cities: An Illustrated Guide to the War Cemeteries and Memorials to the 'Missing' in France and Flanders, 1914–1918* (1929). The King's speech, Kipling's poem, and a description of the tour with photographs, were collected in Frank Fox, *The King's Pilgrimage* (1922), with the profits going to fund bereaved relatives to visit the cemeteries. For more information, see Roger Ayers, notes on 'The King's Pilgrimage', <http://www.kiplingsociety.co.uk/rg_kingspilgrimage1.htm> (last accessed 2 June 2019).
86. Letter to Rider Haggard, 14 March 1925, in *The Letters of Rudyard Kipling, Volume 5: 1920–30*, ed. Thomas Pinney (2004), p. 212.
87. Levenback, *Virginia Woolf and the Great War*, p. 49.
88. Freud, 'Thoughts for the Times on War and Death' [1915], in *Sigmund Freud: Collected Papers, Volume 4*, trans. under supervision of Joan Riviere (1959), p. 304.
89. Isherwood, *The Memorial: Portrait of a Family* [1932] (2012), p. 81. Further references will be included in the text. The novel, dedicated to his father, is semi-autobiographical: Isherwood's father was killed in the war in 1915.

90. Bradshaw, '"Vanished, Like Leaves": The Military, Elegy and Italy in *Mrs Dalloway*', *Woolf Studies Annual*, 8 (2002), quotes from pp. 108–18.
91. Woolf, *To the Lighthouse* [1927] (1964), pp. 146–7. Further references will be included in the text.
92. Marcus, *Writers and Their Work: Virginia Woolf*, p. 103.
93. Virginia Woolf, *To the Lighthouse*, p. 152. Sherry, *The Great War*, p. 295.
94. Sherry, *The Great War*, p. 294.
95. To J. M. Murry, [16 November 1919], *CLVIII*, pp. 97.

CONCLUSION: MODERNISM'S GHOSTS

The final version of Sir William Orpen's *To the Unknown British Soldier in France*, presented to the Imperial War Museum in 1928, features the tomb of the Unknown Warrior lying beneath a chandelier in an ornate marble hall in the Palace of Versailles; in the distant background, the silhouette of a cross outlined in a lit arch gives some light to the scene. This was the third of three commemorative paintings that the British official war artist was commissioned to paint of the Peace Conference in July 1919. The first two paintings depict the political leaders in group settings, where Orpen's deliberate composition makes them appear small in relation to their ostentatious surroundings.[1] In the final painting, Orpen planned to depict the Allied leaders and generals, including Earl Haig, David Lloyd George and Ferdinand Foch before they entered the signing chamber, and claimed he had made thirty portraits of the figures before deciding to paint over them.[2] However, as he records in his memoir *An Onlooker in France* (1921), he was intensely disillusioned with the proceedings of the conference: 'It was all over. The "frocks" had won the war. The "frocks" had signed the Peace! The Army was forgotten. Some dead and forgotten, others maimed and forgotten, others alive and well – but equally forgotten.'[3] Instead, he painted out the political figures and included instead two soldiers guarding the coffin with bayonets, with only their loins concealed on their skeletal frames, with two cherubs floating above the soldiers. Orpen's cynicism is evident: 'after all the negotiations and discussions, the Armistice and Peace, the only tangible result is the ragged unemployed soldier and the Dead' (see Fig. C.1).[4]

Figure C.1 Sir William Orpen, *To the Unknown British Soldier in France* (1921, exhibited 1923). © IWM (Art.IWM ART 4438)

Orpen's key gesture was to return the mass dead, through the new memorial of the Unknown Warrior, and the surviving veterans, to the heart of the Peace Conference. He had drawn the model for the soldiers in an earlier painting, *Blown Up. Mad.* (1917), which depicts the impact of a shell explosion that Orpen witnessed: a soldier who has lost his clothes and mind, wearing rags, his puttees unravelling, one of his shoes blown open. The second version of *To the Unknown Soldier in France*, completed in 1921, was first exhibited at the Royal Academy Summer Exhibition in 1923, where it caused both controversy and acclaim. Despite being voted 'picture of the year' by popular vote, it was turned down for purchase by the Imperial War Museum for not fulfilling its commission. In 1927, Orpen painted over the soldiers and cherubs, leaving only the coffin. It was finally accepted by the Imperial War Museum in 1928 when he donated it in in memory of Haig, 'one of the best friends I ever had' (see Fig. C.2). Looking closely at the painting, some of the original figures of the leaders and the soldiers remain visible under the paintwork: their ghosts remaining within and out of sight, the war dead never far concealed beneath the surface.

Figure C.2 Sir William Orpen, *To the Unknown British Soldier in France* (1927–8). © IWM (Art.IWM ART 4438)

THE RETURN OF THE DEAD

There are multiple ways that war death continued to preoccupy women's writing throughout the 1920s and 1930s (and beyond), which manifested itself in various ways. Allyson Booth's argument that modernism was 'strangely haunted by the Great War' is made literal for many of these writers.[5] For those who were still looking for their dead, the unknown situation of many wartime deaths – particularly those where the soldier remained 'missing' – were particularly problematic. As Bruce Scates has argued, 'Doubts almost always attended the case of the missing. [. . .] "missing" was beyond the comprehension of much of the civilian population', that 'it implied that a body had somehow been "misplaced"'.[6] This meant that many families 'refused to accept the loss of a loved one even long after the war had ended'.[7] Although, as we saw in Chapter 5, a common sentiment was that 'Missing *always* means dead', many families lived in eternal hope that their loved ones would return, that their deaths had been misidentified or that their status as 'missing' would turn into 'found'.[8] Soldiers did continue to return in the postwar period, such as the strange case of Octave Félicien Monjoin (known as Anthelme Mangin), the French amnesiac soldier released from a German prisoner-of-war camp in 1918, who was fought over by dozens of families and not formally identified until 1938, after his father's and brother's death. His identity was confirmed when he walked to his family home from the train station in his hometown, observing, on the way, the changed appearance of the church steeple.[9] Rebecca West's 1918 novel *The Return of the Soldier* provides a wartime fantasy of the amnesiac soldier's return, but whereas the fictional version ends with his being successfully reintegrated into his family and society, the real-life Monjoin died in an asylum in 1942. Others turned up, having been mistakenly recorded as dead after being badly wounded and in hospitals or taken as prisoners of war, without being correctly registered.

For those who practised spiritualism, usually through séances and ouija boards with mediums, communication with the dead remained a much-desired possibility. In contrast to the idea that it was a wartime phenomenon, the continuing popularity of spiritualism throughout the 1920s and 1930s has been demonstrated by historians, with the 1930s described as spiritualism's 'high water mark'.[10] A number of well-known writers were key proponents, particularly Sir Oliver Lodge and Sir Arthur Conan Doyle, who popularised the movement through lectures, radio broadcasts, debates, essays and fictional writings.[11] Reaching across the divide to dead sons, husbands, brothers and lovers, was a means of bringing them back to life, even if only temporarily. This transgression across boundaries is shown on one particularly unusual headstone inscription: 'WILLIE WE ARE CALLING YOU / DAD AND MAM', which, as Sarah Wearne points out, suggests that Private William London's parents were trying to reach him through a medium.[12] As Jennifer Hazelgrove notes, '[o]f more interest to these people than "proof" of survival was information about the experience of death, the nature of a future life, and the whereabouts and condition of deceased loved ones'.[13]

For many, the idea of the ghosts of the dead returning or watching over the living was intensely comforting. The description in *The Times* of the burial of the Unknown Warrior on Armistice Day 1920 leant heavily on the idea of the ghostly omniscient dead, even depicting the dead lying atop their graves, overseeing the homecoming of one of their own:

> Surely, if one was there [in the burial fields in France], one might almost see the shadowy ranks, brown-clad in their old khaki against the brown November earth, dim shapes, each with his trench helmet on, platoon after platoon, brigade after brigade, whole army corps and armies, leaning motionless on their reversed arms and all gazing this way, out of deep eyes which see more than we can see, watching as the coffin that comes to us to-day passes homeward.[14]

There were other instances of the dead appearing at new memorial ceremonies, such as the spirit photographs taken by Ada Deane on Whitehall at the Armistice Day ceremonies. The two long-exposure photographs she took in 1922, just before and during the Two Minutes' Silence, claimed to show the dead men appearing over the crowd. These photographs were commercially printed and distributed, and newspapers bid for the rights to her future Armistice Day photographs, until *The Daily Sketch* exposed Deane's 1924 photographs as a fraud, finding the 'dead' who had appeared were, in fact, living sportsmen.

In more personal terms, ghosts of the dead appeared to women in dreams. Katherine Mansfield dreamt of Rupert Brooke soon after his death in April 1915, telling John Middleton Murry:

> I did not tell you that I dreamed all night of Rupert Brooke. And today as I left the house he was standing at the door, with a ruck-sack on his back & a broad hat shading his face. So after I had posted your letter I did not go home. I went a long very idle sort of amble along the quais. [. . .] You cannot think what pleasure my invisible, imaginary companion gave me. If he had been alive it would never have possibly occurred, but – it's a game I like to play – to walk and to talk with the dead who smile and are silent, and *free*, quite finally free. When I lived alone I would often come home, put my key in the door & find someone there, waiting for me. 'Hullo! Have you been here long?'[15]

In December 1915, while she was in intense grief over the loss of her brother, Mansfield saw her brother as an apparition, writing to Murry from her hotel in the south of France: 'Sitting on the verandah in canvas chairs after supper & smoking & listening to the idle sea. But don't be frightened, dear one, you were not there. It was my brother who sat on the verandah step stroking a kitten that curled on his knee'.[16] A few days later she dreamt

> that I sat by a fire with Grandmother & my brother & when I woke up I still held my brother's hand. That is true. For my hands were not together – They were holding another hand – I felt the weight & the warmth of it – for quite a long time.[17]

Losses remained very real throughout the 1920 and 1930s. In January 1923, Woolf wrote in her diary that Noel Olivier, one of Brooke's former lovers, still seemed to see him: 'She looked at me with those strange eyes [. . .] romantic eyes, that seem to behold still Rupert bathing in the river at Christow'. It is clear that Olivier was still in mourning for Brooke, despite being married to someone else: 'But when she read his love letters – beautiful beautiful love letters – real love letters, she said – she cries & cries'.[18]

In the postwar world soldiers were the most obvious ghosts, but women had become ghosts too. In the same diary entry where she wrote about Olivier,

Woolf described a 'certain melancholy' which 'has been brooding over me this fortnight', which she dates from Mansfield's death in early January.[19] Woolf had previously asked herself: 'Katherine has been dead a week, & how far am I obeying her "do not quite forget Katherine" which I read in one of her old letters? Am I already forgetting her?' Since learning of her death, Woolf's image of Mansfield is a spectral one:

> visual impressions kept coming & coming before me – always of Katherine putting on a white wreath, & leaving us, called away; made dignified, chosen. And then one pitied her. And one felt her reluctant to wear that wreath, which was an ice cold one. And she was only 33.[20]

In her grief, Woolf remembers, or imagines, Mansfield in detailed terms: 'I could see her before me so exactly, & the room at Portland Villas. I go up. She gets up, very slowly, from her writing table'.[21] Two months later, in March 1923, Woolf reported satirically in her diary: 'Poor Katherine has taken to revisiting the earth; she has been seen at Brett's; by the charwoman. I feel this somehow a kind of judgement on her for writing the kind of thing she did'. Woolf's comments about Dorothy Brett's reported experience of Mansfield gives a sense of her cynicism about any kind of spiritual encounter with the dead: 'She feels the "contact" she says; & has had revelations; and there she sits deaf, injured, solitary, brooding over death, & hearing voices, which soon will become, I expect, entirely fabulous'.[22] However, Woolf herself would continue to 'think of [Mansfield] at intervals all through life', as she predicted in January 1923.[23] In October 1924 Woolf wrote of her as 'that strange ghost, with the eyes far apart, & the drawn mouth, dragging herself across her room'.[24] In December 1925, she returned to the image of Mansfield with the wreath: '& yet all this part of Hampstead recalls Katherine to me – that faint ghost, with the steady eyes, the mocking lips, &, at the end, the wreath set on her hair'.[25] In July 1928, Woolf reflected on the ability of dreams to effectively conjure ghosts:

> All last night I dreamt of Katherine Mansfield & wonder what dreams are; often evoke so much more emotion, than thinking does – almost as if she came back in person & was outside one, actively making one feel [. . .] somehow I got the feel of her, & of her as if alive again, more than by day.[26]

Although Woolf wasn't mourning a war death, the recurrent memories and apparitions of her fellow writer throughout the 1920s echoed the experience and popular rhetoric of civilians mourning their lost men.

The figure of the ghost similarly populated postwar novels. The war underlies all four of the Anglo-Caribbean writer Jean Rhys's novels of the late 1920s and 1930s, typically referenced only in passing or through a shared allusion between characters.[27] In *After Leaving Mr Mackenzie* (1930), the protagonist Julia is repeatedly figured as a ghost: 'She walked in – pale as a ghost'; 'silent and ghost-like'; 'an importunate ghost'.[28] Julia's spectral status is explicitly linked with the war: as she sees 'the ghost of herself coming out of the fog to meet her', she realises it doesn't recognise her, like the man selling violets on the corner (a symbol of war remembrance, as we saw in Chapter 5) (49). Julia then immediately passes a cinema where during the war she had watched a film 'with a little Belgian when they had shown some town in Belgium being bombarded. And the little Belgian had wept' (49).[29] Julia's wartime experience seems to have been exhilarating, like many women who experienced freedom from earlier social restrictions: 'My God, that was a funny time! The mad things one did – and everybody else was doing them, too. A funny time. A mad reckless time' (49).

There is a clear sense of the war as a break in time, with the Armistice and the death of Julia's child bound together. She 'had left England immediately after the armistice. She had had a child. The child had died – in central Europe, somewhere' (19). This conflation of the war (specifically the end of the war) and her child is similar to H.D.'s stillbirth in *Bid Me to Live*, discussed in Chapter 4, where in both cases the particular maternal grief represents a mode of female war trauma. Like the distorted sense of time in that novel, Julia in *After Leaving Mr Mackenzie* can't place the war temporally: 'I left London after the armistice. What year was that?', she asks (37). Telling her story to a woman who doesn't believe her, Julia seeks out documents to prove to herself that it happened:

> When I got home I pulled out all the photographs I had, and letters and things. And my marriage-book and my passport. And the papers about my baby who died and was buried in Hamburg.
>
> But it had all gone, as if it had never been. And I was there, like a ghost. (41)

This vagueness is perhaps a type of repression for a particularly traumatic death, one that can be linked to the extreme food shortages in many areas of Europe during the 1920s: 'When you've just had a baby, and it dies for the simple reason that you haven't enough money to keep it alive, it leaves you with a sort of hunger', Julia says (80).

The result of this trauma is that Julia sees herself as a ghost, and she is repeatedly linked with death. In a nightclub she dances with an elderly man whose 'face was cadaverous': 'his face was all bones and hollows in the light of the lamp striking upwards, like a skeleton's face' (106, 107). Like the unwanted transgression of the war into the domestic sphere that we saw in *Bid Me to Live*, here the figure of death is invading Julia's body in a gruesome image of assault: 'Julia was being hugged very tightly by her partner, who hung a little over her shoulder, pervading her, as it were, and smiling' (107). In another scene as she climbs the stairs to get to her bedroom on the top floor, she screams when she imagines 'someone dead [. . .] catching hold of my hand' (120). Julia's sister Norah, who looks after their dying mother, is living a similarly deathly existence: 'My life's like death. It's like being buried alive' (75).

Julia's condition, although specific, is representative of many women cut adrift after the war, living down and out in seedy boarding-houses and cheap hotels in the depressed postwar economies of Paris and London, with men who either exploit them or have nothing to offer them. The men are only marginally better off, being socially, financially or psychologically affected by the war. Julia goes to her uncle in London to ask for money and he tells her: 'Things are very difficult over here, you know [. . .] the truth is that I haven't got any money to give to anybody' (59, 60). Neil James, another man she asks for money, tells her the war 'taught [him] a lot':

> Before the war I'd always thought that I rather despised people who didn't get on. [. . .] I didn't believe much in bad luck. But after the war I felt differently. I've got a lot of mad friends now. I call them my mad friends. [. . .] People who've come croppers [. . .] some women too. Though mind you, women are a different thing altogether. (83)

Another male character in the narrative tells her: 'perhaps I know something about cracking up too. I went through the war, you know' and sends her only a small amount of money, because 'times are a bit hard with me' (111, 130). One of the final men we see is 'a thin man, so thin that he was like a clothed skeleton, drooping in a doorway' (136). In the novel's final scene, the only real moment of intimacy or connection in Julia's meeting with the titular Mr Mackenzie is an implicit reference to a war song:

> '"Good-bye-ee. Don't cry-ee." Do you remember that?' she said.
> 'Yes, I remember.' (125)[30]

This moment of shared war experience is soon dissolved, as though the memory only reinforces their consequent lack of connection: 'For the life of him he was unable to think of anything more sympathetic' (126). The return of the dead appears elsewhere in the narrative: 'A most extraordinary thing! I've just seen a man I thought was dead', a stranger in a café tells Julia.

Like H.D.'s soldiers figured as 'ghosts-to-be', here postwar women are the ghosts, unwilling war survivors whose existences are already determined in bleak terms. The death of Julia's mother – the older prewar generation – in an extended Victorian style deathbed scene is, by comparison to the lives of the women left alive, remarkably peaceful: 'The dying woman breathed three times gently, without any effort. Her head dropped sideways' (88). In the cinema Julia notices 'how many of the older women looked drab and hopeless [. . .] They looked ashamed of themselves, as if they were begging the world in general not to notice that they were women or to hold it against them' (50). In Paris all of the women seem isolated in their grief, visible but inaccessible: 'it seemed to Julia that at each window a woman sat staring mournfully, like a prisoner, straight into her bedroom' (129). The proleptic figure of the old woman Julia sees serves to demonstrate Julia and other women's futures, with her 'white face, white frizzy hair [. . .] In the sun she looked transparent, like a ghost' (131). In Christopher Isherwood's 1932 novel *The Memorial*, the war widow Lily is older but similarly feels redundant and isolated in the postwar world, having lost the wartime sense of fellowship with other mothers and widows: 'While the War was still on it had been different [. . .] her grief had had some meaning. She was one of thousands [. . .] But they no longer counted. No, we're done with now, she thought. There's another generation already'.[31]

For others, the possibility of the return of the dead was something to be feared. The famous scene in Abel Gance's 1919 film *J'Accuse*, where the crosses on a battlefield first morph into the dead bodies of soldiers, and then into living, moving beings as the dead reawaken, is greeted by fear and horror on the part of the survivors. Here there is a distinction between the spirits and the ghosts of the dead: 'Whereas Spiritualists insisted that their spirits were for the most part benign, ghosts were usually regarded as malign'.[32] This fear of the return of the dead made its way into literature in interesting ways. In *The Memorial*, Lily considers her vision of her husband's ghost ('He was as she had last seen him, on his last leave, a slightly bowed figure in the British warm and frayed tunic') as a distinctly unwanted 'creation of her own will': 'She had done something base in wishing to create it [. . .] She never prayed to see Richard again' (57–8). Elizabeth Bowen's ghost story 'The Demon Lover' (first published 1941) embodies this civilian fear of the return of the dead. The story begins as the middle-aged protagonist Mrs Kathleen Drover returned to the 'shut-up' London home that she and her family have been forced to leave because of German bombings during the Blitz.[33] The house, much like the Ramsay home in *To the Lighthouse*, has been damaged – 'some cracks in the structure, left by the last bombing' – and requires restoration (Mrs McNab would be welcome here): 'Though not much dust had seeped in, each object wore a film of another kind' (81, 80). The house is repeatedly aligned with death, from the '[d]ead air' which 'came out to meet her as she went in', to the street's distinction from the nearby square 'where people went on living [. . .] the ordinary flow of life' (80, 87). Seeing a letter on the table addressed to her, Mrs Drover 'stopped dead' (81). The letter delivered seemingly supernaturally is apparently from the woman's 'reported missing, presumed killed'

First World War fiancé, whom she said goodbye to in 1916, twenty-five years earlier (84).

The notion of a letter stopping the reader 'dead' – a letter that notified families of the death or missing status of a loved one – was a familiar wartime experience from both the First and ongoing Second World War. In this case, however, the letter portends something potentially far more disturbing: the return of the dead. Like the horrified gasp of the watching soldier in *J'Accuse*, the contents of the letter fill Mrs Drover with fear: 'her lips, beneath the remains of lipstick, beginning to go white' (82). Her memory of her former fiancé is physical in nature: like Julia's experience of Rafe's in H.D.'s *Bid Me to Live*, he had pressed her hand 'without very much kindness, and painfully, on to one of the breast buttons of his uniform. That cut of the button on the palm of her hand was, principally, what she was to carry away' (83). The hold of the dead over the living remains physical and violent: 'the twenty-five years since then dissolved like smoke and she instinctively looked for the weal left by the button on the palm of her hand' (86).

The promise Mrs Drover made to this man is never made explicit, but the idea of not breaking faith with the dead, was a commonplace of memorial rhetoric. Much postwar poetry is therefore predicated on a promise to eternally remember: 'At the going down of the sun and in the morning / We will remember them', intones Laurence Binyon's 1914 poem 'For the Fallen', the fourth stanza (the Ode of Remembrance) of which became a staple of remembrance ceremonies immediately after the war.[34] 'Lest We Forget', inscribed on the Cenotaph and used in remembrance ceremonies, further instructs its readers of the necessity to remember.[35] In marrying someone else and bearing three sons, and settling down into life in 'this quiet, arboreal part of Kensington', arguably Mrs Drover has forgotten her promise to the soldier (84). The sense that she still has a chance to heed the warning and escape ('As things were – dead or living the letter-writer sent her only a threat') soon disappears (84). The end of the story sees her being carried away in a taxi, screaming and 'beat[ing] with her gloved hands on the glass all round as the taxi, accelerating without mercy made off with her into the hinterland of deserted streets' (87). If we break our bond with the dead, the story tells us, they will return to make us remember it.

Bowen's use of the ambiguous status of the 'missing, presumed killed' First World War soldier provides an ideal plot device for an ex-lover who could return at any point. This particular device of the ghost soldier is also not surprising given her readings of the modernist texts of the 1920s, including Katherine Mansfield and Virginia Woolf, both civilian war writers as we have seen: she referred to Mansfield in 1957 as 'our missing contemporary'.[36] Her choice of a dead soldier as the ghost here demonstrates the longstanding nature of this rhetoric of the return of the dead, brought back into focus by the ongoing war. The ghosts of the First World War haunt those of the Second.

This book has developed two arguments in relation to a wide range of writing by women: that the extent and nature of the enormous death toll of the war changed the way that death was perceived and represented in literature; and that the unprecedented war losses and the subsequent cultures of both private and public commemoration are a crucial yet overlooked context for literary development in this period, including but not limited to the development of literary modernism. More broadly, this book argues for the intertwining of modernist, war and memorial culture, suggesting that much of what we call modernist experimentation in terms of death can be traced to its specific socio-historical wartime and postwar context.

Not all of the writers I examine were modernist writers, but worked within a range of genres. Reading 'modernist' writers alongside non-modernist writers, and 'war writers' alongside non-war writers, is in keeping with a wartime and postwar literary culture where these distinctions did not exist. This book suggests that all the writers examined here were war writers, in line with a broadened definition of war writing to include writing by civilian women. In a culture saturated by total war, writing and other cultural production is necessarily part of that culture, whether explicitly or otherwise. More broadly I argue that modernist culture was inherently a war culture, and that there is more scholarship needed to consider the formal and thematic means in which this was manifested.

The concept of proximity, both in terms of distance and time, structures this project. The tripartite division of this book is based on the imbalance in encounters with death between combatants and civilians, and the necessary distinction between wartime and postwar writings. I suggest that the proximity in which an author encountered the war dead may have influenced their mode of representation: that the writer's physical nearness to or distance from the war dead had consequences for the mode of representation they adopted, producing on the one hand an attempted return to earlier conventions, sites and tropes of literary death and memorialisation, and on the other room for imaginative experimentation. Death represented close at hand was depicted largely, though not always, through traditional motifs and sites such as deathbeds, burial rites, funerals and cemeteries, whereas death represented at a distance often led to abstraction, such as Mansfield's military metaphors or H.D.'s use of the cinema. First World War writing was, in many cases, consonant with, and may be productive of, literary modernism.

Many of these women writers lived long lives after the war ended in 1918. A number of the nurses I examined in Chapter 1 married in the postwar period and had families. Wharton stayed in France after the war, producing one more explicit war novel *A Son at the Front* in 1923 about parental and civilian grief, among many others, and dying in 1937 in her home in the countryside. Mansfield died young, as we have seen, in 1923, as her talent was at its height. H.D. lived until 1961, writing and rewriting the story of her war losses in multiple forms. Woolf continued to write about the war in the late 1920s and 1930s, particularly *The Years* in 1937, before she took her own life in 1941. We wonder how much their wartime experiences and losses continued to preoccupy these writers in those later decades: the numerous men the nurses remembered; Mansfield's brother; Wharton's nephew; H.D.'s brother and her baby; Woolf's brother-in-law; and the ghosts of fellow writers and artists: Rupert Brooke, Henri Gaudier-Brzeska, Frederick Goodyear. When the peace negotiations were concluded and when life seemed to move on, when the 1920s turned into the 1930s and another war became more and more likely, all these personal and broader losses must have stood out all the more.

Notes

1. These two paintings are *A Peace Conference at the Quai d'Orsay* (1919), and *The Signing of Peace in the Hall of Mirrors, Versailles, 28th June 1919* (1919), both held by the Imperial War Museum.
2. My description here is informed by Alex Walton's account of 'Official Memorial Art', in Laura Clouting, *A Century of Remembrance* (2018), pp. 226–9, and the Imperial War Museum Image Label <https://www.iwm.org.uk/collections/item/object/20880> (last accessed 26 May 2019).
3. Orpen, *An Onlooker in France, 1917–1919* (1921), p. 119.
4. Quoted in IWM Image Label, source unknown.
5. Booth, *Postcards from the Trenches: Negotiating the Space between Modernism and the First World War* (1996), p. 6.
6. Scates, quoting Peter Stanley, *Lost Boys of Anzac* (2014), p. 162, in 'Bereavement and Mourning (Australia)', in Ute Daniel, et al. (eds), *1914–1918-Online* (2016), <https://encyclopedia.1914-1918-online.net/article/bereavement_and_mourning_australia> (last accessed 2 May 2019).
7. Scates, 'Bereavement and Mourning (Australia)', *1914–1918-Online*.
8. 'The Gardener' [1925], *Debits and Credits* (1926), p. 405.
9. His case is examined in Jean-Yves Le Naour, *The Living Unknown Soldier: A Story of Grief and the Great War*, trans. by Penny Allen (2005). Jean Anouilh's play *Le voyageur sans bagage* (1937) is based on his story.
10. Geoffrey K. Nelson, *Spiritualism and Society* (1969), p. 161, quoted by Jennifer Hazelgrove, *Spiritualism and British Society Between the Wars* (2000), p. 14. Hazelgrove gives the statistics: 'In 1914, there were 145 societies affiliated to the Spiritualists' National Union (SNU); by 1909 there were 309', and by 1932, there were 500 affiliated societies, *Spiritualism*, p. 14. This figure doesn't include attendance at other major spiritualist meetings not connected with the SNU, meaning the actual number of those practising spiritualism was much higher.
11. Wartime and postwar texts that feature spiritualism and séances include Lodge's *Raymond* (1916), written after the death of his son; Conan Doyle's *The New Revelation* (1918), *The Vital Message* (1919), *The Coming of the Fairies* (1922) and *The Land of Mist* (1926), *The History of Spiritualism* (2 vols, 1926); J. M. Barrie's

play *The Well-Remembered Voice* (1919) and Noël Coward's play *Post-Mortem* (1931, written 1930). Hazelgrove suggests that the most successful spiritualist publication was Arthur Findlay's *On the Edge of the Etheric* 'reprinted twenty-five times between November 1931 and June 1932 and [. . .] sold at the rate of 500 copies per week', p. 15. Tatiana Kontou reads Dorothy Richardson's *Pilgrimage* (1915–67) and May Sinclair's *Mary Olivier: A Life* (1919) as spiritualist texts in *Spiritualism and Women's Writing: From the Fin de Siècle to the Neo-Victorian* (2009).

12. From Sarah Wearne's project <http://www.epitaphsofthegreatwar.com/all/> (last accessed 29 April 2019).
13. Hazelgrove, *Spiritualism*, p. 27.
14. 'Armistice Day, 1920,' *The Times*, 11 November 1920, p. 16. *The Times Digital Archive*, <http://tinyurl.galegroup.com/tinyurl/9fENQ2> (last accessed 3 April 2019).
15. To John Middleton Murry, [c. 13 May 1915], in *The Collected Letters of Katherine Mansfield, Volume I: 1903–1917* (1984), ed. Vincent O'Sullivan and Margaret Scott, pp. 186–7. This description is similar to Woolf's depiction of the ghost of her brother Thoby in 1929: 'that queer ghost. I think of ghosts sometimes as the end of an excursion which I went on when he died. As if I should come in & say well, here you are', 26 December 1929, in *The Diary of Virginia Woolf, Volume III: 1925–30*, ed. Anne Olivier Bell, assisted by Andrew McNeillie [1980] (1982), p. 275.
16. To Murry, [9 December 1915], *CLVI*, p. 204.
17. To Murry, [13 December 1915], *CLVI*, p. 211.
18. Woolf, 28 January 1923, in *The Diary of Virginia Woolf, Volume II: 1920–24*, ed. Anne Olivier Bell, assisted by Andrew McNeillie [1978] (1981), pp. 229–30.
19. Woolf, 28 January 1923, *DVWII*, pp. 227–8.
20. Woolf, 16 January 1923, *DVWII*, pp. 225–6. Mansfield, who had died on 9 January, was, in fact, 34.
21. Woolf, 16 January 1923, *DVWII*, p. 226.
22. Woolf, 6 March 1923, *DVWII*, pp. 237, 238.
23. Woolf, 16 January 1923, *DVWII*, p. 227.
24. Woolf, 17 October 1924, *DVWII*, p. 317.
25. Woolf, 7 December 1925, *DVWIII*, p. 50.
26. Woolf, 7 July 1928, *DVWIII*, p. 187.
27. Rhys, *Postures* (1928), published in the US as *Quartet* (1929); *After Leaving Mr Mackenzie* (1930); *Voyage in the Dark* (1934); *Good Morning Midnight* (1939).
28. Rhys, *After Leaving Mr Mackenzie* [1930], intro. by Lorna Sage (2000), pp. 22, 48. Further references will be included in the text.
29. Rhys shared a close friendship with a Belgian refugee Camille and his wife during the war, and met her future husband Jean Lenglet at one of their social gatherings, which she writes about in *Smile Please: An Unfinished Autobiography* [1979] (2016), p. 120. She volunteered in a canteen near Euston station in London during the war. Although Rhys writes that her memory of 'the 1914 war [. . .] seems disconnected and vague,' she records her concern over one soldier who larked about with her in the canteen: 'I prayed for him every night but I don't suppose it did much good', pp. 116, 119.

30. R. P. Weston, and Bert Lee, 'Good-bye-ee!' (1917).
31. Isherwood, *The Memorial: Portrait of a Family* [1932] (2012), p. 54. Further references will be included in the text.
32. Hazelgrove, *Spiritualism*, p. 29.
33. Bowen, 'The Demon Lover', first published in *The Listener* in 1941, collected in *The Demon Lover and Other Stories* (1945), p. 80. Further references will be included in the text.
34. Binyon, 'For the Fallen', first published in *The Times* (21 September 1914), and included in the anthology *The Winnowing Fan: Poems on the Great War* (1914).
35. From the poem 'Recessional' (1897) by Rudyard Kipling, using a Biblical quotation from Deuteronomy 6:12. The poem was written for Queen Victoria's Diamond Jubilee in 1897, first published in *The Times* (17 July 1897) and subsequently included in *The Five Nations* (1903).
36. Bowen, 'Introduction' to Katherine Mansfield, *34 Short Stories* (1957), p. 10.

BIBLIOGRAPHY

ARCHIVAL MATERIAL

Correspondence between Edith Wharton and Scribner's, 1914–15. Archives of Charles Scribner's Sons (C0101); 1786–2004 (mostly 1880s–1970s), Boxes 193–4, Folders 5 and 6. Manuscripts Division, Department of Rare Books and Special Collections, Princeton University Library

Edith Wharton Collection, Yale Collection of American Literature, Beinecke Rare Book and Manuscript Library, Yale University

Edith Wharton Manuscripts (C0118); 1903–25, Box 1, Folders 1–28. Manuscripts Division, Department of Rare Books and Special Collections, Princeton University Library

Ellen N. La Motte Collection, The Alan Mason Chesney Medical Archives of The Johns Hopkins Medical Institutions

H.D. Papers, Yale Collection of American Literature, Beinecke Rare Book and Manuscript Library, Yale University

Miss M. A. Brown (ARRC), Imperial War Museum Archives, 88/7/1

PRIMARY TEXTS

Aldington, Richard, *Death of a Hero: A Novel* (London: Chatto & Windus 1929)

Aldrich, Mildred, *A Hilltop on the Marne* (Boston, MA: Houghton Mifflin; London: Constable, 1915)

Allatini, Rose [A. T. Fitzroy], *Despised and Rejected* (London: C. W. Daniel, 1918)

Anderson, Sherwood, *Winesburg, Ohio: A Group of Tales of Ohio Small-Town Life* [New York: B. W. Huebsch, 1919], ed. Glen A. Love (Oxford and New York: Oxford University Press, 1997)

Anon., 'Advertisement: "Mr. Heinemann's List"', *The Bookman*, April 1918, p. 29

Anon., *'Mademoiselle Miss': Letters from an American Girl Serving with the Rank of Lieutenant in a French Army Hospital at the Front*, pref. Dr Richard C. Cabot (Boston, MA: W. A. Butterfield, 1916)

Anouilh, Jean, *Le voyageur sans bagage: Pièce en cinq tableaux* (Paris: Impr. de l'Illustration, 1937)

Ashe, Elizabeth H., *Intimate Letters from France during America's First Year of War* (San Francisco: Philopolis Press, 1918)

Asquith, Cynthia, *Diaries, 1915–18*, ed. E. M. Horsley, foreword by L. P. Hartley (New York: Knopf, 1969)

Auden, W. H., *The Orators: An English Study* (London: Faber & Faber, 1932)

Bagnold, Enid, *A Diary without Dates* [London: Heinemann, 1918], intro. Monica Dickens (London: Virago, 1978)

Barrie, J. M., *The Plays of J. M. Barrie* (London: Hodder & Stoughton, 1928)

Beauchamp, Pat (First Aid Nursing Yeomanry), *Fanny Goes to War*, intro. Major-General H. N. Thompson (London: John Murray, 1919)

Binyon, Laurence, *The Winnowing Fan: Poems on the Great War* (London: Elkin Matthews, 1914)

Borden, Mary, *The Forbidden Zone* [London: Heinemann, 1929; New York: Doubleday, 1930], ed. Hazel Hutchison (London: Hesperus, 2008)

Bowen, Elizabeth, 'The Demon Lover' in *The Demon Lover and Other Stories* (London: Jonathan Cape, 1945), pp. 80–7

Bowen, Elizabeth, 'Introduction' to Katherine Mansfield, *34 Short Stories* (London: Collins, 1957), pp. 9–26

Bowser, Thekla, *The Story of British V.A.D. Work in the Great War* (London: Andrew Melrose, 1917)

Brittain, Vera, *Testament of Youth: An Autobiographical Study of the Years 1900–1925* [London: Gollancz, 1933], pref. Shirley Williams (London: Virago, 1978)

Bryce, Viscount James, and the Committee on Alleged German Outrages, *Report of the Committee on Alleged German Outrages appointed by His Britannic Majesty's Government and presided over by the Right Hon. Viscount Bryce* [The Bryce Report] (London: H. M. Stationery Office, 1915)

Buswell, Leslie [publ. anon.], *With the American Ambulance Field Service in France, Personal Letters of a Driver at the Front*, 2nd edn, Printed only for private distribution (Cambridge, MA: The Riverside Press, 1916) [later published as Buswell, Leslie, *Ambulance No. 10: Personal Letters from the Front* (Boston, MA and New York: Houghton Mifflin, 1916)]

Cantlie, James, *British Red Cross Society Nursing Manual, No. 2* (London: Cassell, 1912)
Cather, Willa, *Not Under Forty* (London: Cassell, 1936)
Conan Doyle, Arthur, *The New Revelation: What is Spiritualism?* (London: Hodder & Stoughton, 1918)
Conan Doyle, Arthur, *The Vital Message* (London: Hodder & Stoughton, 1919)
Conan Doyle, Arthur, *The Coming of the Fairies* (London: Hodder & Stoughton, 1922)
Conan Doyle, Arthur, *The History of Spiritualism*, 2 vols (London: Cassell, 1926)
Conan Doyle, Arthur, *The Land of Mist* (London: Hutchinson, 1926)
Conrad, Joseph, *The First News* (London: Privately printed by Clement Shorter, August 1918)
Cournos, John, *Miranda Masters* (New York: Knopf, 1926)
Coward, Noël, *Post-Mortem: A Play in Eight Scenes* (London: Heinemann, 1931)
Cushing, Harvey, *From a Surgeon's Journal, 1915–1918* (Boston, MA: Little, Brown, and Co., 1936)
Dent, Olive, *A V.A.D. in France*, with illustrations by R.M. Savage and others (London: Grant Richards, 1917)
Dickens, Charles, *The Old Curiosity Shop* [London: Chapman & Hall, 1841], ed. Elizabeth M. Brennan (Oxford: Oxford University Press, 1998)
Douglas, James, 'How a Nurse Sees the War' [review of Enid Bagnold's *A Diary without Dates*, 1918] (*Birmingham Gazette*, 19 March 1918), p. 2
Duhamel, Georges, *Vie des Martyrs: 1914–1916* (Paris: Mercure de France, 1917)
Eliot, T. S., 'Short Reviews', *The Egoist*, 4 (December 1917), p. 72
Fisher, Dorothy Canfield, *Home Fires in France* (New York: Henry Holt and Company, 1918)
Fitzwilliams, Duncan C. L., *A Nursing Manual for Nurses and Nursing Orderlies* (London: Henry Frowde, 1914)
Farmborough, Florence, *Nurse at the Russian Front: A Diary, 1914–18* (London: Constable, 1974)
Farmborough, Florence, *Russian Album, 1908–1918*, ed. John Jolliffe (Salisbury: Michael Russell, 1979)
Forster, E. M., 'Our Graves in Gallipoli' [1922], in *Abinger Harvest* (London: Edward Arnold, 1936), pp. 33–5
Forster, E. M., *Selected Letters of E. M. Forster, Volume One: 1979–1920*, ed. Mary Lago and P. N. Furbank (London: Arrow, 1985)
Fox, Frank, *The King's Pilgrimage* (London: Hodder & Stoughton, 1922)
Goodyear, Frederick, *Frederick Goodyear, Letters and Remains, 1887–1917* (London: McBride, Nast & Co., 1920)

Hamilton, Mary Agnes, *Dead Yesterday* (London: Duckworth, 1916)
H.D., *Asphodel* [1921–2], ed. Robert Spoo (Durham, NC and London: Duke University Press, 1992)
H.D., *Bid Me to Live: A Madrigal* [New York: Grove Press, 1960], intro. Helen McNeil, afterword by Perdita Schaffner (London: Virago, 1984)
H.D., *Bid Me to Live: A Madrigal* [New York: Grove Press, 1960], ed. Caroline Zilboorg (Gainesville, FL: University Press of Florida, 2011)
H.D., 'H.D. by *Delia Alton* [Notes on Recent Writing]' [1949–50], in Adalaide Morris (ed.), *The Iowa Review, H.D. Centennial Issue*, 16.3 (1986), pp. 180–221
H.D., *HERmione* [1927], intro. Perdita Schaffner (New York: New Directions, 1981)
H.D., *Paint It Today* [1921], ed. Cassandra Laity, foreword by Karla Jay (New York: New York University Press, 1992)
H.D., *Palimpsest* [Boston, MA and New York: Houghton Mifflin, 1926], pref. Harry T. Moore, note on the text by Matthew J. Bruccoli (Carbondale, IL: Southern Illinois University Press, 1968)
H.D., *Richard Aldington and H.D.: The Early Years in Letters*, ed. Caroline Zilboorg (Bloomington, IN: Indiana University Press, 1992)
H.D., *Richard Aldington & H.D.: Their Lives in Letters, 1918–61*, ed. Caroline Zilboorg (Manchester: Manchester University Press, 2003)
H.D., *Tribute to Freud* [New York: Pantheon, 1956], intro. Peter Jones (Oxford: Carcanet Press, 1971)
Hurst, Sidney C., PASI, *The Silent Cities: An Illustrated Guide to the War Cemeteries and Memorials to the 'Missing' in France and Flanders, 1914–1918, containing 959 illustrations and 31 maps*, preface by Major-General Sir Fabian Ware (London: Methuen, 1929)
Instructions for the Training of Divisions for Offensive Action (40/W.O./3591), issued by the War Office General Staff Great Britain (London: Harrison, 1916)
Isherwood, Christopher, *The Memorial: Portrait of a Family* [London: Hogarth Press, 1932] (London: Vintage, 2012)
James, Henry, *The American* [Boston, MA: James R. Osgood & Co., 1877], ed. Adrian Poole (Oxford: Oxford University Press, 1999)
James, Henry, *Collected Stories*, 2 vols, selected and intro. John Bayley (London: Everyman's Library, 2000)
James, Henry, *The Golden Bowl* [London: Methuen, 1904], ed. Virginia Llewellyn Smith (Oxford: Oxford University Press, 1983; repr. 2009)
James, Henry, 'The New Novel' [1914], in *Notes on Novelists, with Some Other Notes* (New York: Scribner, 1914), pp. 314–61
James, Henry, *The Spoils of Poynton* [London: Heinemann, 1897], ed. Bernard Richards (Oxford: Oxford University Press, 1982; repr. 2008)

James, Henry, *Within the Rim, and Other Essays, 1914–15* (London: W. Collins Sons, 1918)

Joyce, James, *Dubliners* [London: Grant Richards, 1914], intro. Terence Brown (London: Penguin, 1992)

Kenyon, Sir Frederic, *War Graves: How the Cemeteries Abroad Will be Designed* (London: His Majesty's Stationery Office, 1918)

Kipling, Rudyard, *The Five Nations* (London: Methuen, 1903)

Kipling, Rudyard, 'The Gardener' [1925], in *Debits and Credits* (London: Macmillan, 1926), pp. 399–414

Kipling, Rudyard, *The Graves of the Fallen: Imperial War Graves Commission* (London: His Majesty's Stationery Office, 1919)

Kipling, Rudyard, *The Letters of Rudyard Kipling, Volume 5: 1920–30*, ed. Thomas Pinney (London: Macmillan, 2004)

Kipling, Rudyard, 'A Madonna of the Trenches' [1924], in *Debits and Credits* (London: Macmillan, 1926), pp. 239–61

Kipling, Rudyard, 'Mary Postgate' [1915], in *A Diversity of Creatures* (London: Macmillan, 1917), pp. 419–41

Kipling, Rudyard, 'Sea Constables: A Tale of '15' [1915], in *Debits and Credits* (London: Macmillan, 1926), pp. 25–49

Kipling, Rudyard, 'War Graves. Work of Imperial Commission. Mr. Kipling's Survey', *The Times*, 17 February 1919, p. 4

La Motte, Ellen N., *The Backwash of War: An Extraordinary American Nurse in World War I*, ed. Cynthia Wachtell (Baltimore, MD: Johns Hopkins University Press, 2019)

La Motte, Ellen N., *The Backwash of War: The Human Wreckage of the Battlefield as Witnessed by an American Hospital Nurse* (New York and London: G. P. Putnam's Sons, 1916; repr. 1934)

Lake, Captain B. C., *Knowledge for War: Every Officer's Handbook for the Front* (London: Harrison, 1916)

Lasswell, Harold D., *Propaganda Technique in the World War* (London: K. Paul, Trench, Trubner & Co.; New York: Knopf, 1927)

Lawrence, D. H., *Aaron's Rod* (London: Secker, 1922)

Leake, R. E., *Letters of a V.A.D.* (London: Andrew Melrose, 1918)

Lippitt, RN, Louisa C., *Personal Hygiene and Home Nursing: A Practical Text for Girls and Women for Home and School Use* (Yonkers-on-Hudson, NY: World Book Company, 1919)

Lockwood, Preston, 'Henry James's First Interview: Noted Critic and Novelist Breaks His Rule of Years to Tell of the Good Work of the American Ambulance Corps', *New York Times* [Magazine Section], 21 March 1915, pp. 3–4

Luard, Kate, *Unknown Warriors: Extracts from the Letters of K. E. Luard, R.R.C. Nursing Sister in France, 1914–1918*, pref. Viscount Allenby (London: Chatto & Windus, 1930)

Macaulay, Rose, *Non-Combatants and Others* [London: Hodder & Stoughton, 1916] (London: Methuen, 1986)
Mansfield, Katherine, *34 Short Stories*, selected and intro. Elizabeth Bowen (London: Collins, 1957)
Mansfield, Katherine, *The Collected Fiction of Katherine Mansfield*, 2 vols, ed. Gerri Kimber and Vincent O'Sullivan (Edinburgh: Edinburgh University Press, 2012)
Mansfield, Katherine, *The Collected Letters of Katherine Mansfield*, 5 vols, ed. Vincent O'Sullivan and Margaret Scott (Oxford: Clarendon Press, 1984–2008)
Mansfield, Katherine, *The Critical Writings of Katherine Mansfield*, ed. Clare Hanson (Basingstoke: Macmillan, 1987)
Mansfield, Katherine, *The Diaries of Katherine Mansfield, including Miscellaneous Works*, ed. Gerri Kimber and Claire Davison (Edinburgh: Edinburgh University Press, 2016)
Mansfield, Katherine, *The Garden Party: and Other Stories* (London: Constable, 1922)
Mansfield, Katherine [as Kathleen Murry], *In a German Pension* [London: Swift, 1911], ed. Anne Fernihough (London: Penguin, 1999)
Mansfield, Katherine, *Journal of Katherine Mansfield: Definitive Edition*, ed. J. Middleton Murry (London: Constable, 1954)
Mansfield, Katherine, *The Katherine Mansfield Notebooks*, ed. Margaret Scott (Canterbury, NZ: Lincoln University Press; Wellington, NZ: Daphne Brasell Associates, 1997)
Mansfield, Katherine, *The Poetry and Critical Writings of Katherine Mansfield* (Edinburgh: Edinburgh University Press, 2014), ed. Gerri Kimber and Angela Smith
Mansfield, Katherine, *The Urewera Notebook*, ed. Ian A. Gordon (Oxford: Oxford University Press, 1978)
March, William, *Company K* [New York: Smith and Haas, 1933] (New York: Sagamore Press, 1957)
Marsh, Edward, *Rupert Brooke: A Memoir* (London: Sidgwick & Jackson, 1918)
Marvell, Andrew, *The Poems of Andrew Marvell*, ed. Nigel Smith (New York: Longman, 2013)
Millard, Shirley, *I Saw Them Die: Diary and Recollections of Shirley Millard*, ed. Adele Comandini (London: George G. Harrap, 1936)
Mortimer, Maud, *A Green Tent in Flanders* (New York: Doubleday, Page & Co., 1917)
Murry Middleton, John, *Between Two Worlds: An Autobiography* (London: Jonathan Cape, 1935)
Orpen, William, *An Onlooker in France, 1917–1919* (London: Williams and Norgate, 1921; rev. 1924)

Oxford, M. N., *Nursing in War Time: Lessons for the Inexperienced* (London: Methuen, 1914)

Ponsonby, Arthur, *Falsehood in War-Time: Containing an Assortment of Lies Circulated Throughout the Nations During the Great War* (London: Allen & Unwin, 1928)

Porter, Katherine Anne, *Pale Horse, Pale Rider: Three Short Novels* (London: Jonathan Cape, 1939)

Randall, Alec W. G., '"The Little Demon"', *The Egoist*, 4.3 (1 April 1916), p. 52.

Rathbone, Irene, *We That Were Young: A Novel*, pref. E. M. Delafield [London: Chatto & Windus, 1932], intro. Lynn Knight, afterword by Jane Marcus (New York: Feminist Press, 1989)

Rhinehart, Mary Roberts, *Kings, Queens and Pawns: An American Woman at the Front* (New York: George H. Doran, 1915)

Rhys, Jean, *After Leaving Mr Mackenzie* [London: Jonathan Cape, 1931], intro. Lorna Sage (Harmondsworth: Penguin, 2000)

Rhys, Jean, *Good Morning Midnight* [London: Constable, 1939], intro. A. L. Kennedy (Harmondsworth: Penguin, 2000)

Rhys, Jean, *Postures* [London: Chatto & Windus, 1928], published in the US as *Quartet* (New York: Simon & Schuster, 1929), intro. Katie Owen (Harmondsworth: Penguin, 2000)

Rhys, Jean, *Smile Please: An Unfinished Biography* [1979] (London: Penguin Classics, 2016)

Rhys, Jean, *Voyage in the Dark* [London: Constable, 1934], intro. Carole Angier (Harmondsworth: Penguin, 2000)

Richet, Charles, *War Nursing: What Every Woman Should Know, Red Cross Lectures*, trans. Helen De Vere Beauclerk (London: Heinemann, 1918)

Seabrook, William, *Diary of Section VIII*, American Ambulance Field Service, Printed only for private distribution (Boston, MA: Thomas Todd Co., 1917)

Seeger, Alan, *Poems* (New York: Scribner, 1916; London: Constable, 1917)

Sinclair, May, *Journal of Impressions in Belgium* (London: Hutchinson, 1915)

Sitwell, Osbert, 'Corpse-Day, July 19th, 1919', in *Wheels, 1919: Fourth Cycle*, ed. Edith Sitwell (Oxford: Blackwell, 1919), pp. 9–11

Smith, Helen Zenna [Evadne Price], *Not So Quiet . . . Stepdaughters of War* [London: Albert E. Marriott, 1930], intro. Barbara Hardy (London: Virago, 1988)

Smith, Lesley, *Four Years Out of Life* (London: Philip Allan, 1931)

Strachey, Lytton, *Queen Victoria* (London: Chatto & Windus, 1921)

Tayler, Henrietta, *A Scottish Nurse at Work: Being a Record of What One Semi-Trained Nurse Has Been Privileged to See and Do during Four and a Half Years of War* (London: John Lane, Bodley Head; New York: John Lane, 1920)

Toomer, Jean, *Cane* [1923] (New York: Liveright, 2011)
Unwin, Stanley, *The Work of V.A.D., London 1, during the War* (London: Allen & Unwin, 1920)
Walker, Dora M., *With the Lost Generation, 1915–1919: From a V.A.D.'s Diary* (Hull: A. Brown & Sons, 1970)
Warner, Agnes [publ. anon.], *My Beloved Poilus* (Saint John, NB: Barnes, 1917)
Wells, H. G., *Mr. Britling Sees It Through* (London: Cassell, 1916)
West, Rebecca, *The Return of the Soldier* [London: Nisbet, 1918] (London: Penguin, 1998)
West, Rebecca, 'War Nurse: An American Woman on the Western Front. A Vivid Record set down by Rebecca West,' *Hearst's International with Cosmopolitan*, 88.2 (February 1930): 20–1, 24–5, 195–200; 88.3 (March 1930): 40–3, 191–201; 88.4 (April 1930): 82–5, 108, 110, 112, 114, 117–18; 88.5 (May 1930): 88–9, 104, 106, 108, 110, 112; published as *War Nurse: The True Story of a Woman Who Lived, Loved and Suffered on the Western Front* (New York: Cosmopolitan Book Corporation, 1930)
Wharton, Edith, *A Backward Glance* (New York: D. Appleton-Century, 1934)
Wharton, Edith (ed.), *The Book of the Homeless (Le livre des sans-foyer): Original Articles in Verse and Prose* (New York: Scribner; London: Macmillan, 1916)
Wharton, Edith, 'Coming Home' [1915], in *Edith Wharton: Collected Stories, 1911–1937*, ed. Maureen Howard (New York: Library of America, 2001), pp. 26–58
Wharton, Edith, *Edith Wharton: The Uncollected Critical Writings*, ed. Frederick Wegener (Princeton, NJ: Princeton University Press, 1996)
Wharton, Edith, 'The Field of Honour' [1919], with commentary by Alice Kelly, *Times Literary Supplement* (6 November 2015), pp. 15–16
Wharton, Edith, *Fighting France: From Dunkerque to Belfort* [New York: Scribner, 1915; London: Macmillan, 1916], ed. Alice Kelly (Edinburgh: Edinburgh University Press, 2015)
Wharton, Edith, *French Ways and Their Meaning* (New York: Scribner; London: Macmillan, 1919)
Wharton, Edith, *Henry James and Edith Wharton: Letters: 1900–1915*, ed. Lyall H. Powers (New York: Scribner's, 1990)
Wharton, Edith, *Italian Backgrounds*, illustrated by E. C. Peixotto (New York: Scribner; London: Macmillan, 1905)
Wharton, Edith, *Italian Villas and Their Gardens,* illustrated with pictures by Maxfield Parrish and by photographs (New York, Century, 1904)
Wharton, Edith, 'L'Amérique en guerre', *Revue hébdomadaire* [2 March 1918], trans. Virginia Ricard, *Times Literary Supplement* (14 February 2018), pp. 3–5

Wharton, Edith, *The Letters of Edith Wharton*, ed. R. W. B. Lewis and Nancy Lewis (New York: Scribner's, 1988)

Wharton, Edith, *The Marne: A Tale of the War* (New York: D. Appleton; London: Macmillan, 1918)

Wharton, Edith, *My Dear Governess: The Letters of Edith Wharton to Anna Bahlmann*, ed. Irene Goldman-Price (New Haven, CT: Yale University Press, 2012)

Wharton, Edith, 'The Refugees' [1919], in *Women, Men and the Great War: An Anthology of Stories*, ed. Trudi Tate (Manchester: Manchester University Press, 1995), pp. 174–98

Wharton, Edith, *A Son at the Front* [New York: Scribner; London: Macmillan, 1923], ed. Shari Benstock (DeKalb, IL: Northern Illinois University Press, 1995)

Wharton, Edith, *Summer: A Novel* (New York: D. Appleton; London: Macmillan, 1917)

Wharton, Edith, *The Unpublished Writings of Edith Wharton*, ed. Laura Rattray (London: Pickering & Chatto, 2009)

Wharton, Edith, *The Writing of Fiction* [London: Scribner, 1925] (New York: Simon & Schuster, 1997)

Wharton, Edith, 'Writing a War Story' [1919], in *Edith Wharton: Collected Stories, 1911–1937*, ed. Maureen Howard (New York: Library of America, 2001), pp. 247–60

Wharton, Edith, *Xingu and Other Stories* (New York: Scribner; London: Macmillan, 1916)

Wharton, Edith, and Ogden Codman Jr, *The Decoration of Houses* (New York: Scribner, 1897; Macmillan: London, 1898)

Woolf, C. N. S., *Poems*, ed. P. S. Woolf (Richmond: Hogarth Press, 1918)

Woolf, Virginia, 'A Cambridge VAD', *Times Literary Supplement*, 10 May 1917, p. 223

Woolf, Virginia, *The Complete Shorter Fiction of Virginia Woolf*, ed. Susan Dick (London: Hogarth Press, 1989)

Woolf, Virginia, *The Diary of Virginia Woolf*, 5 vols, ed. Anne Olivier Bell, assisted by Andrew McNeillie [1977–1984] (Harmondsworth: Penguin, 1979–1985)

Woolf, Virginia, *The Essays of Virginia Woolf*, 6 vols, vols 1–4 ed. Andrew McNeillie, vols 5 and 6 ed. Stuart N. Clarke (London: Hogarth Press, 1986–2011)

Woolf, Virginia, *Jacob's Room* [Richmond: Hogarth Press, 1922], ed. Sue Roe (London: Penguin, 1992)

Woolf, Virginia, 'The Leaning Tower' [1940], in *The Essays of Virginia Woolf, Volume VI: 1933–1941, and Additional Essays 1906–1924*, ed. Stuart N. Clarke (London: Hogarth Press, 2011), pp. 259–83

Woolf, Virginia, 'The Mark on the Wall' [1917], in Virginia Woolf and L. S. Woolf, *Two Stories* (Richmond: Hogarth Press, 1917), repr. in *A Haunted House and Other Stories* (Middlesex: Penguin, 1973), pp. 43–52

Woolf, Virginia, *Monday or Tuesday* (Richmond: Hogarth Press, 1921)

Woolf, Virginia, *Mrs. Dalloway* [London: Hogarth Press, 1925], ed. Claire Tomalin (Oxford: Oxford University Press, 1992)

Woolf, Virginia, *To the Lighthouse* [London: Hogarth Press, 1927] (London: Penguin, 1964)

Woolf, Virginia, *A Writer's Diary: Being Extracts from the Diary of Virginia Woolf* [1953], ed. Leonard Woolf (New York: Harcourt Brace Jovanovich, 1981)

Young, Violet, *Outlines of Nursing* (London: Scientific Press, 1914)

Anthologies

Poetry

Khan, Nosheen (ed.), *Not with Loud Grieving: Women's Verse of the Great War: An Anthology* (Lahore: Polymer Publications, 1994)

Reilly, Catherine W. (ed.), *Scars Upon My Heart: Women's Poetry and Verse of the First World War*, pref. Judith Kazantzis (London: Virago, 1981)

Prose

Cardinal, Agnès, Dorothy Goldman, and Judith Hattaway (eds), *Women's Writing on the First World War* (Oxford: Oxford University Press, 1999)

Higonnet, Margaret R. (ed.), *Lines of Fire: Women Writers of World War I* (New York: Plume, 1999)

Klein, Yvonne (ed.), *Beyond the Home Front: Women's Autobiographical Writing of the Two World Wars* (New York: New York University Press, 1997)

Korte, Barbara and Ann-Marie Einhaus (eds), *The Penguin Book of First World War Stories* (London and New York: Penguin, 2007)

Marlow, Joyce (ed.), *The Virago Book of Women and the Great War* (London: Virago, 1998)

Smith, Angela K. (ed.), *Women's Writing of the First World War: An Anthology* (Manchester: Manchester University Press, 2000)

Tate, Trudi (ed.), *Women, Men and the Great War: An Anthology of Stories* (Manchester: Manchester University Press, 1995)

Drama

Tylee, Claire, with Elaine Turner and Agnès Cardinal (eds), *War Plays by Women: An International Anthology* (London & New York: Routledge, 1999)

War Letters

Blythe, Ronald (ed.), *Private Words: Letters and Diaries from the Second World War* (London: Penguin, 1993)
Carroll, Andrew (ed.), *War Letters: Extraordinary Correspondence from American Wars* (New York and London: Scribner, 2001)
Figes, Eva (ed.), *Women's Letters in Wartime, 1450–1945* (London: Pandora, 1993)

Secondary Texts

Acton, Carol, *Grief in Wartime: Private Pain, Public Discourse* (Basingstoke: Palgrave Macmillan, 2007)
Acton, Carol, and Jane Potter, *Working in a World of Hurt: Trauma and Resilience in the Narratives of Medical Personnel in Warzones* (Manchester: Manchester University Press, 2015)
Alpers, Anthony, *The Life of Katherine Mansfield* [1980] (Oxford: Oxford University Press, 1982)
Ammons, Elizabeth, *Edith Wharton's Argument with America* (Athens, GA: University of Georgia Press, 1980)
Anderson, Elizabeth, Avril Maddrell, Kate McLoughlin and Alana Vincent (eds), *Memory, Mourning, Landscape* (Amsterdam: Rodopi, 2010)
Ariès, Philippe, *Western Attitudes towards Death: From the Middle Ages to the Present*, trans. Patricia M. Ranum (Baltimore, MD: Johns Hopkins University Press, 1974)
Audoin-Rouzeau, Stéphane, and Annette Becker, *14–18, Understanding the Great War*, trans. Catherine Temerson (London: Profile Books, 2002)
Badenhausen, Richard, 'Mourning through Memoir: Trauma, Testimony, and Community in Vera Brittain's *Testament of Youth*', *Twentieth Century Literature*, 49.4 (2003), pp. 421–48
Barreca, Regina, *Sex and Death in Victorian Literature* (Basingstoke: Macmillan, 1990)
Barthes, Roland, *Camera Lucida: Reflections on Photography*, trans. Richard Howard [1981] (London: Vintage, 2000)
Beauman, Nicola, *Morgan: A Biography of E. M. Forster* (London: Hodder & Stoughton, 1993)
Beauman, Nicola, *A Very Great Profession: The Woman's Novel 1914–39* (London: Virago, 1983)
Beer, Gillian, 'Hume, Stephen and Elegy in *To the Lighthouse*', in Su Reid (ed.), *Mrs Dalloway and To the Lighthouse: Contemporary Critical Essays* (Basingstoke: Macmillan Press, 1993), pp. 71–86
Beer, Gillian, *Virginia Woolf: The Common Ground* (Edinburgh: Edinburgh University Press, 1996)

Beer, Janet, and Avril Horner, 'Edith Wharton and Modernism: *The Mother's Recompense*', in Catherine Morley and Alex Goody (eds), *American Modernism: Cultural Transactions* (Newcastle upon Tyne: Cambridge Scholars, 2009), pp. 69–92

Bell, Millicent (ed.), *The Cambridge Companion to Edith Wharton* (Cambridge: Cambridge University Press, 1995)

Bendixen, Alfred, and Annette Zilversmit (eds), *Edith Wharton: New Critical Essays* (New York and London: Garland, 1999)

Benert, Annette Larson, 'Edith Wharton at War: Civilized Space in Troubled Times', *Twentieth Century Literature*, 42.3 (Autumn 1996), pp. 322–43

Benstock, Shari, 'Introduction', in *A Son at the Front* [1923], ed. Shari Benstock (DeKalb, IL: Northern Illinois University Press, 1995), pp. vii–xv

Benstock, Shari, *No Gifts from Chance: A Biography of Edith Wharton* (New York: C. Scribner's Sons, 1994)

Bergonzi, Bernard, *Heroes' Twilight: A Study of the Literature of the Great War* (London: Constable, 1965; 2nd edn, Basingstoke: Macmillan, 1980)

Bland, Caroline, '"In Case the Worst Comes to the Worst": Letters Home from Berlin, 1942–1945', in Caroline Bland and Máire Cross (eds), *Gender and Politics in the Age of Letter Writing, 1750–2000* (Aldershot: Ashgate, 2004), pp. 225–39

Blau DuPlessis, Rachel, *H.D.: The Career of that Struggle* (Brighton: Harvester Press, 1986)

Blazek, William, 'French Lessons: Edith Wharton's War Propaganda', *Revue Française d'Études Américaines*, 115.1 (2008), 10–22

Blazek, William, 'Reading the Ruins: "Coming Home," Wharton's Atrocity Story of the First World War', *Journal of the Short Story in English*, 58 (2012), pp. 125–42

Blazek, William, 'Trench Vision: Obscurity in Edith Wharton's War Writings', in Françoise Sammarcelli (ed.), *L'Obscur* (Paris: Michel Houdiard, 2009), pp. 66–84

Bloom, Harold (ed.), *Clarissa Dalloway* (New York: Chelsea House, 1990)

Bluemel, Kristin (ed.), *Intermodernism: Literary Culture in Mid-Twentieth-Century Britain* (Edinburgh: Edinburgh University Press, 2009)

Boehmer, Elleke, *Colonial and Postcolonial Literature: Migrant Metaphors* (Oxford: Oxford University Press, 1995; 2nd edn, 2005)

Boehmer, Elleke, 'Mansfield as Colonial Modernist: Difference Within', in Gerri Kimber and Janet Wilson (eds), *Celebrating Katherine Mansfield: A Centenary Volume of Essays* (Basingstoke: Palgrave Macmillan, 2011), pp. 57–71

Booth, Allyson, *Postcards from the Trenches: Negotiating the Space between Modernism and the First World War* (Oxford: Oxford University Press, 1996)

Borg, Alan, *War Memorials: From Antiquity to the Present* (London: Leo Cooper, 1991)

Bostridge, Mark, *Florence Nightingale: The Making of an Icon* (New York: Farrar, Straus, and Giroux, 2008)

Bourke, Joanna, *Dismembering the Male: Men's Bodies, Britain and the Great War* (London: Reaktion, 1996)

Bourke, Joanna, 'Gender Roles in Killing Zones', in Jay Winter (ed.), *The Cambridge History of the First World War*, vol. 3: *Civil Society* (Cambridge: Cambridge University Press, 2014), pp. 153–77

Bourke, Joanna, *An Intimate History of Killing: Face-to-Face Killing in Twentieth-Century Warfare* (New York: Basic Books, 1999)

Bracco, Rosa Maria, *Merchants of Hope: British Middlebrow Writers and the First World War, 1919–1939* (Providence, RI and Oxford: Berg, 1993)

Bradshaw, David, 'The Socio-Political Vision of the Novels', in Susan Sellers (ed.), *The Cambridge Companion to Virginia Woolf*, 2nd edn (Cambridge: Cambridge University Press, 2010), pp. 124–41

Bradshaw, David, '"Vanished, like leaves": The Military, Elegy and Italy in *Mrs Dalloway*', *Woolf Studies Annual*, 8 (New York: Pace University Press, 2002), pp. 107–25

Bradshaw, David, 'Winking, Buzzing, Carpet-Beating: Reading *Jacob's Room*' (Southport: Virginia Woolf Society of Great Britain, 2003)

Brassard, Geneviève, '"War is the greatest of paradoxes": May Sinclair and Edith Wharton at the Front', *Minerva Journal*, 2.1 (2008), pp. 3–21

Braybon, Gail, 'Women, War, and Work', in Hew Strachan (ed.), *The Oxford Illustrated History of the First World War* (Oxford: Oxford University Press, 1998), pp. 149–62

Briggs, Julia, *Virginia Woolf: An Inner Life* (London: Penguin, 2006)

Briggs, Julia (ed.), *Virginia Woolf: Introductions to the Major Works* (London: Virago, 1994)

Bristow, Nancy K., *American Pandemic: The Lost Worlds of the 1918 Influenza Epidemic* (Oxford: Oxford University Press, 2012)

Bronfen, Elisabeth, *Over Her Dead Body: Death, Femininity and the Aesthetic* (Manchester: Manchester University Press, 1992)

Bronfen, Elisabeth, and Sarah Webster Goodwin (eds), *Death and Representation* (Baltimore, MD and London: Johns Hopkins University Press, 1993)

Brookes, Jane, and Christine E. Hallett (eds), *One Hundred Years of Wartime Nursing Practices, 1854–1953* (Manchester: Manchester University Press, 2015)

Brooks, Peter, *Realist Vision* (New Haven, CT: Yale University Press, 2005)

Brunton, Elizabeth, '"I had a Baby, I Mean I didn't, in an Air Raid": War and Stillbirth in H. D.'s *Asphodel*', *Women's Writing*, 24.1 (2017), pp. 66–79

Buck, Claire, 'British Women's Writing of the Great War', in Vincent Sherry (ed.), *The Cambridge Companion to the Literature of the First World War* (Cambridge: Cambridge University Press, 2005), pp. 85–112

Buck, Claire, *Conceiving Strangeness in British First World War Writing* (Basingstoke: Palgrave Macmillan, 2015)

Buck, Claire, *H.D. and Freud: Bisexuality and a Feminine Discourse* (London: Harvester Wheatsheaf, 1991)

Budreau, Lisa M., *Bodies of War: World War I and the Politics of Commemoration in America* (New York: New York University Press, 2010)

Budreau, Lisa M., and Richard M. Prior, *Answering the Call: The US Army Nurse Corps, 1917–1919* (Washington, DC: United States Department of Defense, 2008)

Buitenhuis, Peter, 'Edith Wharton and the First World War', *American Quarterly*, 18.3 (1966), 493–505

Buitenhuis, Peter, *The Great War of Words: Literature as Propaganda 1914–1918 and After* [1987] (London: Batsford, 1989)

Burgan, Mary, *Illness, Gender, and Writing: The Case of Katherine Mansfield* (Baltimore, MD and London: Johns Hopkins University Press, 1994)

Bürger, Peter, *Theory of the Avant-Garde* [1974], trans. Michael Shaw, foreword by Jochen Schutte-Sasse (Manchester: Manchester University Press, 1984)

Campbell, James, 'Combat Gnosticism: The Ideology of First World War Poetry Criticism', *New Literary History*, 30.1, Poetry & Poetics (Winter, 1999), pp. 203–15

Cannadine, David, 'War and Death, Grief and Mourning in Modern Britain', in Joachim Whaley (ed.), *Mirrors of Mortality: Studies in the Social History of Death* (London: Europa, 1981), pp. 187–242

Carden-Coyne, Ana, *Gender and Conflict since 1914: Historical and Interdisciplinary Perspectives* (Basingstoke: Palgrave Macmillan, 2012)

Carden-Coyne, Ana, *The Politics of Wounds: Military Patients and Medical Power in the First World War* (Oxford: Oxford University Press, 2014)

Carden-Coyne, Ana, *Reconstructing the Body: Classicism, Modernism, and the First World War* (Oxford: Oxford University Press, 2009)

Carney, Mary, 'Wharton's Short Fiction of War: The Politics of "Coming Home"', in Farhat Iftekharrudin, Joseph Boyden, Joseph Longo and Mary Rohrberger (eds), *Postmodern Approaches to the Short Story* (Westport, CT and London: Praeger, 2003), pp. 109–20

Christodoulides, Nephie J., and Polina Mackay (eds), *The Cambridge Companion to H.D.* (Cambridge: Cambridge University Press, 2012)

Clewell, Tammy, 'Consolation Refused: Virginia Woolf, the Great War, and Modernist Mourning', *Modern Fiction Studies*, 50.1 (2004), pp. 197–223

Clewell, Tammy, *Mourning, Modernism, Postmodernism* (Basingstoke: Palgrave Macmillan, 2009)

Clouting, Laura, *A Century of Remembrance* (London: Imperial War Museums, 2018)

Cobley, Evelyn, *Representing War: Form and Ideology in First World War Narratives* (Toronto and London: University of Toronto Press, 1993)

Cohen, Debra Rae, *Remapping the Home Front: Locating Citizenship in British Women's Great War Fiction* (Boston, MA: Northeastern University Press, 2002)

Cohen, Milton A. 'Fatal Symbiosis: Modernism and the First World War', in Patrick J. Quinn and Steven Trout (eds), *The Literature of the Great War Reconsidered: Beyond Modern Memory* (Basingstoke: Palgrave, 2001), pp. 159–71

Cole, Sarah, *At the Violet Hour: Modernism and Violence in England and Ireland* (New York and Oxford: Oxford University Press, 2012)

Cole, Sarah, *Modernism, Male Friendship, and the First World War* (Cambridge: Cambridge University Press, 2003)

Collecott, Diana, *H.D. and Sapphic Modernism, 1910–1950* (Cambridge: Cambridge University Press, 1999)

Colquitt, Clare, Susan Goodman and Candace Waid (eds), *A Forward Glance: New Essays on Edith Wharton* (Newark, DE: University of Delaware Press; London: Associated University Presses, 1999)

Condé, Mary, 'Payments and Face Values: Edith Wharton's *A Son at the Front*', in Suzanne Raitt and Trudi Tate (eds), *Women's Fiction and the Great War* (Oxford: Oxford University Press, 1997), pp. 47–64

Connor, Rachel, *H.D. and the Image* (Manchester: Manchester University Press, 2004)

Cook, Tim, 'Black-Hearted Traitors, Crucified Martyrs, and the Leaning Virgin: The Role of Rumor and the Great War Canadian Soldier', in Jennifer D. Keene and Michael S. Neiberg (eds), *Finding Common Ground: New Directions in First World War Studies* (Leiden and Boston, MA: Brill, 2011), pp. 21–42

Cooke, Miriam, and Angela Woollacott (eds), *Gendering War Talk* (Princeton, NJ: Princeton University Press, 1993)

Cooper, Helen M., Adrienne Auslander Munich and Susan Merrill Squier (eds), *Arms and the Woman: War, Gender, and Literary Representation* (Chapel Hill, NC and London: University of North Carolina Press, 1989)

Cooperman, Stanley, *World War I and the American Novel* (Baltimore, MD: Johns Hopkins University Press, 1967)

Cooter, Roger, Mark Harrison and Steve Sturdy (eds), *War, Medicine and Modernity* (Stroud: Sutton, 1998)

Cornish, Paul, and Nicholas J. Saunders (eds), *Bodies in Conflict: Corporeality, Materiality, and Transformation* (London: Routledge, 2014)

Coroneos, Con, 'Flies and Violets in Katherine Mansfield', in Suzanne Raitt and Trudi Tate (eds), *Women's Fiction and the Great War* (Oxford: Clarendon Press, 1997), pp. 197–218

Crane, David, *Empires of the Dead: How One Man's Vision Led to the Creation of WWI's War Graves* (London: William Collins, 2013)

Crosby, Alfred W., *America's Forgotten Pandemic: The Influenza of 1918* (Cambridge: Cambridge University Press, 1989; 2nd edn, 2003)

Damousi, Joy, 'Gender and Mourning', in Susan R. Grayzel and Tammy M. Proctor (eds), *Gender and the Great War* (New York: Oxford University Press, 2017), pp. 211–29

Damousi, Joy, *The Labour of Loss: Mourning, Memory and Wartime Bereavement in Australia* (Cambridge: Cambridge University Press, 1999)

Damousi, Joy, 'Mourning Practices', in Jay Winter (ed.), *The Cambridge History of the First World War*, vol. 3: *Civil Society* (Cambridge: Cambridge University Press, 2014), pp. 358–84

Darrohn, Christine, '"Blown to Bits!": Katherine Mansfield's "The Garden Party" and the Great War', *Modern Fiction Studies*, 44.3 (1998), pp. 513–39

Darrow, Margaret H., *French Women and the First World War: War Stories of the Home Front* (Oxford and New York: Berg, 2000)

Das, Santanu (ed.), *The Cambridge Companion to the Poetry of the First World War* (Cambridge: Cambridge University Press, 2013)

Das, Santanu, *India, Empire, and First World War Culture: Writings, Images, and Songs* (Cambridge: Cambridge University Press, 2018)

Das, Santanu (ed.), *Race, Empire and First World War Writing* (Cambridge: Cambridge University Press, 2011)

Das, Santanu, *Touch and Intimacy in First World War Literature* (Cambridge: Cambridge University Press, 2005)

Das, Santanu, and Kate McLoughlin (eds), *The First World War: Literature, Culture, Modernity* (Oxford: Published for the British Academy by Oxford University Press, 2018)

DeBauche, Leslie Midkiff, *Reel Patriotism: The Movies and World War I* (Madison, WI: University of Wisconsin Press, 1997)

Debo, Annette, *The American H.D.* (Iowa City: University of Iowa Press, 2012)

Deer, Patrick, *Culture in Camouflage: War, Empire, and Modern British Literature* (Oxford: Oxford University Press, 2009)

De Groot, Gerald J., *Blighty: British Society in the Era of the Great War* (London: Longman, 1996)

Dendooven, Dominiek, 'Repatriation, Illegal Repatriation and Expatriation of British Bodies during and after the First World War', in Paul Cornish and Nicholas J. Saunders (eds), *Bodies in Conflict: Corporeality, Materiality, and Transformation* (London: Routledge, 2014), pp. 66–79

Detloff, Madelyn, *The Persistence of Modernism: Loss and Mourning in the Twentieth Century* (Cambridge: Cambridge University Press, 2009)

Dollimore, Jonathon, *Death, Desire and Loss in Western Culture* (London: Routledge, 2003)

Donald, James, Anne Friedberg and Laura Marcus (eds), *Close Up, 1927–1933: Cinema and Modernism* (London: Cassell, 1998)

Donner, Henriette, 'Under the Cross: Why V.A.D.s Performed the Filthiest Task in the Dirtiest War: Red Cross Women Volunteers, 1914–1918', *Journal of Social History*, 30 (1997), pp. 687–704

Dunbar, Pamela, *Radical Mansfield: Double Discourse in Katherine Mansfield's Short Stories* (Basingstoke: Palgrave Macmillan, 1997)

Dwight, Eleanor, *Edith Wharton: An Extraordinary Life* (New York: Abrams, 1994)

Einhaus, Ann-Marie, 'Modernism, Truth, and the Canon of First World War Literature', *Modernist Cultures*, 6.2 (2011), pp. 296–314

Einhaus, Ann-Marie, *The Short Story and the First World War* (Cambridge: Cambridge University Press, 2013)

Eksteins, Modris, 'The Cultural Legacy of the Great War', in Jay Winter, Geoffrey Parker and Mary R. Habeck (eds), *The Great War and the Twentieth Century* (New Haven, CT and London: Yale University Press, 2000), pp. 331–49

Eksteins, Modris, 'Memory and the Great War', in Hew Strachan (ed.), *The Oxford Illustrated History of the First World War* (Oxford: Oxford University Press, 1998), pp. 305–17

Eksteins, Modris, *Rites of Spring: The Great War and the Birth of the Modern Age* (Boston, MA: Houghton Mifflin, 1989)

Englund, Peter, *The Beauty and The Sorrow: An Intimate History of the First World War*, trans. Peter Graves (London: Profile, 2011)

Evans, Suzanne, *Mothers of Heroes, Mothers of Martyrs: World War I and the Politics of Grief* (Montreal: McGill-Queen's University Press, 2007)

Faust, Drew Gilpin, *This Republic of Suffering: Death and the American Civil War* (New York: Knopf, 2008)

Favret, Mary A., *War at a Distance: Romanticism and the Making of Modern Wartime* (Princeton, NJ and Oxford: Princeton University Press, 2010)

Fell, Alison S., 'Nursing the Other: The Representation of Colonial Troops in French and British First World War Nursing Memoirs', in Santanu Das (ed.), *Race, Empire and First World War Writing* (Cambridge: Cambridge University Press, 2011), pp. 158–74

Fell, Alison S., and Christine E. Hallett (eds), *First World War Nursing: New Perspectives* (London: Routledge, 2013)

Fell, Alison S., and Ingrid Sharp (eds), *The Women's Movement in Wartime: International Perspectives, 1914–19* (Basingstoke: Palgrave Macmillan, 2007)

Fernihough, Anne, 'Introduction', in Kathleen Murry [Katherine Mansfield], *In A German Pension* [1911] (London: Penguin, 1999), pp. ix–xxxi
Forter, Greg, *Gender, Race, and Mourning in American Modernism* (Cambridge: Cambridge University Press, 2011)
Fox, James, *British Art and the First World War, 1914–1924* (Cambridge: Cambridge University Press, 2015)
Frank, Lucy (ed.), *Representations of Death in Nineteenth-Century US Writing and Culture* (Aldershot: Ashgate, 2007)
Frayn, Andrew, 'Introduction: Modernism and the First World War', in Frayn (ed.), *Modernist Cultures*, 12.1 (Edinburgh: Edinburgh University Press, 2017), pp. 1–15
Frayn, Andrew, *Writing Disenchantment: British First World War Prose, 1914–30* (Manchester: Manchester University Press, 2014)
Freedman, Ariela, *Death, Men, and Modernism: Trauma and Narrative in British Fiction from Hardy to Woolf* (New York and London: Routledge, 2003)
Freedman, Ariela, 'Mary Borden's *Forbidden Zone*: Women's Writing from No-Man's-Land', *Modernism/Modernity*, 9 (2002), pp. 109–24
Friedman, Alan Warren, *Fictional Death and the Modernist Enterprise* (Cambridge: Cambridge University Press, 1995)
Freud, Sigmund, 'Mourning and Melancholia' [1917], in *Sigmund Freud: Collected Papers, Volume 4*, trans. under supervision of Joan Riviere (New York: Basic Books, 1959), pp. 152–70
Freud, Sigmund, 'On Transience' [1916], in James Strachey (ed.), *Sigmund Freud: Collected Papers, Volume 5* (New York: Basic Books, 1959), pp. 79–82
Freud, Sigmund, 'Thoughts for the Times on War and Death' (1915), in *Sigmund Freud: Collected Papers, Volume 4*, trans. under supervision of Joan Riviere (New York: Basic Books, 1959), pp. 288–317
Froula, Christine, *Virginia Woolf and the Bloomsbury Avant-Garde: War, Civilization, Modernity* (New York: Columbia University Press, 2005)
Froula, Christine, with Gerri Kimber and Todd Martin (eds), *Katherine Mansfield Studies*, 10, *Special Issue on Virginia Woolf and Katherine Mansfield* (Edinburgh: Edinburgh University Press, 2018)
Fussell, Paul, *The Great War and Modern Memory* (London and Oxford: Oxford University Press, 1975; repr. 2000)
Gallagher, Jean, *The World Wars through the Female Gaze* (Carbondale, IL: Southern Illinois University Press, 1998)
Garver, Lee, 'The Political Katherine Mansfield', *Modernism/Modernity*, 8.2 (2001), pp. 225–43
Gay, Peter, *Freud: A Life for Our Time* [1988] (London: Papermac, 1989)
Gibb, Lorna, *West's World: The Extraordinary Life of Dame Rebecca West* (London: Macmillan, 2013)

Gilbert, Sandra M., and Susan Gubar, *No Man's Land: The Place of the Woman Writer in the Twentieth Century*, 3 vols (New Haven, CT and London: Yale University Press, 1988–94)

Gillis, John R., 'Introduction: Memory and Identity: The History of a Relationship', in John R. Gillis (ed.), *Commemorations: The Politics of National Identity* (Princeton, NJ: Princeton University Press, 1994), pp. 3–24

Gillis, Stacy, 'Consoling Fictions: Mourning, World War One, and Dorothy L. Sayers', in Patricia Rae (ed.), *Modernism and Mourning* (Lewisburg, PA: Bucknell University Press and Associated University Presses, 2007), pp. 185–97

Goldman, Dorothy, 'Eagles of the West? American Women Writers and World War I', in Dorothy Goldman (ed.), *Women and World War I: The Written Response* (Basingstoke: Macmillan, 1993), pp. 188–208

Goldman, Dorothy (ed.), *Women and World War I: The Written Response* (London: Macmillan, 1993)

Goldman, Dorothy, with Jane Gledhill and Judith Hattaway, *Women Writers and the Great War* (New York: Twayne; London: Prentice Hall International, 1995)

Goldman, Jane, 'From *Mrs Dalloway* to *The Waves*: New Elegy and Lyric Experimentalism', in Susan Sellers (ed.), *The Cambridge Companion to Virginia Woolf*, 2nd edn (Cambridge: Cambridge University Press, 2010), pp. 49–69

Gómez Reus, Teresa, 'Flânerie and the Ghosts of War: Hidden Perspectives of Edith Wharton's "The Look of Paris"', *Women: A Cultural Review*, 22.1 (2011), pp. 29–49

Gómez Reus, Teresa, 'Racing to the Front: Auto-Mobility and Competing Narratives of Women in the First World War', in Teresa Gómez Reus and Terry Gifford (eds), *Women in Transit through Literary Liminal Spaces* (Basingstoke: Palgrave Macmillan, 2013), pp. 107–22

Gómez Reus, Teresa, and Peter Lauber, 'In a Literary No Man's Land: A Spatial Reading of Edith Wharton's *Fighting France*', in Teresa Gómez Reus and Aránzazu Usandizaga (eds), *Inside Out: Women Negotiating, Subverting, Appropriating Public and Private Space* (Amsterdam: Rodopi, 2008), pp. 205–28

Goodspeed-Chadwick, Julie, *Modernist Women Writers and War: Trauma and the Female Body in Djuna Barnes, H.D., and Gertrude Stein* (Baton Rouge, LO: Louisiana State University Press, 2011)

Goodwyn, Janet, *Edith Wharton: Traveller in the Land of Letters* (Basingstoke: Macmillan, 1990)

Gorer, Geoffrey, *Death, Grief and Mourning in Contemporary Britain* (London: Cresset Press, 1965)

Grayzel, Susan R., *Women and the First World War* (Harlow: Longman, 2002)
Grayzel, Susan R., *Women's Identities at War: Gender, Motherhood, and Politics in Britain and France during the First World War* (Chapel Hill, NC and London: University of North Carolina Press, 1999)
Grayzel, Susan R., and Tammy M. Proctor (eds), *Gender and the Great War* (New York: Oxford University Press, 2017)
Gregory, Adrian, *The Last Great War: British Society and the First World War* (Cambridge: Cambridge University Press, 2008)
Gregory, Adrian, *The Silence of Memory: Armistice Day, 1919–1946* (Oxford: Berg, 1994)
Guest, Barbara, *Herself Defined: The Poet H.D. and her World* (London: Collins, 1985)
Gunsteren, Julia van, *Katherine Mansfield and Literary Impressionism* (Amsterdam: Rodopi, 1990)
Hallam, Elizabeth, and Jenny Hockey, *Death, Memory, and Material Culture* (Oxford and New York: Berg, 2001)
Hallett, Christine E., *Celebrating Nurses: A Visual History* (Hauppauge, NY: Barron's, 2010)
Hallett, Christine E., *Containing Trauma: Nursing Work in the First World War* (Manchester: Manchester University Press, 2009)
Hallett, Christine E., *Nurse Writers of the Great War* (Manchester: Manchester University Press, 2016)
Hallett, Christine E., *Veiled Warriors: Allied Nurses of the First World War* (Oxford: Oxford University Press, 2014)
Hämmerle, Christa, '"You let a weeping woman call you home?" Private Correspondences during the First World War in Austria and Germany', in Rebecca Earle (ed.), *Epistolary Selves: Letters and Letter-Writers, 1600–1945* (Aldershot: Ashgate, 1999), pp. 152–82
Hämmerle, Christa, Oswald Überegger and Birgitta Bader Zaar, *Gender and the First World War* (Basingstoke: Palgrave Macmillan, 2014)
Hammond, Mary, and Shafquat Towheed (eds), *Publishing in the First World War: Essays in Book History* (Basingstoke: Palgrave Macmillan, 2007)
Hammond, Michael, *The Big Show: British Cinema Culture in the Great War, 1914–1918* (Exeter: University of Exeter Press, 2006)
Hammond, Michael, and Michael Williams (eds), *British Silent Cinema and the Great War* (Basingstoke: Palgrave Macmillan, 2011)
Handley, William R., 'War and the Politics of Narration in *Jacob's Room*' in Mark Hussey (ed.), *Virginia Woolf and War: Fiction, Reality and Myth* (Syracuse, NY: Syracuse University Press, 1991), pp. 110–33
Hanley, Lynne, *Writing War: Fiction, Gender, Memory* (Amherst, MA: University of Massachusetts Press, 1991)

Hargreaves, Tracy, 'The Grotesque and the Great War in *To the Lighthouse*', in Suzanne Raitt and Trudi Tate (eds), *Women's Fiction and the Great War* (Oxford: Clarendon Press, 1997), pp. 132–50

Harrison, Mark, *The Medical War: British Military Medicine in the First World War* (Oxford: Oxford University Press, 2010)

Hartley, Jenny, '"Letters are everything these days": Mothers and Letters in the Second World War', in Rebecca Earle (ed.), *Epistolary Selves: Letters and Letter-Writers, 1600–1945* (Aldershot: Ashgate, 1999), pp. 183–95

Haslam, Sara, *Fragmenting Modernism: Ford Madox Ford, the Novel and the Great War* (Oxford: Oxford University Press, 2002)

Haslam, Sara, 'The "moaning of the world" and the "words that bring me peace"': Modernism and the First World War', in *The Edinburgh Companion to Twentieth-Century British and American War Literature*, ed. Adam Piette and Mark Rawlinson (Edinburgh: Edinburgh University Press, 2012), pp. 47–57

Haste, Cate, *Keep the Homes Fires Burning: Propaganda in the First World War* (London: Allen Lane, 1977)

Hattaway, Judith, 'Virginia Woolf's *Jacob's Room*: History and Memory', in Dorothy Goldman (ed.), *Women and World War I: The Written Response* (Basingstoke: Macmillan, 1993), pp. 14–30

Haytock, Jennifer A., *Edith Wharton and the Conversations of Literary Modernism* (Basingstoke: Palgrave Macmillan, 2008)

Haytock, Jennifer A., 'Hemingway's Soldiers and Their Pregnant Women: Domestic Ritual in World War I', *The Hemingway Review* 19.2 (2000), pp. 57–72

Hazelgrove, Jennifer, *Spiritualism and British Society between the Wars* (Manchester: Manchester University Press, 2000)

Henke, Suzette A., *Shattered Subjects: Trauma and Testimony in Women's Life-Writing* (Basingstoke: Macmillan, 1998)

Higonnet, Margaret R., 'Another Record: A Different War', *Women's Studies Quarterly*, 23 (1995), 85–97

Higonnet, Margaret R., 'At the Front', in Jay Winter (ed.), *The Cambridge History of the First World War*, vol. 3: *Civil Society* (Cambridge: Cambridge University Press, 2014), pp. 121–52

Higonnet, Margaret R., 'Authenticity and Art in Trauma Narratives of World War I', *Modernism/Modernity*, 9 (2002), pp. 91–107

Higonnet, Margaret R., 'The Great War and the Female Elegy: Female Lamentation and Silence in Global Contexts', *The Global South*, 1.1 (2007), pp. 120–36

Higonnet, Margaret R., 'Not So Quiet in No-Woman's-Land', in Miriam Cooke and Angela Woollacott (eds), *Gendering War Talk* (Princeton, NJ: Princeton University Press, 1993), pp. 205–26

Higonnet, Margaret R., (ed.), *Nurses at the Front: Writing the Wounds of the Great War* (Boston, MA: Northeastern University Press, 2001)
Higonnet, Margaret R., 'Souvenirs of Death', *Journal of War and Culture Studies*, 1.1 (2008), pp. 65–78
Higonnet, Margaret R., 'Telling Trauma: Women and World War I', in Jean Bessière, ed, *Savoirs et littérature* (Paris: Presses de la Sorbonne Nouvelle, 2002), pp. 1–22
Higonnet, Margaret R., 'Women in the Forbidden Zone: War, Women, and Death', in Elisabeth Bronfen and Sarah Webster Goodwin (eds), *Death and Representation* (Baltimore, MD and London: Johns Hopkins University Press, 1993), pp. 192–211
Higonnet, Margaret, Jane Jenson and Margaret Collins Weitz (eds), *Behind the Lines: Gender and the Two World Wars* (New Haven, CT and London: Yale University Press, 1986)
Hoffman, Frederick J., *The Mortal No: Death and the Modern Imagination* (Princeton, NJ: Princeton University Press, 1964)
Hollenberg, Donna Krolik, 'Art and Ardour in World War One: Selected Letters from H.D. to John Cournos', in Adalaide Morris (ed.), *The Iowa Review: H.D. Centennial Issue*, 16.3 (1986), pp. 126–55
Hollenberg, Donna Krolik, *H.D.: The Poetics of Childbirth and Creativity* (Boston, MA: Northeastern University Press, 1991)
Horne, John (ed.), *A Companion to World War I* (Chichester and Malden, MA: Wiley-Blackwell, 2010)
Horne, John, 'The Living', in Jay Winter (ed.), *The Cambridge History of the First World War*, vol. 3: *Civil Society* (Cambridge: Cambridge University Press, 2014), pp. 592–617
Horne, John, and Alan Kramer, *German Atrocities, 1914: A History of Denial* (New Haven, CT: Yale University Press, 2001)
Hussey, Mark, 'Living in a War Zone: An Introduction to Virginia Woolf as a War Novelist', in *Virginia Woolf and War: Fiction, Reality, and Myth* (Syracuse, NY: Syracuse University Press, 1991), pp. 1–13
Hussey, Mark (ed.), *Virginia Woolf and War: Fiction, Reality, and Myth* (Syracuse, NY: Syracuse University Press, 1991)
Hutchison, Hazel, *The War that Used Up Words: American Writers and the First World War* (New Haven, CT: Yale University Press, 2015)
Hynes, Samuel, *On War and Writing* (Chicago: University of Chicago Press, 2018)
Hynes, Samuel, 'Personal Narratives and Commemoration', in Jay Winter and Emmanuel Sivan (eds), *War and Remembrance in the Twentieth Century* (Cambridge: Cambridge University Press, 1999), pp. 205–20
Hynes, Samuel, *A War Imagined: The First World War and English Culture* [1990] (London: Pimlico, 1992)

Isherwood, Ian Andrew, *Remembering the Great War: Writing and Publishing the Experiences of World War I* (London: I. B. Tauris, 2017)
Jackson, Anna, 'The "Notebooks", "Journal", and Papers of Katherine Mansfield: Is Any of This Her Diary?', *Journal of New Zealand Literature*, 18/19 (2000/2001), pp. 83–99
Jackson, Anna, 'Not Always Swift and Breathless: Katherine Mansfield and the Familiar Letter', in Gerri Kimber and Janet Wilson (eds), *Celebrating Katherine Mansfield: A Centenary Volume of Essays* (Basingstoke: Palgrave Macmillan, 2011), pp. 202–13
Jackson, Kevin, *Constellation of Genius, 1922: Modernism Year One* (London: Hutchinson, 2012)
Jackson, Paul, *Great War Modernisms and 'The New Age' Magazine* (London: Continuum, 2012)
Jalland, Pat, *Death in the Victorian Family* (Oxford: Oxford University Press, 1996)
Jalland, Pat, *Death in War and Peace: Loss and Grief in England, 1914–1970* (Oxford: Oxford University Press, 2010)
Jalland, Pat, 'Victorian Death and its Decline: 1850–1918', in Peter C. Jupp and Clare Gittings (eds), *Death in England: An Illustrated History* (Manchester: Manchester University Press, 1999), pp. 230–55
James, Pearl, *The New Death: American Modernism and World War I* (Charlottesville, VA: University of Virginia Press, 2013)
James, Pearl (ed.), *Picture This: World War I Posters and Visual Cultures* (Lincoln, NE: University of Nebraska Press, 2009)
Jensen, Kimberly, *Mobilizing Minerva: American Women in the First World War* (Urbana, IL: University of Illinois Press, 2008)
Jolly, Margaretta, '"Dear Laughing Motorbyke": Gender and Genre in Women's Letters from the Second World War', in Julia Swindells (ed.), *The Uses of Autobiography* (London: Taylor & Francis, 1995), pp. 45–55
Jolly, Margaretta, 'Myths of Unity: Remembering the Second World War through Letters and Their Editing', in Alex Vernon (ed.), *Arms and the Self: War, the Military, and Autobiographical Writing* (Kent, OH: Kent State University Press, 2005), pp. 144–70
Jolly, Margaretta, 'War Letters', in Jolly (ed.), *Encyclopedia of Life Writing: Autobiographical and Biographical Forms* (London: Fitzroy Dearborn, 2001), pp. 927–30
Jolly, Margaretta, and Liz Stanley, 'Letters As / Not a Genre', *Life Writing*, 2.2 (2005), pp. 91–118
Joslin, Katherine, '"Embattled tendencies": Wharton, Woolf and the Nature of Modernism', in Janet Beer and Bridget Bennett (eds), *Special Relationships: Anglo-American Affinities and Antagonisms, 1854–1936* (Manchester: Manchester University Press, 2002), pp. 202–23

Joslin, Katherine, and Alan Price (eds), *Wretched Exotic: Essays on Edith Wharton in Europe* (New York: Peter Lang, 1993)

Kaplan, Sydney Janet, *Circulating Genius: John Middleton Murry, Katherine Mansfield and D. H. Lawrence* (Edinburgh: Edinburgh University Press, 2010)

Kaplan, Sydney Janet, *Katherine Mansfield and the Origins of Modernist Fiction* (Ithaca, NY: Cornell University Press, 1991)

Keene, Jennifer D., and Michael S. Neiberg (eds), *Finding Common Ground: New Directions in First World War Studies* (Leiden and Boston, MA: Brill, 2011)

Kellehear, Allan, *A Social History of Dying* (Cambridge: Cambridge University Press, 2007)

Kelly, Alice, 'Revising Trauma: Death, Stillbirth and the Great War in H.D.'s Fiction', in Maria Stadter Fox (ed.), *H.D.'s Web*, 4 (Summer 2009), pp. 27–67

Kelly, Alice, 'Katherine Mansfield, War Writer', Introduction to Kelly and Isobel Maddison (eds), *Katherine Mansfield Studies, 6, Special Issue on Katherine Mansfield and World War One* (Edinburgh: Edinburgh University Press, 2014), pp. 1–10

Kelly, Alice, "Can one grow used to death?": Deathbed Scenes in Great War Nurses' Narratives', in Jonathan Vance, Alicia Robinet and Steven Marti (eds), *The Great War: From Memory to History* (Waterloo, ON: Wilfrid Laurier University Press, 2015), pp. 329–49

Kelly, Alice, 'Wharton in Wartime', in Edith Wharton, *Fighting France: From Dunkerque to Belfort*, ed. Alice Kelly (Edinburgh: Edinburgh University Press, 2015), pp. 1–73

Kelly, Alice, 'Words from Home: Wartime Correspondences', in Ann-Marie Einhaus and Katherine Baxter (eds), *The Edinburgh Companion to the First World War and the Arts* (Edinburgh: Edinburgh University Press, 2017), pp. 77–94

Kelly, Alice, 'The American Friends – Nurse, Suffragette, War Writer: Ellen N. La Motte's Life in Letters', *Times Literary Supplement* (31 March 2017), pp. 17–19

Kelly, Andrew, *Cinema and the Great War* (London: Routledge, 1997)

Kelly, Andrew, *Filming All Quiet on the Western Front: 'brutal cutting, stupid censors, bigoted politicos'* (London: I. B. Tauris, 1998)

Kelvin, Norman, 'H.D. and the Years of World War I', *Victorian Poetry, Special Issue on Women Writers 1890–1918*, 38.1 (2000), pp. 170–96

Kennedy, David M., *Over Here: The First World War and American Society* (New York and Oxford: Oxford University Press, 1980; repr. 2004)

Khan, Nosheen, *Women's Poetry of the First World War* (Lexington, KY: University Press of Kentucky, 1988)

Kibble, Matthew, 'The "Still-Born Generation": Decadence and the Great War in H.D.'s Fiction', *Modern Fiction Studies*, 44 (1998), pp. 540–67

Kimber, Gerri, *Katherine Mansfield: The View from France* (Bern, Switzerland and Oxford: Peter Lang, 2008)

Kimber, Gerri, *A Literary Modernist: Katherine Mansfield and the Art of the Short Story*, foreword by Vincent O'Sullivan (London: Centre for New Zealand Studies, 2008)

King, Alex, *Memorials of the Great War in Britain: The Symbolism and Politics of Remembrance* (Oxford: Berg, 1998)

Kingsley Kent, Susan, 'Love and Death: War and Gender in Britain, 1914–1918', in Frans Coetzee and Marilyn Shevin-Coetzee (eds), *Authority, Identity and the Social History of the Great War* (Oxford: Berghahn Books, 1995), pp. 153–74

Klekowski, Ed, and Libby Klekowski, *Edith Wharton and Mary Roberts Rinehart at the Western Front, 1915* (Jefferson, NC: McFarland, 2018)

Klekowski, Ed, and Libby Klekowski, *Eyewitnesses to the Great War: American Writers, Reporters, Volunteers and Soldiers in France, 1914–1918* (Jefferson, NC: McFarland, 2012)

Kloepfer, Deborah Kelly, 'Fishing the Murex Up: Sense and Resonance in H.D.'s *Palimpsest*', in Susan Stanford Friedman and Rachel Blau DuPlessis (eds), *Signets: Reading H.D.* (Madison, WI: University of Wisconsin Press, 1990), pp. 185–204

Kloepfer, Deborah Kelly, *The Unspeakable Mother: Forbidden Discourse in Jean Rhys and H.D.* (Ithaca, NY and London: Cornell University Press, 1989)

Knights, Pamela, *The Cambridge Introduction to Edith Wharton* (Cambridge: Cambridge University Press, 2009)

Kontou, Tatiana, *Spiritualism and Women's Writing: From the Fin de Siècle to the Neo-Victorian* (Basingstoke: Palgrave Macmillan, 2009)

Korte, Barbara, and Ann-Marie Einhaus, 'Introduction', in Barbara Korte and Ann-Marie Einhaus (eds), *The Penguin Book of First World War Stories* (London and New York: Penguin, 2007), pp. vii–xviii

Kuhlman, Erika A., *Of Little Comfort: War Widows, Fallen Soldiers and the Remaking of the Nation after the Great War* (New York: New York University Press, 2012)

Langer, Lawrence L., *The Age of Atrocity: Death in Modern Literature* (Boston, MA: Beacon Press, 1978)

Laqueur, Thomas W., 'Memory and Naming in the Great War', in John R. Gillis (ed.), *Commemorations: The Politics of National Identity* (Princeton, NJ: Princeton University Press, 1994), pp. 150–67

Larabee, Mark D., *Front Lines of Modernism: Remapping the Great War in British Fiction* (New York and Basingstoke: Palgrave Macmillan, 2011)

Le Naour, Jean-Yves, *The Living Unknown Soldier: A Story of Grief and the Great War*, trans. Penny Allen (London: Heinemann, 2005)
Lee, Hermione, *Edith Wharton* (New York: Knopf, 2007)
Lee, Hermione, *Virginia Woolf* (London: Chatto & Windus, 1996; London: Vintage, 1997)
Lee, Janet, *War Girls: The First Aid Nursing Yeomanry in the Great War* (Manchester: Manchester University Press, 2005)
Leed, Eric J., *No Man's Land: Combat and Identity in World War I* (Cambridge: Cambridge University Press, 1979)
Levenback, Karen L., *Virginia Woolf and the Great War* (Syracuse, NY: Syracuse University Press, 1999)
Lewis, Pericles, 'Inventing Literary Modernism at the Outbreak of the Great War', in Michael J. K. Walsh (ed.), *London, Modernism, and 1914* (Cambridge: Cambridge University Press, 2010), pp. 148–64
Lewis, R. W. B., *Edith Wharton: A Biography* (New York: Harper & Row, 1975)
Lewis, R. W. B., 'Introduction to *The Collected Short Stories of Edith Wharton*', in Heather McClave (ed.), *Women Writers of the Short Story: A Collection of Critical Essays* (Englewood Cliffs, NJ: Prentice-Hall, 1980), pp. 32–49
Liggins, Emma, Andrew Maunder and Ruth Robbins, 'The Short Story and the Great War', in *The British Short Story* (Basingstoke: Palgrave Macmillan, 2011), pp. 133–54
Linett, Maren Tova (ed.), *The Cambridge Companion to Modernist Women Writers* (Cambridge: Cambridge University Press, 2010)
Longworth, Deborah, 'Trauma and War Memory', in Laura Marcus and Peter Nicholls (eds), *The Cambridge History of Twentieth-Century English Literature* (Cambridge: Cambridge University Press, 2004), pp. 175–96
Longworth, Philip, *The Unending Vigil: A History of the Commonwealth War Graves Commission* [1967] (rev. and updated edn, London: Leo Cooper, 2003)
Lloyd, David W., *Battlefield Tourism: Pilgrimage and the Commemoration of the Great War in Britain, Australia and Canada, 1919–1939* (Oxford: Berg, 1998)
Lubbock, Percy, *Portrait of Edith Wharton* (London: Jonathan Cape, 1947)
Lubin, David M., *Grand Illusions: American Art and the First World War* (New York: Oxford University Press, 2016)
Luckins, Tanja, *The Gates of Memory: Australian People's Experience of Loss and the Great War* (Fremantle, Western Australia: Curtin University Books, 2004)
Macdonald, Lyn, *The Roses of No Man's Land* [1980] (London and Basingstoke: Papermac, 1990)

MacKay, Marina, *Modernism and World War II* (Cambridge: Cambridge University Press, 2007)
MacKay, Marina, *Modernism, War, and Violence* (London: Bloomsbury Academic, 2017)
Mackay, Polina, 'H.D.'s Modernism', in Nephie J. Christodoulides and Polina Mackay (eds), *The Cambridge Companion to H.D.* (Cambridge: Cambridge University Press, 2012), pp. 51–62
Malvern, Sue, *Modern Art, Britain and the Great War: Witnessing, Testimony and Remembrance* (New Haven, CT and London: Yale University Press, 2004)
Mantz, Ruth Elvish, *The Critical Bibliography of Katherine Mansfield*, intro. John Middleton Murry (London: Constable, 1931)
Mao, Douglas, and Rebecca L. Walkowitz, 'The New Modernist Studies', *PMLA*, 123.3 (2008), pp. 737–48
Marcus, Jane, 'Afterword: The Nurse's Text: Acting Out an Anaesthetic Aesthetic', in Irene Rathbone, *We that Were Young: A Novel* [1932], intro. Lynn Knight (New York: Feminist Press, 1989), pp. 467–98
Marcus, Jane, 'Corpus/Corps/Corpse: Writing the Body in/at War', in Helen M. Cooper, Adrienne Auslander Munich and Susan Merrill Squier (eds), *Arms and the Woman: War, Gender, and Literary Representation* (Chapel Hill, NC and London: University of North Carolina Press, 1989), pp. 124–67 [initially published as Afterword to Helen Zenna Smith, *Not So Quiet . . . Stepdaughters of War* [1930], intro. Barbara Hardy (London: Virago, 1988)]
Marcus, Laura, 'The Great War in Twentieth-Century Cinema', in Vincent Sherry (ed.), *The Cambridge Companion to the Literature of the First World War* (Cambridge: Cambridge University Press, 2005), pp. 280–301
Marcus, Laura, 'The Novel as Elegy: *Jacob's Room* and *To the Lighthouse*', in *Writers and Their Work: Virginia Woolf* (Plymouth, UK: Northcote House, 1997), pp. 82–113
Marcus, Laura, *The Tenth Muse: Writing About Cinema in the Modernist Period* (Oxford: Oxford University Press, 2007)
Marsh Fields, Anne, '"Writing a war story": Edith Wharton and World War I' (PhD dissertation, University of North Carolina, 1992)
Matthews, John T., 'American Writing of the Great War', in Vincent Sherry (ed.), *The Cambridge Companion to the Literature of the First World War* (Cambridge: Cambridge University Press, 2005), pp. 217–42
McCabe, Susan, *Cinematic Modernism: Modernist Poetry and Film* (Cambridge and New York: Cambridge University Press, 2005)
McDonnell, Jenny, *Katherine Mansfield and the Modernist Marketplace: At the Mercy of the Public* (Basingstoke: Palgrave Macmillan, 2010)
McEwen, Yvonne, *It's a Long Way to Tipperary: British and Irish Nurses in the Great War* (Dunfermline, Scotland: Cualann Press, 2006)

McLoughlin, Kate, *Authoring War: The Literary Representation of War from the Iliad to Iraq* (Cambridge: Cambridge University Press, 2011)
McLoughlin, Kate, 'Edith Wharton, War Correspondent', *Edith Wharton Review*, 21 (2005), pp. 1–10
McLoughlin, Kate, 'War and Words', in Kate McLoughlin (ed.), *The Cambridge Companion to War Writing* (Cambridge: Cambridge University Press, 2009), pp. 15–24
McNeil, Helen, 'Introduction', in H.D., *Bid Me to Live* (London: Virago, 1984), pp. vii–xix
Mellor, Leo, *Reading the Ruins: Modernism, Bombsites and British Culture* (Cambridge: Cambridge University Press, 2011)
Mellor, Leo, 'Words from the Bombsites: Debris, Modernism and Literary Salvage', *Critical Quarterly*, 46 (2004), pp. 77–90
Mepham, John, 'Mourning and Modernism', in Patricia Clements and Isobel Grundy (eds), *Virginia Woolf: New Critical Essays* (London: Vision Press, 1983), pp. 137–56
Meyer, Jessica (ed.), *British Popular Culture and the First World War* (Leiden: Brill, 2008)
Meyer, Jessica, *Men of War: Masculinity and the First World War in Britain* (Basingstoke: Palgrave Macmillan, 2009)
Michel, Paulette, and Michel Dupuis (eds), *The Fine Instrument: Essays on Katherine Mansfield* (Sydney and Coventry: Dangaroo Press, 1989)
Mieszkowski, Jan, 'Great War, Cold War, Total War', *Modernism/Modernity*, 16.2 (2009), pp. 211–28
Mieszkowski, Jan, *Watching War* (Stanford, CA: Stanford University Press, 2012)
Minogue, Sally, and Andrew Palmer, *The Remembered Dead: Poetry, Memory and the First World War* (Cambridge: Cambridge University Press, 2018)
Moglen, Seth, *Mourning Modernity: Literary Modernism and the Injuries of American Capitalism* (Stanford, CA: Stanford University Press, 2007)
Montgomerie, Deborah, *Love in Time of War: Letter Writing in the Second World War* (Auckland, NZ: Auckland University Press, 2005)
Morató Agrafojo, Yolanda, 'More than a War Correspondent: Edith Wharton's Chronicles about French Civilians in the Great War and the Beginning of Citizen Journalism', *Oceánide*, 5 (2013), n.p.
Morley, Catherine, and Alex Goody (eds), *American Modernism: Cultural Transactions* (Newcastle upon Tyne: Cambridge Scholars, 2009)
Morley, John, *Death, Heaven and the Victorians* (London: Studio Vista, 1971)
Mortelier, Christiane, 'The French Connection: Francis Carco', in Roger Robinson (ed.), *Katherine Mansfield: In from the Margin* (Baton Rouge, LO and London: Louisiana State University Press, 1994), pp. 137–57

Mosse, George L., *Fallen Soldiers: Reshaping the Memory of the World Wars* (New York and Oxford: Oxford University Press, 1990)
Mulvey, Laura, *Death 24x a Second: Stillness and the Moving Image* (London: Reaktion Books, 2006)
Nathan, Rhoda B. (ed.), *Critical Essays on Katherine Mansfield* (New York: G. K. Hall, 1993)
Nelson, Geoffrey K., *Spiritualism and Society* (London: Routledge & Kegan Paul, 1969)
New, W. H., *Reading Mansfield and Metaphors of Form* (Montreal and London: McGill-Queen's University Press, 1999)
Nicolson, Juliet, *The Great Silence, 1918–1920: Living in the Shadow of the Great War* (London: John Murray, 2010)
Norris, Margot, *Writing War in the Twentieth Century* (Charlottesville, VA and London: University Press of Virginia, 2000)
Norris, Nanette, *Great War Modernism: Artistic Response in the Context of War, 1914–1918* (Madison, NJ: Fairleigh Dickinson University Press, 2016)
North, Michael, *Reading 1922: A Return to the Scene of the Modern* (Oxford: Oxford University Press, 1999)
Nowlin, Michael E., 'Edith Wharton as Critic, Traveller, and War Hero', *Studies in the Novel*, 30.3 (1998), pp. 444–51
O'Brien Schaefer, Josephine, 'The Great War and "this late age of world's experience" in Cather and Woolf', in Mark Hussey (ed.), *Virginia Woolf and War: Fiction, Reality and Myth* (Syracuse, NY: Syracuse University Press, 1991), pp. 134–50
Olin-Ammentorp, Julie, *Edith Wharton's Writings from the Great War* (Gainesville, FL: University Press of Florida, 2004)
Olin-Ammentorp, Julie, 'Willa Cather's *One of Ours*, Edith Wharton's *A Son at the Front*, and the Literature of the Great War', *Cather Studies*, 8 (2010), pp. 125–47
Onions, John, *English Fiction and Drama of the Great War, 1918–39* (Basingstoke: Macmillan, 1990)
O'Sullivan, '"Finding the Pattern, Solving the Problem": Katherine Mansfield the New Zealand European', in Roger Robinson (ed.), *Katherine Mansfield: In from the Margin* (Baton Rouge, LO and London: Louisiana State University Press, 1994), pp. 9–24
Ouditt, Sharon, *Fighting Forces, Writing Women: Identity and Ideology in the First World War* (London: Routledge, 1994)
Ouditt, Sharon, *Women Writers of the First World War: An Annotated Bibliography* (London: Routledge, 2000)
Paris, Michael (ed.), *The First World War and Popular Cinema: 1914 to the Present* (Edinburgh: Edinburgh University Press, 1999)

Paris, Michael, 'The Great War and the Moving Image: Cinema and Memory', in Adam Piette and Mark Rawlinson (eds), *The Edinburgh Companion to Twentieth-Century British and American War Literature* (Edinburgh: Edinburgh University Press, 2012), pp. 58–63

Peach, Linden, *Critical Issues: Virginia Woolf* (Basingstoke: Macmillan, 2000)

Perdigao, Lisa K., *From Modernist Entombment to Postmodernist Exhumation: Dead Bodies in Twentieth-Century American Fiction* (Farnham, Surrey: Ashgate, 2010)

Phillips, Howard, and David Killingray (eds), *The Spanish Flu Pandemic of 1918: New Perspectives* (London: Routledge, 2003)

Piehler, G. Kurt, *Remembering War the American Way* (Washington, DC and London: Smithsonian Institution Press, 1995)

Piehler, G. Kurt, 'The War Dead and the Gold Star: American Commemoration of the First World War', in John R. Gillis (ed.), *Commemorations: The Politics of National Identity* (Princeton, NJ: Princeton University Press, 1994), pp. 168–85

Piep, Karsten H., *Embattled Home Fronts: Domestic Politics and the American Novel of World War I* (Amsterdam: Rodopi, 2009)

Piette, Adam, *Imagination at War: British Fiction and Poetry, 1939–45* (London: Papermac, 1995)

Piette, Adam, 'War Zones', in Kate McLoughlin (ed.), *The Cambridge Companion to War Writing* (Cambridge: Cambridge University Press, 2009), pp. 38–46

Piette, Adam, and Mark Rawlinson (eds), *The Edinburgh Companion to Twentieth-Century British and American War Literature* (Edinburgh: Edinburgh University Press, 2012)

Pilditch, Jan (ed.), *The Critical Response to Katherine Mansfield* (Westpoint, CT and London: Greenwood Press, 1996)

Poggioli, Renato, *The Theory of the Avant-Garde* [1962], trans. Gerald Fitzgerald (Cambridge, MA: Belknap Press of Harvard University Press, 1968)

Potter, Jane, *Boys in Khaki, Girls in Print: Women's Literary Responses to the Great War, 1914–1918* (Oxford: Oxford University Press, 2005)

Potter, Jane, '"Peace could not give back her Dead": Women and the Armistice', in *A Part of History: Aspects of the British Experience of the First World War*, intro. Michael Howard (London: Continuum, 2009), pp. 91–8

Plain, Gill, '"Great Expectations": Rehabilitating the Recalcitrant War Poets', *Feminist Review*, 51.1 (1995), pp. 41–65

Plain, Gill, *Women's Fiction of the Second World War: Gender, Power and Resistance* (Edinburgh: Edinburgh University Press, 1996)

Poustie, Sarah, 'Re-Theorising Letters and "Letterness"', *Olive Schreiner Letters Project: Working Papers on Letters, Letterness & Epistolary Networks*, 1 (2010), pp. 1–50

Pozorski, Aimee L., 'Infantry and Infanticide in *A Farewell to Arms*', *The Hemingway Review*, 23.2 (Spring 2004), pp. 75–98
Price, Alan, 'Edith Wharton's War Story', *Tulsa Studies in Women's Literature*, 8.1, *Toward a Gendered Modernity* (1989), pp. 95–100
Price, Alan, *The End of the Age of Innocence: Edith Wharton and the First World War* (London: Robert Hale, 1996)
Price, Alan, 'Wharton Mobilizes Artists to Aid the War Homeless', in Katherine Joslin and Alan Price (eds), *Wretched Exotic: Essays on Edith Wharton in Europe* (New York: Peter Lang, 1993), pp. 219–40
Prieto, Sara, *Reporting the First World War in the Liminal Zone: British and American Eyewitness Accounts from the Western Front* (Basingstoke: Palgrave Macmillan, 2018)
Prost, Antoine, 'The Dead', in Jay Winter (ed.), *The Cambridge History of the First World War*, vol. 3: *Civil Society* (Cambridge: Cambridge University Press, 2014), pp. 561–91
Pryor, Elizabeth Brown, *Clara Barton: Professional Angel* (Philadelphia, PA: University of Pennsylvania Press, 1987)
Quinn, Patrick J., *The Conning of America: The Great War and American Popular Literature* (Amsterdam: Rodopi, 2001)
Quinn, Patrick J., 'The First World War: American Writing', in Kate McLoughlin (ed.), *The Cambridge Companion to War Writing* (Cambridge: Cambridge University Press, 2009), pp. 175–84
Quinn, Patrick J., and Steven Trout (eds), *The Literature of the Great War Reconsidered: Beyond Modern Memory* (Basingstoke: Palgrave, 2001)
Rabaté, Jean-Michel, *1922: Literature, Culture, Politics* (Cambridge: Cambridge University Press, 2015)
Rae, Patricia (ed.), *Modernism and Mourning* (Lewisburg, PA: Bucknell University Press, 2007)
Raitt, Suzanne, and Trudi Tate (eds), *Women's Fiction and the Great War* (Oxford: Clarendon Press, 1997)
Randall, Bryony, *Modernism, Daily Time and Everyday Life* (Cambridge: Cambridge University Press, 2007)
Rattray, Laura (ed.), *Edith Wharton in Context* (Cambridge: Cambridge University Press, 2012)
Rau, Petra (ed.), *Conflict, Nationhood and Corporeality: Bodies-at-War* (Basingstoke: Palgrave Macmillan, 2010)
Razinsky, Liran, 'A Struggle with the Concept of Death: "Thoughts for the Times on War and Death"', in *Freud, Psychoanalysis and Death* (Cambridge: Cambridge University Press, 2013), pp. 112–30
Reznick, Jeffrey S., *Healing the Nation: Soldiers and the Culture of Caregiving in Britain during the Great War* (Manchester: Manchester University Press, 2004)

Richardson, Ruth, *Death, Dissection and the Destitute* [1987] (2nd edn, London: Phoenix, 2001)
Robinson, Janice S., *H.D.: The Life and Work of an American Poet* (Boston, MA: Houghton Mifflin, 1982)
Robinson, Roger (ed.), *Katherine Mansfield: In from the Margin* (Baton Rouge, LO and London: Louisiana State University Press, 1994)
Roe, Sue, and Susan Sellers (eds), *The Cambridge Companion to Virginia Woolf* (Cambridge: Cambridge University Press, 2000)
Rollyson, Carl, *Rebecca West: A Saga of the Century* (London: Hodder & Stoughton, 1995)
Roper, Michael, *The Secret Battle: Emotional Survival in the Great War* (Manchester: Manchester University Press, 2009)
Rose, Jacqueline, 'Virginia Woolf and the Death of Modernism', in *On Not Being Able to Sleep: Psychoanalysis and the Modern World* (London: Chatto & Windus, 2003), pp. 72–88
Rosenthal, Lecia, *Mourning Modernism: Literature, Catastrophe, and the Politics of Consolation* (New York: Fordham University Press, 2011)
Ryder, Mary R., '"Dear, Tender-Hearted, Uncomprehending America": Dorothy Canfield Fisher's and Edith Wharton's Fictional Responses to the First World War', in Patrick J. Quinn and Steven Trout (eds), *The Literature of the Great War Reconsidered: Beyond Modern Memory* (Basingstoke: Palgrave, 2001), pp. 143–55
Sacks, Peter M., *The English Elegy: Studies in the Genre from Spenser to Yeats* (Baltimore, MD: Johns Hopkins University Press, 1985)
Saint-Amour, Paul K., *Tense Future: Modernism, Total War, Encyclopedic Form* (New York: Oxford University Press, 2015)
Sarnecky, Mary T., *A History of the U.S. Army Nurse Corps* (Philadelphia, PA: University of Pennsylvania Press, 1999)
Schriber, Mary Suzanne, '*Fighting France*: Travel Writing in the Grotesque', in Clare Colquitt, Susan Goodman and Candace Waid (eds), *A Forward Glance: New Essays on Edith Wharton* (Newark, DE: University of Delaware Press; London: Associated University Presses, 1999), pp. 139–48
Scott, Bonnie Kime (ed.), *The Gender of Modernism: A Critical Anthology* (Bloomington, IN: Indiana University Press, 1990)
Scott, Bonnie Kime (ed.), *Gender in Modernism: New Geographies, Complex Intersections*, intro. Bonnie Kime Scott (Urbana, IL: University of Illinois Press, 2007)
Scutts, Joanna, 'Battlefield Cemeteries, Pilgrimage, and Literature after the First World War: The Burial of the Dead', *English Literature in Transition, 1880–1920*, 52.4 (2009), pp. 387–416
Scutts, Joanna, 'Writing a War Story: The Female Author and the Challenge of Witnessing', *Journal of the Short Story in English*, 58 (2012), pp. 109–24

Sebba, Anne, *Enid Bagnold: The Authorized Biography* (London: Weidenfeld & Nicolson, 1986)

Sellers, Susan (ed.), *The Cambridge Companion to Virginia Woolf*, 2nd edn (Cambridge: Cambridge University Press, 2010)

Sensibar, Judith L., '"Behind the Lines" in Edith Wharton's *A Son at the Front*: Re-Writing a Masculinist Tradition', in Katherine Joslin and Alan Price (eds), *Wretched Exotic: Essays on Edith Wharton in Europe* (New York: Peter Lang, 1993), pp. 241–56

Sensibar, Judith L., 'Edith Wharton as Propagandist and Novelist: Competing Visions of "The Great War"', in Clare Colquitt, Susan Goodman and Candace Waid (eds), *A Forward Glance: New Essays on Edith Wharton* (Newark, DE: University of Delaware Press; London: Associated University Presses, 1999), pp. 149–71

Shail, Andrew, *The Cinema and the Origins of Literary Modernism* (Oxford and New York: Routledge, 2012)

Shephard, Ben, *A War of Nerves: Soldiers and Psychiatrists, 1914–1994* (London: Jonathan Cape, 2000; London: Pimlico, 2002)

Sherman, David, *In a Strange Room: Modernism's Corpses and Mortal Obligation* (Oxford: Oxford University Press, 2014)

Sherry, Vincent (ed.), *The Cambridge History of Modernism* (Cambridge: Cambridge University Press, 2017)

Sherry, Vincent, *The Great War and the Language of Modernism* (Oxford: Oxford University Press, 2003)

Sherry, Vincent, 'The Great War and Literary Modernism in England', in Vincent Sherry (ed.), *The Cambridge Companion to the Literature of the First World War* (Cambridge: Cambridge University Press, 2005), pp. 113–37

Siebrecht, Claudia, *The Aesthetics of Loss: German Women's Art of the First World War* (Oxford: Oxford University Press, 2013)

Slevin, Tom, *Visions of the Human: Art, World War I and the Modernist Subject* (London: I. B. Tauris, 2015)

Smith, Angela, 'Katherine Mansfield at the Front', *First World War Studies*, 2.1 (2011), pp. 65–73

Smith, Angela, *Katherine Mansfield: A Literary Life* (Basingstoke: Palgrave, 2000)

Smith, Angela, 'Katherine Mansfield and *Rhythm*', *Journal of New Zealand Literature*, 21 (2003), pp. 102–21

Smith, Angela, *Katherine Mansfield and Virginia Woolf: A Public of Two* (Oxford: Clarendon Press, 1999)

Smith, Angela K., *British Women of the Eastern Front: War, Writing and Experience in Serbia and Russia, 1914–20* (Manchester: Manchester University Press, 2016)

Smith, Angela K. (ed.), *Gender and Warfare in the Twentieth Century: Textual Representations* (Manchester: Manchester University Press, 2004)

Smith, Angela K., *The Second Battlefield: Women, Modernism and the First World War* (Manchester: Manchester University Press, 2000)
Smythe, Karen, 'Virginia Woolf's Elegiac Enterprise', *NOVEL: A Forum on Fiction*, 26.1 (1992), pp. 64–79
Snyder, Paula (ed.), *The Roses of No Man's Land: An Edited Transcript* (London: Channel 4 Television, 1997)
Spilka, Mark, *Virginia Woolf's Quarrel with Grieving* (Lincoln, NE and London: University of Nebraska Press, 1980)
Spinney, Laura, *Pale Rider: The Spanish Flu of 1918 and How It Changed the World* (London: Jonathan Cape, 2017)
Stamp, Gavin, 'Memorials', in *A Part of History: Aspects of the British Experience of the First World War*, intro. Michael Howard (London: Continuum, 2009), pp. 142–52
Stanford Friedman, Susan (ed.), 'H.D. (1886–1961)', in Bonnie Kime Scott (ed.), *The Gender of Modernism: A Critical Anthology* (Bloomington and Indianapolis: Indiana University Press, 1990), pp. 85–138
Stanford Friedman, Susan, *Penelope's Web: Gender, Modernity, H.D.'s Fiction* (Cambridge: Cambridge University Press, 1990)
Stanford Friedman, Susan, *Psyche Reborn: The Emergence of H.D.* (Bloomington, IN: Indiana University Press, 1981)
Stanford Friedman, Susan, 'Return of the Repressed in H.D.'s Madrigal Cycle', in Susan Stanford Friedman and Rachel Blau DuPlessis (eds), *Signets: Reading H.D.* (Madison, WI: University of Wisconsin Press, 1990), pp. 233–52
Stanley, Liz, 'The Epistolarium: On Theorizing Letters and Correspondences', *Auto/Biography*, 12 (2004), 201–35
Stanley, Liz, and Helen Dampier, 'Towards the Epistolarium: Issues in Researching and Publishing the Olive Schreiner Letters', *African Research & Documentation*, 113 (2010), pp. 27–32
Stevenson, Randall, *Literature and the Great War, 1914–1918* (Oxford: Oxford University Press, 2013)
Stevenson, Randall, *Reading the Times: Temporality and History in Twentieth-Century Fiction* (Edinburgh: Edinburgh University Press, 2018)
Stewart, Garrett, *Death Sentences: Styles of Dying in British Fiction* (Cambridge, MA: Harvard University Press, 1984)
Stewart, Victoria, *Crime Writing in Interwar Britain: Fact and Fiction in the Golden Age* (Cambridge: Cambridge University Press, 2017)
Strachan, Hew, *The First World War: A New History* (London: Simon & Schuster, 2003; repr. 2006)
Strange, Julie-Marie, *Death, Grief and Poverty in Britain, 1870–1914* (Cambridge: Cambridge University Press, 2005)
Summers, Anne, *Angels and Citizens: British Women as Military Nurses, 1854–1914* (London: Routledge & Kegan Paul, 1988)

Summers, Julie, *Remembered: The History of the Commonwealth War Graves Commission*, foreword by Ian Hislop (London: Merrell in association with the Commonwealth War Graves Commission, 2007)

Tambling, Jeremy, 'Repression in Mrs Dalloway's London', in Su Reid (ed.), *Mrs Dalloway and To the Lighthouse: Contemporary Critical Essays* (Basingstoke: Macmillan, 1993) pp. 57–70

Tate, Trudi, 'The First World War: British Writing', in Kate McLoughlin (ed.), *The Cambridge Companion to War Writing* (Cambridge: Cambridge University Press, 2009), pp. 160–74

Tate, Trudi, 'H.D.'s War Neurotics', in Suzanne Raitt and Trudi Tate (eds), *Women's Fiction and the Great War* (Oxford: Clarendon Press, 1997), pp. 241–62

Tate, Trudi, *Modernism, History and the First World War* (Manchester: Manchester University Press, 1998)

Tate, Trudi, and Kate Kennedy (eds), *The Silent Morning: Culture and Memory after the Armistice* (Manchester: Manchester University Press, 2013)

Taylor, Lou, *Mourning Dress: A Costume and Social History* (London and Boston, MA: G. Allen and Unwin, 1983)

Taylor, Philip M., *Munitions of the Mind: A History of Propaganda from the Ancient World to the Present Era* (Manchester: Manchester University Press, 1995)

Thom, Deborah, *Nice Girls and Rude Girls: Women Workers in World War I* (London: I. B. Tauris, 1998)

Thwaite, Ann, *A. A. Milne: His Life* (London: Faber, 1990)

Todd, Janet, *Gender, Art and Death* (Cambridge: Polity, 1993)

Todman, Dan, *The Great War: Myth and Memory* (London: Hambledon, 2005)

Todman, Dan, 'Remembrance', in *A Part of History: Aspects of the British Experience of the First World War*, intro. Michael Howard (London: Continuum, 2009), pp. 209–16

Tomalin, Claire, *Katherine Mansfield: A Secret Life* (London: Viking, 1987; London: Penguin, 1988)

Towheed, Shafquat (ed.), *The Correspondence of Edith Wharton and Macmillan, 1901–1930* (Basingstoke: Palgrave Macmillan, 2007)

Towheed, Shafquat, 'Reading the Great War: An Examination of Edith Wharton's Reading and Responses, 1914–1918' in Shafquat Towheed and Edmund King (eds), *Reading and the First World War: Readers, Texts, Archives* (Basingstoke: Palgrave Macmillan, 2015), pp. 78–95

Trott, Vincent, *Publishers, Readers and the Great War: Literature and Memory since 1918* (London: Bloomsbury Academic, 2017)

Trotter, David, 'The British Novel and the War', in Vincent Sherry (ed.), *The Cambridge Companion to the Literature of the First World War* (Cambridge: Cambridge University Press, 2005), pp. 34–56
Trotter, David, *Cinema and Modernism* (Malden, MA and Oxford: Blackwell, 2007)
Trotter, David, *The English Novel in History, 1895–1920* (London: Routledge, 1993)
Trotter, David, *Literature in the First Media Age: Britain between the Wars* (Cambridge, MA and London: Harvard University Press, 2013)
Trotter, David, 'Modernism Reloaded: The Fiction of Katherine Mansfield', *Affirmations: of the Modern*, 1 (2013), pp. 21–43
Trotter, David, *Paranoid Modernism: Literary Experiment, Psychosis, and the Professionalization of English Society* (Oxford: Oxford University Press, 2001)
Trotter, David, *The Uses of Phobia: Essays on Literature and Film* (Oxford: Wiley-Blackwell, 2010)
Trotter, David, Sandra Kemp and Charlotte Mitchell (eds), *Edwardian Fiction: An Oxford Companion* (Oxford: Oxford University Press, 1997)
Trout, Steven, *American Prose Writers of World War I: A Documentary Volume* (Detroit, MI and London: Thomson/Gale, 2005)
Trout, Steven, *Memorial Fictions: Willa Cather and the First World War* (Lincoln, NE and London: University of Nebraska Press, 2003)
Trout, Steven, *On the Battlefield of Memory: The First World War and American Remembrance, 1919–1941* (Tuscaloosa, AL: University of Alabama Press, 2010)
Tuttleton, James W., Kristin O. Lauer and Margaret P. Murray (eds), *Edith Wharton: The Contemporary Reviews* (Cambridge: Cambridge University Press, 1992)
Tylee, Claire M., *The Great War and Women's Consciousness: Images of Militarism and Womanhood in Women's Writing, 1914–64* (Iowa City: University of Iowa Press, 1990)
Tylee, Claire M., 'Imagining Women at War: Feminist Strategies in Edith Wharton's War Writing', *Tulsa Studies in Women's Literature*, 16.2 (1997), pp. 327–43
Tylee, Claire M., (ed.), *Women, the First World War and the Dramatic Imagination: International Essays (1914–1999)* (Lewiston, NY: Edwin Mellen Press, 2000)
Vance, Jonathan, *Death So Noble: Memory, Meaning and the First World War* (Vancouver: University of British Columbia Press, 1997)
Van Dijick, Cedric, 'Time on the Pulse: Affective Encounters with the Wristwatch in the Literature of Modernism and the First World War', *Modernist Cultures*, 11.2 (2016), pp. 161–78

Virilio, Paul, *War and Cinema: The Logistics of Perception*, trans. Patrick Camiller (London: Verso, 1989)

Wagner-Martin, Linda, 'Women Authors and the Roots of American Modernism', in Robert Paul Lamb and G. R. Thompson (eds), *A Companion to American Fiction, 1865–1914* (Malden, MA: Wiley-Blackwell, 2009), pp. 140–8

Waid, Candace, and Clare Colquitt, 'Toward a Modernist Aesthetic: The Literary Legacy of Edith Wharton', in Robert Paul Lamb and G. R. Thompson (eds), *A Companion to American Fiction, 1865–1914* (Malden, MA and Oxford: Wiley-Blackwell, 2009), pp. 536–56

Walsh, Michael J. K. (ed.), *London, Modernism, and 1914* (Cambridge: Cambridge University Press, 2010)

Walton, Alex, 'Official Memorial Art', in Laura Clouting, *A Century of Remembrance* (London: Imperial War Museums, 2018), pp. 219–29

Watkins, Glenn, *Proof through the Night: Music and the Great War* (Berkeley, CA: University of California Press, 2003)

Watson, Janet S. K., *Fighting Different Wars: Experience, Memory, and the First World War in Britain* (Cambridge: Cambridge University Press, 2004)

Watson, Janet S. K., 'Wars in the Wards: The Social Construction of Medical Work in First World War Britain', *Journal of British Studies*, 41.4 (2002), pp. 484–510

Webster Goodwin, Sarah, and Elisabeth Bronfen (eds), *Death and Representation* (Baltimore, MD and London: Johns Hopkins University Press, 1993)

Whalan, Mark, *The Great War and the Culture of the New Negro* (Gainesville, FL: University Press of Florida, 2008)

Whalan, Mark, *World War One, American Literature, and the Federal State* (Cambridge: Cambridge University Press, 2018)

Wheeler, Michael, *Heaven, Hell and the Victorians* (Cambridge: Cambridge University Press, 1994), abridged edn of *Death and the Future Life in Victorian Literature and Theology* (Cambridge: Cambridge University Press, 1990)

Whitworth, Michael H. (ed.), *Modernism* (Malden, MA and Oxford: Blackwell, 2007)

Whitworth, Michael H., *Virginia Woolf* (Oxford: Oxford University Press, 2005)

Whitworth, Michael H., 'Virginia Woolf and Modernism', in Sue Roe and Susan Sellers (eds), *The Cambridge Companion to Virginia Woolf* (Cambridge: Cambridge University Press, 2000), pp. 146–63

Whitworth, Michael H., 'Virginia Woolf, Modernism and Modernity', in Susan Sellers (ed.), *The Cambridge Companion to Virginia Woolf*, 2nd edn (Cambridge: Cambridge University Press, 2010), pp. 107–23

Williams, Deborah Lindsay, 'Women at War: Crossing the Gender–Genre Boundary', in *Not in Sisterhood: Edith Wharton, Willa Cather, Zona Gale, and the Politics of Female Authorship* (Basingstoke: Palgrave, 2001), pp. 125–61

Williams, Lea M., 'Ellen N. La Motte: The Making of a Nurse, Writer, and Activist', *Nursing History Review*, 23 (2015), pp. 56–86

Wilson, Janet, Gerri Kimber and Susan Reid (eds), *Katherine Mansfield and Literary Modernism: Historicizing Modernism* (London: Continuum, 2011)

Winter, Denis, *Death's Men: Soldiers of the Great War* (London: Allen Lane, 1978)

Winter, J. M. (ed.), *The Cambridge History of the First World War*, 3 vols (Cambridge: Cambridge University Press, 2014)

Winter, J. M., 'Forms of Kinship and Remembrance in the Aftermath of the Great War', in Jay Winter and Emmanuel Sivan (eds), *War and Remembrance in the Twentieth Century* (Cambridge: Cambridge University Press, 1999), pp. 40–60

Winter, J. M., *The Great War and the British People* (London: Macmillan, 1985)

Winter, J. M., 'Introduction: Henri Barbusse and the Birth of the Moral Witness', in Henri Barbusse, *Under Fire*, trans. Robin Buss, intro. Jay Winter (London and New York: Penguin, 2003), pp. vii–xix

Winter, J. M., *Remembering War: The Great War between Memory and History in the Twentieth Century* (New Haven, CT and London: Yale University Press, 2006)

Winter, J. M., 'Representations of War on the Western Front, 1914–1918: Some Reflections on Cultural Ambivalence', in Joseph Canning, Hartmut Lehmann and Jay Winter (eds), *Power, Violence and Mass Death in Pre-Modern and Modern Times* (Aldershot: Ashgate, 2004), pp. 205–16

Winter, J. M., *Sites of Memory, Sites of Mourning: The Great War in European Cultural History* (Cambridge: Cambridge University Press, 1995; repr. 1998)

Winter, J. M., *War Beyond Words: Languages of Remembrance from the Great War to the Present* (Cambridge: Cambridge University Press, 2017)

Winter, J. M., and Blaine Baggett, *1914–18: The Great War and the Shaping of the Twentieth Century* (London: BBC Books, 1996)

Winter, J. M., and Jean-Louis Robert (eds), *Capital Cities at War: Paris, London, Berlin, 1914–1919*, 2 vols (Cambridge: Cambridge University Press, 1997–2007)

Winter, J. M., Geoffrey Parker and Mary R. Habeck (eds), *The Great War and the Twentieth Century* (New Haven, CT and London: Yale University Press, 2000)

Wolff, Cynthia Griffin, *A Feast of Words: The Triumph of Edith Wharton* [1977] (rev. edn, Reading, MA: Addison-Wesley, 1995)

Woloch, Alex, *The One vs. the Many: Minor Characters and the Space of the Protagonist in the Novel* (Princeton, NJ and Oxford: Princeton University Press, 2003)

Wood, Jane M. (ed.), *The Theme of Peace and War in Virginia Woolf's War Writings: Essays on her Political Philosophy* (Lewiston, NY: Lampeter Mellen, 2009)

Woollacott, Angela, *On Her Their Lives Depend: Munitions Workers and the Great War* (Berkeley, CA and London: University of California Press, 1994)

Wussow, Helen, *The Nightmare of History: The Fictions of Virginia Woolf and D. H. Lawrence* (Bethlehem, PA: Lehigh University Press, 1998)

Ziino, Bart, *A Distant Grief: Australians, War Graves and the Great War* (Crawley, Western Australia: University of Western Australia Press, 2007)

Zimring, Rishona, *Social Dance and the Modernist Imagination in Interwar Britain* (Burlington, VT: Ashgate, 2013)

Zwerdling, Alex, *Virginia Woolf and the Real World* (Berkeley, CA and London: University of California Press, 1986)

Online Resources

The Bookman via ProQuest: <https://www.proquest.com>

The British Newspaper Archive: <https://www.britishnewspaperarchive.co.uk>

Caloyeras, Aliki Sophia, 'H.D.: The Politics and Poetics of the Maternal Body' (PhD dissertation, University of Pennsylvania, 2012). Publicly Accessible Penn Dissertations: <https://repository.upenn.edu/edissertations/618>

'Design for NZ Memorial in Hyde Park, London', Press Release, New Zealand Government, 2005: <https://www.beehive.govt.nz/release/design-nz-memorial-hyde-park-london>

Fehlemann, Silke, 'Bereavement and Mourning (Germany)', in Ute Daniel, Peter Gatrell, Oliver Janz, Heather Jones, Jennifer Keene, Alan Kramer and Bill Nasson (eds), *1914–1918-Online. International Encyclopedia of the First World War*, issued by Freie Universität Berlin, Berlin 2014-10-08: <https://encyclopedia.1914-1918-online.net/article/bereavement_and_mourning_germany>

Hulver, Richard Allen, 'Bereavement and Mourning (USA)', in Ute Daniel, Peter Gatrell, Oliver Janz, Heather Jones, Jennifer Keene, Alan Kramer and Bill Nasson (eds), *1914–1918-Online. International Encyclopedia of the First World War*, issued by Freie Universität Berlin, Berlin, 2015-08-21: <https://encyclopedia.1914-1918-online.net/article/bereavement_and_mourning_usa>

Imperial War Museum, Grave-Marker (EPH 9029): <https://www.iwm.org.uk/collections/item/object/30088095>

Imperial War Museum, Hall of Remembrance: <https://hall.iwm.org.uk/>

Imperial War Museum, Image Label for Sir William Orpen's *The Unknown British Soldier in France*: <https://www.iwm.org.uk/collections/item/object/20880>
The Kipling Society, Lisa Lewis (ed.), Notes on 'The Gardener': <http://www.kiplingsociety.co.uk/rg_gardener1.htm>
The Kipling Society, Roger Ayers, Notes on 'The King's Pilgrimage': <http://www.kiplingsociety.co.uk/rg_kingspilgrimage1.htm>
Lexico: <https://www.lexico.com>
London weather in 1919: <http://www.london-weather.eu/article.59.html>
Modernist Journals Project: <https://modjourn.org>
The New York Times Historical Archive via Proquest: <https://www.proquest.com>
Oxford English Dictionary Online: <https://www.oed.com>
Punch Magazine – Bernard Partridge, 'A Non-Party Statement': <https://punch.photoshelter.com/image/I0000_GIoPKeXiRQ>
Scates, Bruce, 'Bereavement and Mourning (Australia)', in Ute Daniel, Peter Gatrell, Oliver Janz, Heather Jones, Jennifer Keene, Alan Kramer and Bill Nasson (eds), in *1914–1918-Online. International Encyclopedia of the First World War*, issued by Freie Universität Berlin, Berlin, 2016-11-04: <https://encyclopedia.1914-1918-online.net/article/bereavement_and_mourning_australia>
Scutts, Joanna, 'Virginia and Leonard Woolf Remember Their War Dead': <https://lithub.com/virginia-and-leonard-woolf-remember-their-war-dead>
Smyth, Hanna, 'The Material Culture of Remembrance and Identity: South Africa, India, Canada & Australia's Imperial War Graves Commission sites on the First World War's Western Front' (PhD dissertation, University of Oxford, 2019). Oxford Research Archive: <https://ora.ox.ac.uk/objects/uuid:d851b171-566f-4cee-9005-a3f438ee8f6c>
The Times Digital Archive via Gale: <https://www.gale.com/intl/c/the-times-digital-archive>
The Times Literary Supplement Historical Archive via Gale: <https://www.gale.com/intl/c/the-times-literary-supplement-historical-archive>
Trinity College Chapel, Cambridge – 'War Memorials': <http://trinitycollegechapel.com/about/memorials/war-memorials/>
Vintage Watch Straps (information about trench watches): <http://www.vintagewatchstraps.com/trenchwatches.php>
Violet Day: <http://adelaidia.sa.gov.au/events/violet-day>
Wearne, Sarah: <http://www.epitaphsofthegreatwar.com/all/>

FILM

Griffiths, D. W., dir., *Hearts of the World – The Story of a Village* (UK: Artcraft Pictures, 1917)
Malins, Geoffrey, and J. B. McDowell, dirs, *The Battle of the Somme* (UK: War Office Cinematograph Committee, 1916)

Music

Asaf, George [George Henry Powell], music by Felix Powell, 'Pack Up Your Troubles in Your Old Kit-Bag and Smile, Smile, Smile!' (London: Francis, Day & Hunter, c. 1915)

Cohan, George M., 'Over There' (New York: Leo Feist Inc., c. 1917)

Howe, Julia Ward [Mrs Dr S. G. Howe], 'The Battle Hymn of the Republic: Adapted to the Favorite Melody of "Glory Hallelujah"', originally written for the *Atlantic Monthly* (Boston, MA: Oliver Ditson & Co., c. 1862).

Judge, Jack, and Harry Williams, 'The Immortal "It's a Long Way to Tipperary": The Marching Anthem on the Battlefields of Europe' (London: B. Feldman, 1912)

Weston, R. P., and Bert Lee, 'Good-bye-ee!', sung by Miss Daisy Wood, Miss Florrie Forde and Chas. White (London: Francis, Day & Hunter, 1917)

INDEX

Note: Page numbers in italics are illustrations and those followed by n are notes.

Acton, Carol, 3, 4, 43, 49
Airy, Anna, 19
Aldington, Richard, 154, 155, 161, 182, 186n, 188n
Aldrich, Mildred, 115n
Allatini, Rose [A.T. Fitzroy], *Despised and Rejected*, 187n
ambulance trains 40
American Civil War, 23, 143, 152n, 177
American Magazine, 112
American Red Cross, 41, 42, 86, 133n
Anouilh, Jean, *Le voyageur sans bagage*, 241n
Argonne, 89–90
Armistice Day, *194*, 202, 211, 233–4
ars moriendi, 7, 46, 54
atrocity stories, 83, 85, 97–9, 101, 102, 104, 129
Auden, W. H., 'Address for a Prize Day', xiii
Australia, 17–18, 29n, 32n
'authentic' accounts, 41–3

Bagnold, Enid, 2, 41
  A Diary without Dates, 50–1, 53, 61–2, 68, 69–70, 72, 73, 74n, 77n, 79n
  dismissal from nursing position, 50
  Sassoon, Sir Philip, letter from, 72
Bahlmann, Anna, 87, 97–8, 116n
Baker, Herbert, 13
Baker, Ida *see* L.M.
Bandol, 121, 133, 135–6
Barnes, Djuna, 156
Barrie, J. M., 241–2n
Barthes, Roland, 175
Barton, Clara, 41
The Battle Hymn of the Republic, 177–8, 190n
The Battle of the Somme (1916) (film), 11, 171, 173, 175, 189n
battlefield tourism, 198; *see also* pilgrimage to battlefields and cemeteries
Beatty, David Richard, 141, 152n
Beauchamp, Leslie Heron, 'Chummie', 122, 123, 129, 133–5, 141, 150n, 197, 208–9, 227n, 234, 241

285

Beauchamp, Pat, 41, 43, 51
  Fanny Goes to War, 50
Beauman, Nicola, 215
Begg, Samuel, *174*
Bell, Clive, 148n
Bell, Vanessa, 73, 79n, 207
Bennett, Arnold, 84–5
Benstock, Shari, 82–3
Berry, Walter, 86, *90*
'Big Bertha' (German *Superkanon*), bombardment of Paris, 121, 123, 135–8
Binyon, Laurence, 203, 225n, 239
  Ode of Remembrance (from 'For the Fallen'), 239
Blomfeld, Sir Reginald, 13
Bly, Nelly, 115n
Boer War, 8, 9
The Bookman, 86
Bone, Muirhead, 148n
Books of Remembrance, 14
Booth, Allyson, 16, 232
  'civilian modernism', 5, 25, 124–5, 135, 155
  'corpselessness', 5, 31n, 224n
  'corpsescapes', 9, 31n
  Forster, E. M., 214, 228n
  Postcards from the Trenches: Negotiating the Space between Modernism and the First World War, 6, 24–5
Borden, Mary, 2, 54, 57
  The Forbidden Zone, 39, 41
Botticelli, Sandro, *Primavera*, 182
Bourke, Joanna, 43
Bowen, Elizabeth, 2
  'The Demon Lover', 238–9
Bradshaw, David, 220
  'anti-monuments', 220
Brett, Dorothy, 140, 148n, 235
Bridges, Robert, 86, 99
Bright, Laura Kate, 128–9, 150n
Brissy, Edouard, *95, 96*
British Red Cross, 10
  British Red Cross Society Nursing Manual, No. 2, 44
  Wounded and Missing Department, 10, 215

British War Graves Association, 19
British War Memorials Committee, 19
Brittain, Vera, *Testament of Youth*, 8
Brooke, Rupert, 123, 148n, 200, 214, 234, 241
Brown, M. A., 63, 65
Bryce Report, 97
Buck, Claire, 34n
Buitenhuis, Peter, 85
Burgan, Mary, 123, 138

Canada, 17
Cannadine, David, 6, 8, 9, 11, 16, 140
Cantlie, James, *British Red Cross Society Nursing Manual, No. 2*, 44–5
Carco, Francis, 123, 129–31, 150n
Carden-Coyne, Ana, 43
Carrington, Dora, 224n
casualty clearing stations, 40
casualty lists, 13
Cather, Willa, 196
Cavell, Edith, 41
cemeteries *see* war cemeteries
Cenotaph, 8, 16, 21, 193–6, *194*, 196, 239
censorship, 15, 79n, 126, 128
Chanak Crisis, 213–14
Chaplin, Charlie, 173
charitable organisations, 19, 34n, 82, 114n
Christian Cross of Sacrifice, 13
Churchill, Winston, 214
cinema and film
  literary representation, 6, 27, 57, 100, 102–3, 155–6, 171–2, 171–84, 187n, 190n, 236, 238
  wartime cinema, 72, 79n, 84, 162, 172–5, 189n
civilian experience of war death, 3, 11–13, 154, 156–63, 205
civilian modernism, 27, 122, 124–5, 135, 146–7, 155, 156–7, 164, 168, 169, 185, 196, 198, 204; *see also* Booth, Allyson
civilian war novel, 155, 156, 170, 184, 187n, 199
civilians visiting war zones, 11, 85–6, 123, 146–7

Close-Up, 156, 182, 190n
Clouting, Laura, 20
Cohan, George M., 'Over There', 84
Coke, Dorothy, 19
Colle, Father Alphonse, 94–5
'collective memory', 21–2
combatant experience, 3, 11, 25, 169, 240
  narratives, 5, 20–1, 72, 124–5, 156
commemoration
  in earlier wars, 9
  proto-commemoration, 40, 54, 161, 173
Committee on Public Information (CPI), 84
Commonwealth War Graves Commission, 10
  role of Fabian Ware, 10
Conan Doyle, Sir Arthur, 84–5, 233, 241n
Connor, Rachel, 156
Conrad, Joseph, 101
conscientious objectors, 43, 123, 148n; *see also* pacifism
Conway, Agnes, 34n
Conway, Sir Martin, 20
Cook, Charles, 86
Cooperman, Stanley, 82
corpse
  absent and consolatory, 197, 198–211, 218, 222–3
  damaged, 9, 19, 47, 58–60
  imagined after death, 64, 204–5, 209
  influenza pandemic, 15
  laying out after death, 44–5, 58–60
  revenge narrative, role in, 105–6
  unburied, 63, 92
  Victorian death practices, role in, 7, 47, 60
Cosmopolitan, 73
Cournos, John, 186n, 188n
Coward, Noël, 242n
Crane Arthur, Unveiling of the Cenotaph and the funeral of the Unknown Warrior, *194*
Creel, George, 84
cremation, 8

Daily News, 213
The Daily Sketch, 234
Damousi, Joy, 3, 29n
Darrohn, Christine, 198, 208–9
Das, Santanu, 26, 43
Deane, Ada, 233–4
death
  after First World War, 16–22
  before the First World War, 6–9, 31n
  different experience for women and men, 2
  links with photography and cinema, 173–5
  modernist *see* modernist death
  non-traditional sites and rituals, 6, 122, 156, 185, 209, 212–14, 219–20, 222–3, 240
  traditional sites and rituals, 6, 26–7, 46–7, 54, 58, 69, 73–4, 83, 93, 113, 141–2, 198–9, 204–5, 208–9, 240
  see also war dead
deathbed scenes, 46–58, 221, 240
  anti-deathbed scenes, 54–8
  death rites and religious consolations, 52, 56, 57
  religious tracts, 7
  Victorian, 7, 13, 46–7, 51, 60, 73, 208, 223, 237–8, 251
Defence of the Realm Act (DORA) 1916, 11, 126
Dent, Olive, 41, 51
  A V.A.D. in France, 51, 53–4, 62, 64–5, 66, 72
detective fiction, 196
d'Humières, Robert, 87
Dickens, Charles, *The Old Curiosity Shop*, death of Little Nell, 7
Dickinson, Violet, 211
Directorate of Graves Registration and Enquiries, 10
DORA *see* Defence of the Realm Act
Douglas, James, 'How a Nurse Sees the War', 39
Doyle, Sir Arthur Conan, 84, 233
dreams, 134, 167–9, 171–2, 189n, 208, 234–5

Drey, Anne Estelle, 140
du Breuil de Saint-Germain, Jean, 87
Dunkerque, 88

Edis, Olive, WAACs tending graves at Étaples, 10, *11*
The Egoist, 25, 161, 188n
Eksteins, Modris, 5
elegy, 19, 33, 62, 78n, 93, 99, 134, 199, 220, 225n
Eliot, T. S., 161, 188n, 226n
emptiness, 157, 200, 219, 221, 226n
Étaples, *11*, 28
Evening Post (Wellington, New Zealand), 129

Farmborough, Florence, *Russian Album, 1908–1918*, 71–2
Fehlemann, Silke, 31n, 33n
female body and war, 6, 23, 41, 27, 124–5, 156, 163–72, 184, 236
Festival of Remembrance *see* Royal British Legion
ffoulkes, Charles, 20
Field Service Postcard, 126
field telephone, 57
film *see* cinema and film
First Aid Nursing Yeomanry (FANY), 43, 50
Fitzwilliams, Duncan C. L., *A Nursing Manual for Nurses and Nursing Orderlies*, 45
Flanders, 82, 161, 199, 205, 228n
Foch, Ferdinand, 230
'forbidden zone', 43
Forster, E. M., 2, 10, 28, 196, 215
    'Our Graves in Gallipoli', 198, 212–15, 222, 227–8n
    A Passage to India, 228n
Foulds, John, *A World Requiem*, 19
Four Minute Men, 84
Fox, Frank, *The King's Pilgrimage*, 228n
France, 15, 39, 88–91, 111–12, 121, 123, 129, 162–3, 211, 228n, 240
Frayn, Andrew, 24
Freedman, Ariela, 156

Death, Men, and Modernism: Trauma and Narrative in British Fiction from Hardy to Woolf, 22–3
French Red Cross, 86
Freud, Sigmund, 1, 2, 15, 156, 158, 179, 218
Friedman, Alan Warren, *Fictional Death and the Modernist Enterprise*, 22
Friedman, Susan Stanford, 186n
Froula, Christina, 197
Fry, Roger, 206
Fussell, Paul, 5, 224n
    modern memory, 5

Gance, Abel, *J'Accuse*, 238–9
Garbo, Greta, 190n
Garsington, 148n
gas, 123
    literary representation, 121, 161, 169
Gaudier-Brzeska, Henri, 123, 148n, 241
Germany, 15, 31n
    treatment of bereaved families, 18, 33n, 34n
ghosts, 175, 177–8, 182–3, 190n, 195, 231, 233–41, 242n
Gibbs, Philip, 16
Gilbert, Sandra M., 117n
Gill, Leslie MacDonald, 14
good death, 6–7, 9, 46, 52, 198, 208
Goodspeed-Chadwick, Julia, 156, 172
Goodyear, Frederick, 123, 126, 148n, 241
graves
    British soldiers buried at Abbeville, 4, *4*
    design of headstones, 14
    finding in France, 211–18
    headstones, design and inscriptions, 14, 32n, 214, 233
    photographs of, 10, *11*, 71, 93, 94, 205, 216, 228
    Women's Army Auxiliary Corps gardeners tending, 10, *11*
Graves, Robert, 148n
    Goodbye to All That, 21
Graves Registration Commission (GRC), 10
Gray, Cecil, 155

Gregory, Adrian, 6, 16
  The Silence of Memory: Armistice Day, 1919–1946, 29n
grief, 156, 133–4, 194, 204, 206, 211–12, 220, 234–5, 238
  changing attitudes towards, 6, 26
  emotional burden of, 68
  gendered nature of, 3–4, 41
  of parents, 113, 147, 154, 215–18, 236, 240
  public suppression of, 218–19, 222
  state recognition of, 18, 215–16
  unfocused, 13
Gubar, Susan, 117n
Gurney, Ivor, *War Elegy*, 19

Haig, Douglas, 10, 228n, 230, 231
'Hall of Remembrance', 19
Hallett, Christine, 44, 52, 74n, 75n, 78n
Hamilton, Mary (Molly) Agnes, 193–6
  Dead Yesterday, 195, 223n
Hammond, Michael, 79n, 172, 173–5, 189n
Handley, William R., 199
Harris, Frank, 77n
Haste, Cate, 114n
Hastings, Beatrice, 132
Hattaway, Judith, 199
Hazelgrove, Jennifer, 233
H.D., 2, 27, 125, 240–1
  air raids, 154, 158, 164–6, 175, 178, 184
  Asphodel, 155, 157, 161
  biblical and religious allusions, 158, 167, 177–8, 179, 185, 190n
  Bid Me to Live (A Madrigal), 27, 154–72, 184, 186n, 187n, 190n, 236–8, 239
  brother, death of, 154, 241
  characteristics of H.D.'s modernism, 155, 185n
  'The Cinema and the Classics', 182, 190n
  civilian difficulty in picturing war, 162–3, 177
  as civilian modernist, 155–7, 168, 169, 184
  classical allusions, 180–3, 185, 190n
  female body and war, 163–72, 184, 236
  film and cinema, 27, 57, 155, 156, 172–84, 187n, 240
  ghosts, 177–8, 182–3, 190n, 237
  The Gift, 156
  as imagist, 154, 165
  intoxication, 176–8
  letters, 160, 161, 162
  'Madrigal trilogy', 155, 185n
  use of military discourse, 156–8, 161, 164, 166, 169
  Moore, Marianne, letter to, 9
  nightmares, 167–70, 184
  Paint it Today, 155
  Palimpsest, 157, 167
  Pound, Ezra, on, 186n
  proleptic memorialisation, 180, 184
  proleptic mourning, 156–63, 165, 177
  use of propaganda tropes, 155, 166
  stillbirth, 27, 154, 156, 163–9, 178, 181, 184, 188n, 236, 241
  time, distorted sense in war, 158–63, 184, 188n, 236
  trauma, individual and collective, 155, 164, 167, 168–9, 172, 184, 236, 241
  Tribute to Freud, 156
  Trilogy, 156
  wartime civilian experience, depiction of, 154, 156–63, 184
Henke, Suzette, 156
'high modernism', 196, 198
Higonnet, Margaret R., 4, 40, 41, 43
Hogarth Press, 151n, 200
Holden, Charles, 19
Horner, Lady Frances, 211
hospitals, 26, 39–80, 90–1, 173, *174*, 215
  civilians visiting, 11, 50–1, 61, 68
  L'Hôpital Chirurgical Mobile No. 1, Belgium, 54–8
  mortuaries, 60–1
  Royal Herbert Hospital, 50
Hospital Ship *Devanha*, 63
hospital ships, 40
Hughes, Alfred, Portrait of Katherine Mansfield, *130*

Hussey, Mark, 197
Hutchinson, Mary, 133
Hutchison, Hazel, 5, 78n
Hynes, Samuel, 16, 20–2, 196
   'monument-making', 16–17, 196
   'Myth of the War', 6
   A War Imagined: The First World War and English Culture, 5–6

identity tags, 9
Illustrated London News, 173, *174*
Imperial War Graves Commission (IWGC), 10, 13, 14, 205, 215
Imperial War Museum, 19–20, 230, 231
   appeal for mementos of the war dead, *20*, 34n
   Women's Work Subcommittee, 34n
Infantry Record Office, *12*
influenza pandemic, 15–16
Isherwood, Christopher, 2, 28, 196, 228n
   The Memorial, 198, 219–20, 238
Italy, 15, 17, 122, 127, 128, 142, 172, 180, 182

Jagger, Charles, Sargeant, 19
Jalland, Pat, 6–7, 8, 15, 46
James, Henry, 85, 87, 95, 115n, 116n, 146, 206
   'The New Novel', 101
James, Pearl, *The New Death: American Modernism and World War One*, 23
Jekyll, Gertrude, 13
Jolly, Margaretta, 125
Jones, Ernest, 15

Kelly, Andrew, 172
Kenyon, Sir Frederic
   The Graves of the Fallen, 14
   War Graves: How the Cemeteries Abroad Will be Designed, 13–14
Keynes, John Maynard, 148n, 206
Kibble, Matthew, 188n
King George V, 17, 193–4, 228n
Kipling, John, 218
Kipling, Rudyard, 2, 28, 84–5, 196, 228n

biblical allusions, 217, 243n
   'The Gardener', 13, 198, 215–18, 222–3
   'The Graves of the Fallen', 14
   'The King's Pilgrimage', 228n
   'Known Unto God' (headstone inscription), 201
   literary adviser to IWGC, 13
   'Mary Postgate', 98, 111, 212
   mentioned by Katherine Mansfield, 130
   'Recessional', 243n
   'Sea Constables: A Tale of '15', 98–9
   son, 218
Koteliansky, S. S., 125–6, 131, 133

La Motte, Ellen N., 2, 43, 73, 78n
   The Backwash of War: The Human Wreckage of the Battlefield as Witnessed by an American Hospital Nurse, 54–8
Laqueur, Thomas
   'commemorative hyper-nominalism', 14, 72
Lavery, Sir John, *The Cemetery, Étaples, 1919*, 28
Lawrence, D. H.
   Aaron's Rod, 186n, 187n
   Samuel Hynes on, 6
Leake, R. E. (Mollie Skinner), 41, 52
Lee, Hermione, 83, 85
letters and letter-writing, *12*, 13, 17, 27, 121–53, 160–2, 170, 234, 238–9
   wartime postal conditions, 128, 137–8
Levenback, Karen, 197, 218, 224n
Lion, Flora, 19
Little Nell *see* Dickens, Charles
Lloyd, David W., 34n
Lloyd George, David, 141, 152n, 213, 227–8n, 230
L.M. (Leslie Moore), 136, 138
Lodge, Sir Oliver, 233, 241n
London
   postwar, 207, 219, 237
   wartime, 129, 148n, 154, 157–8, 242n
Loyal Women's Guild (Boer War), 9

Lusitania, RMS, 185n
Lutyens, Sir Edwin, 13, 14, 193, 211

Macaulay, Rose, *Non-Combatants and Others*, 2, 170–1, 187n
McCoy, Arthur G., *If I Fail He Dies, Work for the Red Cross*, 42
MacKay, Marina, 26
McLellan, David, Members of the Women's Army Auxiliary Corps carrying wreaths to place on the graves of British soldiers buried at Abbeville, 4
McLoughlin, Kate, 125, 135
Mansfield, Katherine, 2, 27, 28, 156, 239, 240–1
   air raids, 27, 122, 123, 129–33, 135–8, 148n, 164, 170
   The Aloe, 134, 151n
   'Bank Holiday', 147
   biblical allusions, 210, 227n
   Bliss and Other Stories, 151n
   brother *see* Beauchamp Leslie Heron, 'Chummie'
   as civilian modernist, 27, 121, 122, 124–5, 135–6, 146–7
   Carco, Francis, visit to *see* Carco, Francis
   Collected Letters, 133
   combat in 1918, 135–8
   conversation with French nurse, 73, 148n
   death of, 197, 242n
   death rituals, 141–2
   'A Dill Pickle', 147
   dreams, 134, 234, 235
   epistolarium, Mansfield, 125–8
   'The Fly', 124, 147, 198, 211–12, 222
   'The Garden Party', 23, 198, 207–12, 218, 221, 222
   ghosts, 239
   illness, linking of the war with, 27, 122, 125, 135–8, 139–46, 163
   impact of First World War on literature, xiii, 1, 122, 140, 143–6, 197–8, 199, 209–11
   'An Indiscreet Journey', 123, 124, 147
   Journal, 123
   'Late at Night', 147
   letters, 27, 121–3, 125–8, 143, 160
   letters (March 1915), 27, 122, 128–34, 146
   letters (March 1918), 27, 122, 135–8, 146
   letters (July to December 1919), 27, 122, 139–46
   military discourse, 27, 122, 124–5, 135–8, 140, 142–3, 145, 146, 163, 240
   mixing of genres in war writing, 121
   passport photo, *139*
   'Pictures', 147
   portrait of, 129, *130*
   Prelude, 134, 151n, 200
   propaganda tropes, 129
   reluctance to view Mansfield as a war writer, 124, 197
   response to celebrations of the Peace Treaty, 140–1
   self-representation as combatant, 122, 135–8, 146, 157
   'Spring Pictures', 147
   'tragic knowledge' of death, 209–10
   tuberculosis, 135, 138, 141, 197
   'Two Tuppenny Ones, Please', 147
   war as creative stimulus, 121, 122, 123, 125, 128–33
   war rationing, 135–6, 138
   Woolf, Virginia, *Night and Day*, xiii, 1, 144, 197–8, 199, 209–10
   Woolf, Virginia, relationship with, 144, 197–8, 207, 235
Marcus, Jane, 4, 43, 51, 75n
Marcus, Laura, 156, 172–3, 175, 189n, 199, 221
Marseilles, 136
Marvell, Andrew, 'To His Coy Mistress', 210
Masterman, Charles, 84
Matthews, John T., 84, 86–7
medals, 17–18
memento mori, 204
memorial culture, postwar, 27–8, 196, 198, 219, 222, 240
   and modernism, 1–2, 28, 196, 198, 200, 222–3, 240

memorialisation, public and private modes of, 1, 16–22, 27–8, 65–7, 70–2, 196–7, 206, 240
memorial photography *see* Victorian death
Memorial Plaque (Dead Man's Penny), 17–18, *17*
Memorial Scroll, 17, *18*
memorial volumes, 126, 149n, 200, 225n
memorials, literary representation of, 28, 198, 219–20
Ménil-sur-Belvitte, 94, 116n
    Museum of the Battle of, *95*, *96*
Menin Gate, 21
Mepham, John, 204, 206
Millard, Shirley, *I Saw Them Die*, 72
Milne, A. A., 213
Ministry of Information, 19
missing dead, 14–15, 196, 198, 215, 218, 232–3, 238–9
modernism
    and the First World War, 23–6
    and realism, 2, 5, 47
modernist death, 2, 22–3, 155, 180, 196, 198, 218–23
modernist memorials, 193–229
Mond, Sir Alfred, 20
Monjoin, Octave Félicien (Anthelme Mangin), 232–3
monument-making, 16–17, 19, 196, 218
Moore, Marianne, 9, *157*
Morrell, Ottoline, 127, 140–1, 144, 148n
mortality rates, pre-First World War, 7
Mortimer, Maud, 54
mothers
    Centre for Soldiers' Wives and Mothers (Australia), 29n
    Gold Star Mothers (United States), 3
    Gold Star Pilgrimages (United States), 34n
    Mothers' and Widows' Badge (Australia), 17–18, 33n
    as mourners, 3, 14, 215–18, 238
    public recognition of contribution, 17
    Wives' and Mothers' Tribute (Australia), 29n

mourning
    artefacts and memorabilia, 2
    culturally constructed position of women, 3, 14, 41, 218
    dress, 7–8, 31n
    emblems, 204, 210
    emotional labour, focused on women, 3
    unhealthy or unsuccessful, 23, 93–6, 113, 205, 211–12, 216, 234
Mulvey, Laura, 173
Murry, John Middleton, xiii, 73, 121, 123–31, 133–8, 140, 142–4, 148n, 151n, 209–10, 234

Nash, John, 19
Nash, Paul, 19
National Funeral and Mourning Reform Association, 8
Nevinson, C. R. W., *The Harvest of Battle*, 19
New, W. H., 125
'New Death', 23
New Woman, 41
New Zealand, 32n, 128, 134
New Zealand War Memorial, Hyde Park, 123–4, 149n
Nieuport, Belgium, 93
Nightingale, Florence, 41
nightmares, 167–72
Norton, Sara ('Sally'), 98, 116n
nurses
    attempts to individualise death, 47–50
    consolation of relatives and friends of patients, 68–9
    contradictory roles of, 41, 48–9
    different nursing branches, 74–5n
    emotional burden of attending deathbeds, 39–80
    fear of becoming used to death, 51
    feelings of helplessness or inadequacy, 50, 53
    funerals, 63–5
    laying out the dead, 44–5, 58–60
    liminal status of, 39, 40
    as mourners, 67–8, 70–2
    nursing albums, 70–2, *70*, *71*
    nursing manuals and handbooks, 44–6

popular mythologies of, 41
propaganda images of, 41, 42, 75n
religious needs of patients, 52
'specialing' at deathbeds, 44–6
nurses' narratives, 26–7, 40, 43, 46, 47, 50, 51, 53, 54, 62, 74
  biblical allusions, 50
  burial rites and funeral ceremonies, 58–65, 71, 73
  cemetery scenes, 65–7, 73
  deathbed and anti-deathbed scenes, 46–58, 73; see also deathbed scenes
  influence on experimental writers, 72–3
  modernist versions of, 43, 54–8
  new editions, 43, 76n
  propagandistic elements of, 50, 51, 53–4, 55–6, 60, 64–6, 77n
  reviews of, 72–3
  as trauma texts, 40, 43, 59–60, 74n
  wartime market for, 72

Ode of Remembrance see Binyon, Laurence
Olin-Ammentorp, Julie, 87, 94, 95–6
  Edith Wharton's Writings from the Great War, 83
Olivier, Noel, 235
Orpen, Sir William
  Blown Up. Mad., 231
  An Onlooker in France, 230
  To the Unknown British Soldier in France, 230–1, *231*, 232
O'Sullivan, Vincent, 123
Ouditt, Sharon, 40
Oxford, M. N., *Nursing in War Time: Lessons for the Inexperienced*, 45

pacifism, 213, 215; see also conscientious objectors
pacifist novels, 170, 195
Paris, 96, 98, 121, 128, 129, 135, 138, 146, 148n, 157, 161, 162, 163, 164, 237
Paris, Michael, 162, 172, 189n
Partridge, Bernard, 227–8n
Peace Conference (1919), 230–1
Peace Day, public celebration, 140–1

photography, 227n
  of graves see graves
  links with death, 173, 175, 212
  memorial, 7, 18, 20, 47, 173–5
  spirit photography, 233–4
pilgrimage to battlefields and cemeteries, 18–19, 34n, 198, 211, 212, 215–18, 223n
Poppy Appeal, 16, 196
Porter, Katherine Anne, 'Pale Horse, Pale Rider', 16
post in wartime, 125–6
postwar remembrance, 193–229
Potter, Jane, 43
Price, Alan, 85
  The End of the Age of Innocence: Edith Wharton and the First World War, 83, 114n, 114–15n
Primavera, 182
propaganda, 2, 27, 47n, 84–5, 92, 163
  H.D., use of propaganda tropes, 155, 166
  Mansfield, use of propaganda tropes, 129
  nurses' narratives, propagandistic elements of, 50, 51, 53–4, 55–6, 60, 64–6, 77n
  Wharton, use of propaganda tropes, 27, 82–9, 91–2, 96–100, 103, 107, 112, 114–15n
proximity
  to death, 4–5, 25–6, 28, 37–118, 240
  temporal, 5, 240
Punch, 213, 227–8n

Queen Victoria
  funeral, 8
  'Widow of Windsor', 7

Randall, Bryony, 156, 160–1
refugees, Belgian, 82, 96, 98, 111, 113, 123, 129, 148n, 236, 242n
religion
  lack of consolation, 52, 90–1
  religious beliefs, changing, 8
revenge narrative, 97–9, 104–7, 111, 212
Rhinehart, Mary Roberts, 115n
Rhinelander, Newbold, 87, 115n

Rhinelander, Thomas N., 115n
Rhys, Jean, 2, 242n
  After Leaving Mr Mackenzie, 236–8
  death of child, 236
  film and cinema, 236–8
  ghosts, 235–8
  Smile Please: An Unfinished Autobiography, 242n
  war work, 242n
Richards, Grant, 72
Richardson, Dorothy, 242n
Richardson, Mary, 190n
Richet, Charles, *War Nursing: What Every Woman Should Know*, 45
Rokeby Venus, 190n
'Roll of Honour' films, 72–9, 173–5, 189n
roman à clef, 155, 186n
Royal Academy, *The Nation's War Paintings*, 19
Royal Academy Summer Exhibition 1923, 231
Royal Botanic Gardens at Kew, 13
Royal British Legion, First Festival of Remembrance, 19
Royal Herbert Hospital, London, 50–1
Russell, Bertrand, 148n

Sassoon, Siegfried, 21, 148n
Sassoon, Sir Philip, 72
The Saturday Evening Post, 82, 86, 108, 112
Saturday Westminster Gazette, 128, 211
Sayers, Dorothy L.
  Lord Peter Views the Body, 197
  Unnatural Death, 196–7
  The Unpleasantness at the Bellona Club, 197
  Whose Body?, 196
Scates, Bruce, 33n, 232
Scott, Septimus E., *These Women are Doing Their Bit*, 166
Scribner's Magazine, 82, 86, 99, 108, 112
Scutts, Joanna, 223n, 225n
Seacole, Mary, 75n
Second World War, 156, 238

Seeger, Alan, 188n
  'I Have a Rendezvous with Death', 161–2
Shail, Andrew, 175
Sherman, David, 197
Sherry, Vincent, 23–4, 26, 125, 197, 222
  The Great War and the Language of Modernism, 26
Sinclair, May, 242n
Singer Sargent, John, 19
Sitwell, Osbert, 'Corpse-Day, July 19th, 1919', 141
Smith, Angela, 224n
Smith, Angela K., 43
Smith, Lesley, 41, 47–9, 51, 58–61
  Four Years Out of Life, 47–9, 67
South Africans, 14
Spain, 15
Spearing, E. M., *From Cambridge to Camiers under the Red Cross*, 72–3
Spencer, Stanley, 19
Spinney, Laura, 15
spiritualism, 8, 233, 238, 241n
Stanley, Liz
  epistolarium, 126–9
Stein, Gertrude, 26, 57, 114n, 156
stillbirth, 27, 154–5, 156, 163–72, 178, 181, 184, 236
Strachey, Lytton, 196, 206
survivor guilt, 69, 125, 134

Tate, Trudi, 25, 97, 156, 167, 169
  Modernism, History and the First World War, 25
Tayler, Henrietta, 41
  A Scottish Nurse at Work, 39–40, 52–3, 60–1, 68–9, 212
telegram, 68, 128, 133, 138
  notification of death, 13, 212, 218
telephone *see* field telephone
Thiepval Memorial to the Missing of the Somme, 14
Thomas Cook tours, 19
Thomson, James, *The City of Dreadful Night*, 157–8
Thwaite, Ann, 213
time, military control of, 158–9

The Times, 13, 13–14, 144, 195, 233
   'The Last Journey', *195*
   Woman's Supplement, 207, 226n
The Times Literary Supplement, 72, 72–3, 199
Todman, Dan, 21
Treaty of Versailles, 218
Two Minutes' Silence, 16, 159, 194, 196, 197, 220–1, 223, 234
Tylee, Claire, 77n, 86, 186n
Tyler, Elisina, 114n

United States, 3, 17, 41, 74n, 84
Unknown Warrior, 200–2, 204, 209, 219, 222, 230–3
   burial of, 16, 193–4, *194*
   Versailles, 230–1
   Westminster Abbey, 3, 193–5, 204, 219, 233

Van Dijick, Cedric, 159
Vaughan Williams, Ralph, *Pastoral Symphony*, 19
Victorian death
   culture of, 6–7
   memorial photography, 7, 27, 47, 71, 173–5
   see also deathbed scenes; good death
Victory Day, 16
Victory Parade, 193
Violet Day, 190n, 226n
violets, 182, 190n, 204, 226n, 236
Vogue (American), 41
Voluntary Aid Detachments (VADs), 39–40, 40–1, 47, 70, *71*
   VAD funerals, 64–5

Walker, Dora M., 41, 66–8
'War Books Boom' 1928–30, 5
War Cabinet, 20, 29n, 123, 148n
war cemeteries, 1, 13–14, 28, 64–8, 71, 73, 196, 198, 205, 211–18, 222, 228n, 240
   changing practices of burial in wartime, 9
   Cross of Sacrifice, 13
   design and creation, 13
   pilgrimages *see* pilgrimages

'Silent Cities', 18–19, 228n
Stone of Remembrance, 13
war dead
   American government policy on repatriating dead, 11
   British policy on not repatriating dead, 11
   casualty lists, 13
   changed modes of dying, 9, 47, 74, 92
   commemoration in earlier wars, 9
   consolatory letters to families, 13, 17, 32n
   damage to bodies, 9, 47, 59, 66
   equal treatment in death, 13–14
   funeral ceremonies, 55–6, 58, 63–5
   identification of bodies, 9, 196, 201
   identification tags, 9
   lack of official protocol for, 9
   locating and burying, 196, 198, 211–12, 214–18
   misinformation about, 221, 222, 233
   notification to civilians, 11–13, 239
   numbers, 8–9, 28, 39, 87, 96, 176, 178, 196, 198
   numbers of influenza dead in relation to war dead, 15
   return of the dead, 230–39
   unburied dead, 9, 63
war letters *see* letters and letter-writing
war memorials, 196, 216, 219–20
War Office, 10, 151n, 158–9
War Propaganda Bureau (Wellington House), 84–5
war songs, 155, 161, 162, 170
   'Good-bye-ee!', 237
   'It's a Long Way to Tipperary', 162, 176, 177, 180, 181, 183
   'Over There', 84
   'Pack Up Your Troubles in Your Old Kit-Bag and Smile, Smile, Smile!', 162, 184
Ward, Mrs Humphrey, 206, 226n
Ware, Sir Fabian, 8, 228n
   'Great Commemorator', 10
   role in Commonwealth War Graves Commission, 10
Warner, Agnes, 54
wartime commemorations, 38–119

Wearne, Sarah, 33n, 233
Wellington House *see* War Propaganda Bureau
Wells, H. G., 84–5
  Mr. Britling Sees It Through, 187n
West, Rebecca, 73
  The Return of the Soldier, 110, 171–2, 187n, 189n, 233
  War Nurse: The True Story of a Woman Who Lived, Loved and Suffered on the Western Front, 73, 80n
Westminster Gazette, 72, 227n
  Saturday Westminster Gazette, 128, 211, 227n
Wharton, Edith, 2, 26, 90, 178, 240
  The Age of Innocence, 112
  amount paid for stories, 85, 115n
  anxiety about war dead, 83–4, 87, 96, 109, 112
  A Backward Glance, 81, 115n
  The Book of the Homeless, 82
  cemeteries, 92–3
  claims to be first civilian woman at the front, 86, 115n
  'Coming Home', 27, 82, 83, 85, 97–108, 113
  The Custom of the Country, 82
  death of close friends in war, 1915, 87
  Ethan Frome, 82
  expeditions to the front lines, 85–6
  'The Field of Honour', 27, 82, 83, 108–12, 113, 113n, 117n
  Fighting France, 27, 81–2, 83, 85–97, 108, 113, 178–9
  genres in war writing, 83, 96–7
  The House of Mirth, 82
  Hudson River Bracketed, 108
  literariness of war writing, 83–4, 87, 112
  The Marne, 82, 89, 111
  postwar world, 240
  proleptic mourning, 91
  propaganda tropes, 27, 82–9, 91–2, 96–100, 103, 107, 112, 114–15n
  Raugel, Félix, meetings with, 81–2
  'The Refugees', 82, 108, 111, 113
  revenge narrative, 99–108
  A Son at the Front, 82, 113, 240
  story-telling, motif of, 99–104
  transformation of women in wartime, 108–9, 111, 117n
  use of buildings as metaphors for war dead and wounded, 88–90
  war awards, 82
  war charities, 82, 114n
  war rumours, 97–8, 116n
  women's war work, 110–12
  'Writing a War Story', 82, 99, 108
  Xingu and Other Stories, 99
widow, 8, 17, 29n, 34n, 161, 204, 207, 208, 219, 220, 238
'Widow of Windsor' (Queen Victoria), 7
Wilson, Woodrow, 84
Winter, Jay, 5, 17
  Sites of Memory, Sites of Mourning: The Great War in European Cultural History, 5, 6
Winthrop, Egerton, 87
Woman's Home Companion, 108, 112
women
  carers round Victorian deathbed, 3
  civilian, 2
  commemorative groups, 3
  emotional burden of war on, 154
  image as lifegivers, 3, 40
  as mourners, 2–3, 7, 14, 41, 193–4
  as mourners, literary representation of, 67-8, 70, 161, 182, 204, 208, 210, 216, 218
  in official commemoration, 3, 29n
  in recruiting efforts for war work, 3, 166, *166*
  small number of deaths, First World War, 3
  war work, 110–12, 166
Women's Army Auxiliary Corps, 4, 10, 11
Women's War Shrine, Whitechapel Art Gallery, 34n
women's war writing, 124–5
  accessibility, 3
  female specific tropes, 124–5, 163–7, 184, 222, 236
  surge in critical attention to, 3

Women's Work Subcommittee, 34n
Woodruff, Porter, 41, 75n
Woolf, Leonard, 151n
  death of brother Cecil, 200, 211, 241
  'Three Jews', 224n
Woolf, Virginia, 2, 6, 28, 151n, 234, 239
  Bagnold, Enid, 73, 79n
  Booth, Allyson on, 24
  brother, 242n
  Cenotaph, 193–6
  death rituals, 141–2
  ghosts, 190n, 234–5, 239, 241, 242n
  Hynes, Samuel on, 6
  Jacob's Room, 187n, 197–208, 210, 212, 213, 215, 216, 218–19, 222, 225–6n, 227n
  literary characterisation, 200–3, 206–7
  Mansfield, Katherine, relationship with, 144, 197–8, 207, 235
  'The Mark on the Wall', 198–9, 224n
  Memoir Club, 206
  'Mr. Bennett and Mrs. Brown', 200
  'Modern Fiction', 199
  'Modern Novels', 199
  Mrs Dalloway, 23, 187n, 198, 207, 218–21, 223
  Night and Day, xiii, 1, 144, 197–8, 199, 209–10
  proleptic memorialisation, 219
  Spearing, E. M., 72–3
  To the Lighthouse, 198, 203–4, 221–2, 223, 238
  violets, 190n
  The Years, 241
  wristwatch, 158–60, 169–70, 176, 187n; *see also* time, military control of
Wussow, Helen, 197
Wyndham Lewis, Percy, 19

Yorke, Dorothy, 155
Young, Patricia, nursing albums, 70–1, 70, 71
Young, Violet, *Outlines of Nursing*, 45
Ypres, 87–8

zeppelins, 130–3, 147, 164, 170
Zilboorg, Caroline, 156, 186n
Zimring, Rishona, 207
Zouaves, 93, 116n, 142

EU representative:
Easy Access System Europe
Mustamäe tee 50, 10621 Tallinn, Estonia
Gpsr.requests@easproject.com

www.ingramcontent.com/pod-product-compliance
Lightning Source LLC
Chambersburg PA
CBHW071828230426
43672CB00013B/2790